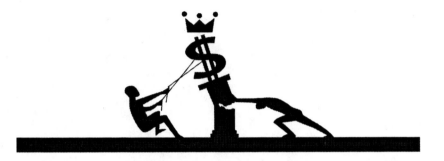

POWER
AND
Powerlessness

Susan Rosenthal

© Copyright 2006 Susan Rosenthal.
All rights reserved. No part of this publication may be reproduced, stored in a retrieval system, or transmitted, in any form or by any means, electronic, mechanical, photocopying, recording, or otherwise, without the written prior permission of the author.

Note for Librarians: A cataloguing record for this book is available from Library and Archives Canada at www.collectionscanada.ca/amicus/index-e.html
ISBN 1-4120-5691-8

Printed in Victoria, BC, Canada. Printed on paper with minimum 30% recycled fibre. Trafford's print shop runs on "green energy" from solar, wind and other environmentally-friendly power sources.

TRAFFORD
PUBLISHING

Offices in Canada, USA, Ireland and UK

Book sales for North America and international:
Trafford Publishing, 6E–2333 Government St.,
Victoria, BC V8T 4P4 CANADA
phone 250 383 6864 (toll-free 1 888 232 4444)
fax 250 383 6804; email to orders@trafford.com

Book sales in Europe:
Trafford Publishing (UK) Limited, 9 Park End Street, 2nd Floor
Oxford, UK OX1 1HH UNITED KINGDOM
phone 44 (0)1865 722 113 (local rate 0845 230 9601)
facsimile 44 (0)1865 722 868; info.uk@trafford.com
Order online at:
trafford.com/05-0589

10 9 8 7 6

*Dedicated to all who struggle for a better life and to the children of the world who **without exception** deserve the fruits of that struggle.*

Contents

Acknowledgments i

Introduction ii

Part One: *What's going on?* 1
    1. Does Anybody Really Care? 2
    2. Compassion Isn't Cost-Effective 6
    3. Who Needs a Heart When a Heart Can Be Broken 12
    4. Nature's Youngest Child 16

Part Two: *How did this happen?* 27
    5. Seize the Surplus 28
    6. Compete or Die 41
    7. Burden the Family 53
    8. Profit From Pain 66

Part Three: *Why do we put up with it?* 81
    9. The Lies that Bind Us 82
   10. Blame the Victim 95
   11. Divide and Rule 112
   12. Suffer the Children 128

Part Four: *What will it take?* 145
   13. Decide Which Side You're On 146
   14. Seize the Power 164
   15. Beware the Middle Ground 185
   16. Claim the Surplus 205

Notes 228

Index 233

Acknowledgements

First and foremost, I want to thank the many people who trusted me with their personal stories. Your courage sustains my faith in humanity and my hope for the future.

I am indebted to the many writers whose works provided a foundation for this book. I hope that I have done justice to your labors. I thank my father, Joe, who taught me that every problem has a solution; my mother, Joyce, who showed me that women can also be fighters; and my brother, Ron, who understood that socialism is about building relationships.

Many people contributed to the creation of this book. For patiently reading the entire manuscript I thank Janna Comrie, Liv Capozzi, Andrea Dawson, Judith Eden, Sophie Hand, Roger Hollander, Selina Mullins, Linda Page, Bill Roberts, Diane Thiel, and Barbara Wilkinson. Thank you Eleanor Dowson, for designing the logo and book cover. Thank you Kim Hanen, for designing and formatting the book's interior.

I want to thank my students, who pushed me to explain everything. Thank you also to Judith Eden, for demanding absolute clarity on the question of human nature. Thank you Janna Comrie, for not letting me wimp out at the end. My greatest debt is to Linda Page. Without her, neither I nor this book would be possible.

Undoubtedly, errors and omissions remain. It could not be otherwise. No depiction of the human condition could be complete without the input of every human being. I invite you, the reader, to contribute your perspective. By putting our heads, hearts, and hands together, we can build a better world and a brighter future.

Susan Rosenthal

Introduction

Their power — our powerlessness.
Our power — their powerlessness.
Each calls the other into being.

The world is a puzzling place. Like Alice in Wonderland, people rush to go nowhere, too many things don't make sense, and the threat of losing one's head is ever present. It seems as if humanity has fallen down the rabbit hole and cannot find a way out. Yet, there is hope. If we can understand how we got here and what keeps us here, we can go forward.

Society is divided into two groups of people: a few who wield immense power and the rest who feel varying degrees of powerlessness. As a result, conflicts over power dominate life. Between individuals, the struggle for power kills intimacy. On a social level, competition drives down living standards. On a global scale, the battle for dominance threatens human survival.

Power over others and lack of power are both corrupting. However, power — the ability to control events — can also liberate. *Power is not the problem; the problem is unequal access to power.* For more than a hundred-thousand years, our ancestors lived in cooperative, power-sharing societies. This book explains how the rule of reciprocity was overthrown and how it can be re-established.

My experience as a physician compelled me to write this book. As the sister of a disabled child, I thought that doctors had the power to end suffering, and I wanted that power. After I graduated from medical school, I learned how powerless doctors actually are. Most of my patients' problems were rooted in family dynamics, financial difficulties, and conflicts at school and at work. I studied psychotherapy in the hope that combining mind and body skills would be more useful. It was — I could help people move from uncommon misery to common misery. The problems created by alienation, oppression, and exploitation remained beyond my control.

After listening to thousands of people's stories, I have concluded that social power is necessary for human health. Most people lack the happy, healthy, fulfilling lives they deserve because they are kept powerless and mistakenly accept this state of affairs as natural or self-inflicted. In fact, *most human suffering is preventable.* This book reveals what must be done.

Part One explains that society does not arise from human nature. On the contrary, current social arrangements violate human nature. Part Two shows how power is divided by class. Part Three investigates how power and powerlessness are perpetuated. Part Four reveals how powerlessness can be transformed into power.

Knowing that the material in this book would be controversial, unbelievable to some, I carefully referenced every fact, every quote, and every contentious statement. To my dismay, the final draft contained more than 1,400 references spanning 70 pages. To make the book shorter and more affordable, I cut out most of these references; however, I will be happy to provide specific references on request.

A just world is possible. Human beings create society, and we can change it. The need for change is urgent. Everywhere, there is injustice, anguish, and anger. This book explains how society shapes people, how people shape society, and how powerlessness can be converted into the power to transform the world.

Part One

What's Going On?

> Many Americans, we know, are horrified by the
> posture of their government but seem to be helpless.
>
> *Harold Pinter*

The 21st century is young and already drips with blood. Washington has launched wars against Afghanistan and Iraq and backed Israel to destroy Lebanon. When Hurricane Katrina hit the Gulf Coast, the most powerful government in the world abandoned its poor to die. Ordinary Americans have lost jobs, pensions, and health care, while oil profiteers reap billions in tax cuts. Secret prisons, systematic torture, and domestic spying confirm the corruption at the heart of the system. Why is this happening? The usual explanations blame human nature, as if nothing can be done.

The inability to change society is an extension of the powerlessness that most people feel every day at the hands of supervisors, bosses, and bureaucrats, at home, at school, in the market, on the street, and at work. How can justice be achieved when so many people feel powerless in so many ways? Do we have the world we deserve, or is there another explanation? Part One addresses these questions.

- Chapter 1. *Does Anybody Really Care* provides evidence that people do care about one another.

- Chapter 2. *Compassion Isn't Cost-Effective* shows how capitalism blocks compassion.

- Chapter 3. *Who Needs a Heart When a Heart Can Be Broken* explains how dissociation helps people endure what they cannot change.

- Chapter 4. *Nature's Youngest Child* reveals how capitalism prevents people from solving social problems.

Chapter 1

Does Anybody Really Care?

Bill Moyers recalls looking at photos of his grandchildren and thinking,

We are stealing their future. Betraying their trust. Despoiling their world. And I ask myself: Why? Is it because we don't care? Because we are greedy? Because we have lost our capacity for outrage, our ability to sustain indignation at injustice? What has happened to our moral imagination?[1]

Such questions demand answers. Every day, crowds of people stream past homeless beggars. Few respond to their pleas for help. One cold Christmas morning, I watched two men walk up to a bank machine. A homeless woman lay sleeping in front of it. They stepped over her to withdraw some money and, as they turned to leave, they stepped back over her again *without interrupting their conversation*. Events like these reinforce the belief that people are naturally selfish and that social problems result from "original sin" or human nature. Is this true? Let's examine the evidence.

Are people heartless?

A poster campaign to raise money for charity shows a half-naked toddler sitting in a pile of garbage with the caption, "How young do they have to be before we give a damn?" The poster implies that people are so indifferent to suffering that they must be shocked or shamed into caring. In fact, people are not indifferent at all. Over 70 percent of Americans think that the government should ensure that no one goes without food, clothing, or shelter.

People also dig into their own pockets to help. The Red Cross and Red Crescent Societies raised over one billion U.S. dollars *in one month* to aid victims of the 2004 Asian tsunami. Eighty-five percent of this money was contributed by the general public. Prisoners donated their wages, and the homeless emptied their pockets. Of the $250 billion donated to American non-profit organizations in 2004, less than five percent came from corporations, while more than 75 percent came from individuals.

People show concern for others every day. Most people prefer to go to work sick than to stay home and increase the burden on their co-workers. Employers literally bank on the altruism of employees. Hospitals and schools are under-funded in the knowledge that workers will expend extra energy to fill the gap. Nearly

55 percent of people working in medicine and education contribute unpaid overtime, and more than half take work home.

People commonly put others' needs before their own. A survey of male and female care-givers of women with advanced breast cancer found that five percent had quit their jobs or turned down a job promotion in order to provide care. Sixty-nine percent had missed days at work, reduced their work hours, and used holidays or taken special leave to support their loved ones. Many of these care-givers suffered anxiety and depression. Despite the strain on their jobs, finances, and health, they reported being very satisfied with their choice to put care-giving first. In everyday human interactions, people who are caring and compassionate are highly valued.

Are people lazy?

Some say that more people don't protest injustice or support social causes because they are lazy. If that were true, there would be no volunteers. Over 80 million Americans donate 20 billion hours of their time every year volunteering in hospitals, hospices, nursing homes, fire departments, rescue squads, shelters, half-way houses, counseling services, and church programs. This does not include the many hours that people spend helping family, friends and neighbors. If people were lazy, no one would participate in bike-athons, walk-athons, and other fund-raising events for charity. If people were lazy, no one would campaign for civil rights or build a union. If people were lazy, they would do nothing after work instead of playing sports, fixing cars, gardening, dancing, painting, and making things for their children. If people were lazy, then the jobs that demand the least work would be the most desirable. In reality, having nothing to do makes people feel useless. Human beings have a strong need to contribute, and many seniors seek work after retirement for that reason.

Do people have it too good?

Some complain that most people are too well off to rock the boat. A few people do benefit from how things are and don't want anything to change. However, most people's living standards are falling. In 2003, the United Nations found that living standards in more than 50 countries had declined over the previous ten years. The World Health Organization estimates that,

> More than 2.6 billion people, about 40 per cent of those on the planet, have no access to basic sanitation or adequate toilet facilities. More than a billion people have no access to clean water sources, and an estimated 4,000 children die every day from illnesses caused by lack of safe water and sanitation.[2]

In rich nations, falling living standards can be seen in the increase in part-time and contract jobs, longer working hours, fewer benefits, rising debt, loss of social supports, more stress, and more poverty. In *America's Forgotten Majority: Why the White Working Class Still Matters,* Ruy Teixeira and Joel Rogers found that a 50-year-old White male high-school graduate earned between $2,000 and $3,000 a year *less* in 1996 than he would have earned ten years earlier.

From 1973 to 1998, in an economy that almost doubled in real terms, the wage of the typical worker in production and non-supervisory jobs (80 percent of the workforce) actually *declined* by 6 percent, from $13.61 to $12.77 an hour. Based on a forty-hour week, this works out to a loss of about $1,750 a year for the typical worker.[3]

In the world's richest nation, more than 11 percent of households have difficulty putting food on the table. More than 45 million Americans cannot afford medical insurance. Twenty-eight percent of uninsured adults with serious medical problems cannot afford to buy the medicines they need. More than 40 percent of working Americans have medical debts, and half of all personal bankruptcies are health-related. With living standards declining for so many people, we can't explain low levels of social protest on people having it too good.

Are people ignorant?

It is commonly thought that if *enough* people knew what was going on, they would never put up with it. This belief motivates some people to dedicate their lives to revealing the truth. Since the 1970's, Dr. Helen Caldicott has campaigned to educate the public about the dangers of nuclear power. Over the same period, Dr. Samuel Epstein has thoroughly documented how industrial pollution creates cancer. Countless others have exposed how the drive for profit creates needless misery for human beings and destroys the environment.

These messages have found an audience. Most Americans think business leaders and politicians are corrupt and self-serving, and 86 percent want stricter laws and regulations to protect the environment. In 2004, Michael Moore's anti-war movie, *Fahrenheit 9/11,* broke the record for the largest grossing documentary ever. By mid-2005, the majority of Americans believed that the U.S. had launched its war against Iraq on false pretenses, that the president and his advisors had lied to the country, and that the war was not worth it. Yet the president remained in office, and the war continued.

Most people do know what is going on. They may not know all the details, but they know the basics — that the world is run for the rich and powerful at the expense of everyone and everything else. If the truth alone could change the world, it would have changed by now. Later chapters will explain how society is structured to keep most people feeling powerless most of the time, *regardless of what they know.*

To care is human

People show kindness and caring every day. We help each other with directions, adopt stray animals, return lost objects, and comfort each other in hard times. Such considerations are ignored by a media machine that provides us with a daily diet of assault, child abuse, murder, war, and other atrocities.

Sometimes, the generosity of ordinary people does hit the news. On 9/11, firefighters raced into the burning World Trade Center with no thought for their own safety and died when the towers collapsed. The bridges to Manhattan were clogged with people rushing downtown to help. Construction workers left their jobs to search for survivors, and volunteers lined up to give blood. Dr. Robert Jones, director of New York City's blood services, described how,

Within an hour of the attack, donors appeared [lining up] around the block wanting to donate blood…Even when you tried to explain to blood donors that…this was not going to be helpful at this time, they still felt compelled by some social value they were experiencing to donate at that time. They just had to do it.[4]

The amount of donated blood overwhelmed the system—500,000 units were collected, while fewer than 260 units were used.

That same day, 17 Canadian towns and cities took in almost 34,000 stranded airplane passengers from the United States. When 38 jets were diverted to a small town in Newfoundland, local people opened their hearts, their homes, and their wallets. Striking school-bus drivers left picket lines to drive plane-loads of passengers to community shelters. Doctors and nurses set up clinics where passengers could get their prescriptions refilled, and pharmacists filled them for free. Canadian air-traffic controllers cooked massive quantities of chili, bacon, and eggs for the visitors. Northwest Airlines Captain Dann Runik told reporters, "I had prepared my passengers to ration their food and their water. For the people of that locale to empty their pantries and open their homes … just took everyone by surprise."[5] Why were they surprised? Because, as the next chapter explains, capitalism cultivates callousness and rewards greed.

Summary

Social problems cannot be blamed on human nature because people can be caring or cruel in different situations. Nevertheless, pessimistic beliefs about human nature persist because the powers-that-be promote this view, and people go along because they need some way to explain what is wrong in the world.

Chapter 2

Compassion Isn't Cost-Effective

It is time to see the world as it really is.
Captain James T. Kirk

During my hospital training, I participated in daily rounds where medical staff moved from room to room assessing the patients. One morning, we examined a 35-year-old woman who was suffering from advanced liver disease. As the convoy of doctors and nurses turned to leave, the patient cried out, "I'm dying! I'm dying! I'm scared!" A nurse responded, "You're not dying. You're going to be fine," and the group moved to the next room. An hour later, I entered the morgue to find this same patient lying on the autopsy table. I was horrified. When I told a senior doctor what happened, he responded, "You'd better get used to it." I got the message: feelings don't matter here. The patient's fears were disregarded, and she was abandoned to die alone. My shock at what happened to her was considered unworthy of discussion.

Medical schools teach students that patients' feelings *are* important. However, in the real world of the busy hospital, feelings are not "cost-effective." When we listen to people and care about how they feel, then we want to provide them with what they need—someone to sit and listen, more detailed explanations, or help with work and family matters. However, *there is no profit to be made from providing these services*.

To maximize productivity, cash-squeezed public hospitals and profit-driven private hospitals treat patients like widgets on an assembly line. Instead of discussing patients by name, medical staff refer to them by diagnosis—"the fibroids" in Room 12 and "the pancreatic cancer" in Room 5—like mechanics working on parts, not people. One psychiatrist describes how compassion is discouraged in his workplace.

> Every few months, all staff psychiatrists receive a compilation of length-of-stay statistics, "savable days" and other related data, listed by individual staff member…Through this process, staff are openly ranked according to the speed with which they discharge their patients, the worst offenders (those who keep their patients in hospital the longest) appearing at the top of the list. These reports, masquerading as "information," represent an example of public shaming…I wait in vain for rankings of humanistic parameters such as compassion, empathy and supportiveness toward patients, or even simpler measures such as providing good treatment or treating other staff well.[6]

The needs of medical staff are no more important than the needs of patients. Hospitals foster a competitive, suck-it-up mentality to squeeze the most work from the fewest people. As a medical intern, I worked between 80 and 120 hours a week. When your own needs are denied, it becomes easier to deny the needs of others. One night, a patient suffered a heart attack. As the team struggled to resuscitate him, I was appalled to find myself hoping that he would die so that I could go to bed. I had been on my feet for 30 hours without a break.

The typical underfunded hospital demands that medical trainees take on overwhelming workloads, suffer persistent sleep deprivation, and abandon any personal life. Under such conditions, it is not surprising that student doctors finish their training significantly more depressed, more hostile, and less empathetic than when they began.

To raise productivity, capitalism glorifies the efficient professional who has no time for feelings. Popular characters, like Spock on *Star Trek,* reject emotions as an obstacle to good decision-making. However, morality, ethics, and values are rooted in emotions or "gut feelings" that move people towards what they believe is right and away from what they believe is wrong. Without emotions, there would be no anger in response to injustice and no shame in behaving badly.

Cultivation of the psychopath

If one were to design a human being that was perfectly suited to the capitalist system, that person would be a psychopath—someone who is disconnected from emotions, having no empathy and no compassion. The American Psychiatric Association defines a psychopath as someone who exhibits "a pervasive pattern of disregard for and violation of the rights of others" as indicated by three or more of the following:

- failure to conform to social norms with respect to lawful behaviors as indicated by repeatedly performing acts that are grounds for arrest.

- deceitfulness, as indicated by repeated lying, use of aliases, or conning others for personal profit or pleasure.

- impulsivity or failure to plan ahead

- irritability and aggressiveness as indicated by repeated physical fights or assaults.

- reckless disregard for safety of self or others.

- consistent irresponsibility, as indicated by repeated failure to sustain consistent work behavior or honor financial obligations.

- Lack of remorse, as indicated by being indifferent to or rationalizing having hurt, mistreated, or stolen from another.[7]

The documentary film, *The Corporation,* explains how this definition applies to corporations. Lying, cheating, stealing, hurting people, having a short-term outlook, aggressive behavior, and lack of remorse are standard business practices, making the psychopath the ideal corporate executive. Albert Dunlap, who was described by his biographer as a vicious psychopath, became the darling of the business world during the downsizing frenzy of the 1990's. Dunlap was called "Chainsaw Al" because he chopped hundreds of thousands of jobs. The more people he laid off, the higher stock prices climbed.

Popular culture presents the psychopath as the villain we love to hate. In the movie *Spiderman,* Norman Osborn is a corporate executive whose greed and ambition cause him to develop an evil persona, the Green Goblin. The Goblin is a psychopath who tells Spiderman, "There are eight million people in this city, and those teeming masses exist for the sole purpose of lifting exceptional people like us on their shoulders."

Hollywood portrays characters like Norman Osborn as freakish exceptions. In reality, the capitalist can maximize profit only by putting business interests ahead of human needs. To make it in business, *all capitalists must behave as if they are psychopaths,* whether they are or not. Consider the following example of how one executive was handsomely rewarded for sacrificing children to meet the needs of his corporation.

In 2002, Cardinal Bernard F. Law, head of the Archdiocese of Boston, was forced to resign for protecting priests who were sexually molesting children. Law had knowingly moved pedophile priests from parish to parish, where they molested even more children. After Law was disgraced for his role in the child-abuse scandal, Pope John Paul II appointed him archpriest of a Basilica in Rome, a highly influential position. Whether or not he was a psychopath, Law advanced his career by behaving like one.

Henry Ford, founder of the Ford Corporation, built an automotive empire by sacrificing human lives. He once stated, "I am not in the business of making cars. I am in the business of making profit." This stance required Ford executives to function like psychopaths. Let's say you had a choice between manufacturing a dangerous vehicle or a safe one. What if the dangerous vehicle was more profitable, even after you included the cost of killing and injuring a certain number of people and generating a predictable number of lawsuits? In the late 1960's, the Ford Motor Company launched the Pinto, knowing that a rear-end collision of more than 30-miles-an-hour would jam its doors and cause a fuel-tank explosion that would incinerate the occupants trapped inside. When asked about the Pinto's exploding gas tank, a Ford engineer admitted:

> That's all true [that the car tends to explode in minor accidents]. But you miss the point entirely. You see, safety isn't the issue, trunk space is. You have no idea how stiff the competition is over trunk space. Do you realize that if we put a Capri-type tank in the Pinto you could only get one set of golf clubs in the trunk?[8]

Ford developed a six-dollar modification to the Pinto that would prevent the gas tank from exploding. The company then did a cost/benefit analysis, based on how many people might die from exploding gas tanks and how much money Ford would have to pay for each death (about $200,000 per person). This sum turned out to be less than the cost of modifying the fuel tanks of *all* Pintos, so Ford chose not to apply the modification. How many people died as a result? The National Highway Traffic Safety Administration began investigating automobile fires shortly after the Pinto began rolling off the assembly line. Every year, 400,000 cars were catching fire and burning more than 3,000 people to death. Even though Ford made only 24 per cent of the vehicles on American roads, its cars accounted for 42 percent of collision-ruptured fuel tanks.

It took ten years for the Department of Transportation to declare that the Pinto had a "safety-related defect." One and a half million vehicles were recalled, and the Ford Motor Company was charged with reckless homicide. However, the judge acquitted Ford on the basis that it could not be convicted for doing what it was designed to do—make a profit.

A society that values profit over people needs policy-makers who act like psychopaths. Of course, most executives have social values; however, the greatest rewards are reserved for those who are willing to do whatever it takes to get ahead. In a society that rewards greed, good guys finish last.

They don't care about us

> We have no obligation to make history. We have no obligation to make art. We have no obligation to make a statement. To make money is our only objective.
>
> *Michael Eisner,* CEO of Disney

Governments claim to represent all the people. In practice, they serve business first and foremost. That is why the minimum wage is kept at $5.15 an hour and why the rich are showered with billions of dollars in tax cuts. Automotive manufacturers continue to deny safety problems, and the State continues to shield them. In 2003, the National Highway Traffic Safety Administration decided to "forbid the public release of some data relating to unsafe motor vehicles" on the basis that "publicizing the information would cause 'substantial competitive harm to manufacturers.'"

Government loyalty to business is clearest in times of crisis. After the bombing of the World Trade Center, Congress authorized $15 billion in emergency aid to the nation's airlines. Thousands of laid-off airline workers got nothing. Even worse, the government's aid package *required* airlines to cut the wages and benefits of workers who remained on the job.

While Congress took 17 days to rush relief to the airlines, it took 11 months to assemble the first compensation packages for victims' relatives. Twenty-five families were offered a total of $34 million, or less than one-quarter of one percent of what the airlines got. More than a year after the tragedy, tens of thousands of people who had applied for emergency assistance were still waiting for their forms to be processed.

If 9/11 left any doubts about government priorities, Hurricane Katrina blew them away four years later. Public officials knew three days in advance that Katrina was going to hit the Gulf Coast. They did nothing. No effort was made to evacuate hundreds of thousands of predominately poor, Black people with no way to leave on their own. Sick and disabled people, old people, patients in hospitals and nursing homes, prisoners locked in cells—all were abandoned to the flood. People desperately searching for supplies to survive were branded as looters, and President Bush gave orders to shoot them on sight.

After Hurricane Katrina, Congress voted $62 billion to kick-start "one of the largest reconstruction efforts the world has ever seen." While well-connected companies lined up for the loot, the poor got a kick in the pants. The Davis-Bacon Act, that prohibits employers from paying sub-standard wages on federally-financed projects, was suspended for contractors working in the Gulf Coast. New federal contractors were also relieved of any obligation to hire minorities, women, Vietnam veterans, and disabled people on Katrina-related projects. These measures were a boon to business while forcing those who had lost everything to work for next to nothing, if they could find any work at all.

Blaming human nature

Capitalism subordinates compassion, contributing, and cooperation to the pursuit of profit and blames the resulting social problems on human nature.

Politicians know that corporate donations butter their bread and return the favor by opening the public purse for whatever business needs—subsidies, tax cuts, war, etc. Meanwhile, there is no "political will" to solve social problems like poverty and unemployment. On the contrary, public officials moan about the deficit and cut funds for education, housing, pensions, social assistance, and medicare.

The people at the top of society set the example for everyone else. When authorities display consistent disregard for human needs, it sends the message that humanity as a whole has no compassion. To support the view that human nature is basically selfish, many so-called experts insist that altruism, or unselfish concern for others, doesn't really exist. Cynics argue that people help others only when it benefits them to do so. Skeptics claim that people offer assistance only to reduce their own distress at witnessing suffering in others. Pessimists insist that people do the right thing only to avoid punishment.

Of course, it feels good to help, and assisting others does reduce one's own distress. The question is whether the decision to help is always based on a cost-benefit analysis. Those who believe this refer to the brutal murder of Kitty Genovese in New York City in 1964. Thirty-eight people heard her screaming, and no one came to her aid or called the police. Does such behavior prove that people care only for themselves? Researchers set out to answer this question.

To test the theory that people aid others only to reduce their own distress, subjects were given the option of reducing their discomfort by escaping from the situation instead of helping. Most people chose to help, even when escape was easier.

To investigate the possibility that people help in order to avoid guilt, shame, or punishment, subjects were provided with various excuses they could use to avoid helping, like being told that others had promised to provide aid. Once again, most people preferred to help, even when they had the option of feeling good about not helping.

Finally, to discover if people help others only to feel good about themselves, researchers compared subjects who helped a victim with subjects who were informed that someone else had helped the victim. Most people felt just as good when they discovered that the victim had been helped as they felt when they were the ones who did the helping.

Other studies show that toddlers as young as 18-months-of-age are eager to help, even when they are not rewarded for doing so. Add the countless examples of people moving to aid others with no thought to themselves, and we must conclude that *human beings have a built-in desire to help that cannot be reduced to personal gain.*

Compassion de-railed

Although caring and cooperation are instinctive in human beings, we are not slaves to our biology. Social influences play an important role in shaping behavior. The need to urinate is biological; however, *where* we urinate is socially conditioned. When hunger strikes, we seldom grab the nearest piece of food. An amorous couple will stop their activities when interrupted by the door bell. Compassion and cooperation are no different—they can be de-railed by social conditions. Researchers into the Genovese murder found that compassion can be negated when people think that no real need exists, that they lack the ability to help, or that someone else will solve the problem.

- **No real need exists:** When is a scream a cry for help, and when is it part of a heated argument? When people are uncertain, they may not react. People are more likely to respond to an obvious emergency, especially when others also show concern.

- **You cannot help:** If people think that they lack the skill, strength, or courage to help, they may hold back. Those who feel less confident are less likely to help, while those who feel good about themselves are more likely to help.

- **Someone else will solve the problem:** If people think that someone has already called for help, they are less likely to call themselves. If they know that others are unable to help, then they are more likely to act.

These three messages—no real need exists, you cannot help, someone else will solve the problem—promote passivity. When President Ronald Regan condemned "welfare queens" living high off the hog on social assistance, he was saying that *no real need exists* because these people are better off than you are. Similarly, the belief that "the poor will always be with us" assumes that *nothing can be done* to eliminate poverty. And when power is concentrated at the top of society, the message is that *someone else will solve the problem.* The few who rule the many must promote such leave-it-to-us passivity if they want to maintain their rule.

Given the extent to which selfishness is modeled at the top of society and passivity promoted in the face of social problems, it is amazing that people care as much as they do. When governments refuse to assist the needy, ordinary people organize fund-raising events and volunteer at distress centers, shelters, and soup kitchens. People spend countless unpaid hours raising children, caring for the sick and elderly, and generally supporting one another. Caring about others is so basic to human nature that most people can't understand how it could be displaced by self-interest. Take the example of Carolyn Kelly, age 81, who dove into deep water to save a fellow nursing-home resident from drowning. Kelly swam out to the victim and held her head above water until paramedics arrived. When questioned by reporters, Kelly explained that she was a good swimmer and felt she had to help. Everyday heroes typically insist that *anyone else would do the same in their place.* The next chapter explains how too much pain can cause people to close their hearts in self-protection.

Summary

When greed is profitable, compassion is not cost-effective. To justify heartless social priorities, "experts" insist that selfishness is basic to human nature. Nevertheless, ordinary people value compassion and generosity because their everyday lives depend on it.

Chapter 3

Who Needs a Heart When a Heart Can Be Broken

Emotional pain can be so unbearable that feeling nothing at all can seem preferable. In a world of pain, nature provides a defense against suffering—dissociation. Dissociation is a double-edged sword: it helps people tolerate what they cannot change, and it also blocks awareness of the need for change.

Dissociation was first identified in the late 19th century by Jean-Martin Charcot, a physician working at an asylum for the sick and destitute in France. Instead of dismissing his patients as raving lunatics, Charcot listened to them and concluded that they had been traumatized.

Charcot's student, Pierre Janet, proposed that some experiences are so traumatic that they cannot be integrated into a person's understanding of the world, so they are split off from conscious awareness. In short, dissociation provides an escape when there is no escape. On hearing that her son had been killed, a mother reported feeling numb and unable to move, as if she were suspended in space. Unfortunately, dissociation has a price.

Janet explained that dissociated fragments of experience can intrude into a person's consciousness as frightening thoughts, feelings, and images; compulsive behaviors; and physical symptoms. Feeling disconnected can also cause depression, anxiety, and low self-esteem. Efforts to counter the distress of dissociation can create more problems, including addictions, self-destructive behaviors, and violence towards others. For example, emotional numbness can be so disturbing that a person may engage in risky activities in order to feel something. Someone else may combat frightening mental images with obsessive thoughts and compulsive rituals. Another person may blame her sense of disconnection on someone else, become angry or violent toward that person, then feel ashamed and get drunk for relief.

Despite the many problems it creates, Janet believed that dissociation helped people to cope with trauma by:

- separating contradictory experiences to avoid inner conflict.

- triggering automatic self-preserving behaviors.

- disconnecting the sense of self from the intolerable experience.

This new, trauma-based approach to illness caused tremendous excitement in the medical world. In 1890 alone, five conferences on dissociation were held in Europe and the United States. In 1906, Janet was invited to give an inaugural series of lectures at Harvard Medical School. Distinguished scientists flocked to study under Charcot, including the 29-year-old Sigmund Freud who traveled to Paris in 1885.

While Charcot believed that any kind of trauma could make people sick, Freud insisted that childhood sexual abuse was the primary cause of nervous disorders. Back in Vienna, this theory proved very unpopular. In response, Freud did an about-turn and proclaimed that patients' stories of childhood sexual trauma were simply fantasies that should not be believed. Freud developed psychoanalysis on the basis that inner conflict, not external experience, was the cause of illness. In *We've Had a Hundred Years of Psychotherapy—And the World's Getting Worse*, James Hillman and Michael Ventura point out that social problems cannot be solved by emphasizing what happens inside people's heads instead of in their lives.

Janet's theory of traumatic dissociation became popular during a time of social rebellion. The following period was more conservative and favored Freud's theory. World War I revived interest in the link between trauma and illness. Today, dissociation remains politically controversial because it places human suffering in a social context.

Everyday dissociation

In *The Stranger in the Mirror,* Marlene Steinberg explains that dissociation is far more common than people think. While severe forms of dissociation occur in response to traumatic events, "mild or moderate experiences of dissociation are as common in otherwise normal people as anxiety and depression." Such experiences include,

> …not recognizing yourself in the mirror; staring into space and losing track of time; being uncertain whether a memory was from a dream or reality; feeling outside one's self as both an observer and a participant; feeling that one was watching a movie of one's progression through life; experiencing a numbing of emotions; missing parts of conversations; and being unable to remember something one had just done.[9]

Dissociation is common because the world is full of contradictory, distressing experiences. Everyday, most people go to jobs where they have no control over what they do. Everywhere, the few dominate the many, and immense wealth exists alongside enormous deprivation. Unfairness normally generates anger that pushes us to set things right. Feeling powerless to correct what is wrong is frightening, so people don't think about it—they dissociate. The media promote such dissociation. A newspaper report on famine is placed next to an advertisement for expensive jewelry. The reader looks at the report and feels bad about people starving, then sees the advertisement and admires the jewelry (or vice versa). The physical separation between the two items encourages this switch in feelings. The question of why some people can't afford food while others can afford diamonds is also avoided.

Dissociation allows people to respond to conflicting aspects of life *as if they were not related*. Through the mechanism of dissociation, divisions within society are reproduced within the human mind. Lack of control over work (called alienation) results in psychological dissociation from the work process. People feel disconnected from their labor, from themselves, from each other, and from the world. While dissociation provides temporary comfort, it allows oppression, exploitation, and inequality to continue. *Dissociation in the face of injustice is mistakenly perceived as a lack of caring instead of what it really is—a psychological defense against the inability to turn caring into action.*

Doublespeak

In the futuristic novel, *Nineteen Eighty-Four,* the main character works at the Ministry of Truth, where his job is deleting facts from the public records. To eliminate internal conflict over what he does, he convinces himself that the version of history he creates everyday is real. The author uses the term "doublethink" to describe how someone can believe two contradictory things at the same time.

"Doublespeak" is a similar form of dissociation that is used to make the unacceptable acceptable, like calling welfare cuts "back-to-work" measures. Doublespeak is used regularly by governments, corporations, media, advertisers, and the military. The more reprehensible the action, the more lies are needed to make it palatable. Not surprisingly, the military takes the prize for doublespeak. War is defense, death is collateral damage, a freedom fighter is a terrorist working for us, and a terrorist is a freedom fighter working for them.

Politicians are especially skilled at doublespeak. While the U.S. was bombing Afghanistan and killing innocent people, President George W. Bush appealed to Americans to send money to the White House to help Afghan children. School students prepared care packages for Afghan refugees, and the United Nations pledged that year's Halloween UNICEF collection to Afghan children. What is wrong with this picture?

Knowing that most people are repulsed by mass murder, war-mongers make humanitarian gestures to present themselves as compassionate people with good intentions. Expressing concern for those you attack, and urging people to rally around your concern, channels distress about war into activities that support war and those who wage it.

When anti-war activists pointed out the contradiction of sending aid to Afghanistan and bombing the country at the same time, many people reacted with hostility. It is impossible to reconcile the image of America as a savior of the oppressed with the image of America as a terrorist State. Official doublespeak made it easier for people to dissociate from the fact that their government was conducting mass murder in their name.

Doublespeak invites people to dissociate, and dissociation helps people to accept contradictions: to love their own children *and* support wars that kill other people's children; to want help when they run into trouble *and* condemn others needing social assistance; to feel anger at being hurt *and* defend those who hurt them. When thinking brings pain, dissociation helps people move through life without thinking.

Doublespeak also helps wrong-doers dissociate. When people in power who are not psychopaths are compelled to act like psychopaths, when they can reach their goals only by harming others, they must dissociate. They cannot allow themselves to feel compassion for their victims or they would be unable to do their jobs. They must convince themselves that they are doing the right thing. They must believe their own lies.

Dissociation as a drug

Under severe stress, the body produces pain-killing chemicals called "internal opiates" that are identical to external opiates like morphine and heroin. These chemicals block fear and pain so the wounded can escape to safety. Injured soldiers and accident victims often report feeling no pain for some time. When there is no escape, these same opiates make death easier.

Internal opiates contribute to the dissociated or altered states of consciousness that occur during severe stress. There may be a sense of detachment ("I floated out of my body"), feelings of unreality ("it was like watching a movie"), an altered sense of time ("time stood still"), automatic movements ("it was like a higher power took over"), and feeling numb. This state of mind is featured in the movie *Fearless*. The main character is a passenger on an airplane that is about to crash. At first he is terrified. When he realizes that he cannot escape death, he becomes calm—even blissful—despite the chaos around him.

In a world of uncertainty, danger, and pain, dissociation functions like a welcome drug. The unbearable can be tolerated when emotions are numbed; however, there is a cost. Dissociation numbs *all* emotions, including the positive ones, making life seem flat and empty. Severe dissociation numbs feelings of compassion and empathy, making it possible for people to do cruel and monstrous things that they would never do in a non-dissociated state.

Milder forms of dissociation make it easier to live *as if* the world were more safe and more fair than it really is. Being comfortably numb also has a price. Recall the cartoon ostrich that buries its head in the sand, only to be kicked in the butt. By numbing fear, anger, and pain, dissociation reduces the motivation to solve problems that should be solved.

It used to puzzle me that people would change the subject when I talked about social problems. At first, I assumed they didn't care. It took some time before I realized that discussing problems can make people feel powerless and frustrated *when they think there is no solution.* People have a limited tolerance for pain, and it makes sense to avoid what you think you cannot change. One man confessed that he dodges beggars on the street because he feels so bad that he can't help. A woman admitted outright, "If I don't care, then it won't hurt so much."

People don't need to care more, they need more solutions. Believing that a problem can be solved makes it possible to bear the pain of that problem. The next chapter explains how people's natural problem-solving abilities are discouraged by society.

Summary

People dissociate in response to painful contradictions and seemingly unsolvable problems. Dissociation makes feeling powerless more tolerable, while allowing intolerable situations to continue.

Chapter 4

Nature's Youngest Child

Some say that human beings are little more than animals in clothing, with savage natures that lurk beneath a thin veneer of civilization. Others insist that people are nothing like animals at all. In reality, the human species is both animal *and more than animal*, with a unique ability to shape its own history.

Animals have amazing abilities. By smell alone, a rescue dog can find someone buried beneath the snow. Some animals can detect cancer in human beings. Others can sense impending earthquakes. Animals are particularly adept at finding food—in the wild, on kitchen counters, and behind cupboard doors. However, no species can match the human ability to transform fantasy into reality. No other animal can look at a field full of stones, imagine biting into a luscious cob of corn, make a plan, enlist others to help and then persevere for months, hauling rocks, plowing, planting, weeding, watering, and waiting, until a field of ripe corn is ready to harvest.

Bees construct hives based on geometric patterns that, while intricate, never change. Human beings can imagine and build an unlimited variety of structures. Furthermore, people accumulate knowledge and skill from generation to generation, so that the ability to imagine and the ability to construct continually evolve.

Compared with dinosaurs who lived for millions of years, the human species is very young—about 150,000 years old. As nature's youngest child, humanity has barely begun to explore its potential.

How important is biology?

All mammals have a biological bonding system because the newborn's connection to its mother is essential for survival. This bonding system functions like an emotional umbilical cord connecting dependent offspring to adults who can nurture and protect them. The human bonding system is especially important. Children take years to learn how to control their bodies, regulate their emotions, use language, and master social skills. This long process of development is rooted in biology and shaped by experience.

The newborn infant has a surplus of connections among brain cells. Experience prunes these connections and organizes the brain. The human attachment system orchestrates this complex dance between biology and experience. In *The Developing Mind: How Relationships and the Brain Interact to Shape Who We Are,* Daniel Siegel explains that interactions between adults and children literally shape the child's brain, determining which nerve cells develop connections; which ones disconnect from lack of use; and how the developing systems of the brain relate to each other, to the rest of the body, and to the external world. For example, all children are born with language abilities; however, they learn to speak only those languages that are spoken to them. In short, our thoughts, feelings, and sense of self are all shaped by our relationships.

Throughout life, the brain shapes and reshapes itself in response to new experiences. A study of dyslexic children found their brain activity to be different from children without dyslexia. (People with dyslexia have difficulty reading, recognizing the meaning of words, and spelling accurately.) After completing a treatment program that improved their reading, the brain patterns of children with dyslexia had become the same as the brain patterns of children without dyslexia.

The adult brain can also reshape itself. When a 35-year-old man lost both hands in an accident, his brain reorganized itself, delegating his elbows to be his new "hands." After he underwent a double hand transplant, his brain reorganized itself again to permit his new hands to function. The lifelong flexibility of the brain makes human beings the most adaptable species on the planet.

Many animals organize themselves into societies. Bees build hives, geese flock together, and wolves live in packs. These species always organize themselves in the same ways. A beehive in one location is like a beehive anywhere else, and beehives have remained basically the same for thousands of years. In contrast, human beings change their social arrangements to meet their changing needs.

People have learned to live in all climates and in every geographic location. We have constructed egalitarian societies as well as societies with sharp class divisions. We have built societies where men and women played equal roles, others where women were superior, and still others where men were superior. People of different origins have lived together as equals, and they have also enslaved one another. We have lived for eons in cooperation and suffered centuries of warfare. Different human societies promote different values. Pre-class societies valued reciprocity, while class societies value competition. Homosexuality was revered by the upper class in ancient Greece and reviled by the upper class in Victorian England.

A flexible brain and a highly social nature make it possible for human beings to solve problems by changing how they live. However, the people in power oppose change because they benefit from the way things are. They and their supporters insist that society can be organized in only one way—the way it is now. Such inflexibility blocks our ability to respond to environmental and social challenges.

A fright-filled world

In the 21st century, most of the threats faced by our ancient ancestors have been eliminated. Rarely is someone eaten by a larger animal. Modern agriculture has made possible an abundant supply of food. We know how to prevent and cure many diseases. We can construct shelters for every possible environment. Our ancestors would be greatly impressed with these achievements and assume that we must live happy lives, free from fear. If only this were true! The dangers of the natural world have been replaced with new dangers created by human beings.

Modern society is divided into antagonistic social classes. Some get rich on the food trade, while others starve because they cannot pay for food. Drug companies make huge profits, while millions die for lack of medicines. Banks, builders, and landlords make fortunes in real estate, while homeless families sleep on the streets. Fortunes are invested in training Olympic athletes, while youngsters lack access to sports programs.

In this class-divided world, the rich and powerful protect themselves at the expense of everyone else. Before Enron declared bankruptcy in 2001, its executives emptied the cash box. About 500 executives took "bonuses" ranging from $1,000 to five million dollars each. When Enron shares plummeted, executives sold their stock, while barring workers from selling theirs. The top dogs at Enron took care of themselves, leaving Enron employees stripped of their jobs, benefits, life's savings, and pensions.

For the majority of people, the world is a dangerous and unpredictable place. Like Enron workers, most people have no control over their jobs, the job market, or the state of the economy. Ordinary people do not control foreign policy or the decision to go to war (although they pay for and die in those wars). People who live without power live in fear.

Animal defenses

A strong fear response is hard-wired into the human brain. Human beings evolved from animals that were prey, not predators. For prey, the best defense is fear. All primates learn fear quickly and easily. Young monkeys who were previously indifferent to snakes acquire an intense fear of them when they observe another monkey display a fearful reaction *even though no actual harm is experienced or observed.* Consider the emotional impact of the movie *Jaws.* The rhythmic, menacing sound that signals the shark's approach produces a strong fear reaction, despite the fact that most people will never see a real shark, let alone be attacked by one.

Animal defenses are rooted in human emotions. The word "emotion" is derived from the Latin verb, *emovere,* which means "to move." Emotions pull us away from what is dangerous (heights, thunderstorms, predators) and push us toward what we desire (food, warmth, companions). Disgust and shame move us away from others while empathy and curiosity move us towards them.

People don't realize how frequently their animal defenses are triggered. Danger activates a fear response that consists of several steps. The first priority is to locate and identify the danger. When a group of people hear a loud crash outside, all conversation stops. All activity stops. People look at each other, asking, "What was that?" They move to a window to find out. Normal activity will not resume until people know whether protective action is required. When this knowledge is withheld or unavailable, people become fearful and unable to concentrate on anything else.

The "orienting response" to danger causes drivers to slow down near accidents and survey the scene. They tie up traffic and irritate those who are trying to clear the roads. Radio announcers make derogatory comments about "rubber-neckers." Police wave cars on and impatiently push onlookers away. Yet, people are compelled to look—the need to assess danger is instinctive.

Once danger has been identified, the brain sets automatic responses into motion. The safest option is to flee. When there is not enough strength, time, or room to run, the brain will ready the body to fight. When neither flight nor fight seems possible, the strategy of last resort is to dissociate, which is also called submitting, freezing, or "playing dead."

Animal defenses are also activated in response to low levels of threat. If reading this book threatens your beliefs, you might put it down and avoid picking it up again (flight). You might get angry and throw the book in the garbage (fight). Or you might go over the same page repeatedly without retaining anything (dissociate). In response to a threatening conversation, you might change the subject (flight), get angry (fight), or appear to listen while you think about something else (dissociate). You take a different route to work to avoid your ex (flight). You fume when your dog chews your shoe (fight). You go blank during an exam (dissociate).

Animal defenses are *instinctive and automatic,* yet society values some reactions over others. The fight response is prized most highly because it is associated with power. Soldiers who enter a fear-induced killing-frenzy (fight reaction) are commended, while those who run or freeze are condemned. Women who fight or flee their rapists are praised, while those who dissociate are wrongly accused of consenting. Dissociated defenses are most disdained as a sign of powerlessness.

Mistaken morality causes people to feel guilty or ashamed about how they react to danger. They may curse themselves for running when they thought they should have fought or for freezing when they thought they should have run. Other people, including professionals, compound the problem when they question why someone "chose" to react one way instead of another. In fact, the type of defense used is determined by subconscious brain centers that rapidly assess the best way to survive, set the response in motion, *and only then* inform the conscious mind of what is happening. By saving time, automatic behavior improves the chance of surviving, and survival is nature's highest value.

The fearsome predators of today are not large animals but corporations, governments, and institutions that devour human lives for profit. Animal defenses cannot protect us from these predators. Recall the Ford Pinto. Most people feel horror when they think about burning to death in their cars. They feel fear that someone they love might die that way. They feel angry that Ford got away with calculated mass murder. When people experience strong emotions, their bodies are pushing them *to do something now.* Unfortunately, emotional responses cannot solve complex social problems.

The emotion of injustice

> Imagine that your town's wealthiest family throws a lavish party costing many times more than your annual income. You're not invited, but you get the bill. Worse, they plan to throw increasingly lavish parties every year and want you to shortchange your family, cash in your savings and postpone retirement to pay for them. You'd be outraged.
>
> *Holly Sklar*

All social animals have a built-in sense of fairness. Two dogs will fight when only one is offered a bone. When treats are equally dispensed, everyone is happy. The sense of fairness is even more developed in primates. Monkeys will refuse to perform when they see other monkeys getting better rewards than they get for the same effort. Human beings can tell the difference between being treated fairly and being cheated. They don't need to be taught this; they feel it in their gut. Who hasn't heard a young child protest, "It's not fair!" and "He got more than I did!"

While fairness is essential for harmonious social living, it takes conscious effort to ensure that relationships are fair. Egalitarian societies develop complex customs to promote fairness. West Coast aboriginal peoples arranged parties where desired goods would be given away, exchanged, and even destroyed to prevent the resentment that results when some have more than they need, while others go without.

At every age, in all cultures, and throughout time, unfairness has evoked anger in human beings. Anger is the emotion of injustice. Anger screams, "Something is wrong!" and provides energy to set things right. The beginning of class divisions marked the beginning of rebellions by the ruled against their rulers. From the slave uprisings of the ancient world through the peasant revolts that swept Europe during the Middle Ages to the working class revolts that rocked the 20th century people have fought for their right to an equal say and an equal share.

Anger results when some are denied what is available to others (jobs, housing, access to education, medical treatment, social support, etc.). The have-nots may live with simmering resentment or rebel openly.

Either way, the *awareness of inequality is a constant irritant*. Because inequality generates rebellion, unequal societies must create penal systems to crush those who rebel.

When anger is stimulated and its expression is blocked, emotions can build to an intolerable level. Anger warns us that something is wrong and provides energy to act. However, no emotion, on its own, can tell us *what* is wrong or *how* to make it right. Without this information, anger can be unleashed in ways that backfire or it can be squandered in useless activities that only blow off steam. A good example is the worker who is humiliated by her supervisor every day and fears she will lose her job if she fights back. Her frustrated anger can become dissociated from her supervisor and misdirected against herself or her workmates, family members, pet, neighbors, or anyone who crosses her path. The phrase "going postal" refers to U.S. postal workers who became so stressed that they "lost it" and attacked their supervisors and co-workers, often killing themselves as well. Misdirected anger does not solve problems. On the contrary, dumping anger on innocent bystanders and loved ones can produce guilt and shame and generate more anger.

Anger is most powerful when it is organized and focused on a specific goal. In 1997, the South African government passed a law allowing it to import or produce cheaper versions of expensive medicines to treat HIV/AIDS. In response, a cartel of 39 drug companies sued the South African government for bypassing their drug patents and threatening their profits. The U.S. government backed the drug companies and threatened to boycott South Africa unless it dropped the law. The injustice of this situation enraged many people around the world. They organized in such large numbers and so effectively that they forced both the U.S. government and the drug cartel to back down.

Emotional hijack

Human beings have a unique ability to analyze and solve complex problems. However, strong emotions release stress hormones that can hijack the brain and prevent clear thinking. Common metaphors like "out of his head with grief," "loose cannon," and "consumed by lust" describe how intense feelings can overwhelm common sense. Automatic reactions helped our ancestors to survive animal predators when taking time to think might have been fatal.

The military exploits the link between stress and automatic reactions to ensure that soldiers will kill on command, without thinking. Such training can be difficult to contain. In 2002, a series of murders and suicides rocked the Fort Bragg military base. Just two days back from the war in Afghanistan, Rigoberto Nieves shot and killed his wife and then himself. Back from the war for only a month, William Wright killed his wife. Six months after returning from Afghanistan, Brandon Floyd shot his wife and then himself. Former Air Force captain Dorothy Mackey explains, "The military members who are committing these attacks are, in fact, trained to be this violent. There is a lack of restraint, a lack of humanity that's drilled into them."

Danger stimulates strong emotions that cause people to behave without thinking. However, *social problems require social solutions based on reasoned problem-solving*. The solution to this contradiction is an organized defense. There is safety in numbers. In response to danger, a group of people can calm each other enough to analyze and solve complex problems. However, when authorities prevent collective problem-solving, people resort to animal defenses, as the following example shows.

Slaughtering chickens is notoriously dirty, dangerous, and low-paid. Anyone doing such work would have to dissociate. In 2004, it was revealed that workers at a chicken-processing plant in Moorefield, West Virginia, were torturing chickens, with the apparent approval of management. The incidents increased when employees were forced to work overtime. No doubt their anger against the chickens was aroused by unbearable working conditions. No doubt their supervisors preferred workers to unleash their anger on the chickens instead of organizing to demand humane conditions for themselves and for the chickens.

Exploiting fear

The world can seem wonderful or horrible, depending on which emotions are stimulated. Advertisers use images of children and animals to evoke positive emotions and attract customers. The media do the opposite. The media slogan, "If it bleeds, it leads" reveals how danger is used to capture people's attention. While a media focus on crime, cruelty, and disaster is profitable, it creates a distorted view of the world that makes people more fearful. In response to the highly-publicized murders of two 10-year-old girls, a couple in England decided to implant a global-positioning microchip in their daughter's arm so they could find her if she was abducted.

The media, the police, and the military exaggerate danger to serve their needs. The automotive industry minimizes danger for the same reason. Automobiles are promoted as safe family fun, despite the fact that children are far more likely to be killed by cars than abducted by strangers. In rich nations, vehicles are the leading cause of child death. Such facts are not allowed to undermine car sales and car profits. When people's emotions are so regularly manipulated, it can be difficult to know what is real.

Politicians are notorious for manipulating people's emotions. During the buildup to the U.S. war against Afghanistan, public officials used fear as a weapon of mass deception. Most Americans viewed the attack on the World Trade Center on television and were in no immediate danger. They wanted to know what had happened and why. However, the mainstream media discouraged thoughtful discussion by emphasizing the horror of the tragedy. Dramatic footage of the towers collapsing and people screaming and jumping out the windows was shown repeatedly, around-the-clock. People were hypnotically glued to their television sets, watching planes strike the buildings hundreds of times, day after day. Gruesome images multiplied on the covers of newspapers and magazines. The entire population was engulfed in a relentless horror. A study conducted a few days after 9/11 found that 71 percent of Americans felt depressed, 49 percent had difficulty concentrating, and 33 percent were suffering from insomnia. The American Psychological Association was concerned about how much fear was being stimulated. Their web site explains,

> If a person can form a mental image of themselves, their children or their loved ones in life-threatening situations, he or she feels vulnerable…Statistics show that while becoming the victim of further terrorism is unlikely for the great majority of Americans, the images of the attacks on the World Trade Center and the Pentagon can supersede people's rational perception of what is dangerous.[10]

Suppressing rational perception was the goal. When a parade of politicians, experts, and media commentators cries that danger is looming and war is the only response, people find this message hard to resist. Fear compels us to *do something now,* even though that something might create more danger. Panic demands that *someone set things right,* even when that someone can't be trusted. A panicked population was pointed in the wrong direction—"the enemy is over there!" Those who tried to think through the situation were denounced as unfeeling, condemned as disloyal, and accused of supporting the enemy. To silence the opposition, President Bush threatened "Whoever is not with us is against us."

In fact, Washington had plans to invade Afghanistan before September 11, when the Taliban rejected a U.S. proposal to construct an oil pipeline through their country. When this information became public a few months after 9/11, Vice-President Dick Cheney and FBI director Robert Mueller warned of the possibility of further terrorist attacks. In a rare fit of honesty, White House officials later told reporters that these warnings were issued not because of any increased threat but to deflect criticism that was coming from political opponents.

The fear of imminent danger was also used to sell the war against Iraq. After the U.S. invasion, when no weapons of mass destruction could be found, when no link between Iraq and Al Qaeda could be found, when it became clear that the president had lied and all the reasons for the war were false, the US continued to occupy Iraq and suppress all resistance. Why?

For years, the U.S. has wanted more military bases in the Middle East to control the world's largest supply of oil. The problem was how to convince the American people to back such a plan. The attacks of 9/11 offered the perfect opportunity. The dog and pony show about weapons of mass destruction, defense of the nation, evil dictators, and promoting democracy provided the needed cover for an oil grab.

Joseph Schumpeter describes how exaggerating the threat of danger to support imperial expansion is a political tactic that dates back to the early Roman Empire.

> There was no corner of the known world where some interest was not alleged to be in danger or under actual attack. If the interests were not Roman, they were those of Rome's allies; and if Rome had no allies, then allies would be invented. When it was utterly impossible to contrive such an interest—why, then it was the national honor that had been insulted. The fight was always invested with an aura of legality. Rome was always being attacked by evil-minded neighbors, always fighting for a breathing-space. The whole world was pervaded by a host of enemies, and it was manifestly Rome's duty to guard against their indubitably aggressive designs.[11]

Today, the United States dominates the world with overwhelming military power. In 2003, the U.S. Department of Defense reported that it had more than 700 American military bases in 130 countries (in addition to the 6,000 bases on U.S. territory). The report did not include bases in Kosovo, Afghanistan, and Iraq. Nor did it include the State of Israel, America's largest and best-funded military base. Furthermore, the number of bases in each country was underestimated; for example, only one of the ten bases in Okinawa, Japan was counted. A more realistic estimate would be 1,000 American military bases outside the United States.

Despite a half-trillion dollar "defense" budget, the United States has not been invaded since 1812, when Canadian forces burned the White House. As serious as it was, the attack on 9/11 pales in comparison to the savage destruction that U.S. forces periodically inflict on other nations. Stoking the fear of further attacks in order to expand the empire does not increase public safety. On the contrary, military aggression increases the risk of retaliation. U.S. wars in the Middle East bring power and profit to the ruling class, while making the world more dangerous for everyone else.

The panic myth

In 1916, Wilfred Trotter wrote *The Instincts of the Herd in Peace and War* in which he argued that anti-war protests and workers' revolts were based on mindless "herd instinct." Trotter was writing for an elite who were terrified that ordinary people might take power into their own hands. His concept of "herd instinct" launched the myth that people in groups behave like wild animals.

Everyone has seen media images of people stampeding over each other in a frenzied effort to escape a fire or a collapsing building. When Hurricane Katrina devastated the Gulf Coast in 2005, the media reported mass murders and rapes in New Orleans. Later investigation found no evidence of such events. During the crisis, official order broke down completely, while ordinary people behaved exceptionally well.

Researchers who study disasters find that panic reactions are extremely rare; most people respond cooperatively and sensibly in a crisis. The "everyone out for himself" phenomenon occurs only when there is great risk of injury or death, little chance of escape, limited resources, lack of organization, and lack of leadership.

Examples of orderly behavior in the face of disaster are seldom reported by the media. There was no mass panic in response to the Three Mile Island nuclear accident. After the bombing of the World Trade Center in 1993, and again in 2001, people evacuated the buildings in an organized fashion. Those who jumped in panic from the windows of the World Trade Center had no other way out.

Another example of calm behavior occurred during the massive power blackout of 2003. When the electrical grid failed in the northeast U.S. and parts of Canada, public officials feared a complete breakdown in law and order, readied militia, and braced for the worst. In contrast, ordinary people gathered to trade news and share perishable food. Individuals helped direct traffic, and drivers offered rides to stranded commuters. Although the blackout was not a disaster, it showed that people don't panic at the first sign of trouble.

Authorities use the panic myth to exclude ordinary people from the decision-making process. After 9/11, scientists expressed concern that,

> The assumption that people will panic or become irrational following an attack has negative consequences. Authorities may provide inaccurate information or unfounded reassurances motivated by a wish to calm the public. The panic myth may also lead to the neglect of the public's role in planning and response.[12]

Scientists urged the authorities to "treat the public as a capable ally" and warned that panic and social disruption are *more likely* when people are kept in the dark or misled. Such advice falls on deaf ears, because the people in power are concerned more with maintaining control than with protecting human lives. Two paramedics who were caught in the flood that destroyed New Orleans experienced this first-hand.

> All the law enforcement agencies appeared threatened when we congregated into groups of 20 or more. In every congregation of "victims," they saw "mob" or "riot." We felt safety in numbers. Our "we must stay together" attitude was impossible because the agencies would force us into small atomized groups.[13]

Authorities fear the prospect of people mobilizing on their own behalf, yet offer no competent alternative. The commission investigating 9/11 found that "the attacks, rather than being bolts from the blue, were preceded by a rising tide of unheard, ignored or mishandled warnings of pending trouble." According to the *New York Times,*

> Most Americans were no doubt stunned to learn how poorly prepared federal agencies and the military were for such an emergency, much as New Yorkers were shocked when the commission spelled out the shortcomings of local first responders. But it's one thing to learn of communications problems

between the Police and Fire Departments, or between city agencies and the Port Authority. It's quite another to learn about communications problems, and chain-of-command confusion, among the White House, the military and other federal agencies as the nation was under attack.[14]

Contrast the bungling of bureaucrats with the heroism of passengers on United Flight 93, who chose to crash their plane rather than let it be used as a missile. The commission found that, in many instances, front-line workers came through where the higher-ups caved. The same scenario was repeated during Hurricane Katrina. While government officials showed their incompetence, ordinary people rose to the challenge:

> The maintenance workers who used a forklift to carry the sick and disabled. The engineers who rigged, nurtured and kept the generators running…Refinery workers who broke into boat yards, "stealing" boats to rescue their neighbors clinging to their roofs in flood waters. Mechanics who helped hotwire any car that could be found to ferry people out of the city. And the food service workers who scoured the commercial kitchens, improvising communal meals for hundreds of those stranded.[15]

The authorities present themselves as intelligent adults, and ordinary people as easily-panicked children who cannot handle the truth. In reality, the deepest fear of public officials is that common people will take over the decision-making process. The panic myth helps to keep information, resources, and control in the hands of the few and out of the hands of the many.

Tend and befriend

The power of people pulling together is rejected by those who sniff that they are not "joiners," as if collective activity posed a threat to their individuality. The conflict between the individual and the collective is played out in TV programs like *Star Trek,* in which the alien Borg have a "hive mind" that does not tolerate individuality. Ironically, the show also provides a model of collectivity that cherishes individuality, both in the crew-as-family on the Starship and the extended family of the Federation of Planets. Preserving one's individuality does not require isolation. On the contrary, human beings require secure connections with others in order to develop their individuality.

The human sense of self is not confined to the physical body, but includes all who are important to us: friends, family, pets, and even places and things. Their loss hurts so much because they are a part of us, and we are not the same without them. In early human societies, the sense of self extended to the whole community and the natural world. This was no romantic fantasy. Strong social bonds support survival.

Many animals display collective defenses. A swarm of wasps will defend a threatened nest. A flock of swallows will attack any who approach their breeding ground. Frightened elephants gather their young behind them and form an outward-facing circle to present an advancing predator with a wall of tusks. Such collective defenses, called "tend and befriend," are especially important for human beings who lack the physical defenses of other animals—sharp claws, a venomous bite, piercing teeth, thick skin. The human species survived by banding together for mutual benefit. A hormone called oxytocin facilitates adult-child bonding and promotes trust between adults. In crises, people are highly motivated to "tend and befriend." On 9/11, people rushed to Ground Zero to offer help, and during Hurricane Katrina people spontaneously organized to provide aid.

Cooperation typically produces positive feelings and increases the sense of power. To find out why, psychologists at the University of Sussex conducted interviews with people who had been involved in "traditional marches, fox-hunt sabotages, anti-capitalist street parties, environmental direct actions, and industrial mass pickets." Their research revealed several factors that contribute to a heightened sense of power: being part of something bigger than yourself; increased hope that change is possible; and having a sense of "unity and mutual support" within the group. Furthermore,

> Empowering events were almost without exception described as joyous occasions. Participants experienced a deep sense of happiness and even euphoria in being involved in protest events. Simply recounting the events in the interview brought a smile to the faces of the interviewees.[16]

Because positive feelings are known to promote mental and physical health, the researchers concluded, "people should get more involved in campaigns, struggles and social movements, not only in the wider interest of social change, but also for their own personal good."

Hope and power

People who feel powerless have been compared to laboratory animals who resign themselves to unavoidable electrical shocks. Even when their cage doors are opened, they do not escape. This phenomenon is called "learned helplessness," where the familiar, no matter how terrible, seems preferable to the unknown, no matter how promising. When people feel hopeless they do not seek solutions, which reinforces their feelings of powerlessness.

Animals have limited ways to extract themselves from powerless situations. Very few can think their way out or recruit others to help them escape. In contrast, there is no limit to the creativity, imagination, and resourcefulness of people who work together. As the saying goes, "A burden shared is a burden halved." People who cooperate feel more hopeful, so they work harder to find solutions, thereby increasing the possibility of success. When people pull together, they generate hope and power, as the following example shows.

There may be no one more hopeless than a condemned prisoner on Death Row. Nevertheless, in 2003, Governor George Ryan commuted all death sentences in the state of Illinois, saving the lives of 163 men and 4 women. What could make a long-time supporter of the death penalty turn against it? Marlene Martin from the Campaign to End the Death Penalty provides the answer:

> We should recognize how important the efforts of death penalty opponents were in setting the stage for a Republican governor—who came to office with no intention of paying any attention to the issue of the death penalty—to make the most sweeping changes on this issue in 30 years. George Ryan admitted that the issue was not even on his radar screen four years ago. It was the work of activists, lawyers, journalists, family members and death row prisoners themselves who put it there.[17]

Hope and power depend on whether people work alone or together. Alone, we cannot protect ourselves from the dangers of exploding cars, abusive priests, corrupt corporations, oppressive institutions, and dishonest governments. As an organized force, we have the power to make a difference. Part Two explains how humanity was robbed of this collective power.

Summary

The human species is nature's youngest child — a problem-solving animal unlike any other. While individuals are limited in their ability to solve problems, there is virtually no limit to the problems that people can solve together.

To maintain exclusive control over society, the people in power strive to keep the majority feeling isolated, fearful, and powerless. However, the incompetent, immoral behavior of public officials compels ordinary people to organize in self-defense.

Part Two

How Did This happen?

What do I care about the law? Haven't I got the power?
Cornelius Vanderbilt (1794–1877)

I've lived my life by the Golden Rule: He who has the most gold makes the rules.
Magna CEO *Frank Stronach (1932–?)*

During the 19th century, a gang of thieves called "robber barons" conspired, bribed, lied, cheated, stole, clawed, and murdered their way to the top of American society. At the beginning of the 21st century, such people rule the world. They are called CEOs, magnates, moguls, capitalists, industrialists, tycoons, captains of industry, policy-makers, and pillars of society. The more wealth they gather into their possession, the more deprivation and misery they create for everyone else. Their power grows out of our powerlessness.

Knowing the past is essential to changing the future. Part Two explains how the majority came to be robbed of its power and what humanity lost in the process.

- Chapter 5. *Seize the Surplus* explains how class divisions developed.

- Chapter 6. *Compete or Die* describes how the drive for profit shapes society.

- Chapter 7. *Burden the Family* outlines how the family system serves capitalism.

- Chapter 8. *Profit from Pain* reveals how social problems are disguised as individual medical illnesses.

Chapter 5

Seize the Surplus

> They have taken untold millions that they never toiled to earn,
> Yet without our brain and muscle not a single wheel would turn.
>
> from the song *Solidarity Forever*

We live on a planet that is rich in natural resources: water, minerals, topsoil, and an abundance of plant and animal life. About 150,000 years ago, a dynamic new species appeared in Africa. Human beings distinguished themselves from other animals by their ability to learn new skills, share these skills with each other, and teach them to their children. Other animals used tools, but no other animal accumulated experience from one generation to another. With such a survival advantage, the human species multiplied and migrated from Africa to every part of the globe.

Human development transformed the environment. An expanding knowledge of plants, soil, weather, seasons, and tools laid the basis for agriculture, more permanent settlements, and a surplus of food. People learned to fire clay pots to store water and food. They learned to shape metals into sharper, harder tools to plow the land. As living standards rose, the population increased.

The industrial revolution pushed production forward at a rapid rate. The 17th-century printing press accelerated the accumulation of knowledge by making individual experiences accessible to thousands of people. The 18th-century steam-driven engine provided power to drive the new machines. A global economy developed by the end of the 19th century. By the end of the 20th century, the annual value of goods and services produced in the world had reached 20 trillion U.S. dollars.

Imagine the benefits of everyone sharing these riches: no one dying from preventable or treatable disease; everyone fed, clothed and sheltered; and people free to develop their potential. Unfortunately, most of the world's wealth is owned and controlled by a handful of powerful ruling families. That giant sucking sound you hear is the global surplus being siphoned into their bank accounts. The majority of the planet's population—about six billion people—scramble to survive. At the beginning of the 21st century, one in five people lives on less than one dollar a day, one billion people do not have adequate shelter, more than two billion people have no access to proper sanitation, and more than one billion people lack access to safe drinking water. It wasn't always like this.

The rule of reciprocity

The human species is about 150,000 years old, while evidence of class divisions, exploitation, oppression, and war appeared only 10,000 years ago. For 95 percent of human history, people lived as hunters and gatherers in sharing societies. Cooperation enhances survival for many species—ants build colonies, fish swim in schools, birds graze in flocks, and so on. For human beings, cooperation is key to survival. Hunters relied on gatherers for their primary source of food, while gatherers relied on hunters for supplements of richer foods. Hunting larger prey required teamwork, and cooperating adults could protect and provide for their dependent offspring more effectively. Most respected anthropologists, including Richard Leakey, Eleanor Burke Leacock and Richard Lee, acknowledge the cooperative nature of early human societies. Lee reports,

> Food is never consumed alone by a family: it is always shared out among members of a living group or band….This principle of generalized reciprocity has been reported of hunter-gatherers in every continent and in every kind of environment.[18]

The rule of reciprocity applied equally to interpersonal relationships and to human relationships with the natural world. No one took anything from another person or from Nature without giving back something in return. The rule of reciprocity was embedded in cultural practices and folklore. All aboriginal societies contain stories that warn of the harm that comes to those who behave in a selfish, greedy, or careless manner. Lee concludes,

> It is the long experience of egalitarian sharing that has molded our past. Despite our seeming adaptation to life in hierarchical societies, and despite the rather dismal track record of human rights in many parts of the world, there are signs that humankind retains a deep-rooted sense of egalitarianism, a deep-rooted commitment to the norm of reciprocity, a deep-rooted…sense of community.[19]

Our early ancestors lived very differently from how we live today, and not because of human nature. If an infant born 150,000 years ago were raised in a modern family, that child would be the same as any other child. Genetically, we are identical. The only difference between us and them is several thousand years of human history.

Around 10,000 years ago, people learned to grow food in addition to gathering it. The development of agriculture dramatically changed the way people lived and related to one another. Foraging societies moved continually in their search for food. Planting crops required landed settlements. The wandering life could support only small groups of people; too many children were a burden. In contrast, farming villages could feed hundreds of people, and more children provided more help on the land. Foraging societies depended on equality and reciprocity to survive. Landed agriculture laid the basis for war.

War

Some people argue that war is inevitable because it is human nature. Throughout history, individual disputes have undoubtedly resulted in death on occasion. However, individual conflict is not the same as the socially organized activity of war. Despite Hollywood fantasies to the contrary, there is no scientific evidence of warfare for most of human history. In *The Birth of War,* anthropologist R. Brian Ferguson explains, the global archaeological record contradicts the idea that war was always a feature of human existence; instead, the record shows that warfare is largely a development of the past 10,000 years.[20]

Why did war appear after eons of cooperative living? In *Origins Reconsidered: In Search of What Makes Us Human,* Richard Leakey examines the evidence and concludes,

> I believe that warfare is rooted in the need for territorial possession once populations became agricultural and necessarily sedentary…I do not believe that violence is an innate characteristic of humankind, merely an unfortunate adaptation to certain circumstances.[21]

People behave differently in different situations. The ability to adapt is humanity's greatest strength and its greatest weakness (when we adapt to harmful conditions instead of changing them). Survival in foraging societies depended on cooperation, so conflict was discouraged and disputes were settled by separating the adversaries. However, separating adversaries could not be done so easily when people had invested labor in the land.

Foraging societies lived from hand to mouth because they had no surplus beyond their immediate needs. In contrast, agricultural villages could accumulate a surplus of food, tools, valued objects, and animals. There is no benefit in stealing when no one has anything worth taking. And there is no benefit in stealing when everyone has all they need. However, when there is a surplus, *but not enough for all,* then the opportunity arises for some to benefit by seizing the goods and lands of others. Humanity did not begin to war for biological reasons, but because warfare became socially advantageous.

Wars of acquisition result in continual conflict, as those who are robbed strive to regain what was stolen. Leakey notes that after warfare appears, violence becomes "almost an obsession." The history of war is emphasized so much that most people can't believe that warfare is such a recent development. Most discussions of human cruelty end with comments like, "That's Man's inhumanity to Man," or "People have always warred against each other," or "It's survival of the fittest." Christianity offers Cain and Abel as evidence that war springs from "original sin." Books and films promote the idea that human beings are naked apes born with a killer instinct, a territorial imperative, and selfish genes. This is nonsense. If war was in our nature, the airways would be filled with songs about war, not love. If war was in our nature, there would be no need to disguise war as humanitarian intervention and no need to censor the gruesome images of slaughter. Historian Howard Zinn points out,

> We don't find people spontaneously rushing to make war on others. What we find instead is that governments must make the most strenuous efforts to mobilize populations for war. They must entice soldiers with promises of money, education, must hold out to young people whose chances in life look very poor that here is an opportunity to attain respect and status. And if those enticements don't work, governments must use coercion—they must conscript young people, force them into military service, threaten them with prison if they do not comply.[22]

Class society

The complexities of agricultural life (including the threat of raids) required more formal methods of decision-making. Differences in status began to appear when selected individuals were given the right to decide some matters for the group as a whole. However, there were still no signs of significant differences in *wealth*. Mutual survival demanded that people with higher status work alongside everyone else.

Eventually, rising productivity created a surplus that was large enough to plan community projects. When enough food could be produced to feed everyone in the village, small groups of people could be assigned to construct irrigation systems to increase next year's harvest. Others might clear roads to improve trade with nearby groups. Time that is freed from food production can also be used to design better ways to do things. Science and technology—astronomy, writing, mathematics, engineering, manufacture, and medicine—developed from the desire to increase production and raise living standards. Releasing some people from food production allowed society to advance when there was not enough surplus to free everyone from regular toil.

People are inventive and creative. Those who were delegated to manage the surplus *for* the community found themselves in a position to impose their will *over* the community. The same armed guards who were hired to protect the village from raiders could also protect the elite from villagers who challenged their power.

Historians estimate that the collectively-produced surplus began to be claimed as the private property of individuals about 6,000 years ago. *The development of a ruling class was possible only because there was not enough surplus for everyone.* People need not submit to the power of wealth when they have their own. Unfortunately, the potential to create that much wealth would not be realized for a few thousand more years.

With the development of private property, humanity split into classes: the majority who labor to produce; the minority who claim ownership of what is produced; and a small group of people in between. Class divisions did not develop because "some people are naturally greedy." The potential for greed is in every human being. However, if greed were a dominant characteristic, class divisions would have appeared along with humanity—150,000 years ago. Human behavior is flexible. When there is no surplus, everyone benefits by sharing. When there is plenty for all, greed provides no benefit. When there is enough to free some from daily labor, but not enough to lighten everyone's load, greed can reward the well-placed few.

Communal living did not succumb easily to class divisions. However, with a ruling elite driving their economies forward, class societies became more technically advanced. North American aboriginals with spears on foot were no match for Europeans with rifles on horseback. The transition from cooperative to class society took different forms in different regions, but the process was always violent and bloody. In some areas, egalitarian societies were completely wiped out. In others, conquered peoples were enslaved or herded onto reservations.

The beginning of class divisions marked the end of thousands of years of sharing the ups and downs of life. As the elite seized the biggest and best for themselves, their living standards rose. As the laboring classes lost a growing proportion of what they produced, their living standards fell. For these people, the division of humanity into classes meant less food, more sickness, and shorter lives.

Private property

Human beings arrange their relationships—their social system—based on how they produce their living. Societies that depend on mutual cooperation develop a culture to support their prime directive, "Share." When the elite seized the surplus, the *rule* of reciprocity was overthrown even though reciprocal relationships remained necessary for the day-to-day survival of the majority.

Class society established a new prime directive: "Seize the Surplus." The ruling class not only claims ownership over the products of labor, but also over the means of making a living that were once commonly owned, such as land, water, science, and technology. Claiming these means of making a living as "private property" removes them from common control. Let me emphasize that *private property is not the same as personal property,* or personal-use items. Throughout history, people have kept, lent, given away, and traded clothing, tools, toys, furniture, homes, and other personal possessions. The term "private property" should be reserved only for the *means of making a living.* Confusion about the difference between personal and private property is widespread because people are encouraged to view their homes as private property (not personal property) so they will feel loyal to the system of private property. In fact, private property consumes personal property. In 2005, the Supreme Court ruled that cities can seize and demolish people's homes to make way for shopping malls and other money-making enterprises.

The emergence of private property marked a fundamental change in human relationships. Pre-class societies used land in common, having no concept of individual land ownership. Once land was declared the private property of some and not others, it became a source of conflict. European peasants were killed for gathering wood and for hunting on previously common lands that were claimed as "the lord's estate." A massive land grab in North America required the decimation of native peoples. Human beings could also become private property; the first signs of slavery appeared about 5,000 years ago.

The biggest problem for every ruling class is preventing private property from reverting to common control. The State was organized for this purpose. An effective State includes a legal system to uphold the rule of private property, police to serve the elite and protect their property, officials to collect surplus in the form of taxes, armies to enforce the rule of the State, a religious system to preach obedience to authority, an education system to prepare children for their roles in the social hierarchy, and a penal system to crush rebels and keep potential rebels under control.

Inheritance laws ensure that ruling families retain their wealth and power. For the "rightful heir" to be determined, the sexuality of women has to be restricted. Class society makes children the property of their parents and distinguishes between "legitimate" and "illegitimate" children.

Private property, the State, and the oppression of women and children developed together in different locations around the world, indicating a common response to the needs of emerging ruling classes.

Simple and complex

You might be wondering how changing the prime directive from "Share" to "Seize the Surplus" could cause such a dramatic change in society. Simple rules can generate complex systems. When simple equations are fed into a computer and repeated in a continual feedback loop, they generate complex geometric patterns called fractals. Nature works in a similar way. Have you ever wondered how a school of fish or a flock of birds could change direction, seemingly all at once, and then change direction again, as if they were one giant organism? It appears as if there must be some master hand at work. Not so. Each fish or bird follows two simple rules: maintain a constant distance from your neighbors and turn when they do. We do not see these rules, only the patterns that result when these rules are applied.

Modern society is similar. Despite its complexity, there is no invisible hand directing things. Of course, corporations collude to set prices and fleece their customers, and politicians conspire to win support for pro-business laws and for wars, but there is no grand conspiracy. There doesn't need to be. Two simple rules, reproduced throughout society, create the complex web of relationships that we experience every day. These rules are Seize the Surplus (where common holdings become private property) and Compete or Die, which is discussed in the next chapter. What we experience as immense social complexity is generated from these two rules being applied in different situations.

Societies based on the same rules can look very different. Before classes existed, there were many different societies based on the rule of reciprocity. These societies varied in appearance because they interpreted the need to share according to local conditions. Nevertheless, the rule of reciprocity dominated them all so that a person from one egalitarian society would feel fairly at home in another. When humanity broke into classes, the rule of private property replaced the rule of reciprocity, leaving no room for those who followed the old ways. Aboriginal peoples could not be assimilated into class societies without destroying their culture and identity. It was easier to move in the opposite direction—people "went native" to escape oppression and exploitation.

Class societies also developed variations in different conditions. The European, Egyptian, Chinese, and Mayan dynasties were early class societies that arose on separate continents. While they varied in many ways, the power relations within them were basically the same—a minority class exploited the labor of the majority. Capitalism also takes many forms: electoral systems like the U.S.A. and Canada; monarchies like Nepal and Saudi Arabia; one-party States like China and Cuba; religious States like Israel and Iran; military dictatorships like Myanmar and occupied Haiti; and so on. A person from one class society can fit into any other class society by accepting the prevailing social hierarchy.

Because complex societies are based on simple rules, changing those rules changes society. Replacing the rule of reciprocity with the rule of private property resulted in a complete transformation of human experience. As the final chapters explain, society can be transformed again, not by changing the behaviors that result from social rules, but by changing the rules themselves.

Capitalism

Capitalism differs from previous class societies in the extent to which it denies the majority *any* control over the means of making a living. In feudal Europe, peasants could own small plots of land, even though the landlord took most of what was produced. Craftspeople also owned their own tools and could make a living selling their products. Capitalism revolutionized the way work was done. Small family farms have been swallowed up by giant farming corporations called "agribusiness." Artisans cannot compete with factory production. With few exceptions, the modern capitalist class controls virtually all the means of production: land, livestock, factories, fisheries, mines, machines, methods, and technology. Even seeds, plants, and animals are patented.

There seems to be no limit to the process of claiming every square inch of the planet as private property. Corporations claim ownership over the water supply and charge for its use. Nations claim ownership of air space. There are even disputes over who owns the moon. Only the national debt is collectively owned. How did the ruling class get so much power?

Like every ruling class before it, the capitalist class established itself by theft, by claiming exclusive possession of what had formerly been held in common. In the United States, land was taken by force from aboriginal peoples, and many founding families built their fortunes by buying and selling this land. Others enriched themselves through slave labor. Such "primitive accumulation" laid the foundation for more sophisticated capital accumulation, as the following example shows.

Profit

Let's say that someone manages, by hook or by crook, to obtain enough surplus to hire workers to construct a factory. The factory-owner then offers a wage to entice people to work in his factory. In exchange for this wage, the capitalist claims ownership over *everything* the workers produce. Security systems ensure that no worker removes "company property."

Let's say that each worker can build one machine every eight hours, or the length of one workday. At the end of the day, the worker takes home her wage and leaves the machine that she made in her employer's possession. Let's say that this machine can be used to build more machines. The next day, the capitalist demands that the worker use the machine she made yesterday to produce two more machines today.

If the worker insists on being paid twice as much to make two machines, or if she insists on working only four hours (the length of time it now takes to make one machine), or if she insists on taking home the second machine, she would enjoy higher wages, a shorter workday, or possession of a growing number of machines. However, the capitalist would make no profit.

The capitalist is not a philanthropist. He invested in the factory to make a profit, not to raise workers' living standards. The capitalist demands that the worker accept the same wage as before *and* work the same eight hours as before *and* give up her right to both machines. That way, the capitalist will enjoy a one-hundred percent profit, equivalent to one additional machine every eight hours. The capitalist wants the worker to be the philanthropist and build the capitalist's fortune.

The essence of class conflict lies in the dispute over who should own what the worker produces. The worker points out that she made the machine. The capitalist claims that he paid for the factory, tools, and raw materials. He neglects to mention (and hopes that we have forgotten) that he or his ancestors stole the assets needed to acquire these things. The State sides with the capitalist, declaring that the factory is his private property, so that everything made there belongs to him. The worker is commanded to relinquish all rights to what she produces. The capitalist is overjoyed. He gets to keep the value of what the worker makes, which is always more than what he pays her in wages.

The process of taking surplus away from those who produce it is called *exploitation*. The surplus taken by the capitalist is called *profit*. Profit that is used to extract more surplus from workers is called *capital*. Capitalists live to accumulate capital.

> Every process of capital accumulation involves repeated changes [of capital] from one form to the other: money capital is used to buy means of production, raw materials and labor power [productive capital]; this is put together in the production process to turn out commodities [commodity capital]; these commodities are then exchanged for money [money capital]; this money is then used to buy more means of production, raw materials and labor power, and so on.[23]

Capitalism is the social arrangement between the capitalist class and the working class where the capitalist takes what the worker produces today in order to more effectively exploit the worker tomorrow.

The social creation of private wealth

Most capitalists would disagree that profits are created by workers. They believe that their profits represent their share of the work. In fact, capitalists do no socially useful work. Their job is to maximize profit:

to get more out of their workers; to outfox their competitors; and to avoid paying taxes. A society that produced for human need would have no use for such "work."

Others say that capitalists are richer because they are smarter or work harder. This is a delusion. In their book, *I Didn't Do It Alone: Society's Contribution to Individual Wealth and Success,* Chuck Collins, Mike Lapham and Scott Klinger explain how important luck is to individual accomplishment. Where you are born, the time in which you live, the family into which you are born, your skin color, and your sex strongly influence the possibility of success. They provide the example of Nick Szabo, who survived a plane crash while the person sitting next to him was killed. Szabo used the insurance money from his injuries to buy Silicon Valley real estate and make a fortune.

No business could prosper and no capitalist could become wealthy without the social support of property laws, laws of inheritance, and patent protection of ideas, methods, and products. Bill Gates built his megafortune by buying and selling software that other people produced. He could do this only because the legal system upholds the right of the capitalist class to privately own the means of production and, therefore, all the wealth that workers create.

Business also depends on the publicly-funded infrastructure of society—roads, highways, bridges, railways, airports, shipping ports, power-grids, communication systems, police, schools, and medical facilities. The auto industry would quickly go belly-up if it had to finance the building and maintenance of roads and bridges.

Billions of dollars of government money fund the research and development that support corporate profits. Ross Perot, who ran for U.S. president in 1992, was called "the welfare billionaire" for using public money to build his fortune. The pharmaceutical industry has become the most lucrative business in America by relying on taxpayer-funded scientific research.

While business profits from the use of social resources, the legion of low-paid workers who pay for and provide these resources receive no portion of the profits. Nor is society repaid in the form of corporate taxes. Tax deductions and loopholes see to that. According to the *New York Times,*

> Almost two-thirds of America's corporations paid no federal income taxes during the late 1990's, when corporate profits were soaring. Nine out of 10 companies paid less than the equivalent of 5 percent of their total income.[24]

If the social basis of private wealth were openly acknowledged, then all of society would have a claim on this wealth. The myth of the "self-made" man or woman helps to keep socially-produced wealth in private hands.

The degradation of work

> God, I hated that assembly line. *I hated it.* I used to fall asleep on the job standing up and still keep doing my work. There's nothing more boring and repetitious in the world. On top of it, you don't feel human. The machine's running you, you're not running it.[25]

Lillian Rubin captured the anguish of this 33-year-old mechanic in *Worlds of Pain: Life in the Working-Class Family.* Workers are rarely allowed to use their creativity and judgment, to be the masters of their machines. What happened to the generations of skilled artisans who took pride in their work?

In *Labor and Monopoly Capital: The Degradation of Work in the Twentieth Century,* Harry Braverman explains that for capitalists to gain control over production, workers had to lose control over the labor process—to become alienated from their own labor. Initially, this was accomplished through the pressure of starvation, the compulsion of the orphanage, the fear of the workhouse, and the force of the prison.

In the late 19th century, Frederick Winslow Taylor developed the concept of "scientific management" (also called Taylorism) to maximize the extraction of profit. Braverman emphasizes that "Scientific management enters the workplace not as the representative of science, but as the representative of management masquerading in the trappings of science." Taylor developed three principles to fragment the work of skilled artisans into small segments that could be assigned to less skilled workers. By de-skilling work, management can remove control from the worker and cut the cost of labor.

Taylor's first principle is to *remove skill from the labor process.* Managers gather all the traditional knowledge previously possessed by workers and reduce this knowledge to simple rules and formulas. Time-and-motion studies are one way to do this. Management can then re-design the work for maximum productivity. The nineteenth-century writer John Ruskin observed,

> It is not, truly speaking the labor that is divided; but the men: divided into mere segments of men—broken into small fragments and crumbs of life; so that all the little piece of intelligence that is left in a man is not enough to make a pin, or a nail, but exhausts itself in making the point of a pin or the head of a nail.[26]

Taylor's second principle is to *separate conception from execution.* All possible brain work is removed from the shop floor to the planning department. In the 1930's one manager boasted, "We hire Chevrolet workers from the neck down." Divorcing mental and manual work severs the connection between brain and hand and sets them against one other. Those who make all the decisions do none of the actual work. Those who do all of the work make none of the decisions. Braverman concludes,

> In this way the remarkable development of machinery becomes, for most of the working population, the source not of freedom but of enslavement, not of mastery but of helplessness, and not of the broadening of the horizon of labor but of the confinement of the worker within a blind round of servile duties in which the machine appears as the embodiment of science and the worker as little or nothing.[27]

Taylor's third principle is to *control each step of the labor process.* Management gives each worker instructions describing in detail the tasks to be accomplished, the method to be used, and the time allotted. The worker is reduced to an animated tool of management, a general-purpose machine, adaptable to a large range of simple tasks. This degradation can be imposed on the worker because property laws grant management power over the workplace.

The lack of worker control over production leads to the dissociated perception that machines, not people, move society forward. Braverman notes, "It has become fashionable to attribute to machinery the powers over humanity which arise in fact from social relations."

> The machine, the mere product of human labor and ingenuity, designed and constructed by humans and alterable by them at will, is viewed as an independent participant in human social arrangements.

[The machine] is given life…is endowed with the power to shape the life of mankind, and is sometimes even invested with a design upon the human race.[28]

Films like *The Matrix* and *I, Robot* exploit fears of machine domination. It seems as though machines have great power, while the people who build and operate the machines are irrelevant. This illusion is shattered when workers strike, the machines stop, and society grinds to a halt. Employers and politicians hate strikes, not only because they disrupt business. Workers who strike challenge the power of the capitalist class to dictate what happens in the workplace.

It wasn't easy for the capitalists to get control of the labor process. Craft unions fought against a fully-managed process that stripped them of skills and subordinated them to machines. However, skilled workers cannot compete with cheaper manufactured goods, and most of them were forced into the factory system.

Today, the de-skilling process continues to penetrate previously unconquered areas of work. Fast-food restaurants function like assembly lines. Classroom courses are scripted "down to instructions on the appropriate hand gestures to make while teaching."[29] Hospitals function like factories where different departments attend to different parts of the body in assembly-line fashion. Physicians and psychotherapists, who were trained to use skill and judgement to treat patients, are provided with manuals listing the services they can and cannot provide.

As work is degraded, life's fulfillment becomes life's drudgery. Workers stripped of their dignity suffer low morale and frequent absenteeism, both of which lower productivity. To boost productivity, medicine, psychology, sociology, and human relations experts serve as the maintenance crew for the human machinery. These professionals do not remedy the degradation of work and the alienation of workers; they manage workers' *reactions* to degradation and alienation. The worker, not the organization of work, becomes the problem.

> These same scientific managers have not ceased to complain bitterly, as is their wont, of the characteristics of a working population which they themselves have shaped to suit their ends, but they have not yet found a way to produce workers who are at one and the same time degraded in their place in the labor process, and also conscientious and proud of their work.[30]

As the de-skilling process advances into each new field, it is bitterly opposed by workers who are more aware of what they are losing than those who have already adapted to the loss. Braverman concludes that until workers fight back as a class, they will "remain servants of capital instead of freely associated producers who control their own labor and their own destinies," and they will "work every day to build for themselves more 'modern,' more 'scientific,' and more dehumanized prisons of labor."

Alienation and dissociation

Richard Sennett and Jonathon Cobb discovered that most of the people they interviewed for their book, *The Hidden Injuries of Class,* felt inadequate and powerless. One worker told them,

> The more a person is on the receiving end of orders, the more the person's got to think he or she is really somewhere else in order to keep up self-respect. And yet it's at work that you're supposed to "make something" of yourself, so if you're not really there, how *are* you going to make something of yourself?[31]

This statement reveals the link between alienation and dissociation. *Alienation* is the condition of being cut off from control over the work process—being "on the receiving end of orders." *Dissociation* is a psychological defense against powerlessness—having to go "somewhere else." Dissociation preserves "self-respect." However, dissociation keeps the worker trapped in his alienated condition—"if you're not really there, how are you going to make something of yourself?" In short, alienation makes dissociation necessary, and dissociation allows alienation to continue.

Alienation and dissociation re-enforce each other in innumerable ways. People who are forced to function like cogs in a machine have dissociated relationships with the other cogs. Instead of relating to each other as fellow producers, directly exchanging what they want and need, workers use their wages to purchase goods and services that are created by other workers. These workers relate to each other as dissociated consumers—you pay my boss for what I made and I pay your boss for what you made. In effect, capitalism transforms human relationships into commodity transactions. *There is no direct and conscious sharing of the creative, productive process.* As a result, despite living, working, commuting, and shopping together, most people feel estranged from one another. We exchange superficial pleasantries, not knowing what else to say.

Lack of control over the work process disrupts the bonds of mutual care that protected our ancestors. Pre-class societies did their best to provide for the elderly, sick, and disabled. Today, workers who become ill or injured discover that employers feel no loyalty to them. People who produce their entire lives are discarded like worn-out machinery, as employers gut pensions and politicians attack Social Security. According to the U.S. National Center on Health Statistics, starvation, dehydration, and bedsores are commonly listed as the cause of death on nursing-home death certificates. Working people are not provided with paid leave to care for elderly relatives at home, nor do they earn enough to pay for private care. The result is helpless anguish as families watch loved ones die of neglect.

How human beings relate to each other is inextricably linked with how they relate to the environment. Before class society, life was governed by the rule of reciprocity. Communal societies viewed the environment as an extension of themselves and treated it the same way they treated each other, with respect and gratitude. They took only what they needed and gave back what they could.

Class society severed the link between humanity and the environment in order to exploit both. Workers are used up and thrown away. Nature has become a source of raw materials to pillage on the one end and a massive toilet in which to dump garbage on the other. Natural resources are designated private property to be exploited for profit, regardless of the impact on people or the environment. We have all seen the result: excessive logging causes lethal mud slides; shoreline development removes natural barriers to storms and tsunamis; the over-use of fossil fuels heats the atmosphere, melts the ice fields, causes sea levels to rise, and creates more turbulent weather. At the same time, there is no profit in reforestation, evacuating people in advance of storms, and relocating residents of flooded coastal areas. Hurricane Katrina demonstrated how disregard for human beings and disregard for the environment go hand-in-hand.

Capitalism encourages people to live as if there were no past, no future, and no consequences. Only the sale is important. Every year, millions of tons of pesticides, herbicides, industrial chemicals, cosmetics, and pharmaceuticals enter the market as commodities, with no consideration for what happens after they are sold. Once used, these products are thrown away, washed away, and excreted from human and animal bodies, entering rivers, streams, and lakes, returning to us in the form of contaminated food and water. In 2001, Bill Moyers hosted a PBS television program that documented widespread chemical pollution of the environment, the link with human disease, and the collusion between government and industry to deny the problem. Moyers' own blood and urine tested positive for 84 different toxic chemicals, including some that had been banned for decades.

People who are denied control over their work and society are forced to live dissociated lives, powerless to counter the growing dangers around them.

Longing to belong

Pre-class societies valued everyone because everyone's contribution was needed to survive. The only worthless people were those who refused to contribute. Individuals did strive for excellence in their work. However, doing something well did not make a person more worthy any more than failing made a person less worthy. While studying the !Kung people of the Kalahari desert, anthropologist Richard Lee observed,

> The !Kung are a fiercely egalitarian people, and they have evolved a series of important cultural practices to maintain this equality, first by cutting down to size the arrogant and boastful, and second by helping those down on their luck to get back in the game.[32]

The !Kung are fiercely egalitarian because survival demands it; life is hard, food is scarce, and lives are short. Cooperation is so important that nature did not leave it to chance. Human beings have an inborn need to contribute. At a very early age, children insist on helping with household tasks and react with delight when their contributions are appreciated. Throughout life, human beings have a biological need to bond with others, making disconnection literally painful. The human brain experiences separation and rejection in the same way that it experiences physical pain; a broken heart hurts just as much as a broken leg. Scientists believe that the system of emotional attachment evolved alongside the system of physical pain because connection is so critical for human survival.

Human beings are such a social species that every society we have created, including capitalism, is based on social labor. Human bonding is literally a matter of life and death. In pre-class societies, banishment from the tribe was equivalent to a death sentence. Today, solitary confinement in prison breaks the mind and the body. Isolated people have higher blood pressure, get sick more often, and suffer higher death rates than those who are socially connected. Strong social bonds protect health. People with Alzheimer's disease who have strong social networks preserve their brain functions better than those with the same severity of the disease and less social support.

Human beings have a biological need to belong, and yet, no species is so divided against itself. Class society shattered the assumption of equal worth by dividing people into classes — the exploiters and the exploited. Capitalism promotes constant competition and measures a person's worth by his or her position in the social hierarchy. Those closer to the top are valued more than those further down. Those who work with their minds are valued more than those who work with their hands. Those who do the hardest, dirtiest work are the least valued. These evaluations are based on the structure of the social hierarchy, not the social usefulness of the work. Doctors who treat disease are well paid and highly respected, while garbage collectors who remove the source of disease are poorly paid and not respected. If an ounce of prevention is worth a pound of cure, then garbage collectors contribute more to social health than doctors.

The conflicted state of humanity creates a conflict inside every human being. Instinct propels us toward others; yet, experience warns that others can hurt us. We vacillate between the need for connection and the need for protection. When this conflict becomes unbearable, we dissociate. And, wrongly, we blame ourselves.

I have been listening to people's problems for more than 30 years and, over that time, thousands of people have revealed to me their secret shame at being (in their minds) inadequate, not loveable, not good enough, failures, losers, worthless, useless, etc. They assume that because they are not rich, successful, educated, good looking, or popular, there must be something wrong with them. Capitalism promotes widespread social shame, so that stories of redemption—sought, denied, lost, and found—have strong appeal (*The Unforgiven, Spiderman, Xena, etc.*). Most people hide their shame at feeling unworthy in the belief that they are the only ones who feel that way. One person told me, "It's easier to keep everyone at bay. It feels safer to love and care for them and not let them love and care for me." The fact that so many people feel the same, yet feel so alone, indicates how disconnected we are from one another.

People are healthier when they feel valued, and they feel valued when they are treated fairly. In one study, people who felt fairly treated at work had lower blood pressure and 30 percent less risk of developing heart disease. Employees felt fairly treated when supervisors told them the truth, considered their point of view, and shared information concerning decision-making. By definition, class society devalues the majority of people. Employers, politicians, and other authorities don't tell the truth, disregard public opinion, and exclude ordinary people from the decision-making process.

Social harmony results when society cherishes, includes, and provides for all of its members. As long as inequality exists, people will hunger to get even (equal). Until all are considered worthy, no one can feel secure. Fortunately, despite the corrupting impact of capitalism, reciprocity has deep roots in the human spirit. Until 2004,

> Conductors on the Long Island Rail Road allowed employees of Madison Square Garden to ride without paying, and in return workers at the arena gave employees of the commuter railroad free admission to sports events.[33]

While workers on both sides of this reciprocal arrangement undoubtedly considered it fair and equitable, officials complained about "lost revenue" and warned that further "violations of policy" would not be tolerated. Behind their official indignation lay the fear that workers would even think of bypassing management to make direct arrangements with each other. The next chapter explains how reciprocity is incompatible with capitalist competition.

Summary

Human survival depends on cooperation. For most of human history, people lived in sharing societies without bosses or rulers. Class society split humanity into two antagonistic groups: the exploited who create surplus and the exploiters who seize it as their private property. Alienation describes the social arrangement where workers labor to create a world that exploits and oppresses them. Dissociation is a psychological defense against alienation. Alienation and dissociation reinforce each other in a cycle of powerlessness. Nevertheless, the longing to contribute, to belong, and to be equal are basic to human nature and cannot be extinguished.

Chapter 6

Compete or Die

Capital is dead labor which, vampire-like, lives only by sucking living labor, and the more labor it sucks, the more it lives…The vampire will not let go while there remains a single muscle, sinew, or drop of blood to be exploited.

Karl Marx

Why do capitalists have such an insatiable thirst for profit? Before capitalism, ruling families *consumed* the surplus, demanding the biggest, the best, and the most of what was produced. Capitalism transformed the goal of production from consumption to accumulation.

Even though the economy of the Middle Ages was dominated by agriculture, there was an embryonic class of capitalists that operated small workshops and bought and sold goods. Over several centuries, this class grew in size and influence until it began to challenge the rule of the landed aristocracy. The French Revolution (1789–1799) marked the first capitalist revolution.

The capitalist class replaced the feudal system of production-for-use with a new system of production-for-profit. To the prime directive of all class societies, "Seize the Surplus," capitalism added a second directive, "Compete or Die." All capitalists are engaged in a race to accumulate capital. As the previous chapter explained, capital is surplus extracted from the worker *that is used to extract more surplus*. There is a limit to how much surplus can be consumed, but there is no limit to how much capital can be accumulated. In the 19th century, Karl Marx described the driving force of capitalism as, "Accumulate, accumulate! That is Moses and the prophets! Accumulation for the sake of accumulation, production for the sake of production."

The capitalist cannot stop competing for profit. Capitalist A buys a knitting machine so that his workers can produce more sweaters at a cheaper rate. As his profits roll in, other capitalists rush to purchase knitting machines. Soon, sweaters glut the market and the price of sweaters plummets. Capitalist A has lost his advantage. If he wants to stay in business, he must find another way to raise his profits.

Raising productivity

The key to raising profits is to increase worker productivity. Productivity is a measure of the value of what workers produce *over and above* the value of the wages they are paid. Compete or Die demands that each capitalist outdo his competitors in raising productivity. Some ways of doing this include:

- lengthen the workday
- increase the number of days worked per year
- increase the speed of production
- redesign the work to increase output per worker
- use machines to increase output per worker
- employ the fewest number of workers
- cut wages and benefits

Employers lengthen the workday by demanding overtime. Unpaid overtime is even more profitable. According to the U.S. Labor Department, the practice of working "off the clock" is illegal and widespread. The workday is also lengthened when wages fall so low that more than one job is needed to make ends meet. Productivity rises when workers don't take holidays and when employers don't replace workers who fall ill, are injured, retire, or quit. Like speeding up the assembly line, deliberate "short-staffing" forces those who remain to work harder for the same pay. As if people weren't working hard enough, performance-enhancing drugs are being developed to keep people working longer and performing better. One study found that a compound called CX717 helped sleep-deprived monkeys perform better than when they were well rested. Non-sleep-deprived monkeys who were given the drug did even better.

It is more profitable to overwork one section of the labor force and keep the rest unemployed than it is to provide jobs for everyone. Maintaining a pool of unemployed workers pressures those with jobs to accept conditions they might otherwise reject. The unemployed are not rewarded for boosting the profits of the capitalist class. On the contrary, the jobless are condemned as "free-loaders," even though the capitalists are the ones getting the free ride.

Productivity rises when more workers accept temporary, part-time jobs that typically pay less, have few if any benefits, and can be easily terminated. In 2001, 31 percent of female and 23 percent of male workers in America were employed in such jobs. Productivity also rises when employers can pay lower wages to young, female, Black, immigrant, and disabled workers.

Employers also increase productivity by cutting wages and benefits. The current attack on unions is being driven by the demand for higher productivity. Even as profits rise, retired seniors are being forced back to work to pay medical bills that are no longer covered by their pension benefits. Employers who hire undocumented immigrants can pay them less than the law demands and sometimes nothing at all. By shafting vulnerable workers, dead-beat bosses make super-profits.

Each new industrial technology is designed to extract more value out of each worker. Each generation of workers is promised that if they accept the new technology, they will enjoy easier work, more leisure time, and a higher standard of living. Between 1973 and 2000, the output per worker per hour nearly doubled in the U.S. In other words, all the goods and services produced in 1973 could be produced in half the time by 2000. In her book *The Overworked American: The Unexpected Decline of Leisure*, Juliet Schor calculates that if workers controlled production,

> We actually could have chosen the four-hour day. Or a working year of six months. Or *every worker in the United States could be taking every other year off from work — with pay*.[34]

Why did this not happen?

More work, less pay

Because the capitalist class owns the means of production, it claims all the benefits that flow from rising productivity. Workers get falling living standards in return for their labors. Between 2000 and 2003, the productivity of American workers rose 12 percent, while the median household income *dropped* three-and-a-half percent over the same period. It has continued to fall every year since then. To compensate for falling wages, people work more hours. By 2000, the average American worker was putting in 199 *more* hours on the job, or five weeks more than in 1973. In 1991 Schor calculated,

> In the last twenty years, the amount of time Americans have spent at their jobs has risen steadily… about nine hours, or slightly more than one additional day of work [every year]…Working hours are already longer than they were forty years ago. If present trends continue, by the end of the century, Americans will be spending as much time on their jobs as they did back in the nineteen twenties.[35]

Most Americans are not only working longer and harder, they are also taking home less money. In the late 1960's, the minimum wage in America was half of what the average worker earned per hour. By 2003, it had fallen to 34 percent of the average wage. A 2004 report called *Working Hard, Falling Short* found that,

> More than one out of four American working families now earn wages so low that they have difficulty surviving financially. By 2003, one in five American workers were in occupations where the median wage was less than $8.84 an hour, which is considered to be a poverty-level wage for a family of four. A full-time job at the federal minimum wage of $5.15 an hour would not be enough to keep a family of three out of poverty…In all, more than 14 million, or 21 percent of all kids under 18, still live in poverty — a higher proportion than in 1975.[36]

Real wages have dropped so low that two people must work to earn the same income that one used to make. By 2000, half of all families were two-earner families, and more than half of low-income working families were headed by married couples. Families that depend on two incomes are less able to provide home-care for young children, the sick, and the elderly. The resulting stress on the family is discussed in the next chapter.

Because the capitalist class seizes the surplus, rising productivity enriches the capitalist class at the expense of the working class. The difference in pay between executives and workers is one measure of this growing inequality. Between 1950 and the mid-1970's, average executive compensation was about 35 times the average wage. By 1999, the average CEO of a major US corporation was taking home 330 times the average wage and

476 times the average blue-collar wage. By 2004, the proportion of the economy going home in workers' pockets had dropped to the lowest level ever recorded.

The land of opportunity should be renamed the land of inequality. Between 1992 and 2000, the incomes of the 400 wealthiest taxpayers in the U.S. increased 15 times faster than the bottom *90 percent,* whose income barely kept up with the rate of inflation. In 2005, the *New York Times* reported that

> The top fifth of earners in Manhattan now make 52 times what the lowest fifth make—$365,826 compared with $7,047—which is roughly comparable to the income disparity in Namibia...Put another way, for every dollar made by households in the top fifth of Manhattan earners, households in the bottom fifth made about 2 cents.[37]

Competition corrupts

In 1869, Thomas Joseph Dunning wrote,

> Capital shuns no profit just as Nature abhors a vacuum. With adequate profit, capital is very bold. A certain profit of 10 percent will ensure its employment anywhere; 20 percent profit will produce eagerness; 50 percent positive audacity; 100 percent will make it ready to trample on all human laws; 300 percent, and there is not a crime at which it will scruple, not a risk it will not run, even to the chance of its owner being hanged. If turbulence and strife will bring a profit it will freely encourage both. Smuggling and the slave-trade have amply proved all that is here stated.[38]

Competition breeds corruption. When only winners are rewarded, people will do anything to win. Businesses cook their books, employers violate health and safety regulations, students cheat on exams, politicians take bribes, and athletes inject performance-enhancing drugs. In 2006, the media reported that hundreds of Americans had been given tissue transplants from illegally-looted corpses. When a corpse can provide thousands of dollars worth of transplantable parts, someone is bound to cut corners.

Corruption is standard business practice and occurs in all sectors of the economy, as those with access to desired goods and services enrich themselves by granting favors. According to *Global Corruption Report 2006,*

> In the health sphere, corruption encompasses bribery of regulators and medical professionals, manipulation of information on drug trials, the diversion of medicines and supplies, corruption in procurement [bribes, kickbacks], and over-billing of insurance companies.[39]

The greed for profit overrides human decency. In 2002, America's largest telecommunications company announced that it was cutting 7,000 jobs on the East Coast. Just a year earlier, Verizon had hailed these same workers as heros for the way they labored around the clock to restore communication networks destroyed on 9/11. The layoffs were not the result of there being too many workers. Quite the opposite. The company was experiencing rising numbers of customer complaints, more service disruptions, and longer waits for installations and repairs. Nor was the company suffering financially. Verizon's net income had more than doubled over the previous quarter, and the company's top executives were making millions of dollars. Driven by Compete or Die, they wanted more. This level of greed is difficult for most people to understand.

Capitalists have no use for reciprocity; they profit only by taking more than they give. In contrast, ordinary people depend on reciprocity to survive. When my car blew a tire on a major highway, a passing truck driver pulled over and changed it for me. He refused my offer to pay him for his time, insisting, "If it was my wife or mother, I would want someone to stop and help her." Life in the working class is precarious, and one needs all the friends one can get. As the saying goes, "It's only the way the cards have been dealt, that I am the helper instead of the helped."

Interpersonal conflict

Compete or Die creates conflict in human relationships. When the elite seize the surplus, everyone else must scramble for the crumbs they leave. There are not enough good jobs and affordable housing. There is stiff competition for higher education and for higher-paid jobs. The competition that dominates our lives is dramatized in "reality" shows like *Survivor, American Idol, The Apprentice,* and *America's Top Model.* The premise of these shows — There Can Be Only One — implies that those who are not chosen have no value. This message is so pervasive that people will even compete for admiration, love, and respect — as if there were not enough to go around. Such competition can take the form of malicious gossip and bigotry, where putting down others is a way to elevate yourself. Children quickly learn that a well-placed "put-down" can bring attention, even admiration, at someone else's expense.

While feeling one-up generates elation, feeling put-down generates resentment and a burning desire to *get even,* fueling interpersonal conflict and law suits. In 2003, four-and-a-half billion dollars were paid to settle medical malpractice claims in the U.S. Doctors are not being sued for making mistakes, because most doctors who make mistakes are not sued. Doctors are sued for being arrogant. When medical errors occur, doctors who express genuine concern for their patients are rarely sued; whereas doctors with a condescending attitude are sued repeatedly.

Personal competition is fierce because success is determined by the ability to surpass or defeat others. The year I applied to medical school, there were 2,000 applicants for 64 places. All 2,000 applicants qualified academically; they could apply only if they had three years of university with a Grade Point Average of 3.6 or higher (out of 4). However, neither the government nor the medical profession wanted to admit all 2,000 applicants. The government wanted to limit the number of doctors to minimize the budget for medical care. The medical profession wanted to limit the number of doctors to keep physician incomes high. Even though society needed more doctors, and all 2,000 applicants were able and willing to contribute in that way, only 64 would be selected.

For 64 hopefuls to win the medical-school lottery, 1,936 would have to lose. The admissions process claimed to distinguish the more worthy candidates from the less worthy ones. *Its actual function was to make the lottery appear less arbitrary,* because there was no significant difference between those who won and those who lost. At no point in this process did the 2,000 cry, "Foul! Unfair! Let us all in!" The few who were admitted believed that they were chosen because they were superior, while those who were rejected believed that they were turned down because they were inferior (or tried again in the belief that their superiority had been overlooked).

In *Disciplined Minds,* Jeff Schmidt recounts how Black and White applicants to U.C. Davis medical school were set against each other when a few minority students with slightly lower test scores were admitted under affirmative action policies. A White student who was not admitted sued the university, claiming "reverse discrimination," because his test scores were higher than some of the minority students. Schmidt concludes,

Such racism takes the anger that springs from the frustrations of a life of limited opportunity and aims it at other victims—the minorities—thus taking the heat off the hierarchical system that by its very nature restricts the number of openings. And so we have ludicrous situations like the one at U.C. Davis, where almost *2,000* rejected whites could think of 16 minorities as stealing their opportunity to become doctors.[40]

They compete and we die

Capitalist competition is deadly because business is concerned only with making profit in the here-and-now. What comes later is of no concern. The necessity for short-term gain explains why beef producers would endanger human lives and risk their own livelihoods.

Mad Cow Disease began in 1986 in Britain as a result of diseased animal carcasses being fed to livestock that were later consumed by human beings. Over a hundred people died and an unknown number were infected with a deadly brain disease. Millions of cows had to be destroyed, and the British beef industry collapsed. How did this happen?

Cows are normally vegetarians. However, they grow faster when they are fed rendered protein. Rendering is the process of pulverizing discarded and diseased animal parts to produce a sludge of raw protein that can be incorporated into animal feed. (Rendered protein is also used to make pet food, fertilizer, cosmetics, concrete, tires, gelatin, candy, and many other products.) The rule of Compete or Die demands that when one rancher starts fattening his cattle on rendered protein, all must do the same to stay competitive.

Despite the British disaster, the lure of profit prolonged the feeding of rendered beef to North American livestock until 1997, when the U.S. Food and Drug Administration banned the practice. However, the FDA continued to allow diseased cattle remains to be fed to pigs and chickens, whose remains could then be fed back to cows. In December of 2003, the first case of Mad Cow Disease surfaced in the U.S. Before the diagnosis was confirmed, meat from the infected animal had been distributed to more than eight states, and the cow's spinal cord had been incorporated into food for pets, pigs, and poultry.

The government's first concern was to protect the beef industry. As the news broke, Agriculture Secretary Ann Veneman stated, "We believe that the food supply is fully protected and that consumers should feel fully confident that the beef supply in this country is very safe to eat." Another diseased cow was identified in December, 2003, and a third was found in June, 2005.

In 2004, the Department of Agriculture refused to allow a Kansas beef company to test all of its cattle for BSE (the infection that causes Mad Cow Disease). The National Cattlemen's Association applauded this decision on the basis that testing all cattle would imply that untested beef might not be safe. While BSE testing is inexpensive, more testing would increase the risk of finding the disease. In 2006, the Department of Agriculture announced that it was *reducing testing* for BSE from the 1,000 tests per day (about one percent of slaughtered cattle) initiated in response to the first sick cow to one-tenth of that. The reason given was that the risk of BSE was "extraordinarily low." With less testing, the risk of identifying sick animals is even lower.

Servant to capital

In the most elementary sense, the State is guarantor of the conditions, the social relations, of capitalism, and the protector of the ever more unequal distribution of property which this system brings about.[41]

The capitalist State has a huge presence in everyday life. The State is more than the government; the State is a complex structure that includes the legislative, executive, and judicial sections of government, the police and the military, the penal and education systems, and government-funded agencies. (The capitalized "State" refers to this complex structure, in contrast to the lower case "state," which refers to the level of government below the federal.)

The State presents itself as a class-neutral force. In reality, the State manages the capitalist system for the ruling class. The State also functions as a capitalist in its own right. The U.S. government is the biggest venture capitalist in the world; three-quarters of all American research engineers and scientists work in federally-funded enterprises.

The capitalist State and the corporate class are inseparable. In 2006, coal industry executive Richard Stickler was appointed head of the Mine Safety and Health Administration. The mines that Stickler had previously managed injured workers at rates that were double the national average. No doubt they were also more profitable.

State officials and corporate executives are interchangeable because they have the same goal — to serve business through favorable legislation and lucrative contracts. Almost half the politicians who leave Congress become lobbyists or "influence peddlers" for business. This is equally true of Republicans and Democrats. Well-connected lobbyists enable the industries they represent to influence State policies: energy companies decide energy policy, chemical industries dictate pollution regulations, drug companies shape drug policy. Former politicians are also valued for their ability to secure government contracts. In 2006, the *New York Times* reported that, in the three years since its founding, more than two-thirds of the senior executives at Homeland Security had become executives, consultants, or lobbyists for private security companies that sell services to the federal government.

The incestuous relationship between the corporate class and the State is exemplified by Dick Cheney, former CEO of energy corporation Halliburton. Shortly after becoming vice-president, Cheney moved to deregulate the power industry, allowing energy corporations to inflate the price of power and pocket billions of dollars in profit. With Cheney as vice-president, Halliburton secured a contract with the Pentagon to service its global military operations. After the U.S. invaded Iraq, Halliburton was awarded a multi-billion-dollar contract to put out the oil fires, rebuild Iraq's oil infrastructure, and provision the military.

The rule of Compete or Die also dominates international relations. To give the advantage to its own capitalist class, each State strives to:

- regulate and maintain the supply of labor
- referee the competition of capitalists within the nation
- provide corporate welfare
- cushion industry from economic crises
- provide military forces to protect (and extend) domestic capital interests.

To regulate the supply of labor, the State sets immigration policy; polices the national borders; regulates and funds education; and licences the skilled trades and professions. When more workers are needed, more immigrants are admitted, and people are encouraged to have more children, or denied the means to control their fertility. To reduce the number of workers, governments clamp down on immigration and restrict the right to have children. During World War II, the federal government passed the Lanham Act, funding daycare for an estimated 600,000 children. This measure enabled more women to enter the workforce to replace men who had been sent to war. When the men returned after the war, the Lanham Act was terminated and women were pushed back into the home.

Slave-owners were responsible for feeding and clothing their slaves, and feudal lords had a duty to care for those they ruled (noblesse oblige). The capitalist class is so obsessed with accumulating capital that it is willing to work its laboring class to death.

The industrial revolution of the 19th century plunged workers into desperate conditions. Slum housing had little or no ventilation. Garbage and excrement littered the streets, and toxic fumes filled the air. Unguarded machinery mangled human limbs, as malnourished men, women, and children worked around the clock. Frederick Engels documents

> Women made unfit for childbearing, children deformed, men enfeebled, limbs crushed, whole generations wrecked, afflicted with disease and infirmity, purely to fill the purses of the capitalist class.[42]

The capitalist class refused to solve these problems, so the State stepped in to prevent total social collapse. Today, the State is responsible for public sanitation, housing standards, public health, and pollution control. Labor laws regulate the hours and conditions of work. The State also provides minimal support to the unemployed, the destitute, the elderly, and the disabled. These measures reduce or cushion the destructive effects of capitalist competition—preserving the beast by preventing it from devouring its own tail.

Referee

Compete or Die locks every capitalist in cut-throat competition with every other capitalist. To prevent complete chaos, the State imposes rules of competition. The State is no neutral referee between warring capitalists; it can be bought. By 2005, there were 34,750 registered lobbyists in Washington—*65 for every member of Congress.* By 2004, over two billion dollars were being spent every year to influence the federal government. This money is distributed fairly evenly between Democrats and Republicans, with more going to whichever party is office. Lobbying is a good investment. The Hewlett-Packard Corporation paid lobbyists hundreds of thousands of dollars to promote federal legislation that saved the company millions of dollars in taxes on overseas profits.

What happens when the interests of different industries conflict and both are lobbying hard? Consider the following example. General Motors spends more money on medical care than it spends on steel for its automobiles. As the *New York Times* points out,

> General Motors covers the health care costs of 1.1 million Americans, or close to half a percent of the total population, though fewer than 200,000 are active workers while the rest are retirees, children or spouses. Not only are such costs escalating rapidly, but GM's rivals, based in Japan and Germany, have virtually no retirees from their newer operations in the United States and, at home, the expenses are largely assumed by taxpayers through nationalized health care systems.[43]

The U.S. auto industry would be more profitable if the State took over the cost of providing medical care; however, a State-funded medical system would put the medical insurance industry out of business.

Both industries make hefty political contributions. The inability of the State to resolve this conflict leads to convoluted bureaucratic dances, like the 2004 proposal to establish a "federally chartered but privately run reinsurance organization" for the purpose of "shielding employers from the most expensive medical cases."

Corporate welfare

The State supports the capitalist class by taking from the poor and giving to the rich—a kind of reverse Robin Hood. Every year, city and state governments give businesses $50 billion to "create jobs" in their localities. Corporations play cities and states against each other to get the maximum pay-outs. North Carolina gave Dell Corporation a $200 million subsidy package for a factory that was expected to cost $100 million. Dell also arranged to get several million more at the local level *for the same facility.*

Corporate subsidies do not require that any jobs be created because these subsidies come without strings. Once they have the money, businesses can use it to downsize, contract work out, eliminate unions, and even move away. Such betrayal is inevitable because the primary function of business is to make profits, not create jobs. Governments understand and support this goal. The hype about job creation is designed to make corporate welfare more acceptable to taxpayers and voters.

Government-funded social services are another form of corporate welfare. After workers in Flint, Michigan, made General Motors the biggest corporation in the world, GM abandoned the city. Instead of forcing GM to meet its obligations, the government subsidized GM's move from the city by providing welfare to thousands of laid-off auto workers.

The State enables employers to pay poverty wages by covering the difference between what workers earn and what they need to survive. Medicaid, Social Security, children's medical insurance, free school lunches, Section-Eight housing assistance, income tax credits, and other social supports are a massive boon to employers. In 2001, the state of California spent $86 million providing food stamps and subsidized housing to Wal-Mart employees alone.

> Of $21.2 billion of public assistance provided to low-income California families in 2002, 48 percent—or $10.1 billion—went to families in which at least one member worked at least forty-five weeks per year.[44]

The State works to shift the tax burden of the capitalist class to the middle and working classes. Waged workers have taxes deducted automatically from their paychecks, while businesses have innumerable ways to avoid paying their share. In *Perfectly Legal: The Covert Campaign to Rig Our Tax System to Benefit the Super-Rich—And Cheat Everybody Else,* David Cay Johnston explains that legal tax-dodges allow the richest 20 percent of Americans to pay the same portion of their income in tax as the poorest 20 percent of Americans. By 2002, less than 10 percent of federal revenue was coming from corporations.

Business tax shelters cost the U.S. treasury an estimated $54 billion in revenue every year. By creating 881 offshore subsidiaries, the Enron corporation paid absolutely no taxes for four of the five years before it collapsed. Between 1998 and 2001, CSX Corporation made $900 million in profits and paid no taxes at all. On the contrary, it received $164 million in tax rebates. Twenty-one states permit utilities to keep the taxes they collect from customers. Between 2002 and 2004, Xcel Energy collected $723 million in taxes, paid none of it to the government, and received $351 million in tax refunds.

In 2005, the Congressional Joint Committee on Taxation calculated that the federal government could increase tax revenues by $311 billion over the following 10 years if it pressed rich individuals and corporations to meet their tax obligations. However, the State has no interest in clamping down on the class that it serves and protects. In 2003, the IRS audited fewer than one quarter of one percent of corporate tax returns. Corporate tax evaders who are caught are seldom punished or even made to pay the money they owe. Furthermore, Congress periodically grants U.S. corporations tax holidays—times when they can import billions of dollars in overseas profits virtually tax free.

The State also cushions the corporate class from market forces. Because production is driven by profit, the economy moves through a "profit cycle" of booms and slumps. When producing steel is profitable, everyone rushes to produce it. The resulting boom in steel eventually creates more product than can be sold *profitably*. "Excess" steel is left to rust, steel workers are laid off, and some steel companies go bankrupt. When steel finally becomes profitable to produce again, capitalists will compete again to produce it. This boom-slump cycle affects every sector of the economy.

Despite talk about "market forces," the State cannot allow large corporations to go bankrupt and take down chunks of the economy with them. In the 1980's, billions of tax dollars bailed out the bankrupt Savings and Loans industry. Twenty years later, the federal government helped ailing industries to offload their pension obligations. In 2004, a federal judge ruled that the nation's fourth-largest coal company no longer had to provide medical and retirement benefits to more than 3,000 workers, many of whom suffer from Black Lung and other occupational diseases. A year later, a federal bankruptcy court allowed United Airlines to walk away from almost seven billion dollars' worth of pension obligations, the biggest pension default in American history.

Competition goes global

> The trouble with America is that when the dollar only earns 6 percent over here, then it gets restless and goes overseas to get 100 percent. Then the flag follows the dollar and the soldiers follow the flag.
>
> *Major General Smedley Butler*

Compete or Die is a global imperative; all capitalists need a home State to support them against their foreign rivals. Small industries rely on their State to protect them from foreign competition by setting up tariff barriers. Larger industries depend on their home State to help them penetrate foreign markets. The opposing interests of small and large businesses drive the conflict between "protectionism" and "free trade." Workers lose either way. Protectionist polices shield smaller industries from having to compete in the world market. Eventually, these less-competitive industries fail anyway, as thousands of laid-off American steelworkers can confirm. Free trade policies make it easier for larger industries to penetrate foreign markets and to set up shop in countries where wages are lower, driving down wages at home. *Workers can defend themselves against free trade and protectionism only by uniting across national borders.*

The "free market" is anything but free because every State does its utmost to further the interests of its own capitalist class. Farm subsidies are a good example. In 2005, the U.S. government paid farmers a record $23 billion in subsidies. These payments allow American agribusiness to dump a surplus of cheap food on the world market. Farmers in poor nations cannot compete with this subsidized produce and are forced out of business, making their countries even more dependent on U.S. food imports.

The stronger the State, the more it can push the interests of its home-based corporations. U.S. corporations dominate the world because the U.S. is the world's strongest military power and can dictate the terms of doing business. According to *New York Times* columnist Thomas Friedman,

The hidden hand of the market will never work without a hidden fist. McDonald's cannot flourish without McDonnell Douglas, the designer of the F-15, and the hidden fist that keeps the world safe for Silicon valley's technology is called the U.S. Army, Air Force, Navy and Marine Corps.[45]

U.S. Major General Smedley Butler (1881-1940), who was decorated with two Congressional Medals of Honor and a distinguished service medal, had this to say about the link between business and the military.

I spent thirty three years and four months in active military service as a member of this country's most agile military force, the Marine Corps...And during that period, I spent most of my time being a high class muscle-man for Big Business, for Wall Street and for the Bankers. In short, I was a racketeer, a gangster for capitalism. I helped make Mexico, especially Tampico, safe for American oil interests in 1914. I helped make Haiti and Cuba a decent place for the National City Bank boys to collect revenues in. I helped in the raping of half a dozen Central American republics for the benefits of Wall Street...I helped purify Nicaragua for the international banking house of Brown Brothers...I brought light to the Dominican Republic for American sugar interests in 1916. In China I helped to see to it that Standard Oil went its way unmolested...During those years, I had, as the boys in the back room would say, a swell racket. Looking back on it, I feel that I could have given Al Capone a few hints. The best he could do was to operate his racket in three districts. I operated on three continents.[46]

War without end

Compete or Die drives nations to war. As economic rivalry grows more fierce, military conflict becomes more deadly. During the 17th century, the dollar rode the sword around the globe in search of resources to exploit. By the end of the 19th century there was no new territory to conquer, and the imperial powers turned on one another. World War I proved that capitalism was as efficient at killing people as it was at producing wealth. World War II was even more deadly. President Franklin D. Roosevelt condemned the German bombing of British cities as inhuman barbarism. Five years later, the U.S. dropped half a million incendiary bombs on Tokyo, killing 100,000 people in the course of one night. Six months after that, America dropped atomic bombs on two Japanese cities, introducing humanity to the prospect of complete annihilation. Instead of being horrified by these new weapons, every ruling class wanted them.

The United States emerged from World War II as the world's dominant nation. Over the next 40 years, the U.S. and the Soviet Union were locked in an economic and military struggle for world domination called the Cold War. Because the Soviet Union was economically weaker to begin with, its efforts to match the U.S. in the arms race weakened its economy even further. When the Soviet Union finally collapsed in the late 1980's, the United States emerged as the number one super-power. However, it wasn't long before a new challenger appeared.

At the beginning of the 21st century, the Chinese economy was growing so fast that it was predicted to match the U.S. economy within 30 years. In 2004, the U.S. produced six times more than China did. Nevertheless, China was producing 70 percent of the world's toys, 60 percent of its bicycles, 50 percent of its shoes, and 33 percent of its luggage. China also accounted for one-third of the global growth in automobile sales and had become the world's third largest producer of personal computers. The lure of profit continues to draw foreign investment to China. The average Chinese wage is five percent of the average American wage, and more than one billion Chinese represent a huge market for goods and services

While China poses a growing economic threat to the U.S., there is no contest when it comes to military power. The American military budget is *greater than all other nations in the world combined.* Not counting Social Security, the federal budget for 2007 was over two trillion dollars, half of which was designated for the military. The U.S. Defense Department budget alone is six times the military budget of Russia, and eight times the military budget of China. Nevertheless, the United States viewed China's attempt to buy an American oil company as a threat to national security. For the U.S., national security means economic dominance, and China's efforts to fuel its growing economy threatens that dominance. Compete or Die is no mere slogan. With economic and military rivalry intertwined, war is inevitable.

The United States will sacrifice everything to maintain its global dominance. In 1980, President Jimmy Carter proclaimed that any attempt by another nation to control the Persian Gulf would be considered an attack against the U.S. and would be repelled by military force. Well before 9/11, the U.S. Department of Defense declared that, "the mission of the U.S. military today and tomorrow" is "full-spectrum dominance," defined as "the ability of U.S. forces, operating alone or with allies, to defeat any adversary and control any situation across the range of military operations." In 2002, President George W. Bush declared the right of the United States to use military measures (including nuclear weapons) against any nation that challenges the United States and to ignore international treaties or agreements that interfere with American interests.

The current wars in the Middle East have the potential to ignite a Third World War that would wipe humanity off the planet. We can prevent that terrifying outcome by replacing capitalism with a sharing, cooperative society that has no need for war. *That is what most people want.* The insistence that war arises from human nature, not capitalist competition, is mistaken. As the next chapter explains, capitalism survives only by overriding the human longing for belonging and security.

Summary

Capitalism is based on the rule, Compete or Die. The competition for capital respects no limits, subordinating everyone and everything to the quest for profit. Economic competition has pushed productivity so high that, if the surplus were shared, everyone could have a decent standard of living. However, the capitalist class controls production so that the more workers produce, the more the capitalists take, and the less workers get in relation to what they produce. Military competition threatens to destroy the world. The only force that stands opposed to this deadly competition is the desire of ordinary people to live in peace.

Chapter 7

Burden the Family

Our culture places tremendous value on self-sufficiency and self-reliance. Just as individuals are esteemed for taking care of themselves rather than relying on others, effective families are glorified as being self-contained, self-regulating, autonomous entities.

Steven Gold

In 2001, Andrea Yates methodically drowned her five children, one by one, in the bathtub of their Texas home. How could a mother do such a thing?

Yates was diagnosed with post-partum psychosis when she tried to kill herself after her fourth child was born. After giving birth to her fifth child, she was prescribed anti-psychotic medications. Three months later, her father died and her mental state deteriorated. A few months after that, she drowned all of her children.

Expecting a grieving, psychotic woman to take care of five young children under the age of seven is a tragedy waiting to happen. Those children might be alive today if their family had been given more support. However, families are not supposed to need support, especially not fundamentalist Christian families like the Yates. Andrea was expected to have as many children as she could and school them at home, which was a 350-square-foot converted bus. She was not to have any friends, interests, or activities outside of her family, and she was to accept her husband's authority in all matters. According to religious commentator Anne Eggebroten,

> The conditions of her life were unbearable, but to challenge them would have been to oppose God's will…She did not see the drownings as a sin in the eyes of God. In fact, she felt she had already committed the greater sins—being a bad mother and producing children who were ruined and would go to hell if allowed to reach adulthood…She had twice tried to kill herself for this sin and failed.[47]

The prison psychiatrist described Yates as severely mentally ill. Nevertheless, she was charged with murder. At trial, the prosecuting attorney warned jurors that a guilty verdict was necessary to deter other mothers from murdering their children. Yates was convicted and sentenced to 40 years in prison without parole. During the trial, no one condemned the burdens that had broken this family.

The big squeeze

Most families suffer from severe stress. In 2001, 84 percent of women and 82 percent of men reported that their lives were moderately or extremely stressful. People between 25 to 44 years of age (the child-raising years) reported the highest stress levels. A 2005 study found that parents of both sexes were more likely to report depression than non-parents. Why is this happening?

The drive to increase productivity and profits sucks the life out of the family. Men's wages have fallen and the cost of living has climbed, forcing women out to work to keep their families afloat. In 2003, 78 percent of women with school-age children worked outside the home, including 59 percent of women with children under the age of five. Women's wages are essential for family survival. In 2003, 62 percent of working women brought home more than half of their entire family's income.

More hours on the job mean fewer hours at home. Between the early 1970's and the later 1980's, one-third of the time that people had off-the-job disappeared. After grocery shopping, cooking, cleaning, and laundry, most people don't have time for themselves, let alone for their children. Joan, a 28 year-old mother of two, describes her situation:

> My husband and I work four jobs between us. We can't afford childcare, so we work staggered shifts seven days a week. When he's at work, I'm at home, and vice versa. I rarely see him—we leave notes for each other—and we never get to be a family together. But it's the only way we can keep a roof over our heads and pay the bills.

Financial necessity forces many parents to work as much overtime as they can get. Bill drives transport trucks and may not see his family for days at a time. Although he misses them terribly, he reasons, "I can spend time with my kids, or I can feed them."

Despite working harder than ever, most families are financially insecure. When women go out to work, families have added expenses, like childcare. A second car may be needed where public transportation is inadequate. In 2004, more than three out of ten Americans named transportation as their biggest monthly expense after rent or mortgage payments.

Medical bills have become a nightmare for families. According to a 2004 survey by the Kaiser Family Foundation:

- Nearly one-quarter of Americans had problems paying their medical bills. More than 60 percent of these people had medical insurance.

- More than one in five Americans had an overdue medical bill, 15 percent were contacted by a collection agency because of medical bills, and eight percent borrowed money or took out another mortgage to pay for medical care.

- Nearly three in ten adults could not afford to pay for medical care at some time over the previous year. This figure is almost double what it was in 1976.

By 2001, total household debt was 10 percent greater than total household disposable income. In *Life and Debt: Why American Families are Borrowing to the Hilt,* Alex Baker writes,

Debt burdens are at record levels because families have been stretched to the limit in recent years. With more income going to housing and other rising expenses related to medical care, education, vehicles, child care, and so forth, families are relying on credit as a way to meet everyday needs. Remarkably, a family with two earners today actually has less discretionary income, after fixed costs like medical insurance and mortgage payments are accounted for, than did a family with only one breadwinner in the 1970's.[48]

According to Elizabeth Warren and Amelia Warren Tyagi, authors of *The Two-Income Trap: Why Middle-Class Mothers and Fathers Are Going Broke*:

This year, more people will end up bankrupt than will suffer a heart attack. More adults will file for bankruptcy than will be diagnosed with cancer. More people will file for bankruptcy than will graduate from college. And, in an era when traditionalists decry the demise of the institution of marriage, Americans will file more petitions for bankruptcy than for divorce.[49]

The decline in real wages, combined with the rising cost of necessities, has caused bankruptcy rates to escalate. Ninety percent of bankruptcies result from excessive medical bills, job loss, and divorce. Compared with their parents' generation, today's families are five times more likely to go bankrupt and three times more likely to lose their homes. Families with children are more than twice as likely to file for bankruptcy and 75 percent more likely to lose their homes than families without children.

The State does not help families that are drowning in debt. On the contrary, a 2005 federal law makes it *harder* for ordinary people to declare bankruptcy and start over. At the same time, a "millionaire's loophole" lets the rich shield their assets from creditors and lets corporations declare bankruptcy to avoid paying pensions and medical benefits.

Women's oppression

Unlike machines that can be worked continuously, human beings need time to rest and recover their energy. And while machines enter the world fully formed, human beings take years to mature. As a result, every society must solve the problem of how to maintain those who labor, how to respond to sick, injured, and old workers, and how to raise the next generation of workers.

Egalitarian societies shared these tasks. Everyone helped to care for the young and supported the disabled and elderly. This changed with class society. To maximize profits, the ruling class shuns responsibility for the maintenance and reproduction of the working class. Consequently, the bulk of this burden falls upon the individual family, primarily upon the women in the family, who cook, clean, do laundry, care for sick and elderly relatives, and raise young children.

The capitalist State provides some social services, but never enough to lift the burden of reproduction from the family. In 1995, it was calculated that if employers and governments had to pay for all the socially-necessary work done in the family, it would cost them $11 trillion world-wide and $1.4 trillion in the U.S. alone. Unpaid domestic labor represents a massive financial gift to the system and is the root source of women's oppression. As long as women must do socially necessary labor in the home, they cannot participate in work and society as equals with men.

Employers take advantage of women's domestic responsibilities to pay them lower wages. Lower wages make women workers more desirable; however, to engage all women in the workforce, employers would have to pay for or provide 24-hour childcare, convenient family eateries, and drop-off laundries. The cost of these services would negate the profits to be made by employing women. Capitalism has a conflict: it wants women in the home providing free social services and it also wants them in the workforce making profits. This conflict is reproduced within each woman's life. A lack of social services compels women to work at home, and financial necessity compels them to also work outside the home. To manage this double burden, 40 percent of employed women work evenings, nights, or weekends on a regular basis. To provide continuous care for their children, one in three employed women works a different shift from her mate.

The reproductive (nuclear) family

The modern family was formed during the industrial revolution. Within feudal societies, extended families lived and farmed together. The intensity of work changed with the seasons, and the length of the workday was determined by the amount of daylight. Capitalism shattered these families, sucking men, women, and children into the factory system and working them around the clock. Each family member might work in a different location, and all labored such long hours that they seldom saw each other. The sick, injured, and elderly were left to fend for themselves. Pregnant women worked until they went into labor, and they returned to work immediately after giving birth. The infant death rate skyrocketed. Surviving children were put to work as young as two years of age. Parents could neither protect nor care for their children, and children, as one investigator at the time remarked, "neither recognized duties to their parents nor felt any affection for them."

In 19th century England, the life span of the average factory worker fell to 18 years. Under such terrible conditions, the working population could not reproduce itself. Something had to be done; however, the capitalist class refused to pay for social supports for the working class. Pressed by workers' demands, government reformers enacted laws that excluded women and children from the most dangerous jobs and prohibited the youngest children from working. These and other laws and practices increased women's financial dependence on men, made men responsible for supporting women and children, held parents responsible for raising children, restricted divorce, and severely punished male homosexuality. The nuclear family was born, and it was very different from what had come before.

Feudal families were units of production and reproduction. Many generations worked and lived together, and their ties to the land made these families relatively stable. By removing production from the family and locating it in the workplace, capitalism created a family system with only one function—reproduction. This kind of family is more vulnerable to disintegration. Today, half of all marriages end in divorce, and this figure would be higher if divorce did not bring so much financial hardship.

World War II showed how easily the reproductive family could break down. In America, the State established a system of comprehensive childcare so that women could take industrial jobs. During this time, same-sex relationships flourished. After the war, during the 1950's, a repressive campaign was launched to re-build the nuclear family. The better-paying jobs were closed to women and funding for childcare was cut off, forcing women back into the home. Psychiatry labeled homosexuality a mental illness to be "treated" with castration, lobotomy, electroshock, and forced confinement in psychiatric institutions. Women who suffered emotional problems from constricted lives were prescribed psychiatric drugs called "mother's little helpers."

The biological need to belong causes people to gravitate towards each other. *How* they live together is socially determined. To maintain the reproductive family, society restricts the ways in which people can live. Housing is designed for nuclear families composed of two parents and their children. Most cities regulate how many "non-related" people can live in one dwelling. Same-sex couples and people designated as "non-related" are denied rights granted to family members, including employment benefits, Social Security, and a say in medical and legal matters that affect their loved ones.

The reproductive family system is maintained by force of law, medicine, religion, and custom. The oppression of women is key. If women were free to work as they pleased, to chose their partners as they felt, and to have or not have children as they wished, the reproductive family system would be replaced by different family forms that actually met people's needs. To sustain the nuclear family system, women must be *compelled* to work in the home by denying them other options. Restrictions on contraception and abortion rob women of control over their reproductive functions. Lack of childcare and other social supports force women to provide cooking, cleaning, and childcare services in the home. Lower wages, the absence of paid maternity leave, and little or no job security after pregnancy keep most women in a state of financial dependence on higher-waged men. Forcing men to support women and children provides the added bonus of controlling male workers. Spouses who want out of marriages and parents who want relief from childcare duties can be prosecuted and held financially responsible for "dependents." Youngsters who run away from home are forcibly returned to their families, placed in alternate families, or confined in detention centers. The American Psychiatric Association persists in designating variations in sexual behavior as mental disorders. And homosexuals continue to be victims of discrimination, violence, and murder.

The systematic under-funding of social services forces a life-long dependence on the family. Those who are sick, injured, unemployed, broke, or in trouble, are expected to rely on their families. Existing social supports are either too expensive (private care), or so inadequate (institutional care) that only the most desperate people use them. To make the absence of alternatives more palatable, the reproductive family is praised as the best way—the only way—to live.

Family values

The phrase, "family values," evokes warm images of love, comfort, and mutual aid—what everyone desires. Ironically, this slogan is used to deprive families of social support. While the State supports the capitalist class in innumerable ways, it provides next to nothing for families. The richest nation in the world does not provide paid leave for workers to care for needy relatives. Currently, twelve percent of women and eight percent of men care for a sick or aging relative. Twenty-nine percent of these care-givers provide more than 40 hours' assistance per week. There is no paid maternity leave and no national system of childcare in the United States. Individual parents are solely responsible for nurturing, socializing, and educating children before they enter the school system. In this privatized system of reproduction, good parents are expected to find the resources they need. Those who cannot are condemned as bad parents lacking family values. Psychologist Steven Gold explains,

> Hidden behind the aura of dominion implied by the term "family values" is the expectation and demand that families be self-sufficient. Not only should they be liberated from the constraints of outside forces, they should be capable of functioning without depending on external supports and should be independent of outside influences.[50]

Advocates of "family values" oppose social support for families. They insist that "a woman's place is in the home," even though most women must work outside the home and need childcare to do so. Publicly-provided childcare has been shown to be as good or better for children than home parenting. Nevertheless, politicians use "pro-family" arguments to oppose funding childcare programs. The lies that "all you need is love" and "love conquers all" serve to deprive working people of social resources.

Media campaigns push the importance of good parenting at the same time that funding for children's programs like Headstart is reduced or eliminated. In 2000, the Invest in Kids foundation organized a mass campaign to "Love your child to launch your child." Parents were urged to spend quality time with their kids and to involve them in music and art. This joint government-corporate crusade was launched *at the same time* that family, recreation, and school-support programs were being scrapped to pay for corporate tax cuts.

Parents want to provide their children with the best start in life, and they need social support to do so. State-funded childcare, unemployment insurance, social assistance, Social Security, Medicare, and paid leave are a form of "social wage" that benefits the entire workforce. Studies show that workers are more productive, absent less often, and stay longer with companies that provide these benefits. For these reasons, some employers do provide family support for difficult-to-replace employees. In general, however, it is more cost-effective not to provide social benefits and to condemn families that cannot manage on their own.

Children pay the price

All mammals have an inborn attachment system that connects newborns to adults who can nurture and protect them. The human attachment system is especially important for the development of the human brain. However, the capitalist family system is designed to replace the labor force, not to promote healthy human development. Let me explain.

At birth, human infants cannot regulate their feelings. When newborns are hungry, they are completely, totally, and desperately hungry, with no memory of not being hungry and no sense that hunger will ever end. *Now* is all there is, and now is filled with hunger. When an adult responds to the infant's hunger-cry with food and soothing touch and voice, the infant's hunger is replaced with satisfaction and comfort. Thousands of such interactions teach the child that food follows hunger, and so he learns to tolerate feeling hungry. The same process applies to other emotions.

Infants need adults to "tune-in" to their needs—feeding them when they are hungry, soothing them when they are distressed, providing them with stimulation when needed, and allowing them to pull away when overstimulated. Embraced in a synchronized emotional dance with the care-giver, children learn how to manage a wide variety of feelings and situations, developing a balanced nervous system that is neither too aroused nor too withdrawn. Adults don't need to be perfect to provide this secure base for children, they only need to be available and responsive *most of the time*. The reproductive family is not structured to provide that time.

It takes a village to raise a healthy child. However, most people live in overburdened, isolated, family units. In a village, children can form bonds with many adults, so that there is always someone available in times of need. The nuclear family has at best two accessible adults and often only one. When parents are busy, stressed, sick, or needy, many children have no one else to turn to.

Unlike adults, children cannot put events into context. When they are pressed into the service of overwhelmed parents ("Take care of your mother/father") children mistakenly conclude that their own needs are unimportant and that they do not deserve to have their needs met.

Children are psychologically more vulnerable than adults because immature nervous systems cannot handle intense emotions. Children in stressed families need more time and attention, more calming and soothing; however, these are the times when parents have the least to give. Not surprisingly, sickness and stress in parents is strongly correlated with emotional problems in children. In such situations, parents and children can become trapped in a cycle of deprivation, where adult stress triggers child distress and child distress elevates adult stress. Whether professionals treat the overwhelmed parent or the distressed child, the social problem of overwhelmed families is rarely acknowledged.

When most people hear the phrase "childhood trauma," they think of child abuse. In fact, most childhood trauma is not abuse. Children are most frequently traumatized by separations—when a parent is injured, imprisoned, deported, or dies, and when family members are dislocated by war and other disasters. Youngsters who seem calm in such crises are actually dissociating, which increases their risk of developing post-traumatic stress disorders later on.

Children who experience too much stress and receive too little nurturing have more difficulty managing strong emotions like fear, grief, and anger. To shift out of intolerable emotional states, these children may bang their heads, engage in prolonged rocking, behave impulsively or violently, and daydream excessively. As adolescents they are more likely to take drugs and engage in risky behaviors. As adults, they are more likely to be violent towards themselves and others. Instead of meeting their needs (and the needs of their families) society punishes and medicates these youngsters to make them "behave."

Capitalism deprives the majority of what they produce. Deprived adults cannot provide what children need to thrive. Deprived children grow up believing that they don't deserve to have their needs met. Employers capitalize on low self-esteem to take even more from workers, creating more deprived adults, more deprived children, and an expanding ocean of misery.

Family violence

> It would be hard to find a group or institution in American society in which violence is more of an everyday occurrence than it is within the family.[51]

People long for their families to be a refuge, the heart of a heartless world. Sadly, families are anything but safe. One is much more likely to be assaulted or murdered by a family member than by a stranger. More than one in three Americans has witnessed an incident of domestic violence, and 80 percent of children experience violence from their siblings. Almost one in three adults has experienced physical assault, sexual assault, or a combination of both during childhood.

While family violence occurs in all social classes, it occurs more frequently as one moves down the social ladder. More stress and fewer options increase the likelihood of interpersonal violence. An overwhelmed parent who can find no relief is more likely to explode in frustration than one who can hire a babysitter and get a few hours off. Families with annual incomes under $15,000 suffer six times more physical and sexual child abuse. This figure may be inflated. Poor families are scrutinized more by authorities, while better-off families can hide their problems more easily. However, severe physical abuse is difficult to hide. One study found that parents who worked in semi-skilled or unskilled jobs were three times more likely than professional parents to seriously physically harm their children.

People commonly dismiss the link between deprivation and violence with comments like, "Not everyone who comes from poverty is violent, so it must be that some people *choose* to behave badly." This is a curious reaction. Everyone accepts that the cold virus causes colds, even though not everyone who is exposed to a cold virus gets a cold. Likewise, not everyone who suffers poverty becomes violent. Nevertheless, in both cases, the probability of being afflicted increases with exposure. One could argue that poverty "creates" violence in the same way that germs "cause" disease.

The probability that any particular individual will be violent (and the probability that any particular individual will get sick) depends on past and present conditions. The developing nervous system is very sensitive to stress. Stable conditions in childhood increase resilience to stress, whereas chaotic conditions increase vulnerability to stress. Family background is one reason why some people remain cool under severe stress while others "lose it" in response to seemingly mild stress.

Strong social bonds increase resilience to stress. Families and individuals who band together for mutual support are more stable and less violent than families and individuals who lack social support. Children who suffered bad treatment, yet grew up to become kind and generous adults, had at least one person along the way—a relative, teacher, neighbor—who treated them well. Adults who were badly parented themselves can become good parents when they are provided with social support. One study found that regular home visits from a nurse, beginning in pregnancy and continuing through a child's second birthday, significantly reduced child abuse among highly disadvantaged families. And the effects were long-lasting.

Those who dismiss social conditions and insist that "People always have a choice," are unrealistic and lack compassion. It is easy to condemn the behaviors of others from a safe distance. As Chapter 4 explained, severe stress causes the brain to react *automatically* with flight, fight, and freeze reactions, providing no time for conscious choice. Like Andrea Yates, people who feel overwhelmed do not make good choices. People make better choices when they have more support. Blaming individuals for family problems undercuts efforts to improve social conditions and provide people with more choices.

The State sanctions family violence by permitting adults to use force against children for discipline and control. In the United States, one-quarter of all children between one month and six months of age are hit, and half of all children between six months and one year of age are hit. As long as "reasonable" force is applied, parents cannot be prosecuted for physically assaulting their children.

Most people think that spanking children is harmless. However, children do not think like adults. In most cases, the harm does not lie in the severity of the violence but in its emotional impact. When a child is completely dependent upon someone who becomes a source of pain and humiliation, that child feels confused and frightened. Long-lasting emotional problems can result.

Nearly 100 studies have documented a link between childhood spanking and adult mental health problems. One study found that almost 80 percent of people had been slapped, spanked, or both by an adult during childhood. Forty percent of the people in this study reported being frequently slapped or spanked as children. This group suffered much higher rates of anxiety and were more likely to have drug or alcohol problems as adults. Keep in mind the strong connection between family deprivation and family violence. The harmful effects of spanking cannot be separated from the impact of living in overly-stressed families.

Societies that foster equality and cooperation suffer less interpersonal violence. In a world where the strong dominate the weak and where diplomacy is backed by force, using violence against children is not surprising. Even though family members have a common interest in cooperating, parents are encouraged to view youngsters as unmanageable and in need of "a firm hand." The possibility that children might want to cooperate, and could be encouraged to cooperate, is dismissed as a nice idea that could never work in practice. In fact, punishment is what doesn't work.

Actions speak louder than words. Physical punishment demonstrates to children that those with more power have the right to use violence against those with less power. Like children, hamsters also learn by example. Studies show that when normally placid hamsters are threatened and attacked as youngsters, they grow up to be cowards when caged with larger hamsters and bullies when caged with smaller ones.

Battle of the sexes?

When people hear the phrase "domestic violence" or "spouse abuse," they usually picture a man hitting a woman. There are many reasons for this. The women's movement of the 1970's brought the issue of violence against women to public attention and secured funding for a network of shelters for battered women. Feminism promotes the view that men seek power over women and children *because it is in their nature to do so.* The assumption that males are naturally more violent than females has caused most research on domestic violence to examine male perpetrators and female victims. In contrast, violence perpetrated by women against men is not considered to be a social problem.

Female-perpetrated violence is under-estimated for several reasons. Female victims are more likely to report spousal violence than males, who are ashamed to admit they were assaulted by females. Most studies do not distinguish between minor assaults, perpetrated by both men and women, and serious assaults that are more commonly perpetrated by men. These factors combine to give the mistaken impression that domestic violence is always serious, if not life-threatening, and that women only attack men in self-defense.

The private nature of relationships makes it difficult to know for certain how much men and women contribute to violent encounters. The problem cannot be attributed solely to a "battle between the sexes" because same-sex relationships are also afflicted with interpersonal violence. Studies show that men in relationships with men are battered as often as women in relationships with men. And between 17 and 45 percent of lesbians report having been the victim of at least one act of physical violence perpetrated by a female partner.

A fuller awareness of the ways that men and women hurt each other would be useful. However, many feminists oppose research on female-perpetrated violence for fear that evidence of battered husbands will undermine efforts to combat wife abuse. They have reason to fear. Anti-feminists have opposed funding for domestic violence programs that refuse to acknowledge females as perpetrators.

I have treated battered women, abused men, and adults of both sexes who were maltreated in childhood by mothers, fathers, brothers, and sisters. It does not help to debate whether men or women are more responsible for domestic violence. *All victims of family violence deserve support, and all perpetrators need treatment.*

Making men tough

To understand why men are violent, we only need to look at how they are socialized. Society directs an astonishing level of violence against males. Teaching males to be tough prepares them for a world of "Compete or Die," where death is preferable to failure.

The most sensitive parts of men's bodies are singled out for attack. Parents are encouraged to circumcise their sons in the first week of life, a traumatic procedure that is commonly performed without anesthetic.

The same surgery done on female infants (removing the skin around the clitoris) is illegal and deplored as cruel and mutilating. More than 13 percent of boys have experienced assaults directed at their genitals, and 10 percent of boys have been kicked in the groin before junior high school. While boys are subjected to physical violence, they are prohibited from expressing pain or vulnerability. In films, a man being kicked in the groin is usually presented as comical, despite the excruciating pain of such trauma. Laughing at someone's pain is a sign of dissociation, and both girls and boys are taught to deny male vulnerability from an early age.

Sexist stereotypes depict real men as strong and powerful, not as victims. To be a victim is to be without power—like a woman—and the most important thing for a man is to *not* be a woman. Males victimized by females are especially shamed and ridiculed. One of my students confessed that she found herself laughing while reading a description of a woman battering her husband until she realized that she would be "screaming bloody murder" if the roles were reversed.

Taunts like "Don't be a cry-baby" and "Don't be a girl" teach boys to feel ashamed of feeling scared or hurt. The belief that even very young boys should be tough causes them to be separated from their mothers much earlier than girls. Males are discouraged from showing feelings other than anger, which is considered a manly emotion because of its power. Consequently, boys learn to respond with anger, even rage, when they feel vulnerable or detect vulnerability in other males. Homophobic bullying is a common way for boys and men to bolster their masculine identity.

The school system plays an important role in promoting violence against young males. Physical abuse during initiation rituals for social clubs and sports teams is justified as "character building." In Columbine High School, site of the 1999 shooting massacre, sports initiation rituals included senior wrestlers twisting the nipples of newcomers until they turned purple and older tennis players sending hard volleys into the backsides of younger ones. School transforms recreational play into war-games, where there is no gain without pain—preferably the other guy's pain.

Sports train young men to hurt others, and to risk being hurt, in order to win. Head injuries and concussions are common in ice hockey, so an injury-prevention video was developed for players aged nine to ten. However, 22 of 34 minor-league coaches refused to show their teams the video because they thought it would "decrease aggressive play," "make players think they will hurt other players on the ice," and "decrease competitive success in the game."

The pressure for men to appear invincible can be lethal. In the summer of 2001, six players died from heatstroke during football practice. One of them was Minnesota Vikings' Pro Bowl tackle Korey Stringer.

> On the day of Stringer's collapse, the heat index peaked at 103 degrees...[yet he]...remained at practice even after vomiting several times, one of the most well-known warning signs of severe heat-related problems.[52]

Despite the publicity surrounding Stringer's death, two days later, Northwestern's Rashidi Wheeler collapsed and died after an intense practice in stifling heat. The pressure not to "wimp out" is so strong that Wheeler spent his last conscious moments protesting his removal from the field.

Shame and rage

Shame plays an important role in interpersonal violence. Shame is the intensely painful feeling of being unworthy or unacceptable—a loser. Intolerable shame can transform into anger or rage that is directed at one's self or at someone else. Rage and shame reinforce each other in a downward spiral that can erupt in violence.

The most common source of shame is the social hierarchy that divides people into a few winners and many more losers. The lower down the ladder you stand, the harder it is to feel good about yourself. Studies show that those most likely to injure their partners are not the most powerful people, but the most powerless. Abusive men are more likely to feel like failures, to be unemployed or intermittently employed, and to have less than high-school education. They are also more likely to suffer from addictions that temporarily soothe their inner anguish, but also increase their shame and consequent rage.

Mothers are usually blamed when their sons have relationship problems. However, researchers have found that fathers play a more important role. In *The Abusive Personality: Violence and Control in Intimate Relationships,* Donald Dutton notes.

> To our surprise, we found that the biggest childhood contributors to adult [male] abusiveness were (in order of importance) feeling rejected by one's father, feeling a lack of warmth from one's father, being physically abused by one's father, being verbally abused by one's father, and feeling rejected by one's mother…It seemed that the emotional aspect of paternal treatment was paramount. Being punished in a rejecting way by your father was the worst thing that could happen, far worse than simply being punished.[53]

The human longing for connection is incompatible with the competition that capitalism demands. Intimacy requires openness and vulnerability, while competition favors secrecy and guardedness. Fathers consider it their duty to toughen their sons to help them succeed in life. A conflict is created between the son who needs his father's affection and the father who has learned to suppress his own emotions and thinks his son should do the same.

The child who is ridiculed by the parent for feeling needy is put in an impossible position; shame at displeasing the parent increases the need for reassurance and the shame of needing reassurance. Both girls and boys learn to avoid this problem by never stating what they want and then punishing those who fail to deliver. This behavior pattern commonly precedes interpersonal violence.

On the surface, wife-battering looks like a display of male power. In reality, most men who batter or kill their female partners feel extremely dependent and extremely ashamed of their dependence. The desire for complete control over the partner is in direct proportion to the sense of unworthiness and the fear of loss. As the longing for love competes with the fear of rejection, frustration is directed at those who fail (as fail they must) to take away the pain. A "battering cycle" can begin where discontent builds to an explosion of rage that drives the partner away. Terror at the prospect of being abandoned leads to acts of contrition to draw the partner back. The return of the partner revives the fear of being shamed through rejection, and anger builds again. These people are at their partners' throats one minute and at their knees the next.

Men are most likely to murder their partners when they feel least powerful—when the partner leaves or threatens to leave. Those who kill their partners often kill themselves at the same time. In general, men are 11 times more likely than women to kill themselves when a relationship breaks up. Such violence is not a result of male power, but the tragic outcome of traumatizing males and then shaming them for feeling hurt and needing comfort. As early as five years of age, males are more likely than females to kill themselves. This difference increases through life. By age 22, men are six times more likely and by age 85 fifteen times more likely to kill themselves.

Shared stress and mutual violence

Interpersonal violence is a defense against feeling powerless, and both boys and girls learn this in the family. Sons of violent parents are 1,000 times more likely to beat their female partners than sons of non-violent parents. Daughters of violent parents are 600 times more likely to assault their male partners than daughters of non-violent partners.

Women suffer more *serious* violence from male partners than men suffer from female partners. This is an undeniable social problem. At the same time, *most violence in intimate relationships is minor and mutual.* Within this more common category, women are as likely to incite the violence as their male partners. The 2003 *Youth Risk Behavior Survey* found that 8.9 percent of boys and 8.8 percent of girls in high school reported being hit, slapped, or physically hurt on purpose by a girlfriend or a boyfriend. Examples of adult mutual violence are routinely found in police reports. Here are a couple of items from my local newspaper:

Domestic dispute. Husband and wife arrested after they started punching each other during an argument. Both are charged with assault.

Couple charged in domestic. A husband, 46, and wife, 45, were both charged with assault after an argument turned physical. Both suffered minor injuries but did not require medical attention.

These are not descriptions of male dominance and female submission. This is mutual aggression that results when overly stressed individuals take their frustrations out on each other. In such disputes, women are generally disadvantaged in size and strength. At the same time, many men refuse to fight back in the belief that only cowards hit women.

When it comes to children, women are more violent than men. One study found that mothers were the assailants in 52 percent of child abuse cases. In another study, mothers were the perpetrators 61 percent of the time. Women who were themselves being battered were *more* likely to hurt their own children. These findings are consistent with the premise that lack of choices and lack of power increase the likelihood of interpersonal violence.

That females can be violent should not be surprising. The double burden of work and family duties falls on women, who also have more financial stress. Anger is a response to injustice, and women's oppression provides a daily diet of injustice. Depression is another response to injustice, and no one disputes that depression is common among women. However, female rage remains controversial, partly because sexist stereotypes define females as nurturing and submissive. It is easier to blame men for family violence. However, in *Myths of Male Dominance,* anthropologist Eleanor Burke Leacock warns,

> To consign the grim brutalities of abused power we see everywhere about us to what amounts to masculine "original sin" not only denies the historical and ethnographic record (plus what we may personally know of individual men), but seriously disarms all of us, as humanity, in the urgency of our need to understand and redirect our social life if we would ensure ourselves a future.[54]

Tainted love

People look to their family and personal relationships for understanding, acceptance, and relief from the rat race. Some find comfort. Many do not. Different social expectations for men and women create barriers to intimacy. Because women are expected to be care-givers in the family, they are raised to be warm and responsive. Because men are expected to compete at work, they are trained to be aggressive and action-oriented. Incompatible gender roles are not the only barriers to closeness. Same-sex couples have just as much difficulty. After many years of pondering why so many relationships fail, I have come to the following conclusions:

Mutually satisfying relationships are based on equality and cooperation; capitalism cultivates inequality and competition. Marriage expert John Gottman discovered that when one or both partners expresses contempt for the other (rolling eyes, condescending tone of voice), the marriage is more likely to fail. Contempt is an expression of superiority and inequality.

Daily frustrations and humiliations increase the need for comfort and reassurance. At the same time, work and domestic chores consume so much time and energy that, too frequently, emotional needs are put on hold. The combination of pressing needs and insufficient time breeds resentment and anger. When there doesn't seem to be enough to go around, people compete for what little there is. Children compete for their parent's time. Adults compete for each other's love. The winners of this competition feel anxious about losing what they have. The losers feel hurt and resentful. Everyone feels cheated. Relationships that begin full of hope break down in anguish. The competition of capitalism reproduces itself in the most private corners of our lives.

When relationships don't work, people wrongly assume that the problem is a lack of love, lack of trying, or a mismatch of individuals. The material and social pressures that make it so difficult for relationships to work are seldom considered. People blame themselves ("I'm not good enough") and each other ("You don't care about me"). The man who feels ashamed of having emotional needs blames his wife for not knowing how to meet them. The woman who is exhausted from her double day blames her husband for not helping more.

Social pressures make it difficult for people to create satisfying relationships and to leave intolerable relationships. There is tremendous pressure to stay together, regardless of the level of suffering. Women's low pay keeps them financially dependent on men, especially when they have children. The State insists that men support women and children, regardless of their ability to do so. People who feel trapped in relationships are more likely to attack each other. The next chapter explains how even the misery created by capitalism is exploited for profit.

Summary

Capitalism organizes the maintenance and reproduction of the labor force in isolated family units. Because social services are inadequate, individual women are compelled to do most of this work in the home. The current family system controls men by forcing them to support women and children and deprives children of the social support they need to thrive.

Human beings seek comfort and connection in personal relationships. However, female oppression, male trauma, lack of support, and a competitive social environment make sustained emotional closeness virtually impossible. Family conflict results from too much work, too little time, too few choices, and the unreasonable expectation that love alone can solve all problems.

Chapter 8

Profit From Pain

I'm standing on the shore of a swiftly flowing river. I hear a scream for help. I dive into the water and pull a woman to shore. As I revive her, I hear another cry. I jump back in the river to save a child. There is another call. Again I rescue. I'm so busy pulling people out of the water that I don't look upstream to see who is pushing them in.

This anecdote describes the predicament of medical workers, social workers, counselors, and therapists who "service the human machinery" for capitalism. We are too busy rescuing people to question why so many are in distress. It is simply assumed that they must have done something wrong: they were too close to shore, they were careless, they never learned to swim, they forgot their life jackets, and so on. An exclusive focus on personal failings ignores the many ways that society makes people sick. This chapter explains how capitalism manufactures disease, and how the medical system is structured, not to eliminate that disease but to contain it politically, and to make a profit in the process.

Blood money

> Go reckon our dead by the forges red
> And the factories where we spin.
> If blood be the price of your cursed wealth,
> Good God! We have paid it in!

The assault on health begins at work. As the ruling class extracts surplus from the working class, it leaves sickness and death behind. To maximize profits, employers compel workers to use cheaper, toxic materials instead of safer, more expensive ones. To raise productivity, managers demand the maximum output per hour, despite the fact that injury rates rise with the intensity of the work. Add shift-work, overtime, and the stress of personal problems, and you have a recipe for disaster.

An estimated six million American workers were injured on the job in 1997. Almost four million workplace injuries were serious enough to be treated in hospital emergency rooms. In 2002, nearly 300,000 new cases of occupational illness were reported; however, the Bureau of Labor Statistics admits that this number greatly underestimates the actual amount of sickness caused by work. One medical study estimated that more than 55,000 Americans die every year from occupational illness and injury—more than die in motor vehicle accidents.

The drive for profit makes work dangerous, despite efforts to promote workplace safety. Industrial laundry workers in Massachusetts were instructed never to put their hands in the machines. Signs in three languages were posted to emphasize this warning. When material got stuck, workers were instructed to shut down the machine and call the maintenance department. At the same time, every worker had a daily production quota, and those who failed to meet it could be fired. Because management had "down-sized" the maintenance department, a worker reporting a jammed machine could wait from 20 minutes to 2 hours for it to be fixed. Lost production during that time was counted against the worker. The *written* rule was: "Don't put your hand in the machine." The *real* rule was: "If you want to keep your job, you must clear the machine yourself." The resulting injuries were predictable.

Between 1993 and 2003, the number of workers who died on the job *every year* ranged between 5,534 and 6,632—more than twice as many as died on 9/11. Despite this shocking level of industrial slaughter, politicians do not denounce employers as "terrorists." Homeland Security does not include the workplace.

Ninety percent of all work sites in the U.S., covering 40 percent of the country's total workforce, are not inspected regularly for health and safety violations. When violations are found, the penalties are too small to force a change in work practices. One corporation was cited for more than 400 safety violations over a period during which 4,600 of its workers were injured and nine were killed. Three deaths were found to be caused by deliberate violations of federal safety standards, yet this company was never threatened with closure.

The State virtually gives employers a license to kill workers. In 1970, Congress declared that causing the death of a worker by *deliberately* violating safety laws is a misdemeanor (not a felony) with a maximum sentence of six months in jail. This is half the maximum for harassing a wild donkey on federal land.

In 2003, *New York Times* journalist David Barstow reported that an excessive number of workers were being "decapitated on assembly lines, shredded in machinery, burned beyond recognition, electrocuted, buried alive…" The Occupational Safety and Health Administration investigated 57 percent of these deaths, and laid charges in only seven percent of them, despite finding that

> Between 1982 and 2002, a total of 2,197 workers were killed on the job because their employers "willfully" violated safety laws. With full knowledge of their responsibilities, they ignored accepted safety precautions, removed safety devices to speed up production or denied workers protective gear.[55]

The body never lies

> Productivity in America shot up in the first quarter of 2002 by 8.6 percent at an annual rate, the biggest leap since 1983. Employees worked longer and harder as unemployment rose.[56]

Higher productivity results from paying workers less than the full value of what they produce. When the media trumpet higher productivity and profits as *great news for everyone,* workers become confused. They are told that surrendering more of what they produce is good, even as their living conditions deteriorate. Do they trust what they are told, that they live in the best possible world? Or do they trust their experience, that life is getting harder? Going with your gut puts you in conflict with the system. Going with the system puts you in conflict with your gut. When people face such seemingly unsolvable problems, their bodies cry out in protest.

The biological stress response developed as an emergency measure—you kill the bear or the bear kills you. But what happens when you cannot get away? What happens when the threat you face comes from your job and from the society in which you live? Bodies subjected to continual stress adapt by dissociating from the awareness of being stressed so that stress feels "normal." No matter how well people seem to adapt to stressful conditions, the body never lies about the true state of an organism.

Bodies flooded with stress hormones respond with backaches, headaches, insomnia, fatigue, anxiety, depression, digestive and respiratory problems, chest pains, high blood pressure, recurring infections, rashes, allergies, muscular spasms, sexual and menstrual difficulties. These symptoms can be relieved with medicines, but there can be no cure as long as the individual is unjustly treated by society. As Michael Schneider wrote in *Neurosis and Civilization,*

> As long as the working class does not rebel against these new and intensified forms of exploitation, heart, stomach and circulatory diseases of individual workers will rebel for them. Even though the worker may still 'go along,' his circulation, in any event, will not. Even if he says, 'actually I feel alright,' his stomach ulcer will prove the contrary.[57]

Inequality kills

As wealth flows upwards to the few, the many who produce it are increasingly impoverished. In 1970 the richest 0.1 percent of Americans took in 100 times the average annual income. By 2001, this same group enjoyed 560 times the average annual income. As surplus accumulates at the top of society, sickness and misery accumulate at the bottom, and not only from injuries, illnesses, and fatalities at work. Inequality itself is deadly.

Human health is inextricably linked with equality. More unequal socieities have *overall* higher death rates. A study of 282 metropolitan areas in the United States found that the greater the difference in income, the more the death rate rose *for all income levels,* not just for the poor. And the rise in death rates was substantial. Researchers calculate that reducing income inequality to the lowest level found in the United States would save as many lives as would be saved by eradicating heart disease, or by preventing all deaths from lung cancer, diabetes, motor vehicle crashes, HIV infection, suicide, and homicide put together! Even greater benefits would flow from eliminating inequality completely.

Consider the lives that would be saved by eliminating racism. Black people in the United States suffer almost 300 more deaths per 100,000 people than White people do. If there were no racism, the death rate for Blacks and Whites would be the same. Compare these 300 additional deaths with the much smaller U.S. murder rate of about 10 people per 100,000. *Every year, racism kills 30 times more people than die at the hands of individual murderers.*

Inequality kills children. Even though the United States is the richest nation in the world, 42 nations have lower infant death rates. The infant mortality rate in Washington, D.C. is more than double the infant mortality rate in the capital of China. There are also 25 nations where the average life span is longer than it is in America.

In *Unhealthy Societies: The Afflictions of Inequality,* Richard Wilkinson found that inequality is so harmful that poor people who live in nations with less inequality tend to be healthier and live longer than better-off people who live in more unequal nations. Bangladesh is one of the poorest countries in the world, yet Bangladeshi men are more likely to reach age 65 than Black men living in Harlem, New York. Harlem men have greater incomes and a higher standard of living than Bangladeshi men; however, the U.S. is a much more unequal society. For one thing, Black men in Harlem suffer more cardiovascular disease, which is linked with class and racial oppression.

A classic study of the British civil service found that health deteriorates as social status falls. This deterioration in health cannot be explained by factors like smoking, exercise habits, and body weight. Most surprising, those *near* the top of the power structure have worse health than those *at* the top, even though their life-styles are essentially the same. This relationship between power and health has been found in every nation studied, including the United States. Income differentials cannot explain these findings. The non-professional who earns as much money as the professional has significantly more health problems. The difference is one of power. Your place in the social hierarchy determines how much control you have over your life, and the less control people have, the more stress and stress-related illnesses they suffer.

Those with little control over demanding jobs, like public servants and social service workers, have more than double the rate of cardiovascular disease compared with those who have more control. Those with less control are more likely to be overweight and develop high cholesterol regardless of age, amount of exercise, and smoking habits. Demanding work, on its own, is generally not related to poor health unless there is also a lack of power. The most health-damaging jobs saddle workers with great responsibility (like finding housing for the homeless) while denying them the resources required to do the job (affordable housing). People working under sustained conditions of high demand and low control suffer three times as many heart problems, three times as much back pain, five times as many cancers, two to three times as much interpersonal conflict, two to three times as many mental health problems, two to three times as many infections, two to three times as many injuries, and twice as much substance abuse.

Feeling powerless is linked with higher death rates from cardiovascular disease; the more powerless a person feels, the faster the disease progresses. Bosses live the longest, healthiest lives because they have the most power. As power diminishes, stress rises and health deteriorates. Less education, lower income, and higher unemployment are all linked with more deaths from cardiovascular disease.

Children show rising levels of stress hormones as their social position falls. Nurses who work under "unfair and unreasonable" bosses suffer higher blood pressure. Simply speaking with someone whose social status is higher will raise a person's blood pressure. Higher rates of chronic disease in the working class, and especially in its oppressed sections, are not only the result of obvious factors—inferior nutrition, less medical care, more dangerous work, greater exposure to environmental toxins, etc. Continuous, damaging stress results when people are put down and ordered around their entire lives.

> Stress triggers a higher heart rate, a release of adrenaline, glucose and other neurological responses to help the body respond to a short-term threat. But when extended over long periods of time, they can harm the cardiovascular and immune systems, making individuals more vulnerable to a wide range of conditions including infections, diabetes, high blood pressure, heart attack, stroke, asthma and aggression.[58]

It makes sense that inequality would make people sick. Human survival has always depended on cooperation and strong social bonds. Social support is linked with better health and longer life. Strong social ties may explain why Hispanic Americans have less chronic illness than White Americans, despite having lower incomes. Inequality ruptures social bonds. Exclusion from the decision-making process is strongly linked with heart disease. Since capitalism excludes the majority from the decision-making process, it is not surprising that heart disease has become a leading cause of death. No matter how you look at it, *ending inequality would reduce the burden of disease and raise the level of health more than any other single measure.*

Our early ancestors preserved social ties by valuing equality and reciprocity. Cultural practices of gift-giving, food-sharing, and making collective decisions were accompanied by social taboos against selfishness, snobbery, and greed. By rejecting these ancient values and setting people against one another, capitalism has created a world of sickness. Sadly, the medical system is designed not to eliminate this misery, but to profit from it.

Caring for profit

In medicine, business comes first. I learned this as a medical intern in a big city hospital. One morning, a 67-year-old man who was waiting for a hernia repair asked me to cancel his surgery because he had a strong feeling that he would die on the operating table. When I conveyed this information to the surgeon, he became furious. Storming into the patient's room, the doctor berated the patient for wasting his time. The patient submitted, the surgery proceeded, and the patient died. The surgeon was paid just the same.

In a social system where human needs come first, the medical system would be organized to promote health and prevent disease. Under capitalism, the medical system is organized to produce profit, and there is no profit in health. Healthy people don't need doctors, hospitals, and medicines. In contrast, disease is a highly profitable gold mine. People will pay anything to relieve their suffering and care for their loved ones. Our "health-care" system is really a disease-care system because most medical spending is devoted to treating disease, not preventing it. Consider the following example.

Over a 100 years ago, Louis Pasteur discovered the link between germs and disease. Today, modern hospitals spread disease because it is not profitable to keep them clean.

> Hygiene is so inadequate in most American hospitals that one out of every 20 patients contracts an infection during a hospital stay. Hospital infections kill an estimated 103,000 people in the United States a year, as many as AIDS, breast cancer and auto accidents combined.[59]

In 2005, New York City's Mount Sinai Hospital experienced an outbreak of illness that is caused when fecal material from one person enters another person's mouth. The germs were being transmitted by nursing assistants who wore the same clothes while emptying bed pans and delivering food trays. These workers were not provided with enough time to change their clothes between duties.

Most infections caught in hospitals could be prevented by basic sanitation; however, keeping hospitals clean is labor-intensive work. Sanitizing surfaces, changing clothes, and washing hands absorbs time that could be invested in profit-making activities. As a result, budget-squeezed hospitals tend to cut cleaning staff and rely on antibiotics to manage infections. The overuse of antibiotics has caused more than 70 percent of hospital-acquired infections to become antibiotic-resistant and more deadly.

The greatest profits flow from denying people medical treatment. While medical insurance companies promise to provide care in times of need, they profit by withholding care: charging high premiums; enrolling only the healthiest individuals; denying coverage for "pre-existing" ailments; demanding co-payments an deductibles; limiting pay-outs; and reserving the right to abandon programs and regions that provide them with insufficient profits.

In the movie *John Q,* the lead character is a factory worker whose insurance company refuses to pay for his son's heart transplant. In real life, former Humana Evaluator Dr. Linda Peeno testified before Congress that she was pressured to deny a heart transplant to a patient who died as a result. She stated, "Humana's only concern was cost. The young man fit all the criteria, a donor had been found, his doctor was ready to do the operation." Humana proved that it had no heart when it purchased a sculpture for its head office that cost as much as the transplant would have cost.

As medical care becomes more expensive, more employers are shifting the cost to workers, who then have less money for housing, food, transportation, and childcare. A Harvard study found that half of U.S. bankruptcies, affecting two million people annually, are caused by sickness or medical bills. Three-quarters of those bankrupted by illness had medical insurance when they first got sick. One doctor concluded, "It's a cruel irony that in trying to help our patients we often ruin them financially. We heal their bodies, but inflict lasting financial wounds."

Medical capitalism

Organizing medicine as a business is profitable for some and lethal for many others. In 2003, *New York Times'* reporters Walt Bogdanich and Eric Koli revealed how Bayer pharmaceutical company knowingly allowed hemophiliacs to be infected with HIV.

Hemophilia is caused by a lack of clotting factors in the blood and is treated with regular injections of a blood product that is concentrated from pools of donors. In March of 1983, the U.S. Centers for Disease Control reported that 74 percent of hemophiliacs who were using unheated blood concentrate were testing positive for HIV. Bayer had developed a heat-treated product that was free of HIV. Nevertheless, for more than a year, the company continued to sell its unsafe product in Argentina, Japan, Hong Kong, Malaysia, Singapore, Indonesia, and Taiwan.

According to company documents, Bayer did not want to be stuck with large supplies of a product that could not be sold in the U.S. and Europe. So Bayer instructed its Hong Kong distributor to "use up stocks" of the old product before switching to the newer, safer one. Even after it began selling the heat-treated product, Bayer continued to make the unheated product for several months because it was cheaper to produce, and the company had several fixed-price contracts. In total, Bayer exported more than 100,000 vials of unheated concentrate *after* its safer product was available. In May of 1985, an official at the U.S. Food and Drug Administration stated that "It was unacceptable for [Bayer] to ship that material overseas," but requested that the issue be "quietly solved without alerting Congress, the medical community and the public." Bayer continued to ship unheated concentrate for another two months. Bayer was not unique in selling death for profit. Three other American-based companies, Armour Pharmaceutical, Baxter International, and Alpha Therapeutic also sold unheated blood concentrate after developing a heat-treated product. Bogdanich and Koli cite the case of 42-year-old hemophiliac, Lee Ching-Chang, who lived in Taiwan and became HIV-positive after using Bayer's unheated blood concentrate. Who knows how many more hemophiliacs were infected?

No amount of regulation can stop the production of harmful drugs and devices if enough profit can be made by selling them. In 2003, the Guidant Corporation pleaded guilty to 10 felonies, admitting that it lied to the U.S. government and hid thousands of serious health problems, including 12 deaths, caused by a defect in one of its medical devices. Guidant was rushing to compete with a company whose medical device was approved by the FDA the same day that Guidant's device was approved. As of this writing, Guidant is still in business, despite continuing problems with defective devices.

It is a sick fact that corporations profit by suppressing evidence that their products can kill. GlaxoSmithKline knowingly marketed anti-depressants that increased the risk of suicide in children. Merck knowingly produced a pain-killer that doubled the risk of heart attack and stroke. Pfizer knowingly sold a similar pain-killer that more than tripled the risk of heart attacks, strokes, and death. AstraZeneca knowingly promoted an anti-cholesterol drug that resulted in 75 times more kidney failure than all of its competitors combined. This is a partial list of incidents in one year from one industry. As long as profit rules, the safety of products cannot be guaranteed.

The role of the State

The State has a conflict regarding matters of health. To preserve the capitalist system, the State must ignore the systemic causes of disease. At the same time, sick workers are less productive. One U.S. study found that time off work due to illness cost the economy $260 billion a year. To counter this loss, the State must ensure some level of medical care. In the United States, about 100 million people, one in three, have access to medical care through government-funded programs like Medicaid, Medicare, the military, and government employee health plans. These programs make the U.S. government the largest provider of medical care in America. However, providing *everyone* with medical care would undermine the profitability of the American medical system. Dr. David Himmelstein calculates,

> There's something like $50 billion a year in profit extracted from the health care system, and that's only about one-sixth as much as the bureaucratic costs of actually extracting that profit. In fact, we spend each year about $320 billion or $340 billion on useless bureaucratic work in order to apportion the right to health care according to ability to pay, enforce inequality in care, and enforce the collection of profit by insurance companies, for-profit hospitals, the drug industry—a whole panoply of players.[60]

To generate profits, people must be denied medical care. In 2005, the average annual insurance premium for a family of four was $10,880—more than the entire annual income of a full-time minimum-wage worker. (This fee does not include the cost of deductibles, co-payments, and non-insured medical treatments.) As a result, 28 percent of Americans had no medical insurance at all; more than 40 percent of Americans making between $20,000 and $40,000 had no medical insurance for some portion of the year; and 67 percent of the uninsured lived in families with at least one full-time worker.

People without medical insurance are more likely to be admitted to hospital for preventable conditions, and they die at almost twice the rate of those with insurance. The Institute of Medicine estimates that *18,000 unnecessary deaths result every year from a lack of medical insurance*. When the Institute recommended that the federal government provide medical coverage for *all* Americans, Health and Human Services Secretary Tommy Thompson replied that universal medical coverage was unrealistic. He did not say that it wasn't affordable.

In 2004, the U.S. government spent two trillion dollars on medical care—an average of $6,820 per person—which is more than any other government in the world, including those that offer universal medical care. In effect, the U.S. government could provide top-notch medical care for all Americans without spending a penny more than it already does. Dr. Steffie Woolhandler points out,

> We pay the world's highest health care taxes. But much of the money is squandered. The wealthy get tax [deductions for medical care]. And HMOs and drug companies pocket billions in profits at the taxpayers' expense. But politicians claim we can't afford universal coverage…We already pay for it, but we don't get it.[61]

Politicians have no problem with police, emergency, military and fire-fighting services being publically funded and administered. Health-care is treated differently because big business insists on it. To defend their profits, medical insurance companies contribute more money to federal politicians than banks, military contractors, oil and gas companies, and the real estate industry. The top lobby group is the pharmaceutical industry, which is also the most profitable business in America. In 2004 alone, drug companies paid 1,291 lobbyists $123 million to influence various levels of government. Favorable legislation is not the only result. The U.S. government contributes more money to the development of new drugs than any other government in the world.

There is a revolving door between Washington and the pharmaceutical industry with a pot of gold on both sides. A 2005 report by the Center for Public Integrity found that one-third of 3,000 lobbyists employed by the drug industry were former federal government employees, with more than 75 being former members of Congress. Here is one example of how it works. Over 15 years, the drug industry donated more than $200,000 to Congressman Billy Tauzin's election campaigns. In return, Tauzin designed a Medicare law that expressly forbids government from negotiating lower drug prices. In 2004, Tauzin's loyalty was rewarded when he traded his $158,100 legislative post for a two-million-dollar-a-year job as president of the drug industry's chief lobby group, the Pharmaceutical and Research Manufacturers of America.

The tight relationship between Washington and the drug industry makes a joke out of the Food and Drug Administration's mandate to protect the public from harmful drugs. The FDA serves the drug industry by providing rapid drug approval with minimal testing and by covering up problems that occur after drugs are approved. When a class of FDA-approved anti-arthritis drugs were found to increase the risk of death, the FDA did not rush to protect the public. On the contrary, an FDA scientist was pressured not to publish his finding that one of these drugs had caused as many as 140,000 incidents of heart disease and 56,000 deaths over a period of five years. When the bad news finally broke, Washington protected the drug industry, not the public. Drug companies had made billions of dollars selling these dangerous products, and they could afford to pay for the harm they had caused. Nevertheless, the White House ruled that drug companies did not have to pay punitive damages caused by drugs and medical devices that the FDA had approved.

A pill for every ill

Eliminating class divisions would be the best way to improve human health. However, the medical system does not challenge the class system because it is an integral part of it. The treatment of disease is limited to the treatment of individuals. In essence, the *symptoms* of class inequality—sickness, injury, and premature death—are dissociated from their social roots and classified as individual medical problems. This approach is highly profitable for the pharmaceutical industry.

When continuous stress elevates blood pressure and cholesterol and irritates the stomach lining, these symptoms are given medical diagnoses—Hypertension, Hypercholesterolemia, Hyper-Acidity—that suggest they are distinct diseases. Once a symptom is labeled as a disease or medical condition, a drug can be developed to treat it. (Sometimes the drug comes first and the "disease" comes later.) The nine top-selling drugs in the world treat symptoms: one lowers blood pressure; two lower cholesterol; three reduce stomach acid; two are anti-depressants; and one reduces pain and inflammation. In the United States, the top three selling drug categories are anti-depressants, stomach-acid reducers, and cholesterol reducers. Lipitor, a drug that lowers blood cholesterol, is the top-selling drug in the U.S., with sales of nearly $10 billion in 2003.

The $500 billion-a-year U.S. drug industry works hard to ensure that the preferred treatment for every ailment is a drug, preferably an expensive one. Consider the problem of child bed-wetting. Ferring Pharmaceuticals promotes a drug that claims to prevent this problem. One advertisement shows a smiling child underlined with the caption, "Not only is there hope for bed-wetting, but now it can happen as early as age five." The ad concludes, "Bed-wetting is a medical condition that when left untreated can be harmful to a child's self-esteem."

In fact, most children wet their beds because their urinary systems are not fully developed, and bed-wetting stops as children mature. At age five, about 16 percent of children wet their beds. By age eight, this figure has dropped by half. By 12 years of age, only three percent wet the bed and by age 15, only one percent have wet beds. Experts advise that patience and understanding are the best response to childhood bed-wetting. The problem is that most parents do not have time to change the bed every morning, do extra laundry, and reassure their kids. Physicians are not paid to reassure parents or to teach them how to use non-drug methods to reduce bed-wetting. Instead of providing reassurance, Ferring plays up the shame of bed-wetting and offers to rescue parents, children, and physicians with a drug that costs about $200 per month. Adverse effects listed for this drug include: headaches, nosebleeds, chills, dizziness, nausea, abdominal pain, wheezing, skin rash, and, in rare cases, lethargy, mental impairment, seizures, and coma.

Treating social problems as individual medical conditions has made the pharmaceutical industry the most profitable business in America. Forty-four percent of Americans take at least one prescription medicine, and 17 percent take three or more. Sixty-two percent of people visiting doctors' offices or hospital outpatient departments leave with a prescription, regardless of the reason for their visit. Retail pharmacies dispense close to $200 billion worth of drugs a year. The top 10 drug companies enjoy a 30 percent profit margin, almost double the profit margin of commercial banks. Their products are so expensive that 26 percent of seniors take less medicine than they are prescribed or go without entirely.

Both the drug industry and the government insist that high profits are necessary to develop new medicines. In reality, the industry spends about $60 billion a year marketing drugs, which is nearly double what it spends on research and development. Manufacturers of brand-name drugs employ 80 percent more people in marketing than in research. And, between 1995 and 2000, drug companies hired 59 percent more marketing employees, while cutting back the number of research workers. Under capitalism, the function of the pharmaceutical industry is to make profit, not treat disease.

To promote their products, drug companies finance or directly provide the bulk of physician education. In 1997, the FDA made it easier for the pharmaceutical industry to market prescription drugs directly to consumers. By 2005, drug companies were spending $4 billion a year on television and print ads to give their products the same level of brand recognition enjoyed by popular soft drinks and breakfast cereals. The more drugs are advertised, the more patients request them and the more doctors prescribe them. One study found that more than 70 per cent of doctors prescribed the drug their patients demanded. In half of these cases, doctors admitted that they prescribed the drug *only* because the patient asked for it.

Some drug companies go so far as to offer coupons, free samples, free trials, and money-back guarantees for prescription drugs. One group of Florida residents found a month's supply of Prozac in their mail boxes. The recipients were not taking this drug, had not requested it, and had no idea why they received it. Information from medical and pharmaceutical records had been used to identify people who *might* try this anti-depressant.

It is more profitable for drug companies to re-package existing medicines than to invest in developing new ones. Since the 1990's, the number of new drugs approved by the Food and Drug Administration has fallen steadily. Most of the 1,035 drugs approved by the FDA between 1989 and 2000 were "me too" drugs that were basically more expensive versions of already-existing medicines. For instance, advertisements tout Clarinex as a superior anti-allergy medicine. In fact, Clarinex is a re-make of Claritin, a drug that was about to lose its patent protection, drop in price, and provide less profit.

Poor people cannot afford medicine, so there is no profit in developing treatments for diseases that afflict them. Consequently, only 10 percent of global medical research is devoted to finding treatments for 90 percent of diseases. In 1990, eflornithine hydrochloride was licensed as a medicine to treat sleeping sickness, a disease that kills thousands of people in Africa every year. In 1995, production was stopped because African patients could not afford to buy this medicine. When eflornithine was found to reduce unwanted facial hair, the drug was repackaged as a skin cream and marketed to women in the U.S.

Inventing disease

While people die from diseases that are not profitable to treat, drug companies invent medical conditions to sell drugs to those who can pay. A letter from Merck Frosst informs physicians,

> A new campaign to promote disease awareness for male pattern hair loss is now appearing on television and other media…A follow-up to last year's radio campaign, this latest undertaking is expected to motivate an increased number of male patients to speak to their doctors about hair loss…[62]

Since when is baldness a disease? Since Merck developed a drug to treat hair loss. One month's treatment costs about $60, and the product remains effective only with continual use. Merck's "campaign to promote disease awareness" aims to increase *discontent* with baldness, thereby creating the very condition that Merck aims to treat.

The more drug companies blur the boundary between normal processes and disease states, the more drugs they can sell. Wyeth manufactures Premarin, a hormone designed to treat symptoms of menopause. Many women have no problem with menopause; however, some suffer hot flashes, night sweats, insomnia, and other distressing symptoms. For those who can find no relief, hormone treatment can be helpful. However, Wyeth's profits would be much greater if *all* menopausal women took hormone replacement therapy (HRT) for the rest of their lives. To make this happen, menopause itself would need to become a disease.

Wyeth found the man for the job in Dr. Robert Wilson, whose 1968 best-seller, *Feminine Forever,* insists that "menopause is both unnecessary and harmful" and promotes estrogen as a fountain of youth for the "dull and unattractive" menopausal woman. In a separate article, Wilson warns that declining female hormones constitute a potentially fatal "deficiency disease." Wyeth was more than happy to fund Wilson's book, his research foundation, and his promotional tours.

Wyeth joined with other pharmaceutical companies to fund the North American Menopause Society, a major promoter of HRT. Physicians and medical researchers were funded by the drug companies to give talks praising HRT at scientific conferences. Scientists were commissioned to write articles promoting HRT for respected medical journals, and these articles were used as medical education for doctors.

The campaign to promote HRT was so successful that an advisory committee to the FDA recommended that HRT be approved to prevent heart disease, despite the complete absence of any evidence to support this claim. The National Women's Health Network opposed this mass experiment on women and demanded that studies be done to assess the actual benefits and risks of HRT. Over the objection of Wyeth-funded scientists, the FDA finally launched a study in the fall of 1997. The study was stopped prematurely when it was discovered that women taking HRT showed *higher* rates of coronary artery disease, stroke, and breast cancer than women who took the placebo. Women taking HRT were also twice as likely to develop Alzheimer's Disease. It was a huge scandal. For 25 years, doctors had been prescribing harmful drugs to millions of healthy women. National Women's Health Network Director, Cynthia Pearson, explained,

> There was never one single clinical trial that showed that HRT prevented cardiovascular disease or stroke…The belief that hormones are good preventive medicine has been a triumph of marketing over science…Women [who took HRT] were placed in the way of harm by their physicians, who acted as unsuspecting patsies for pharmaceutical companies.[63]

Wyeth suffered no penalty. Barely a year later, a full-page ad in a medical publication announced that Wyeth was "proud of past accomplishments" and trumpeted its "commitment to a single mission: leading the way to a healthier world."

The entire HRT scandal might as well have happened in the *Twilight Zone*. At its 2002 annual conference, the Endocrine Society recommended that every man over age 50 be screened for testosterone deficiency. This conference was funded by Solvay Pharma, a pharmaceutical giant that manufactures testosterone gel. This same company provides research grants, speaking fees, public relations communications, and direct-to-consumer advertising urging tired, depressed men with low sex drive to ask their doctors about testosterone replacement. This HRT campaign for men was launched despite the fact that testosterone can increase the risk of prostate cancer and cardiovascular disease.

A pattern has developed where medical conditions "appear" as drugs are developed to treat them: Social Phobia to sell Paxil; Erectile Dysfunction to sell Viagra; Pseudobulbar Affect (uncontrollable laughing or crying) to sell Neurodex; Overactive Bladder to sell anticholinergic drugs; and Hyperhidrosis (excessive sweating) to sell Botox. As pharmaceutical companies push the boundaries of disease, the healthy person becomes someone who has not yet been diagnosed with a medical condition that can be treated with a drug.

Constructing mental illness

The definition of mental illness has always been political. During slavery days, experts argued that Black people were psychologically suited to a life of slavery, so that there must be something wrong with those who rebelled. The diagnosis of Drapetomania (an intense desire to run away) was developed in 1851 to explain why slaves kept trying to escape. The racist delusion that Black people like being slaves could also be considered a sign of mental illness. Who decides which behavior is normal or healthy and which behavior is sick or deviant?

Before the 20th century, the stresses of life were considered to be either spiritual issues or physical illnesses, and people turned to either their religious advisors or their physicians for relief. Medical doctors treated "hysteria" and "nerves" as physical problems. Psychiatry was restricted to the treatment of severely disturbed people in asylums. There was no concept or treatment of mental illness outside of institutions. In 1918, the first classification of psychiatric disorders in the United States contained 22 categories, and all but one referred to various forms of insanity.

During the early 20th century, Sigmund Freud revolutionized psychiatry by breaking down the barrier between mental illness and normal behavior. In his 1901 book, *The Psychopathology of Everyday Life,* Freud argued that commonplace occurrences—slips of the tongue, what people find humorous, what they forget, and the mistakes they make—indicate repressed sexual feelings that lurk beneath the surface of normal behavior. By linking everyday occurrences with mental illness, Freud and his followers released psychiatry from the asylum and began to treat people with a broad range of problems. Between 1917 and 1970, the proportion of psychiatrists practicing outside institutions swelled from eight percent to sixty-six percent.

The social movements of the 1960's opposed psychiatry's exclusive focus on inner conflict and highlighted the social sources of human misery. Dr. Alvin Poussaint recalls the 1969 convention of the American Psychiatric Association (APA),

> After multiple racist killings during the civil rights movement, a group of black psychiatrists sought to have murderous bigotry based on race classified as a mental disorder. The APA's officials rejected that recommendation, arguing that since so many Americans are racist, racism in this country is normative...[64]

In 1980, the APA greatly expanded its *Diagnostic and Statistical Manual of Mental Disorders (DSM).* According to the Task Force established to create the new manual, any disorder could be included

> If there is general agreement among clinicians, who would be expected to encounter the condition, that there are significant number of patients who have it and that its identification is important in the clinical work.[65]

In other words, the new *DSM* was not based on science but on the need to maintain existing patients and to include new ones who might seek treatment for any number of problems. A profitable and self-perpetuating industry was born. By 1994, the *DSM* listed 400 distinct mental disorders covering a wide range of behaviors in adults and children.

Racism, homophobia (fear of homosexuality), and misogyny (hatred of women) have never been listed as mental disorders in the *DSM.* Homosexuality was listed. In *They Say You're Crazy: How the World's Most Powerful Psychiatrists Decide Who's Normal,* Paula Caplan protests,

> In a culture that scorns and demeans lesbians and gay men, it is hard to be completely comfortable with one's homosexuality, and so the *DSM-III* authors were treating as a mental disorder what was often simply a perfectly comprehensible reaction to being mocked and oppressed.[66]

The women's movement condemned labeling the effects of oppression as symptoms of mental illnesses. Paula Caplan describes efforts to prevent Masochistic Personality Disorder (MPD) from being included in the *DSM*. Among other things, this disorder assumes that women who stay with abusive spouses do so because they like to suffer, not because they lack the resources to leave. Despite protest, MPD was included in the 1987 edition of the *DSM*, although it was later dropped. The *DSM* inclusion of Pre-Menstrual Dysphoric Disorder (PMDD) also raised a protest. According to Caplan,

> The problem with PMDD is not the women who report premenstrual mood problems but the diagnosis of PMDD itself. Excellent research shows that these women are significantly more likely than other women to be in upsetting life situations, such as being battered or being mistreated at work. To label them mentally disordered — to send the message that their problems are individual, psychological ones — hides the real, external sources of their trouble.[67]

Eli Lilly campaigned to have PMDD listed in the *DSM* so that it could repackage its best-selling drug Prozac in a pink-pill format, rename it Serafem, and promote it as a treatment for PMDD. By creating Serafem, Eli Lilly was able to extend its patent (and its profits) on the Prozac formula for another seven years. PMDD continues to be listed as a mental disorder.

Is everybody crazy?

Capitalism denies most people control over their lives, *and needs them to believe that this condition is normal.* Anxiety, depression, and other stress-reactions are treated as signs of personal inadequacy, biological defects, mental illnesses — anything other than reasonable responses to unreasonable conditions. The result is a highly profitable form of social control.

In 2005, American researchers announced that "About half of Americans will meet the criteria for a *DSM-IV* disorder sometime in their life." How can we explain this? Has it become normal to be mentally ill or has the definition of mental illness expanded beyond reason? Both are true. Capitalism produces an immense amount of suffering. At the same time, defining more people as mentally ill takes the focus off social problems and boosts drug sales.

Most people know the difference between normal behavior (such as grief over the death of a loved one) and abnormal behavior that could indicate an internal disorder (such as grief for no apparent reason or beyond what would normally be expected). However, the *DSM* lists and categorizes symptoms *without regard to what is happening in people's lives.* As a result, surveys based on *DSM* categories inflate the number of people who can be classified as mentally ill. This is no accident.

In 2006, a medical journal revealed that most of the scientists, psychiatrists, and other experts who worked on the *DSM* had financial ties to the pharmaceutical industry. Every new mental disorder listed in the *DSM* is worth millions to drug companies. The FDA will not approve a drug to treat a mental condition that does not appear in the *DSM,* giving the pharmaceutical industry a financial interest in maximizing the number of mental disorders listed.

Along with inflated rates of mental illness comes the warning that too many mentally ill people are not getting treatment. The question of whether all the people who are designated as sick are actually sick is never raised. Many people suffer from overwork, unemployment, excessive family responsibilities, illness, death of loved ones, and severe financial stress—all of which can cause feelings and behaviors that are similar to those seen with mental illness.

Rates of mental illness are also inflated by equating the extent of an illness with the number of prescriptions for drugs used to treat that illness. By this measure, the rate of depression in the U.S. has gone through the roof. In 1980, there were 10 million prescriptions dispensed for anti-depressant drugs. Twenty years later, this figure had jumped to 170 million prescriptions. Antidepressants are the top-selling category of drugs in America, with billions of dollars in retail sales every year. This dramatic rise in drug sales is the result of increasing human misery plus highly successful marketing. Studies have shown that the number of prescriptions written for anti-depressants is linked to the amount of money spent on promoting them. One drug company runs full-page, glossy ads urging doctors to "Look for the Paxil spectrum in every patient" in the hope that physicians will prescribe this anti-depressant for more troubled people.

Sick people, healthy profits

As living standards decline, the emphasis on drugs increases. Between 30 and 40 thousand people die from influenza every year in the U.S. Instead of correcting the social conditions that favor the spread of infectious disease—people pressured to go to work sick, stressed families, crowded classrooms, poor nutrition, and increased pollution—public officials push the flu vaccine. This strategy has neither lessened the incidence of flu nor reduced the number of flu-related deaths. Nevertheless, President Bush asked Congress for seven billion dollars to stockpile vaccines and other drugs to fight avian flu. It may be a coincidence that the Secretary of Defense, Donald Rumsfeld, owns $25 million worth of shares in the company that developed the avian flu vaccine.

The pharmaceutical industry, the medical system, and the State all treat illness not as a social problem that requires social solutions but as an individual problem that requires individual treatments. A good example is schizophrenia, an illness that is assumed to be genetic and commonly treated with drugs. Studies from several countries show that living in a city gives a person a higher probability of developing schizophrenia than having a family member with the disease. Moving from rural to urban centers increases the risk of developing schizophrenia, while moving in the other direction reduces the risk. What could explain such patterns? City living is associated with increased exposure to lead, infection, malnutrition, stress, trauma, and racial discrimination—all of which have been linked with higher rates of schizophrenia. Instead of demanding improved social conditions to reduce schizophrenia, the medical system extracts the individual from society, splits the brain from the body, severs the mind from the brain, and drugs the brain. Why people put up with such treatment is the subject of Part Three.

Summary

The cost of doing business under capitalism is disease, disability, and premature death. Inequality on its own is a major source of sickness. The medical system disguises social problems as individual medical illnesses and services only those who can pay. The most effective way to improve human health is to improve social conditions. Under capitalism, drugs are preferred because they support the status quo and provide profits in the process.

Part Three

Why do we put up with it?

> Why do we tolerate them? Why do we tolerate these men who use nuclearweapons to blackmail the entire human race?
>
> *Arundhati Roy*

Knowing what is wrong with society is not the same as being able to change it. To change the world we need to know how the few maintain their power over the many and how this hold can be broken. The capitalist class is so small in numbers that they would drown if we all spat at them at the same time. It sounds so simple. However, accomplishing such a feat would require: a) agreement about who should be spit on; b) agreement about who should not be spit on; c) agreement that spitting is the preferred action; and d) sufficient numbers to organize and participate in the spitting. The people in power are determined to prevent this level of clarity and organization. By keeping the majority confused and divided so they don't know who are their enemies, who are their friends, what should be done, and who should do it, the status quo can be maintained.

Part Three examines four basic methods for keeping the majority subordinate. Each is powerful on its own; in combination, they present a formidable barrier to change. However, as Part Four explains, these barriers have been overcome in the past and can be overcome again.

- Chapter 9. *The Lies That Bind Us* reveals the deceptions that keep the elite in power.

- Chapter 10. *Blame the Victim* explains how blaming the victim protects the system.

- Chapter 11. *Divide and Rule* exposes how the few divide the many in order to rule them.

- Chapter 12. *Suffer the Children* shows how the oppression of children maintains the system.

Chapter 9

The Lies that Bind Us

To tell deliberate lies while genuinely believing in them, to forget any fact that has become inconvenient, and then, when it becomes necessary again, to draw it back from oblivion for just so long as it is needed, to deny the existence of objective reality and all the while to take account of the reality which one denies—all this is indispensably necessary.

George Orwell

More than 50 years ago, Orwell wrote this passage from *Nineteen Eighty-Four* to describe how the elite manipulate information to stay in power. The novel's main character works at the Ministry of Truth, where he deletes facts from the public records. In 2005, the Chief of Staff for the White House Council on Environmental Quality was discovered editing government reports to minimize the connection between fossil fuel emissions and global warming. In 2004, more than 60 leading scientists issued a public statement condemning the Bush administration for "distorting and censoring scientific findings that contradict its policies." Among other things, the government was accused of

> repeatedly censoring and suppressing reports by its own scientists, stacking advisory committees with unqualified political appointees, disbanding government panels that provide unwanted advice and refusing to seek any independent scientific expertise in some cases.[68]

Orwell wrote *Nineteen Eighty-Four* shortly after World War II, when the so-called "glorious war" turned out to be a horrific slaughter. In Orwell's novel, as in life, nothing is as it seems. The Ministry of Truth dispenses lies; the Ministry of Peace conducts war; the Ministry of Love operates the penal system; and the Ministry of Plenty supervises the exploitation of workers. The ruling party has three slogans: WAR is PEACE, FREEDOM is SLAVERY, and IGNORANCE is STRENGTH. One could add a fourth slogan for today: IMPERIALISM is DEMOCRACY. This chapter explains why the capitalist class lies and why we believe them.

The birth of capitalism

The Middle Ages is commonly portrayed as a stagnant period where nothing much happened. In fact, a gradual accumulation of discoveries and inventions laid the foundation for industrial society. By the 16th century, innovations in mechanics, engineering, metal working, and navigation had increased productivity so much that an abundant future seemed inevitable. However, industrial capitalism had reached the limit of what it could achieve within the social framework of feudalism. Feudalism was based on the land. Capitalism built cities. Feudalism revered custom and tradition. Capitalism promised progress. Feudalism feared science. Science was essential to industry, and industry was the motor of capitalism. Conflict was inevitable.

During the French Revolution, the capitalist class overthrew the lords of the land and took power. Being too weak to depose the aristocracy on its own, the capitalist class mobilized the working population to fight under the banner of Liberty, Equality, and Brotherhood. However, once they secured power, the new capitalist rulers called a halt to the revolution. When workers pressed to continue the fight, their former leaders turned on them in a bloody slaughter. As it turned out, the two classes define Liberty, Equality, and Brotherhood quite differently. For capitalists, Liberty means freedom from restrictions on trade and commerce, Equality means an end to the privilege of birth (replaced by the privilege of money), and Brotherhood lasts only as long as it serves their interests. For working people, Liberty means freedom from exploitation and oppression, Equality means no class divisions, and Brotherhood means a sharing society. None of these is possible under capitalism.

Capitalists in England were horrified by the French Revolution. Like their counterparts in France, they longed to break free of feudal restrictions; yet, they feared to rouse a working class that could rebel against capitalist masters as easily as feudal lords. They had reason to fear. The Chartist movement in Britain was organizing tens of thousands of workers to demand democratic rights. In 1842, workers in Lancashire organized the first general strike in history. Five years later, the *Communist Manifesto* urged workers to build a new society based on workers' control of production.

In the spring of 1848, there were mass revolts against Europe's remaining autocracy. Again, workers joined with capitalists to break down feudal restrictions. The growing power of the working class frightened the capitalists, who switched sides and joined the aristocrats in crushing the revolt that threatened to sweep them both away. Seeing the writing on the wall, the European monarchies agreed to cede power to the capitalist class in exchange for retaining some of their privileges.

The capitalist bid for power revealed a central weakness in the capitalist order. Feudalism had Church doctrine to justify class inequality. Having broken the power of the Church, capitalism needed some other way to control the masses.

Freedom is Slavery

America was built on slavery, indentured servitude, and the theft of native land. The 1705 *Virginia Slave Code* declared all non-Christian servants entering the colony to be slaves, defined slaves as real estate, and acquitted masters who killed slaves during punishment. By 1763, almost half the population of Virginia were slaves.

As the American colonies struggled to free themselves from British domination, they raised the cry for freedom and democracy. However, the elite had no wish to free the slaves who produced their wealth. So, the Founding Fathers enshrined the first official lie of the fledgling nation in the 1776 *Declaration of*

Independence. To proclaim that "all men are created equal" while maintaining a slave-based economy equates freedom with slavery. The doctrine of racial inferiority was designed to resolve this contradiction. As historian Barbara J. Fields explains, "Bondage does not need justifying as long as it seems to be the natural order of things. You need a radical affirmation of bondage only where you have a radical affirmation of freedom."

The second contradiction was to promote democracy while denying the majority any control over the direction of society. To keep power in the hands of the elite, the Constitution denied the vote to all women and to all men without property. When official policy declares that all people are created equal *and* denies rights to some people, then additional doctrines are needed to designate some people as less-than-human. The doctrine that Blacks, women, and working class people are inferior served this purpose.

Lies built on lies. In 1791, Congress amended the Constitution to guarantee the right to free speech. A few years later, Congress passed the *Sedition Act* of 1798, making it a crime to say or write anything against the government. (Ignorance is strength.) Despite this law, slave revolts and workers' rebellions continued to rock the nation.

The Civil War interrupted the class struggle, but not for long. In 1872, a strike by 100,000 workers in New York City won the 8-hour workday and 150,000 people paraded through the streets in celebration. Beginning in the mid-1890's the number of strikes per year rose steadily to reach 4,000 in 1904. Between 1899 and 1904, union membership quadrupled to more than two million.

Capitalism had broken feudalism's constraints on society and roused people's longing for a better life. It had also organized workers into large industries where they had their hands on the levers of production. To stay in power, the capitalist class needed absolute control over production. Union organizers were threatened, beaten, jailed, tortured, deported, and killed. In 1914, the National Guard machine-gunned and then set fire to the tents of miners striking against Rockefeller's Colorado Fuel and Iron Corporation. Twenty-six men, women, and children died in what came to be known as the Ludlow Massacre. Such actions only deepened people's hatred of the robber barons and the government officials who served them. The working class had become too large and too powerful to be controlled by force alone.

Ignorance is Strength

> If you can control people by force, it's not so important to control what they think and feel. But if you lose the capacity to control people by force, it becomes more necessary to control attitudes and opinions.
>
> *Noam Chomsky*

The capitalist class did not see the prospect of a better world in workers' rebellions, only the loss of their power and privilege. The feudal aristocracy had thought the same thing when the capitalists threatened to depose them. All ruling classes want history to end with their rule, and the capitalist class is no different. Capitalism was confronted with an inescapable problem—class-divided societies are incompatible with genuine democracy. A numerically small ruling class cannot impose its will on a larger population *as long as that population is actively involved in political life*. A section of the middle class proposed a solution: control the majority by manipulating their minds. As early as 1895, French sociologist Gustave Le Bon warned in *The Crowd: A Study of the Popular Mind*,

Today the claims of the masses are becoming more and more sharply defined, and amount to nothing less than a determination to destroy utterly society as it now exists…The divine right of the masses is about to replace the divine right of kings.[69]

In 1916, Wilfred Trotter wrote *The Instincts of the Herd in Peace and War* in which he argued that workers' revolts and anti-war protests were based on mindless "herd instinct." Sigmund Freud built on LeBon and Trotter's work. In *Group Psychology and the Analysis of the Ego,* Freud argues that being in a crowd overrides the social constraints that keep animal instincts under control. In 1930, he wrote *Civilization and Its Discontents,* warning that "civilization" must control the "savage forces" that would otherwise rise up to destroy it. In *The Future of an Illusion,* he argues that "these dangerous masses must be held down most severely and kept most carefully away from any chance of intellectual awakening."

In 1920, in *The Behavior of Crowds: A Psychological Study,* Everett Dean Martin warns that "crowd-behavior" poses a "serious menace to civilization" that can be countered only by the "rational" middle class. As he put it,

We must become a cult, write our philosophy of life in flaming headlines, and sell our cause in the market. No matter if we meanwhile surrender every value for which we stand, we must strive to cajole the majority into imagining itself on our side…[70]

In *PR!: A Social History of Spin,* Stuart Ewen explains that "corporate PR starts as a response to the threat of democracy and the need to create some kind of ideological link between the interests of big business and the interests of ordinary Americans." One of the first PR-men in America was journalist Ivy Lee, who was hired by the Rockefeller family to defuse public outrage over the Ludlow Massacre. Lee provided the media with false information, claiming that striking miners had deliberately provoked the National Guard who fought back only in self-defense. However, the first person to formulate a theory of public relations was Edward Bernays, the nephew of Sigmund Freud. In *Propaganda,* Bernays argues that "propaganda is the modern instrument by which [intelligent men] can fight for productive ends and help to bring order out of chaos." Bernays began his career in public relations promoting World War I.

Engineering consent to war

Never before in history had such a campaign of education been organized; never before had American citizens realized how thoroughly, how irresistibly a modern government could impose its ideas upon the whole nation.[71]

One week after the United States entered World War I, Washington established a Committee on Public Information (CPI) to mobilize journalists, artists, advertising experts, and social scientists to "sell" the war. The CPI faced an uphill battle; Americans did not want the war. Ordinary people saw no reason to be involved in a dispute between rival empires fighting for territory and power. Just a few months earlier, President Woodrow Wilson had been re-elected on a promise to keep America out of the war. Anti-war meetings were drawing thousands of people. To turn the country around, the CPI used a two-punch strategy — promoting the war with one fist and crushing the anti-war movement with the other.

To sell the war, the CPI constructed a giant propaganda machine with a Domestic Section and a Foreign Section. Each Section had multiple Divisions. The News Division sent press releases to every form of media on a 24-hour basis. The Advertising Division employed advertising agencies to flood the nation with pro-war posters and billboards. The Division of Pictorial Publicity and the Bureau of Cartoons provided pro-war images. The Division of Films conscripted Hollywood to produce pro-war movies. Academics were assigned to write material promoting the war. Pro-war exhibits were mounted at fairs, in schools, and in churches. Teachers were given pro-war material to teach, and students were enrolled in speaking contests to support the war.

The CPI's Division of Four-Minute Men recruited 75,000 businessmen and professionals to deliver short and seemingly spontaneous pro-war speeches in movie theaters, at picnics, and everywhere people gathered. (Junior Four-Minute Men made pro-war speeches in primary and secondary schools.) An estimated 750,000 four-minute speeches were delivered in 5,000 American cities and towns. Hatred of the Germans was whipped to a fever pitch.

While one hand of the State promoted the war, the other hand silenced those who opposed it. To sell the war as a glorious venture binding rich and poor in a common cause, the CPI hid the truth about war profiteers, soldiers' mutinies, and anti-war protests. Most importantly, the unprecedented level of slaughter could not be acknowledged—10 million lives were lost on the battlefield and 20 million more died from hunger and disease. Fifty thousand American soldiers perished in fewer than 19 months.

The Director of the CPI sat on the U.S. Censorship Board. Before publication, all newspapers and magazines had to submit articles to this Board for approval. Editors who refused to cooperate could be prosecuted, their publications could be denied mail service, and their source of newsprint could be cut off. No anti-war material was allowed through the mails. The mainstream media did not protest. On the contrary, the *New York Times* proclaimed, "It is the duty of every good citizen to communicate to proper authorities any evidence of sedition that comes to his notice."

When the U.S. entered the war, Congress passed the *Espionage Act* that made it a federal crime to oppose the war. Four-Minute Men implored their audiences to report anyone expressing anti-war views. The American Vigilante Patrol attacked those who opposed the war. With a membership of 100,000 people in 600 towns and cities, the American Protective League claimed to uncover three million cases of such "disloyalty." Two thousand anti-war activists were prosecuted and 900 were imprisoned. Socialists at the core of the anti-war movement were targeted. Prominent labor leader and socialist, Eugene Debs, was sentenced to 10 years in jail for speaking out against the war.

America got behind the war. As one writer observed, "We hated with a common hatred that was exhilarating." At one church meeting, "a speaker demanded that the Kaiser, when captured, be boiled in oil, and the entire audience stood on chairs to scream its hysterical approval. This was the kind of madness that had seized us." To the delight and relief of the ruling class, the CPI had made the unthinkable acceptable.

Practice makes perfect. Over the following century, Washington had many more opportunities to push unpopular measures and disable the opposition.

"The Communist Menace"

In the two years following the end of [World War II], the CIO [Congress of Industrial Organizations] launched the greatest strike wave in the history of the United States. Millions of workers in the steel, auto, railroad, mining, maritime, and tobacco industries were among those who took part… Workers had kept their "no-strike" pledge during the war as an act of patriotism, but now the war was over, a new era was beginning, and these industrial workers were determined to shape it.[72]

The ruling class was enraged. The demands of American workers were standing in the way of a U.S. victory over Russia in the Cold War.

To fight the Cold War, the U.S. had to maintain a huge military establishment on a near-permanent war footing. Supporting that military establishment required the diversion of billions of dollars from pressing domestic needs. To sell this kind of sacrifice to a population that had just emerged from the Second World War, Truman would have to "scare the hell out of the country."[73]

Anti-communist propaganda was used to purge the labor movement of socialists and other radicals and to get America behind the Cold War. This period was known as the McCarthy Era, named after the most zealous anti-communist, Senator Joseph McCarthy (R-Wis.).

McCarthyism was the most widespread and longest lasting wave of political repression in American history. In order to eliminate the alleged threat of domestic Communism, a broad coalition of politicians, bureaucrats, and other anticommunist activists hounded an entire generation of radicals and their associates, destroying lives, careers, and all the institutions that offered a left-wing alternative to mainstream politics and culture. That anticommunist crusade…used all the power of the state to turn dissent into disloyalty and, in the process, drastically narrowed the spectrum of acceptable political debate.[74]

Between March 1947 and December 1952, *seven million* federal government workers were fingered as potential Russian spies. The investigations relied on secret evidence and paid informers and were conducted without judge or jury. Although not a single case of espionage was confirmed, the witch-hunt intensified, penetrating every level of society.

State governments, colleges and universities, trade unions and civic organizations purged workers and members who refused to sign loyalty oaths. The repression reached absurd levels. People applying for licenses to fish in New York reservoirs had to sign loyalty oaths. Physics students at the University of Chicago feared that signing a petition calling for the installation of a Coke machine in the laboratories would signal their "disloyalty."[75]

Conservative union leaders were happy to cooperate in removing militants who challenged their leadership. Between 1949 and 1950, the CIO expelled 11 Communist-Party-led unions—more than 10 percent of its total membership. By 1954, 59 unions barred communists from holding union office, and 40 unions prohibited communists from being union members.

The witch-hunting frenzy reached its peak when Julius and Ethel Rosenberg were charged with "conspiracy to commit espionage" and sentenced to death, despite the absence of any credible evidence that they were spies. Around the world, people campaigned to save the Rosenbergs. Unions submitted protest petitions. The Pope appealed for clemency. Albert Einstein and other Nobel-Prize-winners protested, along with many famous writers and artists including Pablo Picasso, Jean-Paul Sartre, Dashiell Hammett, Diego Rivera, and Frida Kahlo. Washington refused to back down and executed the Rosenbergs in 1953.

> Their execution case sent a chill through the ranks of the left. "From the point of view of a young person, we all thought that it could be our parents," recounts Arlene Tyner, a longtime activist whose family was involved in the Rosenberg clemency movement. "Everybody felt, especially if you were Jewish, during the witch-hunts that the government could come and take away your parents and execute them. It was a direct threat to your survival."[76]

By the end of the 1950's, thousands had lost their jobs and countless families were ruined. Most important, the union movement had lost its best fighters. Operation Dixie, the CIO's project to organize Black and White workers in the American South, was scuttled. With unions gutted and the working class divided, the capitalist class could drive up productivity, make the U.S. the strongest economy in the world, and win the Cold War. And that was the real purpose of the anti-communist campaign. More than 50 years later, the American labor movement and the American Left still have not recovered.

The anti-communist campaign proved so successful that it was repackaged for use in the 21st century; only the terms have changed—"terrorist" has been substituted for "communist." Like the Cold War, the War on Terror demands that ordinary people support U.S. foreign policy. Those who resist the militarization of the economy, the destruction of other nations, and the loss of civil rights at home are denounced as terrorists and terrorist sympathizers. The War on Communism and the War on Terror both serve to keep the ruling class firmly in control.

The Great Lie

The great lie of the 20th century was that the Cold War was a conflict between American Democracy and Russian Communism. In reality, the Cold War was a power struggle between two super-powers to determine which one would rule the world. Democracy had nothing to do with it and neither did communism, as I shall explain.

In 1917, the Russian working class revolted against a corrupt ruling class and the horrors of World War I. The working class took power but could not hold onto it. Economic ruin caused by the war, the devastation of the civil war, and a subsequent trade blockade combined to strangle the revolution. With no food for the people, no raw materials for the factories, and no other revolution in Europe to come to its aid, the Russian Revolution was defeated. During the 1920's, capitalism was restored in Russia in the form of State capitalism. The State controlled production, and everyone worked for the State. "Russia Incorporated" fulfilled the two directives of capitalism: to Seize the Surplus produced by the working class; and to Compete or Die in the Cold War with the United States.

Both sides portrayed the Cold War as a conflict of ideologies. Russia called itself Communist, which was equated with State control over the economy. The United States called itself Democratic because it had an electoral system. In fact, State intervention was important to the economy of both nations, and neither nation exposed its top decision-makers to the risk of popular elections. *Masking the commonality between the U.S. and Russia was important for both ruling classes.*

Because conditions for Russian workers were so oppressive, Washington could claim that capitalism was better, despite mass inequality and savage racism at home. Those who organized for social change or opposed America's wars could be denounced as agents of communism. Moscow reaped parallel benefits. Because conditions for American workers were so oppressive, Moscow could claim that communism was better, despite mass oppression at home. Those who organized for social change or opposed Russia's wars could be denounced as agents of capitalism.

Pretending that they represented fundamentally different social systems (instead of variations on the capitalist model) made it easier for both the U.S. and Russia to advance their empires. In 1947, President Truman announced that America had a duty to combat communism (the Truman Doctrine) and promptly sent the Marines to Latin America to spread "democracy." Not to be outdone, Russia dispatched the Red Army to Eastern Europe to "liberate" the population from capitalism.

Portraying the United States as democratic and Russia as communist was brilliant propaganda that served both forms of capitalism, East and West, and confused people everywhere. Chris Harman writes,

> Many socialists in the West and the Third World were misled into believing the rulers of the USSR were on their side, while many dissidents in the Eastern bloc believed Western leaders who claimed to stand for "freedom" and "democracy." Those who stood out against this nonsense at the beginning of the 1950's were tiny in number.[77]

Imperialism is Democracy

Inspired by the French Revolution, slaves in Haiti fought to free themselves from French domination. You would think that a nation committed to democracy would welcome such a struggle. Not so. President Thomas Jefferson was horrified by the prospect of an independent Black Republic so close to American shores, and he supplied the French army with munitions to put down the rebellion. Against all odds, the slaves won their independence in 1804.

Real democracy is a threat to capitalism. In 1915, U.S. marines invaded Haiti and occupied it continuously until 1934. The invasion was justified by the racist argument that Haitians needed to be taught how to govern themselves. Before the troops left, Haiti's Constitution was re-written to allow American corporations to plunder the island's natural resources and exploit its population. In 2004, the U.S. invaded the island again, forced the democratically-elected president into exile, imprisoned democratically-elected government officials, and installed a U.S.-friendly military dictatorship. Again, the invasion was disguised as humanitarian intervention. Why the need for deceit?

Ordinary people won't support wars that benefit the rich and powerful, so imperial ventures must be given a noble character. As historian Howard Zinn points out,

> President Polk lied to the nation about the reason for going to war with Mexico in 1846. It wasn't that Mexico "shed American blood upon American soil" but that Polk, and the slave-owning aristocracy, coveted half of Mexico. President McKinley lied in 1898 about the reason for invading Cuba, saying we wanted to liberate the Cubans from Spanish control, but the truth is that he really wanted Spain out of Cuba so that the island could be open to United Fruit and other American corporations…And everyone lied about Vietnam—President Kennedy about the extent of our involvement, President Johnson about the Gulf of Tonkin, and President Nixon about the secret bombing of Cambodia. They all claimed the war was to keep South Vietnam free of communism, but really wanted to keep South Vietnam as an American outpost at the edge of the Asian continent.[78]

After the U.S. defeat in Vietnam, it became more important to counter anti-war sentiment so U.S. wars of conquest were promoted as humanitarian missions: removing a "tyrant" from power in Panama in 1989; countering an "illegal" invasion by Iraq in 1990-1991; saving Somalians in 1992-1993. In 1999, Washington bombed parts of Yugoslavia, supposedly, to stop ethnic cleansing. As had been predicted, the bombing increased the flood of refugees; however, Washington achieved its real objective—to plant military bases in former Russian territory, *without arousing mass opposition at home.* As Noam Chomsky points out, "When you've got your boot on somebody's neck, you can't just say, 'I'm doing this because I'm a brute.' You have to say, 'I'm doing it because they deserve it. It's for their own good.'"

Compete or Die ensures that the biggest bully rules. However, this cannot be admitted. The U.S. claims the right to impose its will on the world because it is morally superior to all other nations. The 20th century slogan, "What's good for General Motors is good for America" has become the 21st century slogan, "What's good for America is good for the world." Because it is the world's most heavily-armed nation, the U.S. can dictate who can have nuclear weapons (the U.S. and its allies) and who cannot (opponents of the U.S.), who can invade and occupy other countries (allies like Israel) and who cannot (enemies like Iraq), which brutal dictators should be removed from power (Panama's uncooperative General Noriega) and which should be placed in power (Chile's cooperative Augusto Pinochet), which crises to respond to (civil war in strategic areas like the Middle East) and which crises to ignore (civil war in less strategic areas like Africa), who are terrorists (opponents of the U.S.) and who are freedom fighters (supporters of the U.S.).

Lies build on lies. The U.S. bombing of Afghanistan was named, "Operation Enduring Freedom." When weapons of mass destruction could not be found in Iraq, the invasion was recast as a war against tyranny and renamed "Operation Iraqi Freedom." During his second inauguration speech, President Bush proclaimed, "The best hope for peace in our world is the expansion of freedom in all the world." Neglecting to mention U.S. military domination of the Balkans, the Middle East, the Philippines, and much of Latin America, Bush uttered the words "free" or "freedom" more than 25 times in fewer than 20 minutes. Such lies secure domestic support for war and seduce young people into the military, in the mistaken belief that war can make the world a better place.

War is Peace: The soldier betrayed

> I think when the world's most powerful medium colludes with the world's most powerful military to put propaganda in mainstream films and television shows, that has to have an effect on the American psyche.
>
> *David L. Robb*

In *Operation Hollywood: How the Pentagon Shapes and Censors the Movies,* David L. Robb explains how Hollywood collaborates with the Pentagon to show the U.S. government and military in the best possible light. Movie producers who want access to military ships, tanks, planes, bases, weapons, uniforms, or troops must accept Pentagon control over their film scripts. After the script is approved, a military advisor is stationed on the set to ensure that no unauthorized changes are made. The Pentagon also claims the right to pre-screen the film before its public release. Producers who reject Pentagon censorship are denied access to military props, and their films can be barred from military theaters and U.S. bases. Not surprisingly, Pentagon-approved war films are sanitized and Disneyfied. As Robb explains,

Hollywood producers have been known to turn villains into heroes, remove central characters, change politically sensitive settings, or add military rescues to movies that require none. There are no bad guys in the military. No fraternization between officers and enlisted troops. No drinking or drugs. No struggles against bigotry. The military and the president can't look bad.[79]

Pro-war films encourage young people to join the armed forces. When soldiers discover the brutal reality of war, they feel deceived. In *Achilles in Vietnam: Combat Trauma and the Undoing of Character,* Jonathon Shay explains how people of good character can go berserk when they are betrayed by their superiors. The betrayal of the soldier takes many forms: lying about the reason for the mission; inadequate training and faulty equipment; incompetent officers; and having to kill innocent people. All these things happened to American soldiers in Vietnam, and are happening again in Afghanistan and Iraq. Living under constant attack, never feeling safe, and suffering the loss of one's closest comrades can combine with the bitterness of betrayal to unravel the most upstanding person. Such conditions provoke the atrocities of war. More than one parent of a veteran has cried, "I gave them a good boy, and they sent me back a murderer."

The army has total control over its soldiers and should be held accountable for their behavior. Shay explains how officers encourage soldiers to turn their grief into revenge, yet, superiors take no responsibility when grief-stricken soldiers go berserk and lose their restraint, their morality, and their humanity. In 2005, Spc. Charles A. Graner Jr. was sentenced to 10 years in a military prison for torturing prisoners at Iraq's Abu Ghraib Prison. Graner was condemned as a "torture ringleader," while the top officers who supervised the prison system were cleared of any responsibility. Meanwhile, the mastermind of U.S. torture policy, Alberto Gonzales, was rewarded with the top job at the Department of Justice. Betrayal doesn't come any bigger than that.

While the people in power promote war as necessary for peace, prosperity, and security; peace never comes, only the wealthy prosper, and life becomes increasingly insecure. The ordinary American, the American soldier, and the people they are supposed to hate—all are victimized by the powerful people who call the shots.

Pay the piper, pick the tune

> This is an industry, it's a business. We exist to make money. We exist to put commercials on the air. The programming that is put on between those commercials is simply the bait we put in the mousetrap.
>
> *ABC Nightline* anchor *Ted Koppel*

The media are supposed to be objective and unbiased. In reality, the mainstream media are the voice of Corporate America. A handful of corporations dominate radio, and five giant conglomerates command the print and television media. Business also controls the media through advertising dollars. Magazines obtain half their revenues from advertising, newspapers get three-quarters of their income from advertising, and radio broadcasting depends almost entirely on advertising.

The media avoid stories that might offend corporate sponsors. Fearing a lawsuit, Fox Network refused to air a report on the health risks of milk produced using Monsanto Corporation's growth hormone. According to reporters Steve Wilson and Jane Akre, Fox's lawyer told them, "it doesn't matter if the facts are true." When Wilson and Akre protested, Fox's manager replied, "We paid three billion dollars for these television stations. We will decide what the news is. The news is what we tell you it is."

Journalists are not allowed to challenge the media's pro-business, pro-Washington bias. Fox fired Wilson and Akre. The *New York Times* fired Pulitzer-Prize-winning journalist Sydney Schanberg for writing about corporate power and corruption. The *San Jose Mercury* fired Gary Webb for reporting how the CIA brought cheap cocaine into the U.S. to fund anti-government terrorists in Nicaragua. Most of the time, such discipline is not necessary because most journalists share their employer's pro-capitalist, anti-labor views.

Media bias becomes most obvious in times of war. Amy Goodwin, host of radio program *Democracy Now!*, explains,

> The media are the same corporations that profit from war. During the 1991 Gulf War, CBS was owned by Westinghouse, and NBC was owned by General Electric. They made most of the parts for most of the weapons used in the war, so it's no accident that what we were watching on TV was a military hardware show.[80]

In *Manufacturing Consent: The Political Economy of the Mass Media,* Edward S. Herman and Noam Chomsky explain that the media depend predominately on "information provided by government, business, military and other 'experts' who are funded and approved by these primary sources and agents of power." Journalists who rely on the establishment for information inevitably become the voice of the establishment. Reflecting on his experience as a correspondent during World War II, John Steinbeck wrote,

> We were all part of the war effort. We went along with it, and not only that, we abetted it. Gradually, it became a part of us that the truth about anything was automatically secret and that to trifle with it was to interfere with the war effort. ...at that time we believed, fervently believed, that it was the best thing to do.[81]

To ensure that its policies are promoted, the U.S. government pays individuals and PR firms to plant stories in the media. In 1991, the public relations firm of Hill and Knowlton brought a 15-year-old Kuwaiti girl to testify before a Congressional Caucus. The girl stated that she personally witnessed Iraqi soldiers invading Kuwaiti hospitals, ripping infants from their incubators and leaving them to die on the floor. This atrocity was used to justify the U.S. war against Iraq. In fact, there was no atrocity. The girl turned out to be the daughter of the Kuwaiti Ambassador to the United States, and subsequent investigations found not a shred of evidence for her claims. The story was pure PR.

In 1991, the CIA hired a different PR firm to spread the story that Iraq had weapons of mass destruction. After the 2003 invasion, the Pentagon hired more PR firms to plant pro-American stories in the Iraqi media. Although these stories were written by U.S. troops, they were presented as unbiased reports by independent journalists. One Pentagon official confessed to reporters, "Here we are trying to create the principles of democracy in Iraq. Every speech we give in that country is about democracy. And we're breaking all the first principles of democracy."

Washington also plants propaganda in the media at home. Between 2003 and the first half of 2005, the Bush administration paid public relations firms, advertising agencies, media organizations, and individuals almost two billion dollars to promote its policies. Journalists were paid to write articles supporting the government's viewpoint and PR firms were hired to create favorable "video news releases" that were broadcast as if they were independent news reports. Ironically, Washington was spending more to produce fake news than media networks were budgeting for real news. When the Congressional Government Accountability Office ruled that such activities were illegal and deceptive, "covert propaganda," the Justice Department instructed all government agencies to disregard the ruling.

The government doesn't have to tell the media what to say—they already know. During the U.S. bombing of Afghanistan, the chairman of CNN sent a memo to his staff stating that, "it seems perverse to focus too much on the casualties or hardship in Afghanistan." He instructed them to "balance" coverage of civilian devastation with reminders that "it is that country's leaders who are responsible for the situation Afghanistan is now in." CNN's head of standards and practices suggested various ways to convey that information such as, "We must keep in mind...that these U.S. military actions are in response to a terrorist attack that killed close to 5,000 innocent people in the U.S." He emphasized that, "Even though it may start sounding rote, it is important that we make this point each time." The result is media grief over the deaths of Americans and media silence in response to the deaths of non-Americans.

Why we believe them

> You can say anything you want during a debate, and 80 million people hear it. So what if it's not true. Maybe 200 people read [the correction] or 2,000 or 20,000.[82]

Before the 2003 invasion of Iraq, 80 percent of Americans thought that the president was saying that Iraq either had weapons of mass destruction (WMD) or was in the process of developing them. Seventy percent believed that the administration was saying that Iraq was directly or indirectly responsible for the attacks on the World Trade Center. These beliefs crossed party lines and were linked with support for the war. At the same time, a series of UN inspectors found no evidence of WMD, a CIA report concluded that Iraq's "WMD capability" had been destroyed in 1991, and the 9/11 Commission found no connection between Iraq and the bombing of the World Trade Center. Nevertheless, on the eve of the 2004 presidential election, 49 percent of Americans still believed that Iraq had WMD, and 52 percent still believed that Iraq was involved in the attack on New York.

We know why Washington lied about the reasons for the war; they knew that the American public would not support a war for oil. The more important question is, why do people believe these lies? Why do they believe a president who assures them that America has no interest in building an empire, only in promoting democracy and freedom around the world?

Part of the answer is because we want to believe this. We want to believe that the people in power have the best of intentions and are genuinely concerned for our safety and our future. *We want to trust them because we want to feel safe.*

Trust connects people. Because human beings are social creatures, we want to give others the benefit of the doubt. Every con artist relies on this willingness to trust. At the same time, all social species have a built-in ability to detect when they are being unfairly treated. The successful con artist must avoid triggering the victim's sense of being cheated or deceived. The best way to disarm distrust is to build a relationship. Very wealthy politicians will mimic the dress and speech patterns of ordinary folks to imply, *"I'm just like you."* To preserve an important relationship, people will ignore their gut feeling that something is wrong and refuse to believe that a spouse is unfaithful, that a child is stealing, or that a president is lying.

The willingness to trust is bolstered by the desire to avoid the pain of betrayal. The American public had the option of believing the president or feeling massively betrayed, so they gave him the benefit of the doubt. Consider the fable of the emperor who wore no clothes. Everyone went along with the lie that he was clothed because they feared to admit the truth.

In relationships where one person is more powerful and the other is less powerful, *and there seems to be no alternative to this arrangement,* the less powerful person will protect the connection with the more powerful person, even when that person cannot be trusted. This phenomenon is called the Stockholm Syndrome after a 1973 bank robbery in Sweden where hostages defended their captors. The same phenomenon can be seen in maltreated children who defend the adults who hurt them. These children will "forget" the abuse, forgive the abuser, and blame themselves instead. Battered adults who cannot escape will also make excuses for their abusers and blame themselves. There is some logic to this. *As long as people feel powerless, it feels safer to trust the people with power.* A captive who turns against a captor, a child who turns against an abusive parent, and a battered spouse who turns against the batterer all risk greater harm and possible death.

The more dependent we feel on our rulers, the more willing we are to reject evidence that discredits them, no matter how convincing it is. When authorities reassure us that their greatest concern is our well-being, we long to believe them. No matter how often they swindle us, we look for signs that they are right and we are wrong. We forgive them again and again. Our "amnesia" flows from the mistaken belief that submission is the only option.

If people acknowledged that the president, his administration, and the media were all lying to them, what would they do? Facing the truth is an option only when there is some alternative (or some hope of an alternative) to the existing social arrangement. In terms of the Middle East wars, the American people saw no alternative. During the 2004 election, the Democrats supported the invasions of Afghanistan and Iraq and viciously attacked the only anti-war candidate, Ralph Nader. The anti-war movement collapsed to support the Democrats, and the revolutionary left was too small to make a difference. When Bush was re-elected, many people turned from politics to religion, needing something to believe in and someone they could trust.

No one can stand alone against the system. When people organize to fight for their rights, they find it easier to reject the lies that bind them to their oppressors. Social support helps to clear the brain, allowing people to see the world as it is and the possibility of creating a better world.

While lies keep the majority confused, lies are not enough to keep the ruling class in power. Someone must take responsibility for social problems. The next chapter explains how the ruling class protects the system by blaming its victims and convincing them to blame themselves and each other.

Summary

If the structure of society were ordained by God or Nature, there would be no need for rulers to lie. However, society is created by human beings and can be changed by them. The capitalist class needs the consent of the majority to rule so it cannot tell the truth—that its primary concern (to maximize profit) conflicts with what most people want (to meet human needs). The majority will believe the lies they are fed as long as they see no alternative and feel powerless to create one.

Chapter 10

Blame the Victim

CUT POWER OR LOSE IT

…screamed the headlines. In August, 2003, an unprecedented power blackout pulled the plug on 50 million people living in a 9,300 square-mile triangle bounded by New York City in the east, Detroit in the west and Ottawa in the north.

Officials warned of further blackouts if people didn't start conserving energy. After the power returned, a radio-journalist in Toronto dubbed "the hydro vigilante" roamed the streets interrogating people she found "wasting" energy, including a man pushing an electric lawn mower and an old woman sitting in front of her air conditioner. Media stories blasted irresponsible "juice hogs." I overheard a bus driver and a passenger agree that *we could not return to our wasteful ways.* People felt justified in scrutinizing their neighbors' habits. After all, didn't *our* wanton use of power cause the problem and weren't *we* responsible for fixing it? The answer is no—on both counts.

Ever since the U.S. power industry was deregulated in the 1980's, energy experts had warned of the probability of large-scale blackouts. Before deregulation, government controlled the generation and distribution of electricity. After deregulation, no one was accountable for making sure the system worked. Freed from enforceable operating standards and hungry for profit, power companies cut every corner they could. Between 1994 and 1996, there were three major blackouts affecting western North America.

A joint US-Canada investigation into the 2003 blackout found no evidence of excess power use by consumers; the power went out because of managerial incompetence, poorly trained workers, lack of coordination, and numerous violations of operating standards. In short, *an electricity grid designed to produce power was being operated to produce profit.*

Electricity users got no apology for being falsely accused. Ordinary people continue to be blamed, and to blame themselves, for systemic problems over which they have no control. The reason why goes back to the beginning of capitalism.

The myth of scarcity

When France's Queen Marie Antoinette was informed that her people were starving, she replied that if they lacked bread they should eat cake instead. Her arrogance enraged the people, and they chopped off her head. The lesson was not lost. Rulers who wish to keep their heads cannot openly thumb their noses at those they exploit.

Minister Thomas Robert Malthus (1766-1834) was determined to prevent a revolution in England by providing explanations for social problems that protected the capitalist class and its system. To explain poverty and deprivation, he argued that there are too many people and not enough to go around. To explain why wealth could not be shared, he insisted that the poor were biologically inferior and that improving their condition would only cause them to multiply. According to Malthus, "natural law" made it impossible to achieve the ideals of the French Revolution—liberty, equality, and brotherhood.

Malthus believed that what was good for the capitalist class was good for society and that any threat to the flow of profits threatened society. In *The Legacy of Malthus,* Alan Chase writes,

> To Malthus, any measures that eased the lot of the greatest number of people—from sanitary reform to medical care to birth control and, above all else, higher wages—were not only immoral and unpatriotic but also against the laws of God and Nature. According to Malthus, all such social instruments for the improvement of the individual, family, and public health shared the common and fatal "tendency to remove a necessary stimulus to industry."[83]

Malthus is known as the founder of "scientific racism" because he was the first to use scientific-sounding language to legitimize prejudice and bigotry. His 1798 publication, *Essay on the Principle of Population as it Affects the Future Improvement of Society,* argues that workers are not impoverished by capitalism but by their inferior biology—in essence, that their poverty is genetic. Chase observes,

> With or without Malthus…people of means would still hate to pay the taxes required to fund effective legislation for social welfare. However, by demeaning the intrinsic worth to society of most newborn children and their families, as well as by denigrating the value to the greater society of any and all human welfare legislation, scientific racism and its propagandists have for two centuries served successions of greedy men and penny-pinching governments.[84]

Malthus laid the basis for modern victim-blaming. He was the first PR-man for capitalism, promoting fictions like: people starve because there are too many of them; they are poor because they are lazy; they are in prison because they make bad choices; they suffer inequality because they are inferior; they destroy the environment because they consume too much; they get sick because they don't take care of themselves; and they are injured because they are accident-prone. Before we examine these arguments, let's look at how Malthus' ideas were propagated.

The genetic superiority of wealth

Francis Galton (1822-1911) was a wealthy man who perverted genetics to support class inequality. In *Hereditary Genius,* Galton declares that intelligence is hereditary because the children of the rich are more likely to rise to the top of society. (He ignores the fact that they inherit their families' wealth.) Because the rich are healthier, Galton argues that they must be biologically superior. Therefore, society could be improved if those of "superior breeding stock" have more children and the poor are prevented from having any. Galton opposed all social programs that might allow more "ineffectives" to survive and breed.

He coined the term "eugenics," meaning "well born," to describe his efforts to improve humanity through selective breeding.

Herbert Spencer (1820-1903) also corrupted science to justify class inequality. He created "Social Darwinism," a fraudulent science that applies "natural laws" to human society. It was not Darwin but Spencer who coined the phrase "survival of the fittest." Spencer insisted that the poor are biologically unfit to live and that supporting them only burdens the wealthy with taxes. On this basis, he campaigned against State-funded education and medical care, opposed all laws to improve working conditions, and rejected all forms of charity, including food for the starving.

Galton, Spencer, and other followers of Malthus (Malthusians) rejected all scientific evidence that improved social conditions improved people's health. Cholera epidemics had plagued England since 1831. By 1866, a network of clean water and sewage systems ended these epidemics. In Liverpool, basic sanitation measures had dramatically reduced deaths due to small pox, measles, scarlet fever, and typhoid fever. Nevertheless, Malthusians continued to insist that poverty and inequality are rooted in biology and cannot be altered because *they did not want to raise workers' expectations that they had a right to a better life.* Like all charlatans, they understood that a well-crafted lie vigorously defended by influential people can triumph over the truth. This strategy continues to serve the capitalist class.

A 1969 memo from the Brown and Williamson tobacco company observed, "Doubt is our product since it is the best means of competing with the 'body of fact' that exists in the mind of the general public. It is also the means of establishing a controversy." A 1998 memo from the American Petroleum Institute outlined its strategy to promote doubt about global warming, "Victory will be achieved when…recognition of uncertainty becomes part of the 'conventional wisdom.'" The strategy of sowing doubt keeps genuine scientists on the defensive, trying to prove the merits of their findings. In fact, these battles have nothing to do with truth or science. They are about protecting the right of the rich and powerful to run society in their own interests.

Eugenics in America

Malthus' theories found a home in 19th century America, where the class struggle was raging. To bolster their side, the capitalist class embraced the theory that the rich are superior beings with a natural right to rule society. In 1910, the Rockefeller, Carnegie, and Harriman families funded Charles Davenport, a professor of biology at Harvard University, to document the hereditary basis of poverty and inequality.

At the turn of the century, poor people in the American South were suffering an epidemic of pellagra, a disease that causes skin rashes, muscular weakness, dizziness, and mental deterioration. Davenport was a devout Malthusian who argued that pellagra and other diseases of the working population were hereditary. Appointed head of the Pellagra Commission, Davenport promoted a do-nothing policy on the basis that treating "pellagrins" would only allow them to survive to breed more "pellagrins." In 1916, Dr. Joseph Goldberger, head of the Public Health Service, showed that pellagra was a form of malnutrition that could be cured by eating foods rich in Vitamin B6. Davenport rallied influential doctors and politicians to reject Goldberger's findings, with the result that pellagra was ignored for another 17 years.

Davenport's mission was to reduce the numbers of poor and rebellious people in society. Allowing them to die from disease was one strategy. Eugenics was another. Davenport's Eugenics Records Office was instrumental in shaping the two arms of American eugenics policy: forced sterilization and racist immigration controls. In 1907, the state of Indiana passed the world's first compulsory sterilization law in the belief that "heredity plays a most important part in the transmission of crime, idiocy and imbecility." In 1913, President Theodore Roosevelt declared, "it is obvious that if in the future racial qualities are to be improved, the improving must be wrought mainly by favoring the fecundity of the worthy types…At present we do just the reverse. There is no check to the fecundity of those who are subnormal…" In 1927 the U.S. Supreme Court upheld the constitutionality of forced sterilization, declaring "It is better for all the world if instead of waiting to execute degenerate offspring for crime, or let them starve for their imbecility, society can prevent those who are manifestly unfit from breeding their kind."

By 1931, thirty states had passed laws to sterilize members of the "socially inadequate classes." Compulsory sterilization was promoted for: the "feeble-minded;" anyone thought to be insane, criminal, or delinquent; epileptics, alcoholics, and drug addicts; the deaf, blind, and crippled; anyone with tuberculosis, syphilis, leprosy, or any other chronic infection; and dependents upon the State including inmates of government institutions, paupers, orphans, and the unemployed. People could be designated as feeble-minded and sterilized simply for doing poorly on I.Q. tests. Recent immigrants, those who knew little English, and the poorly-educated fell into this category.

In the midst of the Great Depression, the Third International Congress of Eugenics convened in New York City. The Congress called for the mass sterilization of unemployed workers and their children to eliminate "the existence among us of a definite race of chronic paupers, a race parasitic upon the community, breeding in and through successive generations." One speaker declared that, "a major portion of this vast army of unemployed are social inadequates, and in many cases mental defectives, who might have been spared the misery they are now facing if they had never been born." By 1935 an estimated 20,000 people in the U.S. had been forcibly sterilized.

In theory and practice, the United States had become the world's foremost advocate of racial purity. Germany's 1933 *Nazi Act for Averting Descendants Afflicted with Hereditary Diseases,* was openly modeled on Davenport's 1922 model sterilization law. Between 1933 and 1945, Nazi Germany sterilized an estimated two million people and exterminated millions more in Race Hygiene death camps.

Instead of being horrified, American eugenicists praised Germany's bold pursuit of racial improvement. In 1934, the editor of the prestigious *New England Journal of Medicine* proclaimed, "Germany is perhaps the most progressive nation in restricting fecundity among the unfit." Psychiatrists were especially enthusiastic. In 1931, the president of the American Psychiatric Association advised, "I believe the time has arrived when we should, as an Association, again most strongly express our approval of the procedure of sterilization as an effective effort to reduce the number of the defective population" Between the 1930's and the 1950's, the *American Journal of Psychiatry* published numerous articles in support of eugenic sterilization and euthanasia. A 1942 article recommended euthanasia for severely mentally disabled children, who "should never have been born—nature's mistakes." An editorial in the same issue advised psychiatrists to convince parents of such children "that euthanasia is the most humane solution."

Both American and German eugenics policies were based on the belief that some "races" are superior to others, and that social problems can be solved by preventing the most disadvantaged people from having children. Historian Howard Zinn points out that the U.S. did not enter World War II to fight Hitler's ideas of "white Nordic supremacy." On the contrary,

> The United States' armed forces were segregated by race. When troops were jammed into the *Queen Mary* in early 1945 to go to combat duty in the European theater, the Blacks were stowed down in the

depths of the ship near the engine room, as far as possible from the fresh air of the deck, in a bizarre reminder of the slave voyages of old.[85]

After the war, when the full horror of the Nazi genocide came to light, talk of racial purity was discredited in the U.S. Facing a public relations crisis, the American eugenics movement re-invented itself as a campaign against "overpopulation." The poor would still be blamed for social problems, not for being genetically defective but for being morally deficient — lazy, criminal, and, most importantly, too numerous.

Culling the poor

After World War II, America's campaign to sterilize the poor escalated, bolstered by a new generation of Malthusians like William Vogt. Published in 1948, Vogt's book, *The Road to Survival,* warns that the greatest threat facing humanity is too many poor people. According to Vogt, the United Nations "should not ship food to keep alive ten million Indians and Chinese this year, so that fifty million may die five years hence." Special venom was reserved for advocates of the poor who, "Through medical care and improved sanitation …are responsible for more millions living more years in increasing misery." Alan Chase points out how influential these arguments were.

> Every argument, every concept, every recommendation made in *The Road to Survival* would become integral to the conventional wisdom of the post-Hiroshima generation of educated Americans…would for decades to come be repeated, and restated, and incorporated again and again into streams of books, articles, television commentaries, speeches, propaganda tracts, posters and even lapel buttons.[86]

In the 1950's, the U.S. began testing "population control" measures on poor people in Puerto Rico. By the end of the 1960's, more than one-third of women of child-bearing age on the island had been sterilized. By 1980, Puerto Rico had the highest rate of female sterilization in the world. Population control methods developed in Puerto Rico were exported for use in other poor nations.

The social movements of the 1960's opposed mass sterilization programs, arguing that high rates of poverty were caused by economic exploitation, not overpopulation. In 1968, Paul Erlich wrote *The Population Bomb* to counter these arguments. Like Vogt, Erlich insisted that overpopulation (not poverty) is the greatest threat facing humanity, and he opposed giving food aid to famine-stricken nations unless they agreed to sterilize their poor. The *Population Bomb* became a best-seller.

By the late 1960's, America was pouring millions of dollars into foreign and domestic sterilization programs. In the United States, poor people, First Nations' peoples, and Black people were targeted. Poor Black women were sterilized so frequently that the procedure was nicknamed, "the Mississippi appendectomy." In 1974, federal judge Gerhard Gesell ruled that "…poor people have been improperly coerced into accepting a sterilization operation under the threat that various federally supported welfare benefits would be withdrawn unless they submitted to irreversible sterilization." According to the judge, "Over the last few years, an estimated 100,000 to 150,000 low-income persons have been sterilized annually under federally funded programs."

Despite such condemnation, forced sterilization continued. In the 1990's Medicaid paid for poor women to have hormone-releasing contraceptive devices implanted under their skin. Removing the device was not funded. In 2000, a Louisiana woman convicted of child abuse was given the "choice" of medical sterilization or lengthy jail time.

Too many people?

Today, sections of the environmental movement continue to promote the false doctrine of overpopulation. The website of Support a Comprehensive Sierra Club Population Policy (SUSPS) states, "Unending population growth and increasing levels of consumption together are the root causes of the vast majority of our environmental problems." This is a dangerous argument. If you believe that too many people are destroying the planet, then you would have to cheer every famine, war, flood, and earthquake that reduced the population. You would also have to welcome diseases that kill millions every year.

Contrary to popular belief, environmental destruction is not caused by too many people on the planet. Environmental damage is accelerating despite falling global birth rates. The average number of children born per woman (the fertility rate) needs to be 2.1 to keep a population from declining over time. Between 1970 and 2000, the fertility rate in the world's poor nations dropped more than half, from 6.2 down to 3. In Europe, the fertility rate has fallen to 1.4, which is below replacement level. The United States has the greatest impact on the environment, yet its fertility rate has been below the replacement level for the past three decades.

There are several reasons for declining fertility. More people are moving from rural to urban centers. Rural families benefit from more children helping on the farm, while urban families can achieve higher living standards by having fewer children. Also, women who gain access to education and jobs have fewer children. Poverty is not caused by people having too many children; people have more children when they are poor.

Malthus was also wrong about hunger being the result of too many people and not enough food. There is only one reason people go hungry: food is produced for profit, not for need. We can produce enough to feed twice the number of people living on the planet, but if all that food came to market, the price of food would plummet. To keep prices high, States restrict food production or keep what is produced off the market. To keep farmers on the land, they are paid not to produce. The ridiculous result is that some people pay inflated food prices and higher taxes for farm subsidies, while others cannot afford to eat at all. In India, where more than half the children are malnourished, the State spends more to stockpile food than it does to feed the hungry.

People are not the problem. Environmental destruction is caused by social policies that put profit first—it is profitable to pillage natural resources and to use the environment as a dumping ground. The belief that social and environmental problems are caused by too many people persists, not because it is true, but because it serves the ruling class. Part Four explains how production could be reorganized to meet the needs of people *and* the environment.

The twin myths of scarcity and overpopulation provide false explanations for class inequality. The more the majority can be convinced to tighten their belts, the more the elite can stuff under theirs. Malthusian lies make the unacceptable seem inevitable: beggars on the streets of the world's most prosperous cities; millions starving while mountains of food are left to rot; people dying because medicines are priced out of reach; one part of the population being overworked, while the other part is desperate for work; obscene wealth growing alongside desperate poverty.

Class struggle

The war between the classes is conducted in two dimensions. In the material realm, the capitalist class extracts surplus from a working class that resists exploitation. In the realm of ideas, the doctrines of the capitalist class do battle with opposing ideas. For capitalism to survive, the capitalist class must dominate both dimensions.

Opposition to the ruling class and its ideas ebbs and flows, depending on the relative strength of the opposing classes. During the 1950's, the ruling class was more confident and smashed the opposition and its ideas. During the 1960's, the working class pushed back, challenging the ruling class and its ideas. Over the past few decades, the ruling class has taken back the ground it lost during the 1960's and strengthened ideas that blame the victim. To win the next round, we need to understand how we lost the last one.

After World War II, Black American veterans believed that they had earned the right to equality at home. Over the next two decades, their struggle for civil rights merged with other struggles to form a general working-class rebellion. During the 1960's, millions of Americans demanded racial equality, women's liberation, aboriginal rights, gay liberation, safer conditions at work, more affordable housing, better schools, and more access to medical care. There was organized opposition to poverty, pollution, nuclear power, the arms race, the death penalty, and U.S. foreign policy. A massive anti-war movement challenged U.S. imperialism, and American cities were shaken by Black rebellions. The belief that ordinary people could change the world was in the air, and it was intoxicating. Support for capitalism was cracking in the heart of the system.

The ruling class fought back on two fronts: granting limited reforms to promote confidence in the system and moving to crush the opposition. Let's look at the reforms first. In 1964, President Lyndon Johnson announced a War On Poverty and launched social programs like Head Start, food stamps, Medicare, and Medicaid. Passage of the 1965 *Voting Rights Act* made it easier for Black people to vote. The *Civil Rights Act* made racial discrimination illegal. To counter past discrimination, affirmative action policies set aside some jobs, admissions to higher education, and other opportunities for members of oppressed groups. In 1967, a moratorium was placed on executions. That same year, the Supreme Court ruled that children had the right to due process. In 1973, women won the legal right to abortion. In 1970, Congress enacted the *Occupational Safety and Health Act* (OSHA) to improve workplace health and safety. And all over the country, employers raised wages and benefits. These social improvements were no act of charity. They were won by masses of people who fought and died for them.

The ruling class also met the call for social justice with repression. Civil rights demonstrators were attacked with water hoses, dogs, clubs, and guns. Black churches were bombed and civil rights workers were murdered. Malcolm X was assassinated in 1965, and Martin Luther King was killed three years later. Between 1967 and 1968, dozens of leading members of the Black Panther Party were imprisoned and murdered. Chicago police viciously attacked demonstrators during the 1968 Democratic National Convention. Deadly force was used to suppress anti-war campus protests. In 1970, the National Guard killed four students at Kent State University and wounded nine others. At Jackson State University, police killed two students and wounded 12 others.

Despite reforms and repression, the social crisis deepened. The U.S. was losing the war in Vietnam. The North Vietnamese forces refused to be beaten, the American people had turned against the war, and the U.S. Army was in revolt. The Watergate scandal exposed the corruption at the heart of the system. In 1973, the U.S. withdrew from Vietnam. In 1974, President Nixon resigned in disgrace. That same year, the economy went into recession.

The employers' offensive

Battered by social protest, imperial defeat, and economic crisis, the capitalist class was desperate to restore its credibility and its profitability. In 1972, the heads of major U.S. corporations organized a Business Roundtable to "enable chief executives from different corporations to work together" to influence public policy. Founders of the Business Roundtable included the chief executives of Alcoa, General Electric, and U.S. Steel. In 1974, *Business Week* described the difficulty of their task,

> It will be a hard pill for many Americans to swallow—the idea of doing with less so that business can have more.... Nothing that this nation, or any other nation, has done in modern economic history compares in difficulty with the selling job that must be done to make people accept the new reality.[87]

And sell they did, through newspapers, magazines, radio, and television stations, book publishers, and movie studios. The new reality was called "neoliberalism" or "trickle down economics." The plan was for workers to accept less in the present in order to build the economy, which would then reward them with higher living standards in the future. This was not a new idea. In 1961, President Kennedy had claimed that "a rising tide would raise all boats." It was pure PR, designed to get the majority to back the goals of the ruling class. It was also a lie. Under capitalism, wealth produced at the bottom flows up; it never trickles down.

As one chorus, the ruling class touted economic growth as the best way, *the only way,* to solve social problems. However, neoliberalism was never about solving social problems; it was the beginning of a one-sided class war to restore the power and profitability of American capitalism. This war had two fronts: to restructure the economy in favor of the capitalist class; and to undercut resistance by blaming the victim. The more that ordinary people blamed themselves and each other for social problems, the less they would challenge the system.

By the late 1970's, the employers' offensive was in full swing. To restructure the economy, governments gave massive tax cuts to Corporate America and removed many of the restrictions on business that had protected workers and the environment. Deregulation and "downsizing" spelled the end of hundreds of thousands of good jobs. Employers demanded concession contracts to roll back wages and benefits they had previously granted. Union-busting companies proliferated. In 1980 alone, the National Labor Relations Board reinstated 10,000 workers who had been illegally fired for union organizing. The massive upward transfer of wealth caused the 1980's to be known as "the looting decade," which was followed by the even greater plunder of the 1990's. Between 1981 and 2000, the average annual compensation of the 10 highest-paid executives in the United States soared from just under four million dollars to $154 million.

A rising economic tide was lifting the yachts by sinking the rowboats. Never before had real wages fallen while the economy was booming. Life for ordinary people became harder and meaner. Someone had to take the blame for falling living standards, and it was not going to be the capitalist class.

Assault on the poor

The second front of the employers' offensive was to blame the victim. Blaming the victim shifts criticism away from unjust social policies and onto the victims of those policies. Victim-blaming also makes it easier to transfer tax revenue from social programs into the pockets of the rich.

During the 1960's, right-wing groups and individuals pumped out blame-the-victim propaganda; however, pressure from the social movements kept these ideas on the fringe of society. The employer's offensive brought them back into the mainstream. When Charles Murray wrote *Losing Ground* to attack social welfare programs, the ruling class embraced it as gospel. President Ronald Reagan concocted the outrageous myth that women on welfare were living high off the hog, wearing fur coats, and driving Cadillac cars. As the media jumped on the poor-bashing bandwagon, the image of the "welfare queen" became a symbol of the undeserving poor.

In 1994, *The Bell Curve: Intelligence and Class Structure in American Life* became a best seller. Reviving Malthus' equations, authors Charles Murray and Richard Herrnstein claim that the growing gap between the classes is caused by smarter people rising to the top of society, marrying each other and having even smarter children, while duller people fall to the bottom of society, marry each other and have even duller children. The authors conclude that social resources should be shifted from those at the bottom of society (who will always be dull and poor) to the better-off, who have better prospects of fulfilling their potential. *The Bell Curve* contained hundreds of pages of scientific-looking charts and graphs—all bogus. Like *Losing Ground*, *The Bell Curve* was Malthusian propaganda masquerading as science. That suited the ruling class just fine, and Murray was invited to address the House of Representatives. Another book, *Inequality by Design*, demolished every argument in *The Bell Curve*; however, its authors were not invited to address Congress. Politicians embraced *The Bell Curve* because it suited their slash-and-burn approach to social programs.

The extent of inequality is determined by the balance of class forces, not by biology. The rebellions of the 1960's raised the standard of living so that, by 1969, income inequality fell to a post-war low. In the 1970's, the employers' offensive drove down the standard of living of working people and caused inequality to rise again. Today, the gap between the super-rich and everyone else is greater than ever.

People don't accept being robbed easily. The ruling class needs some way to keep the growing numbers of poor and angry people under control.

The injustice system

> The prisoner is the visible symbol of *crime contained*—the criminal caged and restrained—to give the unwitting citizen the feeling that the cops and jails are preserving his safety.
>
> *William Ryan*

Everyone wants justice, and everyone wants to feel safe. Unfortunately, human needs are irrelevant to the "justice" system. Defense attorney Clarence Darrow explains:

> a jail is evidence of the lack of charity of the people on the outside who make the jails and fill them with victims of their greed…Those men who own the earth make the laws to protect what they have. They fix up a sort of fence or pen around what they have, and they fix the law so the fellow on the outside cannot get in. The laws are really organized for the men who rule the world. They were never organized or enforced to do justice. We have no system for justice, not the slightest in the world.[88]

The "justice" system exists to legalize the crimes of capitalism—class inequality and deprivation. It is perfectly legal for the capitalist class to commit theft by taking what workers produce, to assault workers to raise productivity, and to commit murder through wars of acquisition. Crime is defined in ways that target the working class. If you take something from your workplace, that is considered stealing. If the power company raises its rates every month, that is considered business. In 2006, Las Vegas declared it a crime to feed homeless people in public parks. Failing to provide housing for the homeless, jobs for the jobless, medicine for the sick, and food for the hungry are not considered crimes. Governments and corporations can legally withhold life's essentials from those who cannot pay. Parents who treated their children this way would be thrown in jail.

In *The Rich Get Richer and the Poor Get Prison,* Jeffrey Reiman calculates that corporate crime costs ordinary people far more money and causes many more deaths than common street crimes. Executives market dangerous and defective products like the Ford Pinto, manufacturers dump toxic chemicals into the environment, managers destroy jobs to raise profits, and drug company barons price medicines out of reach.

> Unlike many murderers sitting in prison for life, these gentleman bandits, these intelligent, educated men and women who slowly and methodically plan the crimes that wreck the future of untold numbers of people, know exactly what they are doing and who will be hurt. Their crimes of cold, selfish greed reflect, in their own way, even more indifference to life than murder.[89]

Darrow defined a criminal as "a person with predatory instincts who has not sufficient capital to form a corporation." Those who do form corporations can ignore the law. General Electric has been convicted of 282 counts of contract fraud, and not a single GE executive sits in jail. A common criminal with 282 convictions would be incarcerated for life. Under California's "three-strikes" law, Gary Ewing was sentenced to 25 years in prison for stealing three golf clubs, and Leandro Andrade was sentenced to 50 years in prison for stealing nine children's videotapes.

The definition of violence also serves the system. If you kill someone, it's called murder. If the State kills someone, it's called justice. Politicians who demand that we "get tough on crime" never talk about cracking down on the causes of crime because the class system is the cause of crime. The poorest neighborhoods have similar (high) murder rates, whether they are predominately Black, White, or Hispanic. Drug addiction, prostitution, theft, assault, and murder are the result of no jobs, no money, no future, and no hope.

A 2004 national survey of American cities revealed a direct relationship between deprivation (unemployment, less education, and lower income) and serious crime, including murder, rape, and robbery. The safest city was Newton, Massachusetts and the most dangerous city was Camden, Pennsylvania. Newton's employment rate was more than five times higher than Camden's. More than two-thirds of Newton residents had a university degree, compared with only five percent of Camden residents. And the median household income in Newton was more than three times that of Camden's. The real crime in Camden is deprivation. If Camden residents had the same living standards as Newton residents they would enjoy the same low crime rates.

The violence that capitalism perpetrates is perfectly legal. In contrast, rebellion against injustice is not tolerated. As a result, prisons are filled with the victims of the greedy people who run society.

The world's biggest jailer

The fuse of America's prison explosion was lit in the late 1960's. With a war raging in Vietnam, riots sweeping major cities, and protests roiling college campuses… Congress responded with a major anti-crime bill that doled out millions of dollars to local police and increased the federal government's involvement in local law enforcement. Crime had never been much of an issue in federal politics before, but Richard Nixon made it a central campaign theme that year.[90]

In 1971, President Nixon announced that the nation's greatest problem was illegal drug use (not the poverty and desperation that cause people to use drugs). The subsequent War on Drugs was a War on the Poor in disguise. Previous administrations had sterilized the poor and left them to die from preventable diseases. The Nixon administration launched a campaign to imprison them in record numbers.

In 1973, New York Governor Nelson Rockefeller dramatically raised the penalties for drug offenses, so that anyone caught selling one ounce of narcotics, or possessing two ounces, would get an automatic *minimum* sentence of 15 years in prison. Elaine Bartlett, a 26 year-old mother of four young children was sentenced to 20 years to life-in-prison for her first offense, selling four ounces of cocaine. To those who moralize that Brown shouldn't have sold drugs, reggae artist Bounty Killer replies, "We do what we do so we stay alive. We sell what we sell because we want to survive."

Mass incarceration went hand-in-hand with the assault on the gains of the 1960's. Troublemakers could be locked up. The victims of heartless social policies could be painted as dangerous instead of deprived. A population that feared the criminal-next-door would be more willing to back the criminals-in-power. In 1976, the Supreme Court reinstated the death penalty, and over the next 30 years, more than a thousand people were executed by the State. All were poor, and almost all were people of color.

Anti-drug laws and longer sentences filled America's prisons. Between 1970 and 2001, the national crime rate did not rise, yet the number of people in prison exploded from 200,000 to over two million, most of them nonviolent drug offenders. By 2001, the Rockefeller Drug Laws had resulted in an additional 325,000 person-years of incarceration in New York State alone. These years of life lost to prison were equivalent to 9,848 deaths, or more than three times the losses suffered in the bombing of the World Trade Center.

By 2004, one out of every 138 U.S. residents was in jail. About five million Americans are arrested every year, and one in every five Americans has a criminal record. The victims of the penal system are the most vulnerable members of the working class, as the Reverend Jesse Jackson explains,

> Sixty-five percent of all prisoners are high school dropouts, 70 percent are functionally illiterate, and 63 percent recidivate. We are often tempted to think of China as an oppressive country, but we incarcerate 500,000 more people in this country—despite the fact that we have less than one-fourth the population of China. We lock up our poor, our uneducated, our unruly, our unstable and our addicted, where other countries provide treatment, mental hospitals and care.[91]

Mass incarceration is socially harmful. Like the workhouses of the 19th century, modern prisons are giant incubators for disease, confining sick people in crowded quarters with poor food and little or no medical care. Imprisoned addicts are denied clean drugs and clean needles, and all prisoners are denied condoms. As a result,

> The number of prisoners with HIV is 10 times the rate in the general population…Hepatitis C, an often-lethal liver disease spread by blood exchange, infects an estimated 41 percent of inmates in California prisons, compared to less than 2 percent of the population at large.[92]

The law-enforcement approach to drug use is directly responsible for soaring rates of HIV/AIDS in America. Every year, hundreds of thousands of released prisoners take their diseases out of prison with them, endangering family, friends, and co-workers. In the early 1990's, a deadly strain of Tuberculosis swept through the New York prison system killing 35 prisoners and infecting more than 1,000 people outside.

The employers' offensive has transformed the 1960's dream of liberation into a nightmare of persecution, incarceration, and disease. With only five percent of the world's population, the United States holds more than 25 percent of the world's prisoners. The Twin Towers Correctional Facility in Los Angeles is the biggest jail on the planet. The ruling class undoubtedly feel safer. However, the prison system does not prevent violence, it strengthens the greatest source of violence—the system itself. Martin Luther King Jr. acknowledged this when he said,

> I knew that I could never again raise my voice against the violence of the oppressed in the ghettos without having first spoken clearly to the greatest purveyor of violence in the world today—my own government.[93]

Blaming Blacks

Inequality in America is not just a matter of class. Whole sections of the population are treated like second-class citizens solely because of their skin color. The ruling class needs to explain the oppression of Black people in a way that does not implicate the system. The solution is blame-the-victim racism.

In 1965, a U.S. government report titled, *The Negro Family: The Case for National Action,* blamed the depressed condition of Blacks on their weak family structure. The report claimed that "unless this damage is repaired, all the effort to end discrimination and poverty and injustice will come to little." Instead of pointing out that weak family structure is a result of racism and poverty, influential publications like *Life, Look,* and the *New York Times* supported the attack on anti-poverty programs. William Ryan wrote *Blaming the Victim,* to protest "the resurgence of ideas about hereditary defects in Blacks, the poor, and working people in general."

In 1967, a trio of Harvard professors claimed that the urban rebellions that were rocking American cities could not be attributed to poor social conditions because most people who shared those conditions did not participate in the uprisings. Therefore, there must be something "peculiar" about those who rebelled, and that peculiarity should be studied. (They showed no interest in why more people did not rebel against injustice. Under capitalism, submission is not considered to be a social problem.) The Department of Justice rushed to fund the professors' quest to identify a "violence gene" and "chemical imbalances" that could be corrected by psychiatric drugs and brain surgery. One prisoner was recommended for psychosurgery because he was disrespectful, led a work strike, read revolutionary material, and refused to stop teaching Karate and judo to his fellow inmates.

In 1972, the National Institute for Mental Health decided to study the biological roots of violence in Black youth. A national opposition movement closed down this project two years later; however, a number of states launched their own programs. California planned several Centers for the Study of the Reduction of Violence that would conduct genetic research and do brain surgery. Activists made sure they never opened. As Peter and Ginger Breggin point out,

The argument used to be that blacks were docile and hence biologically predisposed to slavery. Now, in a few generations, they're supposed to be genetically predisposed to rebellion. This is not science… This is the use of psychiatry and science in the interest of social policy.[94]

Washington was not deterred. In 1993, the National Research Council recommended mass psychiatric screening of Black children *as young as four months old* to identify those who might be "violence-prone" so they could be treated with "medications that reduce violent behavior."

The insistence that Black = Criminal has long been used to persecute and incarcerate Black people. White people form 70 percent of the U.S. population and commit the majority of inter-personal crimes, so that the "typical" American criminal is White. However, only 35 percent of the prison population is White. Black and Hispanic people fill the nation's prisons, not because skin color is genetically linked with criminality, but because the penal system has a history of targeting people-of-color, from the Black Codes of the early 1800's, through Jim Crow segregation, to the War on Drugs. Continuing efforts to paint all Blacks as criminals have reversed the gains of the civil-rights movement and driven a wedge of fear between the Black and White populations.

Modern "racial profiling" is a form of blaming-the-victim that goes something like this: most people in prison are Black; therefore, Blacks are more likely to be criminals; therefore, the penal system is justified in targeting Black people. Racial profiling has made it a crime to drive-while-Black. Every day, thousands of Black drivers are pulled over by police, searched, and abused simply because of their skin color. According to the Justice Department, police are more than twice as likely to search vehicles driven by Blacks, even though Whites are more than twice as likely to be found with illegal items. A report for the New Jersey State Police found that,

African-Americans and Latinos account for 78 percent of those searched, [yet] troops found evidence [of drugs] in the searches of whites 25 per cent of the time, of blacks 13 percent of the time, and of Latinos only 5 percent of the time.[95]

A 1998 national survey found that affluent, educated Whites are more likely to be drug users and drug addicts. Nevertheless, police looking for illegal drug activity target Blacks and Black neighborhoods. Blacks are more likely than Whites to be arrested, convicted, and sent to prison. Anti-drug laws victimize the poor who are also more likely to be Black. Probation is the only penalty for possessing five grams of expensive powdered cocaine. In contrast, possessing five grams of cheaper crack cocaine carries a mandatory five-year prison sentence. Because of such systemic racism, 90 ninety percent of the people in prison for drug possession are Black.

In 1980, there were three times as many Black men in college as there were in prison. By 2000, *there were nearly 200,000 more Black men in prison than there were in college.* On any given day, nearly one in three young Black men in America is in prison, on probation, or on parole. In some places like Baltimore, Maryland, and Washington, DC, more than half the Black male population is under the thumb of the judicial system.

More victim-blaming

The demand for greater productivity leads to more workplace accidents, injuries, illnesses, and fatalities. Instead of taking responsibility for these problems, employers blame workers for being careless and accident-prone. In 1966, the term "accident-prone personality" was listed as a psychiatric diagnosis in the *American Handbook of Psychiatry*. Blaming the worker is more cost-effective than providing a safe workplace. Consider the following example:

Thirty-year-old lineman Brent Churchill died when he reached for a 7,200 volt cable with his bare hands. His boss blamed Churchill's death on his failure to put on his insulating gloves. The story behind the story was that the company had "down-sized" the lineman department and was caught short-handed during a major storm. Instead of calling back the laid-off workers, management forced the existing crews to work overtime. For 55 of the 60 hours before he died, Churchill was climbing up and down 30-foot poles in freezing weather. He was neither careless nor lazy. He was overworked and exhausted.

Human beings are not machines. It is normal for people to become absent-minded and distracted by stress, fatigue, family problems, and other worries. At times, everyone misunderstands, misinterprets, and misreads. A workplace that functions safely *only when no one ever makes a mistake* is a dangerous workplace. A safe workplace protects workers when they make inevitable human errors.

Medicine under capitalism has a strong element of victim-blaming—the assumption that people who become sick must have done something wrong or be defective in some way. The protest movements of the 1960's challenged this view, emphasizing social conditions as a cause of poor health and demanding a national health-care system. To counter this movement, the Rockefeller Foundation sponsored a conference in 1975 to set a new direction for health policy that would cut medical costs, crush the expectation that medical care should be a right, and divert attention from the social causes of disease. All three goals could be accomplished by blaming the victim. Speakers at the conference condemned "irresponsible individuals" who indulge in "sickness-promoting behaviors" and burden "responsible" people with excess taxes and higher medical insurance premiums. Following this conference, the Rockefeller group wrote a series of policy papers promoting individual responsibility for health. In 1979, *Healthy People: The Surgeon General's Report on Health Promotion and Disease Prevention* blamed "personal excesses" for "the lion's share of runaway health costs." Subsequent government health-promotion campaigns instructed the public to eat right, get active, stop smoking, drink responsibly, say no to drugs, abstain from sex, work safely, etc.

The nation's medical journals fell in line with the new policy, treating health as an individual responsibility and sickness as a personal failure. One journal article blamed the lead poisoning of poor children on the "permissive socialization of oral behavior." Instead of demanding that landlords remove lead-based paint from low-income apartments, parents were held responsible for letting children put their hands in their mouths after touching objects coated with lead dust. Blame-the-victim articles increased as more research funding was dedicated to study how poor people make themselves sick.

The campaign to blame the sick found an ally in the self-help movement of the 1970's. People practicing holistic health care rejected the use of medicines and vaccines. Self-care was promoted as the way to free oneself from reliance on doctors and potentially harmful medical treatments. The New Age emphasis on personal responsibility meshed with the employers' efforts to dismantle state-funded medical care. While social activists fought for more access to the medical system, self-help advocates like Ivan Illich argued that less access would be more beneficial.

When it comes to epidemics like cancer, victim-blaming is rampant. While industries flood the environment with cancer-causing chemicals and the State dismantles environmental protections, cancer research concentrates on modifying individual behaviors (drinking, smoking, nutrition) and developing individual treatments. Cancer prevention is dismissed as unrealistic. According to the website of the Centers for Disease Control and Prevention, "Breast cancer cannot be prevented, however, studies show that early detection of breast cancer saves lives." Preventing cancer would require removing carcinogens from production, cleaning up toxic waste dumps, closing down the nuclear power industry, and prohibiting the military from using chemical and radioactive weapons. In other words, *cancer prevention is impossible under capitalism.*

With cancer prevention blocked at the social level, experts concentrate on advising individuals what they should and should not do to prevent cancer. These recommendations are as useful as "duck and cover" exercises during the Cold War, where school children were instructed to duck under their desks and cover their heads in case of a nuclear attack. Personal protective measures don't prevent cancer, they blame people for getting cancer by focusing on individual behavior. Even personality can be targeted. Some experts warn that the risk of cancer increases for people who repress their emotions and ignore their needs. (Ironically, the same behaviors that employers demand of workers, especially women.) In fact, the "cancer-prone" personality is a myth. Scientific studies on two continents found absolutely no connection between personality type and susceptibility to cancer. Nevertheless, the myth endures because it offers (false) hope to people who want to avoid cancer, makes money for those who sell hope, and takes pressure off the primary source of cancer—the capitalist system.

It would be wonderful if people could be healthy simply by making the right choices. However, most illnesses arise from social conditions—overwork, unemployment, workplace hazards, excess stress, inadequate housing, poverty and malnutrition, environmental toxins, and lack of medical care. As long as people live in health-damaging conditions, it is impossible to distinguish how much the individual contributes and how much society contributes to any particular problem.

Do individuals have *any* responsibility for their health? People should be held responsible only for what they control. They cannot be held responsible for what they do not control. Capitalism turns this principle upside down. Those with the most power take no responsibility for social problems. Those with the least power get all the blame. During the Great Depression of the 1930's, Henry Ford blamed lazy workers for high unemployment, "the average man won't really do a day's work unless he is caught and cannot get out of it. There is plenty of work to do if people would do it." A week later, he laid off 75,000 auto workers.

An unjust world

> The pyramid-shaped socioeconomic hierarchy, and the power elite at the top of it, will be secure as long as those at the lower levels blame one another for their lack of access to jobs with greater decision-making power—and as long as they fail to question the system that makes the decision-making power scarce in the first place by holding so much of it at the top.
>
> *Jeff Schmidt*

We want to think that we live in a just world, where people reap what they sow, where what goes around comes around, and where those who play by the rules are rewarded. Belief in a just world is shaken by tragedy and secured by blaming the victim. When Andrea Yates killed her children in a psychotic state, I overheard someone say, "She shouldn't have had so many children if she couldn't take care of them." Such blaming comments shield people from thinking about the desperate conditions that could drive a mother, possibly any mother, to kill her children. It is more comforting to condemn Yates than to think about how trapped she was and how trapped we are.

People blame themselves for the problems in their lives because, in a strange way, self-blame offers the illusion of control ("I could have made something of myself, if only I had…"). Blaming implies responsibility, that a person had the power to make things right and just messed up. People would rather blame themselves than to think that forces beyond their control could pull the rug out from under them *no matter what they do.*

If there is no justice in society, if people can be harmed through no fault of their own, then we are powerless to protect ourselves and our loved ones. Powerlessness is so frightening that people dissociate from reality and believe what they want to believe. It is more comforting to believe that misfortune visits only those who make bad decisions so that one can be safe by making good decisions. In reality, the world is a dangerous place because the people in charge protect themselves at the expense of everyone else.

The struggles of the 1960's exposed capitalism as a sick system, and masses of people began to see that they were in the same boat. To take back control, the ruling class had to change that perception. Hollywood did its part, producing films like *Easy Rider* and *Up in Smoke* that portrayed the 1960's as a continuous orgy of drugs, sex, and rock-n-roll. ("If you remember the 1960's then you weren't there.") The fact that millions of people had organized to change the world was belittled and then erased from public memory. When the social matrix in which we are embedded is invisible, it is easier to blame individuals for social problems and for individuals to blame themselves and each other.

Ordinary people do not benefit from victim-blaming. By 2001, the annual cost of police, courts and prisons had reached $167 billion, up from $36 billion in 1982. This money was taken from social programs known to reduce crime—education, job-training, recreational programs, better housing, and treatment for mental illness and drug addiction. Persecuting poor people doesn't make society safer; it results in more desperation and less public safety.

Criminalizing drug use leads to more drug use and more drug-related crimes. Illegal drugs are so expensive that poor addicts must sell them to pay for their own supply. Others resort to theft and prostitution. One study of a crackdown on illegal drug use found that as police cleared one area, drug-related activity moved into new areas.

A 1994 study funded by the White House recommended that funds be transferred from law enforcement to drug treatment programs because "Treatment is seven times more cost-effective than domestic drug enforcement in reducing cocaine use and 15 times more cost-effective in reducing the social costs of crime and lost productivity." The Clinton administration rejected this advice because the War on Drugs is not about stopping drug use; its purpose is to impose social control. That same year, President Clinton ended educational grants for prisoners even though education is the single most important factor in whether a released prisoner returns to jail.

Prisons are big business—the public foots the bill, and private corporations reap the profits, not only from government contracts but also from convict labor. In 1979, Congress created the Prison Industry Enhancement Certification Program that allows businesses to employ inmates and sell prisoner-made goods. The prison labor system is modern, legal slavery. Prisoners are compliant, disposable labor with no legal rights. Inmate workers earn just pennies an hour, so the profits are huge—billions of dollars every year. More prisoners and longer sentences mean even more profit.

At the beginning of the 21st century, class inequality has never been greater. The race to incarcerate reflects the determination of the capitalist class to continue squeezing the working class and to prevent them from rebelling against this injustice. Criminalizing drug use allows the State to intervene in the daily activities of the working class. More cops, more prisons, and harsher laws give the ruling class more power to dominate society.

Blaming the most exploited and oppressed for social problems is like blaming the canaries in the mine who keel over when toxic gas levels rise. The canaries warn the miners that their lives are in danger. The poor and the persecuted are like society's canaries; their suffering warns everyone else that they are next. We can shoot the messenger by blaming the victim, or we can heed the message.

Portraying victims as villains works only when the majority is divided. The next chapter explains how the capitalist class divides in order to rule.

Summary

Feudalism attributed class inequality to God's will. Capitalism attributes class inequality to the superiority of the few and the defectiveness of the many. Blaming the victim protects the system. As long as ordinary people blame themselves and each other for problems that are created by the ruling class, there will be more problems and more victims.

Chapter 11

Divide and Rule

> They divided both to conquer each.
> *Frederick Douglass*

One day when I was five years old, I saw a Black man walking down the street. Delighted, I cried, "There's a chocolate man!" and ran to get a closer look. Fourteen years later, while working as a receptionist, my boss handed me a stack of job applications and instructed me to discard forms submitted by Black applicants. When I asked why, he replied, "The shippers don't want to work with those people." These two stories demonstrate opposite reactions to human differences. One is delight and curiosity. The other is fear and hate. In order to divide and rule, the capitalist class promotes fear and hate.

Death by a thousand cuts

Capitalism splinters humanity. The first cut is the deepest—the horizontal divide between the many who labor and the few who confiscate the fruits of labor (Seize the Surplus). This class division traverses the globe to create an international ruling class, an international working class, and a buffer class in the middle. In every nation, a minority ruling class dominates a majority working class. Even the poorest nations have their elite. In 2005, Latin America had 300,000 millionaires with combined assets of more than four trillion (U.S.) dollars. Africa had 100,00 millionaires worth a total of $800 billion (U.S.) dollars.

Hundreds of vertical cuts slice humanity into nations that compete economically and militarily (Compete or Die). There is no such thing as a "community of nations" or an "international community." Stronger nations exploit weaker ones using methods that range from unfair trade policies to direct military occupation.

Within each nation, the class-divided population is chopped vertically into multiple segments based on race, sex, language, religion, national origin, sexual orientation, politics, age, geographic location, state of health, and practically any other characteristic you can think of. Each segment retains the horizontal class divisions. For example, in all nations, the majority of Black people are working class, some are middle class, and a tiny few inhabit the ruling class (Supreme Court Justice Clarence Thomas and Secretary of State Condoleezza Rice in the U.S.).

In order to rule, the capitalist class portrays all these divisions as fixed and indisputable. Class inequality is explained as the superiority of the few and the inferiority of the many ("the cream rises to the top" and "survival of the fittest"), while racism, sexism, xenophobia, and homophobia are declared to be instinctual. None of this is true. Throughout history, human behavior, values, and social structures have changed repeatedly.

The truth is that when two classes have opposing interests, the smaller one can rule only by dividing the larger one. This chapter examines some of the divisions that sustain the capitalist order.

How different are we?

Humanity is one species that capitalism has fragmented into many different races and nations, even though our similarities far outweigh our differences. Compare any two people in the world and you will find that 99.8 percent of their genetic material is identical and only 0.2 percent is different. People are so similar because our species has one origin—Africa. According to geneticist Svante Pääbo, "From a genetic perspective, all humans are Africans, either residing in Africa or in recent exile."

As people migrated from the Mother Land, isolated groups developed minor physical variations. Anthropologist James Shreeve notes that skin and eye color, the shape of eyes, nose, and mouth, and the color, texture, and distribution of hair are biological variations that "do vary from region to region, but they do so independently, not in packaged sets." Most people who live in Asia have skin folds on their eyelids, as do the Bushmen of southern Africa. Black-skinned people can have kinky hair and poker-straight hair. There are Black people with thin lips and narrow noses, and White people with full lips and broad noses. As more people migrate through the world, even these regional variations are disappearing.

The Human Genome Project discovered that "racial differences" make up only 0.01 percent of the body's genes. These differences are so superficial that someone who looks very different from you and lives on the other side of the world could be a better organ donor for you than someone who resembles you and lives on your street. The American Anthropological Association concludes,

> … human populations are not unambiguous, clearly demarcated, biologically distinct groups…. Throughout history, whenever different groups have come into contact, they have interbred. Any attempt to establish lines of division among biological populations is both arbitrary and subjective.[96]

The biological concept of race has no scientific basis; however, it does serve a political purpose—to divide people by maximizing their differences and minimizing their similarities. Racist assumptions are deeply embedded in the English language. The designations "Black" and "White" divide people by skin color *and exaggerate that difference.* In fact, White people are not really white, they are various shades of beige. This can be demonstrated by holding a sheet of white paper against the skin. Similarly, Black people are not really black, they are various shades of brown, including beige. It would be more color-accurate to use the labels "Brown" and "Beige." Using the terms, "Black" and "White" implies polar opposites; when *all human beings are actually shades of the same color.* To indicate that "Black" and "White" are political labels, not colors, I have capitalized them throughout the text (except in quotations that appear as originally written).

How natural is the tendency to classify people by skin color? A clever two-part experiment set out to answer this question. In the first part of the experiment, volunteers were shown photographs of individuals that were matched with specific sentences. Then the sentences were shown out of order and the volunteers had to reunite each sentence with the photograph of the person it was originally paired with. The volunteers tended to connect sentences with individuals based on the color of their skin.

In the second part of the experiment, the individuals and their matching sentences were grouped in two color-coded teams, one wearing gray shirts and one wearing yellow shirts. Both teams contained Black and White members. This time, volunteers matched the sentences to their owners by shirt color more than by skin color. The researchers concluded that "less than four minutes of exposure to an alternate social world was enough to deflate the tendency to categorize by race." Racial categories are so artificial that they need constant reinforcing to be maintained. The history of racism in America reveals how important racial divisions are to capitalism.

Slave republic

The United States of America was founded on the destruction of aboriginal peoples through ethnic cleansing (forcing them onto reservations); biological warfare (distributing blankets contaminated with disease); and outright genocide to steal their land. The wholesale massacre of men, women, and children was supported by racist propaganda portraying them as sub-human ("The only good Indian is a dead Indian").

Having seized control of the land, large land-owners needed people to work it. Free laborers kept leaving the plantations to establish their own farms, so indentured servants, aboriginals, and convicts were pressed into service. Poor people were literally kidnaped off the streets of England to work in America. Still, the demand for labor outstripped the supply. The solution was slavery. An unlimited number of slaves could be captured from Africa and forced to work with no hope of a better life. The business of kidnaping poor Whites shifted to the even more lucrative business of kidnaping African Blacks. In *Capitalism and Slavery*, Eric Williams describes how

> Kidnaping in Africa encountered no such difficulties as were encountered in England. Captains and ships had the experience of the one trade to guide them in the other. Bristol, the center of the servant trade, became one of the centers of the slave trade. Capital accumulated from the one financed the other. White servitude was the historic base upon which Negro slavery was constructed.[97]

In *A People's History of the United States*, Howard Zinn notes that, "Africa lost 50 million human beings to death and slavery in those centuries we call the beginnings of modern Western civilization." Black slavery financed the Industrial Revolution in England and built the fortunes of America's ruling families. Being essential to the economy, the slave system was enshrined in the U.S. Constitution.

Racism

> Slavery was not born of racism: rather, racism was the consequence of slavery.
>
> *Eric Williams*

Racism is the practice of discriminating against a group of people and the beliefs that justify that practice. The feudal ruling class had no need for a theory of racial difference. Feudal inequality was justified as God's will (the divine right of kings). Being rooted in science and industry, the capitalist class needed a secular explanation, so it attributed inequality to biology (human nature). However, a specific theory of racial inferiority did not develop until "the Land of the Free" needed to justify Black slavery. According to historian Barbara J. Fields,

> It was the prevalence of freedom rather than the fact of slavery that created [American racism]. English people might find Africans and their descendants to be heathen in religion, outlandish in nationality, and weird in appearance but that did not become an ideology of racial inferiority until one further ingredient became part of the mixture, and that was the incorporation of Africans and their descendants into a society in which they lacked rights that others not only took for granted, but claimed as a matter of self-evident natural law.[98]

In 1857, the U.S. Supreme Court ruled that slaves were property, not people, and that "the Negro might justly and lawfully be reduced to slavery for his benefit."

The American Civil War did not begin as a war against slavery. On the contrary, Northern armies were instructed to return fleeing slaves to their masters. Frederick Douglass observed that, "The South was fighting to take slavery out of the Union, and the North fighting to keep it in the Union…" President Lincoln wrote,

> My paramount object in this struggle is to save the Union, and is not either to save or destroy slavery. If I could save the union without freeing any slave, I would do it; and if I could save it by freeing all the slaves, I would do it; and if I could do it by freeing some and by leaving others alone I would also do that.[99]

In 1862, Lincoln threatened to free the slaves if the South did not surrender. As an added incentive, he promised that states pledging allegiance to the Union could continue using slaves. A year later, the *Emancipation Proclamation* freed slaves only in states that remained hostile to the Union. However, the need to defeat the South forced Lincoln to abolish slavery altogether. After the Civil War, laws were passed to prohibit racial discrimination and grant Black people the right to vote, to own land, and to hold public office.

Hungry for cheap labor, Southern plantation owners organized the Ku Klux Klan and other vigilante groups to beat, burn, lynch, and terrorize Blacks into accepting conditions that were not much better than slavery. In this matter, Northern industrialists allied with Southern landowners. In 1883, the Supreme Court nullified the *Civil Rights Act* of 1875. Thirteen years later, it established legal segregation by ruling that Blacks and Whites could be "separate but equal." The Smithsonian Institute and the American Association for the Advancement of Science gave credibility to segregation legislation by reviving the claim that Blacks were subhuman. More than 400 "Jim Crow" laws, constitutional amendments, and city ordinances made it a crime for Blacks to mingle with Whites in hotels, hospitals, restaurants, washrooms, marriage, military service, and even in cemeteries. If it were natural for people to stick with "their own kind," such measures would have been unnecessary.

The civil rights movement of the mid-20th century abolished legal segregation; however, actual or *de facto* segregation continues in employment, housing, education, medicine, banking, sports, prisons, the military—virtually every aspect of American life. Racism persists because it is necessary to divide the working class. Capitalism could not survive the challenge of a unified majority. By pitting Black and White workers against each other, employers can control both groups. Racism is so important to capitalism that it permeates all classes and all social institutions.

Medical racism

The American medical system is deeply racist. Medical statistics are collected primarily on the basis of race and rarely on the basis of social class, occupation, income level, or access to medical care even though *these factors have the greatest impact on health.* In *Backdoor to Eugenics,* Troy Duster warns that using racial categories to measure infant death rates, disease rates, and life expectancy supports the myth of racial inferiority. By emphasizing race, medicine transforms social problems into biological defects.

Medical research typically compares Whites, Blacks, Hispanics, and Asians, when there is no scientific way to decide who fits into which group or how to distinguish between these groups. The 1890 Census established the "one drop" rule that decreed that an individual with one Black ancestor was considered Black even if that person had white skin, blond hair, and blue eyes. Later on, people were categorized by appearance. Beginning with the 2000 Census, Americans could check more than one of six races, including "some other race," to produce a total of 63 combinations of race and a total of 126 possible categories or combinations of race and ethnicity. Migration and intermarriage make it so difficult to decide one's racial group that many people change their racial category with each survey.

Business has never let science interfere with profit. Linking illness with race creates a market for race-specific drugs. Researcher Jonathan Kahn describes how a combination drug named BiDil was rejected by the FDA for treatment of heart failure and subsequently reinvented as a specific treatment for Blacks. In 2002, Bidil was granted the first U.S. patent for a "race-specific" drug. In granting this patent, the federal government declared African-Americans to be a distinct biological group.

There is no evidence that BiDil will help Black people. The drug trial enrolled only Black subjects, so no one knows if BiDil is more beneficial for Blacks than for Whites. Furthermore, the study assumed that if some Blacks respond well to BiDil, then all Blacks will. We come back to the question of who is Black. Because there is no biological way to differentiate between the races, subjects in the BiDil study were categorized as Black *if they said they were Black.* Bad science can be good economics. If BiDil had been approved for general use, its patent would have expired in 2007. When BiDil was approved as a race-specific drug, its patent was extended to 2020.

There are some biological differences in how people metabolize drugs; however, these differences do not correspond to skin color. An analysis of 15 studies that compared Black and White reactions to blood-pressure-lowering drugs found that the difference between Whites and Blacks was much smaller than the variations *within* each color group. Another study compared 23 drug-metabolizing genes among 354 people representing eight classically-defined races. The genes fell into four groupings that did not match any of the race categories. The researchers concluded, "There is no clear link between skin pigment and drug metabolism genes. Skin pigment is a lousy surrogate for drug metabolism status or most any aspect of human physiology." But never mind the facts; the federal government is determined to link race and health.

The Department of Health and Human Services funded a study to determine the effect of race on calcium metabolism. One researcher announced that,

> While we found a racial difference in calcium retention in adolescents, we also confirmed that blacks retain more sodium on a high-salt diet than whites....This proves that salt is processed differently in the races...[100]

This sweeping conclusion was based on a study of "22 African-American girls and 13 Caucasian girls." The results of this study were considered to be valid because the girls' diets were strictly monitored; however, no one revealed how the racial categories were determined. This study was published in the *American Journal of Clinical Nutrition,* and its conclusion—"Calcium retention is significantly greater in black girls than in white girls"—was headlined by the media.

People who are identified as Black do suffer more medical problems, not because of different biology but because they live in a racist society, and racism has biological consequences. Inequality creates disease, and medical problems multiply as one moves down the social ladder. While the overall U.S. poverty rate is 12 percent, 24 percent of American Blacks are poor. Black unemployment is double the rate of White unemployment, and the median income for Black households is almost 40 percent less than for White households. Black babies die at more than double the rate for White babies. Black women are almost four times more likely to die from pregnancy-related causes. Black people as a whole are more likely to die of heart disease, stroke, cancer, and diabetes than White people of the same age.

Despite their greater need, Black people get second-rate medical care. Studies show that Black patients with congestive heart failure and pneumonia receive inferior medical treatment. Black people with early-stage lung cancer are less likely to have surgery and are more likely to die as a result. Blacks are more likely to be mis-diagnosed as schizophrenic and to be institutionalized for mental illness. The only medical procedure that Blacks receive more than any other group is limb amputation, as a result of neglected health problems.

Because of racism, the average life expectancy of Black Americans is six years shorter than that of White Americans. Racism causes an estimated 84,000 additional deaths in the United States every year, more than the equivalent of a Hurricane Katrina every week. The editor of the Harvard School of Public Health's *Minority Health Today,* declares "This is nothing short of a national medical emergency. When are we going to stop talking about it and start doing something about it?" The problem is what to do.

Race-based medical research and race-specific treatments fail to address the social conditions that kill Black *and* White people. All Blacks experience special oppression. But that doesn't mean that all Whites are doing fine. Most poor people in America are White; most people without medical insurance are White; most homeless people are White; and most people on welfare are White. In deprived areas where more Black babies die, more White babies also die. The medical focus on skin color avoids the political issue of why so many people, Black and White, live and work in harmful social conditions. The best way to improve the health of Black people is to end the deprivation that makes people sick *regardless of their skin color.*

Imperial racism

Empires rule by dividing the populations they conquer. A many-times-conquered people, Africa knows the terrible cost of divide-and-rule. In Rwanda in the spring of 1994, as many as one million people were "hacked, shot, strangled, clubbed and burned to death." The American media attributed the massacres to age-old tribal feuding. In fact, imperial powers sowed the seeds of this slaughter.

Before Germany and Belgium dominated Rwanda, there were three occupational groups: the Hutu were farmers, the Tutsi raised cattle, and the Twa were hunter-gatherers. These were not class divisions; one could be a poor Tutsi or a rich Hutu. All spoke the same language, intermarriage was common, and a person could shift from one group to another simply by changing occupation.

The colonial period that began in the 1890's transformed Rwanda's occupational groupings into racial divisions. Because they looked the same and spoke the same language, people were forced to carry identity cards designating them as Tutsi or Hutu, and movement between the groups became more difficult. The Belgians praised the Tutsi as racially superior and gave them privileges in the colonial hierarchy, even though the majority of Tutsi remained poor.

> The racialization of consciousness affected everybody, and even the 'small Tutsi,' who did not benefit from the system in any way, started to believe they were indeed a superior race and that under the same rags as their Hutu neighbors wore, a finer heart was beating. The Hutu, deprived of all political power and exploited by both the whites and the Tutsi, began to hate all Tutsi, even those who were just as poor as they.[101]

When the Tutsi elite decided to run Rwanda independent of Belgian control, the Belgians backed a Hutu rebellion to oust the Tutsi from power. Civil conflict intensified as the World Bank and the International Monetary Fund imposed economic "shock therapy" that impoverished the country. As Rwanda slid into bankruptcy, it disintegrated into warring factions. Weapons from France, Egypt, and South Africa poured into the country. Disregarding warnings of impending massacres, the United Nations pulled most of its troops from Rwanda. This move was viewed as a green light to escalate the slaughter.

The tragedy of Rwanda has been, and continues to be, replayed throughout Africa and the world. To control India, the British empire played Hindu, Muslim, and Sikh against each other. To control Iraq, the U.S. is playing Shiite Muslims, Sunni Muslims, and Kurds against one another.

Imperial conquest has divided and re-divided the Balkans. After World War II, Yugoslavia established a fairly integrated society. In the 1980's, the economy began to sink under the burden of international debt. Factional leaders staked out their territory and provoked a civil war. The greater the social cohesion, the more terror is needed to shatter those bonds. The most atrocious interpersonal violence was used to turn friends, family, and neighbors against each other so decisively that no reconciliation seemed possible. Like vultures, other nations armed whichever side they thought would position them most favorably. The United States emerged as the primary beneficiary of the war, obtaining military bases in territory previously controlled by the Soviet Union. The former-Yugoslavia remains divided under military occupation.

Duplicity is basic to divide-and-rule. Imperial powers befriend and betray based on their own interests, regardless of the harm they cause. During the Cold War, the U.S. armed and trained Osama bin Laden, the Taliban, Al-Qaeda, and other Islamic fundamentalists to fight the Russians in Afghanistan and to promote U.S. interests in the Middle East. These former friends are now enemies. During the civil war in Yugoslavia, the U.S. backed the Muslims, claiming they were the under-dogs. Muslims later became villains when the U.S. invaded Afghanistan and Iraq. During the 1980's, the U.S. backed and armed both sides of the Iran-Iraq war. Now both countries stand in the way of America's plans to control the Middle East. When today's allies are tomorrow's enemies, the result is war without end.

Nations divide

It seems as if the world has always been divided into nations. In fact, the nation-state is a recent invention of capitalism. People in feudal societies lived and worked in a multitude of small fiefdoms, each ruled by a wealthy family, most having their own language and customs. As capitalism developed, this patchwork of independent economies presented a barrier to trade and commerce. The capitalist revolutions of the 18th century began to consolidate this hodgepodge into the system of nation-states we know today.

As the global economy becomes more international, you would think that capitalism would welcome more open national borders, or no borders at all. However, competition compels capitalists to rely on the financial, political, and military support of their home States. Corporate America dominates the world economically because the American State dominates the world militarily.

To improve their economic clout, nations have banded together in formal and informal trade blocks like the European Union, Mercosur (Brazil, Argentina, Uruguay, Paraguay and Venezuela), and the North American Free Trade Agreement (United States, Canada, Mexico). These blocks do not reduce competition; they take it to a higher level. As long as capitalism exists, the economic pressure to integrate the world economy will strain against the national divisions that are necessary for capitalist competition. Like a volcano building up steam, these pressures periodically erupt in wars that redraw national boundaries.

The capitalist class compares the nation to a family, with itself in the role of parent; however, this is a false comparison. Most families are composed of people from the same social class, while nations are composed of people from antagonistic classes. When President Bush says, "You're either with us or against us," he uses "us" to mean "the nation as a whole," when he actually means "me and my class." The myth of the nation-as-family seduces workers into supporting the policies of the capitalist class as if they were good for everyone.

Like sports teams, nations unite and divide. Sports fans are typically loyal to their own teams and hostile to competing teams. Flag-waving is practiced in sports and reaches a frenzy in times of war. Nationalism unites the people in one country by dividing them from the people in other countries. Concepts like 'nation' and 'national identity' assume that people inside a set of borders share a common culture and common values that other people do not share. This is fiction. People living in the same apartment building don't share the same beliefs and practices, let alone nations of millions.

Because national divisions are necessary for capitalist competition, each capitalist class tries to convince its working class that "our" nation is the best. By fostering emotional bonds between capitalists and workers, patriotism divides and weakens the working class.

Border wars

Patriotism and nationalism are forms of racism — the belief that the differences between people on either side of a border are more important than their common interests. These differences are as artificial as the borders themselves, which move back and forth in response to political conflict and territorial conquest. ("We didn't cross the border, the border crossed us.") Any map more than ten years old is already out of date.

The capitalist class polices national boundaries to separate "us" and "them" and, supposedly, to protect "us" from "them." To exaggerate the fear of outsiders, foreigners and immigrants are called "aliens," a term used to describe non-humans from outer space. The result is the kind of paranoia displayed by U.S. Immigration and Customs Enforcement,

> We believe it is a very serious vulnerability when there are illegal aliens working at Air Force bases, nuclear power plants, chemical plants and airports. They have access to some of the most sensitive work sites in the U.S. Our job is to take actions to immediately remove them from positions where they can do harm.[102]

The racist assumption that immigrants are dangerous, even terrorists, has created a major conflict inside the United States. Rich nations need immigrants because their birth rates are too low to supply the demand for labor. The National Research Council calculates that immigration results in a net *gain* to the U.S. economy of $10 billion a year. Instead of appreciating immigrants for their contribution, the State has declared war on them. A 2003 Supreme Court ruling allows Congress to pass laws against immigrants that would violate the Constitution if they were applied to citizens. Homeland Security has a plan called "Endgame" to apprehend, incarcerate, and deport all "removable aliens" from the U.S. by 2012; however, the economy would be crippled if this goal were actually achieved. The capitalist class does not want to remove all immigrants; it wants a fearful, disposable, low-waged workforce with no legal rights. So the State attacks immigrants and ignores those who hire them.

To survive, workers must move to where there are jobs. The 1994 *Free Trade Agreement* between the U.S. and Mexico devastated the Mexican economy and forced Mexican workers to seek jobs in the U.S. *That same year,* the Clinton administration launched Operation Gatekeeper to make it harder for Mexican workers to enter the U.S. By 2006, the U.S. Border Patrol had a $1.6 billion budget to turn the boundary between the U.S. and Mexico into a war zone. Anti-immigrant attacks coming from the top of society emboldened the far right, and vigilante border patrols formed, bolstered by White supremacist groups like the Ku Klux Klan. Since 1994, more than 4,000 migrant workers have been killed trying to cross the border, and this number continues to rise.

The capitalist class profits from the oppression of immigrants. Workers without rights can be paid less, or not at all, and deported when they complain or try to organize unions. Promoting competition between native-born and foreign-born workers makes it easier to exploit both groups and drive down wages in a "race to the bottom."

Immigrants also make convenient scapegoats for social problems like crime, unemployment, and falling living standards. What are the facts? In terms of crime, Harvard sociologists found first-generation immigrants to be "45 percent less likely to commit violence than third-generation Americans." They concluded that increased immigration in the 1990's could explain why the murder rate during that decade dropped to levels not seen since the 1960's.

Immigrants do not cause unemployment. Areas with higher immigration offer more job opportunities. Immigrants increase the demand for goods and services, and many immigrants start businesses that provide jobs. Nor do immigrants cause wages to fall. The capitalist class is responsible for keeping the minimum wage at $5.15 an hour while the cost of living rises. Twelve million undocumented workers cannot be held responsible for the existence of 40 million low-waged jobs. On the contrary, immigrant workers have launched union organizing drives that benefit all workers. Lies about immigrants are used to divide workers and prevent a revival of the labor movement.

Many people think that immigrants use more public services than they pay for in taxes, when the opposite true. Most undocumented immigrants work for established companies and pay taxes just like other workers. Undocumented immigrants pay about seven billion dollars more into Social Security than they get back and one-and-a-half billion dollars more into Medicare than they receive in services. Over a lifetime, each immigrant pays on average $80,000 more in taxes than he or she will ever use in government services.

The ruling class tries to convince those who have little that they will have less if others have rights. Experience shows that the opposite is true. In 1994, half the Black voters in California endorsed an anti-immigrant measure that denied undocumented workers basic social services like welfare and emergency medical care. Keeanga-Yamahtta Taylor points out,

...most of the African Americans thought that voting yes on Proposition 187 would improve their own economic status—operating from the assumption that Latino immigrants were taking limited resources away from poor and working class Blacks. Instead, Proposition 187 helped to foster an environment of racism and scapegoating that no doubt contributed to the passing of an anti-affirmative action referendum two years later.[103]

In late 2005, the House passed a bill making it a felony to be an undocumented immigrant or to assist one. There are an estimated 12 million undocumented immigrants in the United States. This measure would have criminalized all of them and all who helped them—family, friends, neighbors, clergy, social workers, medical workers, and lawyers. In response to this outrageous attack, millions of people poured into the streets to demand rights for immigrants. Repeated nation-wide demonstrations emptied schools and closed workplaces. There were general strikes in Chicago and Los Angeles. Chanting "We are America" and "No human being is illegal," the working class rose up and punched the ruling class in the face. Reeling from this blow, both the House and the Senate failed to pass their anti-immigrant bills before the 2006 summer recess.

The "Great American Boycott" reclaimed the mass strike as a legitimate weapon of protest. The ruling class retaliated with anti-immigrant raids and the deployment of thousands of National Guards on the border. However, there is no going back. The American working class is multinational; as long as goods and services can cross borders freely, then the workers who create those goods and services will want the same right.

In the 19th century, Karl Marx concluded that working people have no nation because all nations are anti-worker. Employers can shift production to countries where wages are lower, because borders prevent workers from going where wages are higher. Capital can flow freely across borders in search of profits because borders block workers from uniting to raise their living standards. A workers' nationality is like a dog-tag that specifies which ruling class has the right to take what the worker creates and to make the worker fight its wars. Capitalism forces workers to choose: be loyal to your nation and betray your class or to be loyal to your class and betray your nation.

Who is the enemy?

All capitalist wars require a parallel war at home against those who resemble the enemy. In order for England to dominate Ireland, it must promote discrimination against the Irish to prevent unity between English and Irish workers. For the United States to dominate Latin America, it must promote discrimination against Hispanics to prevent unity between American and Latin American workers. During the U.S. war against Japan, more than 110,000 Japanese-Americans were forced into internment camps and their homes and property were confiscated. The official purpose of this measure was to protect America from domestic traitors. In fact, only 10 people were convicted of spying for Japan during the war and not one was of Japanese or Asian descent. The persecution of Japanese-Americans created an internal enemy to boost support for the war and prevent a unified anti-war movement. The persecution of American communists served a similar purpose during America's Cold War with Russia.

U.S. wars in the Middle East demand the persecution of Arabs and Muslims in America. *This has nothing to do with keeping America safe.* When Timothy McVeigh bombed the federal building in Oklahoma City in 1995, there was no mass round-up of White American veterans. According to the Southern Poverty

Law Center, right-wing individuals and groups have attempted at least 60 terrorist plots since then, including plans to bomb or burn government buildings, banks, refineries, utilities, clinics, synagogues, mosques, and bridges; to assassinate judges, politicians, and civil rights leaders; and to acquire machine guns, missiles, explosives, and biological and chemical weapons. The extent to which the mainstream media ignore White, home-grown terrorists is astonishing.

Arabs and Muslims were targeted after 9/11 to build public support for Washington's plan to invade the Middle East. To promote paranoia, American airport security were warned that anyone from the Middle-East could be a terrorist. It didn't take long for all brown-skinned people to be included. By 2004, Amnesty International reported,

> Racial profiling of citizens and visitors of Middle Eastern and South Asian descent, and others who appear to be from these areas or members of the Muslim and Sikh faiths, has substantially increased since September 11, 2001....Approximately thirty-two million Americans, a number equivalent to the population of Canada, reported they have already been victims of racial profiling.[104]

One U.S. airport official confiscated a bundle of cooking spices that my East Indian friend was bringing back from her visit home. She was told that the spices were a potential weapon that could be thrown in the pilot's eyes. From the ridiculous to the outrageous, people are being questioned, humiliated, detained, interrogated, strip-searched, imprisoned, deported, and tortured for the "crime" of having brown skin, being Arab, or being Muslim.

President Bush responded to the increase in attacks against Arab-looking people by stating that all Arabs and Muslims are not enemies. But actions speak louder than words. The U.S. bombing of Iraq made no distinction between military and civilian, friend and foe. The State encouraged anti-Arab racism by imprisoning people on the *suspicion* of being terrorists, holding them without charge or access to legal counsel in what the Justice Department later ruled were mentally and physically abusive conditions. The aim of such measures was to send the message that all Arabs and all Muslims are possible terrorists.

Those who oppose State policies are also treated as enemies. ("Whoever is not with us is against us"). In 2002, the Department of Justice launched Operation TIPS (Terrorism Information and Prevention System). The plan was to recruit "a million letter carriers, meter readers, cable technicians, and other workers with access to private homes as informants to report to the Justice Department any activities they think suspicious." That same year, the Pentagon launched its own spy program, Total Information Awareness (TIA), to monitor all electronic transaction data in the United States and internationally. While Operation TIPS and TIA were officially dropped, domestic spying continues on a massive scale. Washington spends more than $40 billion a year to fund its spy agencies. FBI counter-terrorism units monitor civil rights groups like the American Civil Liberties Union, peace groups like United for Peace and Justice, environmental organizations like Greenpeace, charities, churches, and thousands of individuals who have committed no crimes.

War brings the iron fist of the State out of its velvet glove. Police attack anti-war demonstrators to show what happens to those who oppose the government. Under the Patriot Act, political dissenters can be charged with "domestic terrorism" and treated like terrorists. A man finds federal agents at his door to question his opposition to the war. A youngster is suspended from school for wearing a political T-shirt. Secret Service agents question a high-school student about anti-war drawings he made in art class. The demand for conformity is expressed by the slogan, "America: Love It or Leave It." Anyone who protests this loss of civil liberties is considered a traitor. As Attorney General John Ashcroft warned, "To those who scare peace-loving people with phantoms of lost liberty, my message is this: Your tactics only aid terrorists."

Losing humanity

The strategy of divide-and-rule dehumanizes society by breaking human bonds and turning people against each other. It isn't easy to convince ordinary people to kill people just like them or to support such killing. The targeted population must be painted as less-than-human. Britain's Prime Minister Tony Blair defended the invasion of Iraq by insisting, "These are not people like us. They are not people who abide by the normal rules of human behavior." Perverse logic justifies brutalizing "them" on the basis that they are not as civilized as "we" are. The ordinary soldier gets the message. Photographs of U.S. and British soldiers torturing Iraqi prisoners show the victims with hoods over their heads, reduced to faceless objects. Writer Luc Sante observed,

> The pictures from Abu Ghraib [prison] are trophy shots. The American soldiers included in them look exactly as if they were standing next to a gutted buck or a 10-foot marlin…There was something familiar about that jaunty insouciance, that unabashed triumph at having inflicted misery upon other humans. And then I remembered: the last time I had seen that conjunction of elements was in photographs of lynchings.[105]

Every war comes home. Methods developed to subdue foreign populations are inevitably used domestically. As a military policeman in Vietnam, Jon Burge was trained to torture suspects. Back in America, he joined the Chicago police force and found a new use for his skills. In 1993, Burge was fired for supervising the systematic torture of more than 100 Black men over a period of more than 20 years. Thirteen of these men had been sentenced to death on the basis of confessions obtained through beatings, burnings, suffocations, electric shock, and mock executions.

A 2004 *New York Times'* investigation found that prisoners in the United States were being treated much the same as prisoners in Iraq. This is no coincidence. Prison officials with experience torturing American inmates were selected to run Iraqi prisons and train Iraqi prison guards.

Torturing prisoners is not an aberration, nor is it caused by a few bad apples. Those who profit by dominating others will do whatever is necessary to secure their power. The people at the top set the example by dehumanizing the enemy. General James Mattis, commander of U.S. forces in Afghanistan and Iraq, was quoted as saying, "It's fun to shoot some people." Admiral Harris, commander of the American prison at Guantánamo, told reporters that three prisoners being held without hope of release had killed themselves because, "They have no regard for life, neither ours nor their own." With leaders like these, it's no wonder that ordinary soldiers assault, torture, and murder. In *An Open Letter to GIs in Iraq,* Stan Goff describes his experience in Vietnam.

> We had to dehumanize our victims before we did the things we did. We knew deep down that what we were doing was wrong. So they became dinks or gooks, just like the Iraqis are now being transformed into ragheads or hajjis. People had to be reduced to 'niggers' here before they could be lynched. No difference…so long as they were human beings, with the same intrinsic value we had as human beings, we were not allowed to burn their homes and barns, kill their animals and sometimes

even kill them. So we used these words, these new names, to reduce them, to strip them of their essential humanity…[106]

Goff's warning to soldiers stands as a warning to us all. When you take away the humanity of another, you kill your own humanity. *You attack your own soul because it is standing in the way.*

Their gain, our pain

> You tell me the truth. You tell me that my son died for oil. You tell me that my son died to make your friends rich. You tell me my son died so you can spread the cancer of imperialism in the Middle East. You tell me that.
>
> *Cindy Sheehan*

In 1995, when *60 Minutes* host Lesley Stahl asked Secretary of State Madeleine Albright, "We have heard that a half a million children have died [because of the sanctions against Iraq]. I mean, that is more children than died in Hiroshima. And, you know, is the price worth it?" Albright replied, "I think this is a very hard choice, but the price, we think, is worth it." Ten years later, President George W. Bush claimed that the mounting death toll in Iraq was worth it. Most parents of dead Iraqis and dead American soldiers would not agree. The elite reap the power and profit that are paid for with other people's lives and other people's suffering.

It is commonly believed that ordinary Americans benefit from U.S. imperialism. This is not true. What the U.S. capitalist class takes from the poor people of the world does not "trickle down" to American workers. On the contrary, this surplus is invested in extracting more wealth from *all* workers, including those in the United States. While U.S. oil companies were reaping billions in oil profits from the war, ordinary Americans were paying record high prices at the gas pumps.

In no way does capitalism at home or imperialism abroad benefit ordinary workers. Workers' living standards rise and fall based on their willingness to fight the employers to keep more of what they produce. The living standard of American workers reached a peak in the late 1960's as a result of class struggles. Conditions have deteriorated since then because workers have submitted to employers' demands for higher productivity and more profits.

Capitalist competition is always waged at the worker's expense. On the economic front, each employer goads his employees to produce more and faster than his competitors' employees. The capitalist who can pressure his workers to give up the most surplus wins. The workers of the losing enterprise are laid off, and the workers of the winning enterprise have increased their own exploitation. On the military front, each State goads its workers-in-uniform to fight harder and kill more people than the workers-in-uniform of the opposing State. Rulers who command the most brutal and destructive military forces win, while the workers of both nations lose, as the following examples reveal:

In 2003, the U.S. launched its war against Iraq on the pretext of protecting America from further terrorist attacks. By 2004, the number of terrorist attacks reached a record high. In 2005, the number of terrorist attacks had more than tripled over the previous year. (Attacks on military personnel were not included.) *The war on terror has made the world more dangerous.* Washington refuses to admit this, and the State Department has stopped publishing the data.

The primary beneficiary of the war against Iraq is the U.S. capitalist class, which has seized control of one of the world's richest sources of oil. American corporations have also reaped a windfall in war-profits. The primary losers of the war are ordinary Iraqis and ordinary Americans. The U.S. tax dollars being spent to conquer Iraq represent a transfer of wealth from the American working class to a few wealthy U.S. corporations and individuals. The web site of the National Priorities Project keeps a running total of how much money Congress is appropriating to wage the war in Iraq and what that money could provide in terms of medical care for America's uninsured children, public education, public housing, and stopping HIV/AIDS. The costs are broken down by state, by U.S. household, and by individual American. *Every social issue in America today is linked with this war.*

When Hurricane Katrina slammed into the Gulf Coast, most of the Louisiana and Mississippi National Guard were deployed in Iraq, along with essential equipment like high water vehicles and refueling tankers and generators. A nearby army brigade from Fort Polk was not mobilized to help the flood victims because it was preparing to go to Afghanistan. By March of 2006, Congress had appropriated more than $245 billion for the Iraq war, while hundreds of thousands of Americans displaced by Hurricane Katrina remained homeless. One anti-war demonstrator made the connection when she held up a sign, "No Iraqi left me on a roof to die."

Whether they live in the invading or the invaded country, ordinary people pay for war with their blood. The people in power do not send their children to war; they send the children of the working class. By 2005, over 2,000 American soldiers had been killed in Iraq, and tens of thousands were disabled with horrible injuries. The proportion of U.S. soldiers in Iraq suffering from depression, anxiety, and post-traumatic stress disorder is approaching the one-in-three ratio suffered by Vietnam veterans.

Soldiers and their families get shabby treatment in return for their sacrifice. For months at a time, active-duty soldiers are paid late or not at all. The General Accounting Office found the Defense Department's payroll system to be "so primitive and error-prone that few people fully understand it." Many returning soldiers have lost their jobs, homes, and families. According to the National Coalition for Homeless Veterans, nearly 200,000 veterans are homeless on any given night and more than half a million are homeless over the course of a year. More than one out of every three homeless males in America is a veteran. While the military gets billions of dollars to develop new weapons, the Department of Veterans Affairs is starved of funds to treat the sick and wounded.

The bombs produced in America leave behind toxic waste that pollutes our air, water, and food. Soldiers also bring the war home. During the 1991 Gulf War, Timothy McVeigh was ordered to kill surrendering Iraqi soldiers. Four years later, he bombed the federal building in Oklahoma City. In October 2002, Gulf War veteran John Allen Muhammad went on a shooting rampage in Washington, D.C. that left ten people dead. Other veterans have killed family members, strangers, and themselves. The war machine that turned these men into murderers is not put on trial.

Soldiers and anti-war activists have a common interest; both want to end the war and bring the troops home. The ruling class dreads such an alliance. The film, *Sir! No Sir!,* documents the scale and heroism of the soldier's revolt that forced the U.S. defeat in Vietnam. To keep soldiers out of the anti-war movement, war mongers attack anti-war activists as traitors who despise their own soldiers and root for the enemy. (They just as falsely portray all soldiers as gung-ho for war and hostile to the peace movement.) The myth that anti-war activists spat on soldiers returning from Vietnam is pure PR. Vietnam veteran Jerry Lembcke, author of *The Spitting Image: Myth, Memory, and the Legacy of Vietnam,* insists that "stories of spat-upon Vietnam veterans are bogus."

The Veterans Administration commissioned a Harris Poll in 1971 that found 94 percent of Vietnam veterans reporting friendly homecomings from their age-group peers who had not served in the military. Moreover, the historical record is rich with the details of solidarity and mutuality between the anti-war movement and Vietnam veterans. The real truth, in other words, is that anti-war activists reached out to Vietnam veterans and veterans joined the movement in large numbers.[107]

The benefits of unity

To prevent the majority from uniting against them, the capitalist class pits groups of people against each other: White against Black; men against women; citizen against immigrant; Christian against Muslim, and so on. By fostering such competition, employers divide, rule, and profit.

In a divided society, some people are better off than others, including within the working class. It is easier to be White than Black, to be male than female, to be a citizen instead of an immigrant, to be heterosexual instead of homosexual, to be able instead of disabled, and so on. It can seem that those who are better-off benefit from those who have it worse. This is the point of divisions—*to keep ordinary folks so busy measuring whose crumb is bigger that nobody notices who ran off with the bakery.* Of course, some crumbs are preferable to others. It is better to be educated than to be illiterate, to have a home than to be homeless, to have a job than to be unemployed, to be free than in prison. However, these differences are insignificant compared with the humongous difference created by class.

In 1999, the world's 225 richest people had a combined wealth of one trillion dollars. That's as much as the combined annual income of the world's 2.5 billion poorest people. The wealth of the world's three richest individuals is greater than the combined Gross Domestic Product of the 48 poorest nations. If the height of the Washington monument (555 feet) represented the average income of the top 500 American CEOs, the average American worker's income would be 16 inches tall in comparison. Now, that's a *real* difference.

Talk of "White privilege" and "male privilege" makes it seem that all Whites benefit from Black oppression and that all men benefit from women's oppression. This outlook ignores the class divide and who really benefits. The Grand Canyon between the wealthy elite and everyone else is possible only because the majority is divided. Instead of fighting for crumbs, a united majority could take control of the world's wealth and share it.

Those who argue that Whites benefit from Black oppression ignore the fact that *no benefit from this division could possibly compare with what both could have if they pulled together.* Consider the American South.

> The South remains the region… where discrimination against Blacks is most severe. The South is also the region where incomes of white workers are lowest and poverty among whites is highest…where the rights of labor, white and Black, have been most trampled; where trade union membership and influence have been most drastically curtailed.[108]

The capitalist class *does* benefit from oppression. The difference between the wages of higher-paid and lower-paid workers goes to the employers. The bosses also pocket the difference between what these workers make and how much more they could make if they were not divided. Like Frederick Douglass said, "They divided both to conquer each."

By insisting that all men benefit from the oppression of women, feminist politics divides the working class. In reality, workers of both sexes are exploited and oppressed by capitalists of both sexes. During a strike, women workers understand that class comes first. They fight beside their male co-workers instead of seeking allies with their female employers or with the female relatives of their male employers.

The power and privileges of upper-class women depend on the exploitation of male and female workers. In contrast, the oppression of women makes life *more* difficult for ordinary men. Women's lower wages pull down the family income. When women suffer, the men in their lives also suffer. Men whose wives have stressful jobs, unsupportive bosses, and few promotions are seven times more likely to develop heart disease regardless of the status of their own jobs. When women advance, the men in their lives benefit. Having a wife with more education lowers the husband's risk of smoking, being overweight, having high blood pressure, high blood cholesterol, and dying of heart disease.

Where social conditions are better for women, they are also better for men. One study examined the status of American women in all fifty states, measuring political participation, employment, wages, and reproductive rights. Expecting to find a link between better conditions for women and lower female death rates, researchers were surprised to find that,

> Strikingly, male mortality rates were even more strongly linked to the status of women than female death rates, suggesting that men are better off, health-wise, where women's status is more equal to men's…The critical finding is that gender inequality has costs for men, as well as women. In general, a society that tolerates greater gender inequalities is more likely to be less healthy for both men and women.[109]

There is strength in unity. The union movement has a saying, "United We Stand; Divided We Fall." The belief that ordinary people benefit from imperialism, racism, sexism, and homophobia is just as mistaken as the belief that more police, more prisons, and more wars will keep us safe. Only the ruling class benefits from divisions that keep the majority subordinate. The next chapter explains how people are indoctrinated from childhood to accept the world as it is.

Summary

The few can dominate the many only by dividing them—by minimizing similarities and magnifying differences. However, the differences between ordinary people are insignificant compared with the colossal chasm between the classes. The capitalist class profits from divide-and-rule, while ordinary people are prevented from working together to build a better life.

Chapter 12

Suffer the Children

> Weakening the parent-child bond and disintegrating families within a group are a means of subordinating the entire group.
>
> *Dorothy Roberts*

In 1860, the U.S. government began forcibly removing aboriginal children from their homes and placing them in residential schools far from their families. These schools punished children for speaking their native languages, and physical and sexual abuse were common. Untold numbers died of cold, malnutrition, and disease. Those who made their way home lacked the skills to contribute to their communities. Launched in 1958, the Indian Adoption Project removed over one-third of all aboriginal children from their families. These and other assaults on the aboriginal family have left a legacy of domestic violence, addiction, mental illness, and suicide.

In *Shattered Bonds: The Color of Child Welfare,* Dorothy Roberts explains how disrupting family ties is a weapon of social control that has been used since slavery days. Because family loyalties undermined the slave-owners' control, slave children were sold apart from their parents and slave parents were punished in front of their children. As Roberts explains,

> Slave law installed the white master as head of an extended plantation family that included his slaves... Slaves, on the other hand, had no legal authority over their children. Naming a slave after his owner reenforced the child's ultimate subservience to his master rather than to his parents.[110]

After Emancipation, Black parents tried to re-unite with their children. However, plantation owners used apprenticeship laws to keep as many former slaves as they could. In Maryland, 10,000 of the 90,000 emancipated slaves were re-enslaved under apprenticeship laws. It was argued that,

> ...Black children needed the supervision afforded by apprenticeship because the Black race "was not prepared for freedom yet." A key component of Blacks' presumed need for continued white supervision was a 'theory of black parental incompetence.'[111]

Today, the American prison system and child welfare system are responsible for the largest separation of families since slavery. Half the parents in prison are Black, and 90 percent of the children in long-term foster care have a parent in prison. An estimated 10 million American children have lost a parent to prison at some point in their lives. Parents can be imprisoned in locations far from their children, and children may have no way to visit. Many children of prisoners suffer shock and show symptoms of post-traumatic stress from prolonged separation. According to the Los Angeles-based Center for Children of Incarcerated Parents,

> Across the country, an estimated 1.5 million children have a parent behind bars—an increase of more than half a million since 1991, according to the federal Bureau of Justice Statistics. No one knows the exact number, because in virtually every jurisdiction nationwide, *no official body—not police, courts, or prisons—is responsible for even asking if prisoners have children.*[112] [italics added]

Parent to the nation?

How did the State get so much power over families? The doctrine of *parens patriae* (parent to the nation) originated in feudal England, where the King decided the fate of orphans and others who could not care for themselves. In 1838, this policy was adopted by the United States. *Parens patriae* gave the State the right to intervene in family life. Social workers, police, and judges could apprehend, detain, interrogate, institutionalize, and adopt out children without the knowledge or consent of their parents.

Just as there were more slaves than masters on the plantations, there were also more workers than bosses in the cities. Breaking up families helps to control the urban working class. The *Truancy Act* of 1853 allowed children to be arrested simply for being poor. That same year, the Reverend Charles Loring Brace founded the New York Children's Aid Society (CAS) to serve as a "moral and physical disinfectant" against the "multitude of…boys swarming now in every foul alley and low street" who might "come to know their power and use it." During its first 25 years, the CAS received government funding to remove more than 50,000 poor and homeless children from New York City and place them on farms where they were commonly mistreated and overworked.

Children sent to reform schools were seldom returned home. Parents seeking to retrieve their children were told that they had been given away. An 1864 Massachusetts state report noted, "We have felt it our duty generally to decline giving [children] up to their parents and have placed as many of them as we could with farmers and mechanics." The *Bill of Rights* did not apply to minors until 1967, when the Supreme Court granted them the right to due process.

Breaking up families

State policies assume that those needing government support must be lazy, losers, or cheats. Condemning the poor serves three functions: to blame poverty on the victim not the system; to justify withholding resources from the working class; and to increase State control over society. The American child welfare system serves all three functions.

> The underlying philosophy of the present child welfare system is that *all* families *should* be able to function adequately without the assistance of society…and that failure to perform the parental role without such assistance is indicative of individual pathology.[113]

In America, poverty is considered proof of parental incompetence. It is assumed that parents who care about their kids will find a way to take care of them. In reality, as previous chapters explained, families are pushed into crisis by social policies that overburden them on the one hand and deprive them on the other. To prevent families from seeking government assistance, those that do risk losing their children. Let's look at how this happens.

The capitalist system does not provide social support to all. To emphasize that support is not a right, a great deal of effort is spent to distinguish the worthy poor, who presumably deserve relief, from the unworthy poor who do not. The profession of social work was developed for this purpose. Screening families for eligibility gives the State a licence to inspect homes, scrutinize lives, and judge parenting practices. It is assumed that the poor are trying to cheat the system. It is never acknowledged that the system is looking for ways to cheat the poor.

Social workers are under pressure to separate children from parents. Failing to remove a child who is later harmed can cause a social worker to be disciplined, demoted, fired, and prosecuted. Even when there is no evidence of harm in the present, social workers are urged to remove children *on the possibility of harm in the future*. To make this decision easier, there is no penalty for wrongfully removing children from their families.

Better-off families in crisis can avoid police and social workers because they can pay (or have insurance that pays) for physicians, therapists, counselors, childcare, and so on. In contrast, poor families who are temporarily unable to look after their children can lose them to foster care. The courts view "failing to provide for a child" as a parental crime that is equivalent to physical or sexual abuse. Portraying poverty as a parental deficit allows the state to remove children from any poor family. *In America, poverty, not maltreatment, is the single most important factor in the decision to place a child in foster care.* According to the National Coalition for Child Protection Reform,

> Far more common than a child who comes into care because he was beaten are children who come into foster care because the food stamps ran out or because an illness went untreated after parents were kicked off Medicaid or because a single mother trying to stay off welfare could not provide adequate supervision while she worked…some children are taken just because their parents are down on their luck, out of work, or unable to provide adequate shelter.[114]

The State pays for respite care for foster parents of children with serious mental illness. It does not provide this same relief for biological parents. Some parents with sick children become so desperate that they falsely claim to be neglectful or abusive, so their children can enter foster care and receive state-funded medical treatment. A federal investigation found that, in 19 states, parents had relinquished custody of more than 12,700 children so they could receive mental health services. Parents who give up their children lose any say over where the child is sent or what kind of treatment is provided. Tragically, despite their parents' sacrifice, many of these children get no treatment at all.

In 2003, Congressional investigators found that 15,000 children with psychiatric disorders, some as young as seven years old, were incarcerated in juvenile detention centers because mental health facilities were unavailable. A full eight percent of all youth in detention centers were mentally-ill youngsters waiting for treatment.

Biological parents have parental rights that guarantee them access to their children, even after divorce. Parents of children in foster care enjoy no such protection. On the contrary, seemingly endless bureaucratic hurdles prevent families from reuniting. The courts assume that parents with children in foster care are incompetent until proven otherwise. Psychologists and psychiatrists probe them for character flaws. They must prove they are free of addiction. If they are working, they must have approved child care arrangements. The State imposes housing requirements that discriminate against the poor — a separate bedroom for the parent(s) and different bedrooms for male and female children. At the same time, the State does not provide addiction treatment, accessible childcare, or affordable housing. Roberts points out that

> Inadequate housing is frequently at the center of caseworkers' decisions to place children in foster care…children from families with housing problems are also more likely to stay in the system longer…The court-appointed administrator of the District of Columbia's foster care system determined that as many as half of the children in foster care could be immediately re-united with their parents if housing problems were resolved.[115]

When reunification takes too long, the courts can permanently terminate the parents' rights. *Delay in reunification, not parental fitness, is the most common reason why parents lose all legal rights to their children.*

Some prominent psychiatrists support breaking the bonds between parents and their children who are in foster care. In *Beyond the Best Interests of the Child*, Anna Freud (Sigmund Freud's daughter) contends that children can form such strong psychological bonds with their foster parents that serious psychological damage can result when these children are returned to their original families. The bonds that children maintain with their original parents are treated as having little or no value. The option of preserving the child's relationship with both sets of parents is not even considered.

On the basis of such "expert" advice, American courts regularly deny competent parents custody of their children in favor of "continuity of care" by foster parents. One Iowa court ruled that a strong bond between parent and child is not an overriding factor in considering whether or not to terminate all parental rights, in effect preventing the birth parents from ever seeing or communicating with their children again. Severing parental rights is supposed to help move foster children into permanent homes. In reality, the number of children available for adoption far exceeds the number of people looking to adopt.

Assault on the Black family

Racism and poverty intersect in the American child welfare system. Proportionally, there are three times as many Black children in foster care as there are in the population as a whole. In contrast, there are half as many White children in foster care as there are in the population as a whole. A government-sponsored fact sheet states, "No differences have been found in the incidence of child abuse and neglect according to racial group." If there is no difference in the rate at which Black and White parents mistreat their children, why are so many more Black children removed from their families?

Because of racism, Black American families suffer less education, higher unemployment, lower wages, more medical problems, and less access to medical care than White families. About 54 percent of Black children live below the poverty line, compared with 15 percent of White children. As a result, Blacks are more likely to live in substandard housing in unsafe neighborhoods.

Racism also causes Black parents to be scrutinized more often and more harshly than White parents. Black families are more likely to be reported than White families when their children suffer the same injuries. A Florida study of pregnant women found that the rate of drug abuse was similar for Black and White women; yet 10 times as many Black women were reported to government authorities for drug use.

> Black children were more likely to be placed in foster care even when their parents were employed, drug-free, and not receiving welfare; even when they came from small families and safe neighborhoods; and even when they had no disabilities or mental health problems.[116]

Roberts points out that, once Black children are removed from their families, they "remain in foster care longer, are moved more often, receive fewer services, and are less likely to be either returned home or adopted than other children." The double whammy of racism and poverty results in a predominately Black foster care population. In New York City, one of every 22 Black children is in foster care. In Central Harlem, one of every 10 children is in foster care. In Chicago, 95 percent of the children in foster care are Black. Almost all Chicago families who have lost their children are clustered in two zip code areas that are very poor and almost exclusively Black.

Roberts concludes, "Placing so many Black children in the state's custody implements the quintessential racist insult—that Black people are incapable of governing themselves and need white supervision." Malcolm X, whose own family was dismembered by the welfare system, called it "Nothing but legal, modern slavery—however kindly intentioned."

Saving children?

The strongest argument for taking children from their families is to remove them from danger. How much harm does the child welfare system prevent? Roberts explains that,

> For every child placed in foster care because she was malnourished or unsupervised, there are hundreds more who suffer the same deprivations… The system haphazardly picks out a fraction of families to bludgeon, while it leaves untouched the conditions that are really most damaging to children.[117]

In 2003, eighteen percent of American children were living below the official poverty level of $18,810 for a family of four. According to the U.S. Department of Health and Human Services, poverty is the most important cause of child maltreatment. Child abuse is 14 times more common and child neglect is 44 times more common in families with annual incomes under $15,000 compared with families whose annual incomes are over $30,000. The best way to prevent child maltreatment would be to raise family incomes and improve social services. However, the child welfare system emphasizes punishment over support. As a result, parents who fear that they might harm or be unable to provide sufficiently for their children are *less likely* to seek help. Concerned relatives will hesitate to contact an agency if doing so might result in the loss of the child.

When case workers are kept busy supervising families simply because they are poor, the children who are in real danger of being harmed or killed by their parents are more likely to fall through the cracks. The recommended standard for social workers is no more than 17 cases at any one time. In Newark, New Jersey, a seven-year-old boy died and his two brothers were found almost starved. The worker assigned to that family had over 100 children in her caseload and was working nights, weekends, and holidays.

Sometimes children need to be removed from dangerous families, and the State does provide some children with safer places. However, even more are removed from the frying pan and dumped into the fire. Imagine the agony of parents whose children are taken from them, supposedly for their own good, only to die in foster care.

In Los Angeles, the pipes in a grandmother's rented house burst, flooding the basement and making the home a health hazard. Instead of helping the family find another place to live, child protective workers take away the granddaughter and place her in foster care. She dies there, allegedly killed by her foster mother. The child welfare agency that would spend nothing to move the family offers $5,000 for the funeral.[118]

Social agencies are quick to prosecute birth parents for child abuse, while ignoring the more serious problem of foster-parent abuse.

National data on child abuse fatalities show that a child is twice as likely to die of abuse in foster care as in the general population…A study of reported abuse in Baltimore found the rate of 'substantiated' cases of sexual abuse in foster care more than four times higher than the rate in the general population.[119]

State-run group homes and orphanages have a horrific record of child neglect and abuse. A 1997 Los Angeles County Grand Jury report found that "Many of the nearly 5,000 foster children housed in Los Angeles County group homes are physically abused and drugged excessively while being forced to live without proper food, clothing, education, and counseling." An investigation of all 50 states did not find one that was fully compliant with federal standards for protecting children.

The State is an incompetent parent. A 1991 national survey found that 46 percent of former foster children did not complete high school and 51 percent were unemployed. More recent studies have found similar results. Thirty percent of the nation's homeless population were in foster care as children. The welfare of children should not be entrusted to a State that impoverishes families and then removes their children, only to neglect, abuse, and abandon them.

Poverty is the greatest source of childhood trauma. In the United States, 13 million children and youth live in poverty. Seventeen percent of American children do not receive adequate nutrition. The State gives billions of dollars in tax cuts to the capitalist class, while turning children into the largest destitute group in the nation. For that reason alone, the State is the single greatest perpetrator of child abuse.

Welfare as social control

In *The Children of Neglect*, Margaret Smith and Rowena Fong conclude,

The traditional view of both poverty and child neglect is that they are due to personal problems of parents, and therefore, not the responsibility of the community to resolve…thus children are condemned to live in poverty because the child welfare system is about the culpability of parents, not about providing resources to resolve the issues associated with poverty.[120]

The *Social Security Act* of 1935 entitled poor families to social assistance as long as they needed it. In 1996, the Clinton administration placed a time-limit on how long anyone could get welfare, regardless of need. Families that exceed their time-limit and become destitute can lose their children to foster care. Ironically, the State pays foster parents twice as much to look after other people's children as it pays biological parents to look after their own children.

The Clinton welfare laws also require welfare recipients to find waged work. Most women on welfare are single parents, yet the State provides no funds for childcare. In New York City, most of the families investigated for "lack of supervision" had no access to affordable childcare.

In Genesee County, Michigan, which includes Flint, the foster-care population has doubled…One of the main reasons is they're removing children from women forced to leave their children with unsuitable caretakers while they go to jobs they must take under the state's welfare laws.[121]

The State won't provide adequate welfare because the capitalist class needs a low-waged work-force, and people won't work for low wages if social assistance is available. Most importantly, the working class cannot be allowed to think that it has a *right* to anything. As a result, the State spends more money to break up families than it spends to keep them together.

…a 1998 Michigan Auditor General report found that the average cost for family preservation services was $4,367 per family, compared to the annual cost per child of $12,384 for foster care and $56,206 for institutional care.[122]

Welfare policies are not designed to help people; they are designed to help the State control "the dangerous classes." The threat of losing financial support instills fear and submission in the needy. Funding religious organizations to deliver aid to the poor adds another layer of control, forcing people to submit to religious doctrine as a condition of receiving support. While welfare polices target the poorest families, the entire working class gets the message — Don't expect any help from the State.

Teach them their place

Education as social control goes back to slavery days, when it was a crime to teach Black slaves to read and write. By the time slavery was legally abolished in 1863, more than 95 percent of Blacks were illiterate. Newly-freed slaves were hungry to learn.

Few were too young, and none were too old, to make the attempt to learn. As fast as any kind of teachers could be secured, not only were day-schools filled, but night schools as well…Day-school, night-school, and Sunday-school were always crowded and often many had to be turned away for want of room…[123]

Teachers flooded down from the North; however, the Southern establishment tried to block their efforts. "In the interior of Texas, Alabama, Mississippi, Louisiana, Kentucky, Tennessee and Maryland…Negroes were disposed of their school buildings, teachers were not allowed to enter upon their duties and churches and schoolhouses were sometimes burned."

The Black civil rights' movement won the legal integration of public schools in the 1950's; however, the employer's offensive has eroded that victory. As the courts lifted desegregation laws and attacked affirmative action, the proportion of Black students attending integrated schools dropped. In Chicago today, almost 90 percent of public school students are Black or Latino. In *The Shame of the Nation: The Restoration of Apartheid Schooling in America,* Jonathan Kozol explains how education-funding policies perpetuate a race-segregated school system. Education is funded primarily through property taxes, so schools in poor neighborhoods are starved for money, teachers, books, and other resources. Because of racism, Blacks and Hispanics are more likely to live in poor neigborhoods. A vicious cycle is created where Black and Latino children are deprived of educational opportunities that could help them get better-paying jobs as adults.

The education system is designed to keep all working-class people down. Before industrial capitalism, young people learned by watching and listening, by exploring the world on their own, by apprenticing themselves to those who had something to teach them, and by trial and error. This kind of learning—directed by curiosity and embedded in society—is incompatible with a work system that demands repetitive movements and unquestioning obedience.

In *The Underground History of American Education,* John Taylor Gatto explains that the modern school system developed in response to working-class rebellions that shook capitalism in 1848 and again after World War I. The ruling class needed a school system to keep the masses in their place—working for capitalism. This was no secret conspiracy. President Woodrow Wilson announced,

> We want one class to have a liberal education. We want another class, a very much larger class of necessity, to forego the privilege of a liberal education and fit themselves to perform specific difficult manual tasks.[124]

To preserve the class system, schools teach children only what they will need to do their future jobs *and no more*. A few creative critical thinkers are needed at the management and professional level; however, the majority are expected to work in low-waged, mind-numbing jobs. These students cannot be allowed to develop their potential. William Torrey Harris, U.S. Commissioner of Education between 1889 and 1906, writes approvingly,

> Ninety-nine [students] out of a hundred are automata, careful to walk in prescribed paths, careful to follow the prescribed custom. This is not an accident but the result of substantial education, which, scientifically defined, is the subsumption of the individual.[125]

The de-skilling of work has been accompanied by a rising rate of illiteracy. Based on American military testing, 98 percent of adult men could read or write in the 1930's. By World War II, this number had dropped to 96 percent. During the Korean war, the literacy rate declined to 81 percent. By 1973, only 73 percent of recruits for the Vietnam war had a minimal level of literacy. Literacy rates have fallen faster for Whites than for Blacks. Between 1940 and 1992, Black illiteracy doubled, while White illiteracy quadrupled.

A 1992 nation-wide survey conducted by the U.S. Department of Education found that 21 percent of the adult population did not have basic reading and writing skills, and eight million people were unable to perform even the simplest literacy tasks. A 2003 survey found that prose literacy among adults had fallen at every level of education. Is the school system failing? In *Dumbing Us Down: The Hidden Curriculum of Compulsory Schooling,* John Taylor Gatto quotes David Albert:

Schools are not failing. On the contrary, they are spectacularly successful in doing precisely what they are intended to do, and what they have been intended to do since their inception. The [school] system, perfected at places like the University of Chicago, Columbia Teachers College, Carnegie-Melon, and Harvard, and funded by the captains of industry, was explicitly set up to ensure a docile malleable workforce to meet the growing, changing demands of corporate capitalism.[116]

In *Savage Inequalities: Children in America's Schools,* Jonathan Kozol explains how working-class youth are denied education. Schools in more affluent areas can hire the best teachers and provide the most engaging learning experiences. Schools starved of funds cannot feed hungry minds. In some states, the difference between rich and poor schools is more than $2,000 per student per year.

The U.S. has one of the highest high-school dropout rates in the industrialized world. Only two-thirds of all students, and only half of minority students, graduate from high school. In New York City, only 18 percent of students, and nine percent of Black students, qualify for admission to college. These statistics are the result of a school system that preserves racial and class inequalities, providing just enough education to prepare children for their pre-determined roles in society. Youngsters naturally resent such unfairness. Kozol quotes a high-school student from the South Bronx.

Most of the students in this school won't go to college. Many of them will join the military. If there's a war, we have to fight. Why should I go to war and fight for opportunities I can't enjoy—for things rich people value, for their freedom, but I do not have that freedom and I can't go to their schools?[127]

What did you learn in school today?

In 1964, Tom Paxton wrote *What Did You Learn in School Today?,* a song that describes how schools create a distorted view of the world. History lessons highlight the deeds of "great men" and ignore the contributions of regular folks. The message is that ordinary people have nothing to offer society. Eleven-year-old Oliver Maynard-Langedijk recounts his experience:

I came into school and most of my friends had their backpacks on. I asked them where they were going, and they told me that it was a special kids' trip, to this comic book convention. The principal selected them. Most of them had something special about them. They were really quiet, or they were really, really, smart. I don't know. No one told me how they got to go. It made me feel left out. The other kids who didn't get to go felt the same as me. I was really mad, so I told my mom. Some other parents were mad too, so they all went to the principal and he said that they wouldn't do it again. But they did.

Oliver is learning that some people get special privileges and others don't and that you're not supposed to question this arrangement. He is learning that people in authority do as they please, that they cannot be trusted, and that parents are powerless against them. The school system is designed to teach these lessons to working-class children. A few students, those who seem eager to please the authorities, are groomed for professional training; the rest are channeled into low-paying jobs. To prepare youngsters for life under capitalism, schools must:

- discipline children to obey without question. (Think and do as we say)
- pressure children to conform to external expectations. (Be who we want you to be)
- accustom children to competition. (Fight over the crumbs we throw you)
- grade and sort children into categories based on future functions. (Adapt to the needs of the machine)
- groom a few students to manage and control the others. (Workers need managers)
- degrade and humiliate the rest for not being good enough. (You don't deserve better)

Schools teach dissociation

To accomplish the tasks listed above, schools must remove children from sources of independent learning. Huck Finn did not attend school, and look at the trouble he got into (freeing a slave and all). Homework ensures that children stay busy with school-directed chores. For most children, school attendance is compulsory—there is no choice.

Schools claim to help children fulfill their creative and intellectual potential. In practice, most schools are run like assembly-line factories without regard for students' needs. Government-mandated programs and standardized testing demand that every child learn the same thing at the same time in the same way. As one Los Angeles principal told his teachers, "When I stand in the hallway, I should be able to hear all fourth grade teachers saying the same thing. Do not deviate from the scripted program and do not fall behind in the pacing plan."[128]

To condition them for the workplace, students are trained to obey the clock. Bells ring periodically to signal a change of station. At the ring of the bell, students must drop what they are doing and move to the next classroom. No thought, conversation, or project can continue beyond the time allotted. When concentration is continually interrupted, only now matters. Repeated disengagements of this kind teach children not to think too long or care too much about anything. Television re-enforces the immediate and the temporary. Politicians appreciate voters who don't recall past betrayals.

Schools promote dissociation when they divide subjects into arbitrary categories with no seeming connection, divorce facts from their historical context, and make no effort to relate material to the child's world. Large numbers of students in each classroom keep teachers busy enforcing discipline instead of responding to students' individual needs.

Schools teach children to rely on and take direction only from experts. Students confined in age-segregated classrooms can neither learn from older children, nor teach younger ones. They must sit quietly and not talk to one another. Only the teacher is presumed to have anything important to say.

Students are not allowed to speak, to move from their seats, or to go to the toilet without permission. "Big Brother" surveillance reinforces authoritarian control. In 2002, three-quarters of the 950 new public schools that opened across America were equipped with spy cameras. Continual electronic monitoring of classrooms and corridors sends the message that youngsters cannot be trusted.

Schools enforce the rules that govern male and female behavior. Males are shamed for being quiet or emotional, while females are shamed for being loud or aggressive. Males are groomed to act tough and disdain everything female, while females are pressured to look sexy and defer to males. No ambiguity is tolerated. Rigid sex-role expectations keep children focused on their "performance." The more they censor themselves, the less they relate to each other in genuine ways. These rigid sex roles, that are reinforced throughout life, block compassion, prevent intimacy, and contribute to marriage break-down.

Schools teach bigotry and intolerance. The Human Rights Watch publication, *Hatred in the Hallways: Violence and Discrimination against Lesbian, Gay, Bisexual and Transgender Students in U.S. Schools,* explains how "more than two million school age youth in the United States who are different from the majority of their peers soon learn that the principle of equality does not apply to them." In one Iowa school, gay students reported hearing anti-gay epithets about every seven minutes. The report condemns

> the abject failure of the United States government to protect lesbian, gay, bisexual, and transgender youth who attend public schools from harassment and violence. Government at the local, state, and federal levels has refused to dismantle the laws and policies and to eliminate the practices that effectively discriminate against these youth.[129]

Bullying 101

A 1998 survey of more than 15,500 public- and private-school students in grades six through ten found that 40 percent of boys and 30 percent of girls had been bullied in school. About half of the boys and one third of the girls reported that they bullied others. Most were bullies and victims at different times. Why is bullying so common among young people?

Children learn by mimicking adults. Schoolyard bullying fits with a world where might makes right (regardless of what adults say). In response to the 1999 shooting at Columbine High School, President Bill Clinton pleaded on national television, "We must teach our children to resolve their differences with words, not weapons." While the president was preaching non-violence, the U.S. military was bombing Yugoslavia.

Children are keen observers, and they copy what adults do. In 2002, a bystander videotaped four police officers beat a handcuffed Black teenager, drag him along the ground and slam him against a police car. What provoked this savage attack? Sixteen-year-old Donovan Jackson was "slightly built," and had hearing and speech problems. It seems that the officers became enraged when the youngster did not respond quickly enough to their verbal commands.

Actions speak louder than words. A "do as I say, not as I do" model of behavior establishes two standards: one for those with more power and a different one for those with less power. The lesson is not lost on children who 'practice' the three roles of powerful persecutor, helpless victim, and passive bystander. These roles are acted out at home when parents attack each other and children feel helpless to intervene, when a parent singles out one child for punishment and forces the rest to watch, and when a parent punishes a child over the protests of the other parent. In the classroom, the teacher humiliates one student to discipline them all. In the workplace, management targets a few workers to control the rest. On a world scale, stronger nations destroy weaker ones to demonstrate their power. *Schoolyard bullying is a 'copycat' response to the bullying that saturates the child's world.*

The most effective response to bullying is for people to unite against it. Schools don't want youngsters learning this lesson. Eighth grader, Anthony Soltero, stood up to the bullies in March of 2006, when he helped to organize a student walkout in Los Angeles to protest anti-immigrant legislation. After the march, the school administrator threatened to send Antony to jail for three years and fine his mother $250. In despair, Anthony killed himself. To honor Soltero's commitment to justice, LA students organized another march for immigrant rights and called on students across the country to do the same.

Winners and losers

> I'm the king of the castle, and you're the dirty rascal

Every child has proudly chanted this ditty on top of the tallest mound and has also been humiliated by someone else who got there first. Through games and chants, pre-school children prepare for a world of competition. As soon as they enter school, they are immersed in win-lose situations. By means of tests, contests, games, and sports, teachers evaluate, rank, and sort youngsters, advancing the winners and de-grading the losers.

Schools hold out the promise that hard work will be rewarded, but win-lose competitions teach children otherwise. My six-year-old grandson loves to spell, and he works hard at it. One day he came home from school dejected. He had spelled two words wrong and was denied a gold star. His mother reassured him, but he remained sullen. After dinner, he hit his sister. When reprimanded, he began to howl and would not be consoled. Children have an innate sense of fairness and know when promises are not kept ("It's not fair!") My grandson was learning that hard work counts only when it results in perfection. There is no recognition for hard work or for learning through trial and error. He was treated like a loser and that made him angry. As Oliver observed, "You feel mad, so you take it out on other people."

Schools produce bored and angry children. When adults reward the efforts of only a few children, those who see their efforts ignored or belittled lose interest in learning. Children who cannot win at school will compensate by trying to win the recognition of their peers, often by defying the system that is excluding and humiliating them. "Uncooperative" and "misbehaving" children are like red flags that signal serious social problems.

When children have problems with school, teachers and parents are blamed. Teachers are squeezed between the needs of their students and the demands of the administration. If they provide engaging opportunities for children to learn, they are disciplined for not following the curriculum. If they impose the curriculum, they become the enemies of the students. Parents are treated like extensions of the school. They are supposed to "make" their children do homework and provide extra support for those who fall behind. When children rebel, parents are pressured to give them drugs to make them more compliant.

Say "yes" to our drugs

The school system neglects, oppresses, and humiliates children, and then labels those who rebel as sick or defective. The *Diagnostic and Statistical Manual of Mental Disorders (DSM)* considers child rebellion to be a sign of mental illness. Conduct Disorder and Oppositional Defiant Disorder are psychiatric diagnoses listed under the category of Disruptive Behavior Disorders. The following study exposed how absurd these diagnoses are.

In North Carolina, a gambling casino opened midway through an eight-year study of child psychiatric illness. Because the casino was owned by the First Nations, it paid each aboriginal family a financial bonus that rose every year. These payments elevated 14 percent of the families out of poverty, while 53 percent remained poor. Thirty-two percent of the families were not poor to begin with. Before the casino opened, the poor children had more than four times as many psychiatric symptoms as the children who had never been poor. After the casino opened, psychiatric symptoms among children who were no longer poor fell to the same level as children who had never been poor. In contrast, psychiatric symptoms remained high among the children who remained poor. Similar results were found in non-aboriginal children whose families moved out of poverty during the same period. Why would rising income levels solve child behavior problems?

Chapter 7 explained that all children have difficulty regulating emotions. At times, all children are impulsive, hyper-active, aggressive, and defiant. Supportive adults must teach children how to manage their feelings. Deprived and overly stressed parents cannot do this. The resulting child "misbehavior" signals a crisis in the family. Money does not solve all family problems; however, it can meet enough of the parents' needs so that they, in turn, can meet their children's needs. Unfortunately, society refuses to support families and drugs kids instead.

Cuts in funding for education, family support, and child services have led to an escalation in the number of children being prescribed psychiatric drugs. The psychiatric diagnosis of Attention Deficit Disorder (ADD)—also called Attention Deficit Hyperactivity Disorder (ADHD)—was created to permit doctors to drug children who act out in school. Drug prescriptions for school-aged children peak in September and drop in June—the duration of the school year. One program offered an alternative to drug treatment—a trained social worker met weekly at home and at school with children diagnosed with ADD and their parents. While they were participating in this program, none of the children needed medication. When funding for the program ended, all the children began to have problems and went back on medication.

The drugs most commonly prescribed for ADD are powerful stimulants, like amphetamines and methylphenidate [Ritalin]. According to the U.S. Drug Enforcement Administration,

> In clinical studies…neither animals nor humans can tell the difference between cocaine, amphetamine, or methylphenidate when they are administered the same way at comparable doses. In short, they produce effects that are nearly identical.[130]

Between 1991 and 1999, U.S. production of amphetamines increased more than 2,000 percent, and sales of methylphenidate increased nearly 500 percent. About 80 percent of all prescriptions for both these drugs are for children diagnosed with ADD. In some areas, one in four school children is taking these drugs. Twice as many boys are given drugs for ADD, compared with girls, who are more likely to be given anti-depressants. Every year, an estimated 500,000 American children are prescribed anti-depressant drugs. A national survey found that increasing numbers of children are also being prescribed anti-psychotic drugs that have been linked with serious health problems. In 1993, 275 children out of every 100,000 were taking these drugs. By 2002, the number had risen to 1,438 out of every 100,000 children. While politicians call for "a drug-free America," the nation's children are being drugged at an unprecedented rate.

The American Academy of Pediatrics estimates that between four and twelve percent of school-aged children suffer from ADD. It is more likely that politicians and bureaucrats are afflicted with ADD because they pay no attention to the harm caused by their slash-and-burn social policies. In contrast, children are fully aware of their suffering, and they protest in the only ways they can—with anger, agitation, anxiety, depression, and defiance.

Who hears the cries of our children? Teachers are tied to a restrictive curriculum and deprived of resources. Doctors prescribe drugs instead of protesting oppressive conditions. Courts force children to take mood-altering drugs. Parents who refuse to medicate their kids have been charged with child abuse and threatened with losing custody. When medication fails, there is always punishment.

School as prison

> We are breeding a generation of children who think they are criminals for the way they are being treated in school...School used to be a refuge. Now it's a lockdown environment. We are bringing the practices of criminal justice into the schools.
>
> Annette Fuentes

Today's youngsters are being criminalized by policies of "zero tolerance" in schools. Making mistakes is human and unavoidable, especially during adolescence, which is a time to explore and experiment. By forcing youngsters into behavioral strait-jackets, zero-tolerance policies invite rebellion, beginning a cycle of punishment and defiance that turns children into criminals. Students in Texas can be suspended for "cheating, violating dress codes, horseplay, excessive noise and failure to bring homework to class." Because student suspensions are reported to the county juvenile justice board, a child could be saddled with a criminal record for being rowdy. In 2003, journalist Annette Fuentes investigated the impact of zero-tolerance policies in public schools.

> Every year, more than 3 million students...are suspended and nearly 100,000 more are expelled, from kindergarten through twelfth grade. Of those, untold thousands...face police action for disciplinary problems that were previously handled in school, because forty-one states now require that certain acts committed in school be reported to the police.[131]

Boys are the primary targets, and Black males are singled out. Even though they do not break the rules more often, two to three times more Black students than White students are suspended from school.

> African-American students are 17 percent of the entire public school population but account for 34 percent of all out-of-school suspensions and 30 percent of expulsions. White students, by contrast, are 62 percent of the student population but account for 48 percent of out-of-school suspensions and 49 percent of expulsions.[132]

Zero-tolerance policies are enforced by police, police dogs, and metal detectors in schools that feel like prisons. Public officials insist that such heavy-handedness is necessary to prevent youth crime. In fact, rates of school violence are much lower now than when the parents of today's youth were in school. There is only a one-in-two-million chance of anyone being killed at school. Seventy-five percent of all murders of youngsters under age 18 are committed by adults. One would never know this from the media.

Demonizing youth

Portraying youngsters as criminals helps to justify more police, more prisons, and more social control. In 1995, John DiIulio of Princeton University wrote, "The Coming of the Super-Predators," in which he predicted the rise of an especially violent type of juvenile criminal. In 1996, Bill Bennett, co-chair of the Council on Crime in America predicted that "America is a ticking violent crime bomb. Rates of violent juvenile crime and weapons offenses have been increasing dramatically and by the year 2000 could spiral out of control."

In 1997, Florida Congressman William McCollum stated that today's youth are "the most dangerous criminals on the face of the Earth." The facts said otherwise. Crimes committed by young people had been falling for years. According to FBI statistics, in 1999 (the year of the Columbine High School shooting) incidents of school violence and juvenile violent crime had hit their lowest level in twenty years. There had been an increase in youth embezzlement. Perhaps DiIulio should have titled his report: "The Coming of the Super-Embezzlers," but people might have thought he was referring to Corporate America.

In "The Myth of the Grade-School Murderer," Mike Males provides the following statistics.

> In raw numbers, about 60 grade-school kids were arrested every year for homicide during the 1960's, 70 per year during the 1970's, 40 per year in the 1980's and 1990's, just 22 in 1998, and 17 in 1999. A grade-school child was arrested for murder once a week, on average, in the halcyon days of 1965 when *Father Knows Best* and "I Want to Hold Your Hand" ruled the airwaves. Today, when ultra-violent video games, slasher movies, gangsta rap, explicit TV, internet savagery, more poverty and family disarray, and automatic firearms are rampant, grade-school kids are 65 percent less likely to murder.[133]

Despite the facts, the mainstream media revel in the image of youngsters as dangerous criminals. A group of New York high-school students studied the *New York Times'* coverage of youth and crime. They found that over a three month period, 54 percent of the articles portrayed youth as perpetrators of crimes, and 44 percent portrayed them as victims of crime. A study of the *San Francisco Chronicle* found that stories on youth and crime portrayed youth as perpetrators almost 75 percent of the time. The hype against youngsters is so effective that when people hear the words "youth" and "violence," they think of youth as violent—not as victims of violence. (Test this yourself.) In reality, young people are victims of violent crime more than 12 times more often than they are perpetrators. The media all but ignores the estimated 2,000 deaths and 475,000 incidents of violence that adults inflict on youngsters every year.

What about teen drug abuse? Adults suffer far more drug abuse and addiction than young people. Eighty percent of drug overdose deaths occur in people over 30 years of age. Fewer than three percent of these deaths occur in people under age 20. Today's 40 year-olds are three times more likely to suffer serious illegal-drug abuse problems than today's 16 year-olds. Males concludes,

> Nearly all the imagined youth crises of today—from guns to heroin to suicide—are hallucinations… The fastest growing population in terms of drug abuse, criminal arrest for violent, property, and drug offenses, and imprisonment is persons aged 35 to 59, mostly white…Teens comprise perhaps 2 percent of America's drug problem, but 90 percent of the raging controversy over drug use. That is scapegoating.[134]

The flood of negative hype against youngsters has an impact. A 1999 survey found that most adults in the United States have disapproving and negative attitudes towards teenagers, *and most believe that the next generation will not make the world a better place.* By demonizing young people, the ruling class drives a wedge between the generations. When people lose faith in the future, they resign themselves to the way things are.

Child convicts

During the 1960's, schools and communities provided a variety of music, art, and athletic programs for young people. Since then, cuts to social programs have left many youngsters with no organized activities. As a result, 75 percent of teens report hanging out with their friends with nothing specific to do. No one thinks twice when adults hang out with their friends; however, teens are condemned for doing the same thing. When parents are working two and three jobs, peer acceptance becomes more important for young people. Instead of condemning the lack of social support for youngsters, politicians and the media condemn youth "gangs" and call for a crackdown on young people, including harsher penalties, trying youngsters as adults, and jailing them in adult prisons.

Between 1994 and 2000, the rate of juvenile violent crime *fell* 40 percent in the U.S., and the juvenile homicide rate *fell* 70 percent. Yet from 1990 to 1999, the number of incarcerated juveniles *rose* 74 percent. Juvenile detention centers are filled with children convicted of under-age drinking and smoking, truancy, breaking curfew, running away, and other minor offenses *that are illegal only for minors.*

The racism of the adult prison system extends to the youth prison system. Between 1988 and 1997, the rate of increase in detentions for Black youth was more than double the rate of increase for White youth. In 1997, judges sent 27 percent of Black delinquents to juvenile prisons compared with just 15 percent of White delinquents. Young people of color form one-third of the total youth population and two-thirds of youngsters in criminal detention.

A two-way conveyor belt runs between the foster care and prison systems. Dorothy Roberts observes, "The prison system supplies children to the child welfare system when it incarcerates their parents. The child welfare system then supplies young adults to the prison system when it abandons them after years in foster care." Foster children form fewer than two percent of the general population, yet they make up 15 percent of all the children in detention. In some states, the rates are much higher. In Connecticut, 75 percent of youth in the state criminal justice system had been in foster care. In Illinois, 80 percent of adult prisoners were in foster care as children.

All 50 states allow juveniles to be tried as adults. Young defendants are less likely to have adequate legal representation, with the result that youth sentences average 60 percent longer than adult sentences *for the same crimes*. In 1999, 12-year-old Lionel Tate killed his six-year-old playmate while showing her wrestling moves he had seen on television. He was tried as an adult and convicted of first-degree murder. When he was 13 years old, a Florida court sentenced him to life in prison. Young Black males like Tate are three times more likely to be charged with violent crimes, six times more likely to be tried in adult court, and seven times more likely to be sentenced to prison when they are tried as adults. Frightened, defenseless, subject to all manner of abuse, children in adult jails are up to eight times more likely to kill themselves than those held in juvenile detention centers. Nothing condemns capitalism more than its barbaric treatment of children.

The kids are all right!

Children are the future. Despite efforts to drive a wedge between the generations, most adults think that helping kids get a good start in life is extremely important—more important than preventing crime. Seventy-five percent of adults agree that "given enough help and attention, just about all kids can learn and succeed in school." Eighty-nine percent think that "given enough attention and the right kind of guidance, almost all teenagers can get back on track." This belief in youngsters runs counter to social policies that treat troubled youth as unmanageable and in need of harsh punishment.

Young people deserve support and admiration. What society gives them instead is neglect and abuse. The powers-that-be fear the energy and moral indignation of youth. Young people who organize against injustice are maligned by the media and assaulted by police. Some are even killed as a warning to the rest. When 23-year-old Carlo Guiliani was murdered by police during a demonstration in Genoa, Italy, his father praised him.

> Carlo was the exact opposite of what people have written about him. He was a boy of great generosity who was opposed to injustice. He read, he studied, he discussed, and he protested for his ideas. He always cared about others. And he always worked, if irregularly. He worked in the jobs that all young people are forced to take—in the black economy, without any security, without any rights. Carlo didn't accept the notion that eight leaders of the world should decide the life and deaths of hundreds of thousands of people.[135]

In the story of the emperor who wore no clothes, the adults admired the emperor's invisible threads, while the child could see that he was stark naked. When the child spoke up, the adults were faced with a choice. Should they confront the emperor or force the child to conform? The next chapter explains why it is necessary to take sides.

Summary

A society that oppresses the majority must also oppress its children. Children question everything and do not tolerate injustice. To maintain the status quo, the potential of youth to build a better world must be suppressed. Schools demand subservience to prepare most youngsters for low-waged work. Youth who rebel against their oppression are slandered by the media, torn from their families, drugged by doctors, brutalized by authorities, and incarcerated by the State. Despite efforts to drive a wedge between the generations, belief in the potential of youth remains strong and provides hope for the future.

Part Four

What Will it Take?

How will we find a way out?
We walk and talk with Babylon's mouth.

Faith Nolan

In her song, *How Will We Find a Way Out?*, Faith Nolan wonders how we can create a new society when every aspect of our lives is shaped by the old one. The answer to this question lies in the question itself. Those who are completely dominated do not question the way things are. Questioning reveals a desire for change. The last part of this book shows how the elements of a new society exist within the old, creating pressure for change.

At some point in their development, all species face problems that they must solve or they will perish. The most important question humanity faces today is the question of power — who will control society, the minority or the majority? Part Four explains how humanity can break free of capitalism and create a classless society based on equality, reciprocity, and cooperation.

- Chapter 13. *Decide Which Side You're On* explains why we must take sides.

- Chapter 14. *Seize the Power* shows how the working class could take control of society

- Chapter 15. *Beware the Middle Ground* reveals the danger of compromise.

- Chapter 16. *Claim the Surplus* outlines the prospect of producing for human need.

Chapter 13

Decide Which Side You're On

I don't believe it's possible to be neutral. The world is already moving in certain directions. Wars are going on. Children are starving. And to be neutral, to not take a stand in a situation like that is to collaborate with whatever is going on, to allow it to happen.

Howard Zinn

Why do we have to take sides? Wouldn't *everyone* benefit from an end to famine, preventable disease, pollution, and war? It's a lovely thought; however, class divisions exist because the two major classes have conflicting goals. The prime directive of the capitalist class is to Seize the Surplus at the expense of the working class, which can resist only by raising its own demand, Share. Because it is impossible to seize the surplus and share it at the same time, only one class can rule. Which one should it be? This chapter explores which class best represents the interests of humanity.

Defining class

Forty percent of Americans think that it's easier to move up the class ladder now than it was 30 years ago. America is described as the land of opportunity, where people can better themselves if they try hard enough. In reality, fewer American families improved their conditions over the 1980's compared with the 1970's, and even fewer moved up during the 1990's. Between 1980 and 2002, the proportion of U.S. income earned by 90 percent of the population fell, while the share going to the top 0.1 percent more than doubled.

Stories of individual success support the myth of upward mobility. A newspaper article titled "McJob can lead to career: McDonald's employee worked his way up" highlights Glen Steeves, a top McDonald's executive who started off as a restaurant worker. The message is that entry-level jobs can lead to professional careers for those with the right stuff. Lotteries use the same logic. Someone has to win; why not you? In reality, corporations hire few executives, and even fewer people win lotteries. Nevertheless, the lure of success draws many into a game that enriches only a few. No matter how hard people work, a hierarchical society cannot provide a decent life for all.

A 2005 investigation by the *New York Times* concluded, "class is still a powerful force in American life. Over the past three decades, it has come to play a greater, not lesser, role in important ways." Those who insist that "you can't reduce everything to class" fail to understand how profoundly class affects every aspect of life, from birth to death. Health and life-span decline as you go down the social ladder. Raising children is much easier with nannies, maids, and regular vacations. Retirement with health and wealth is very different from retirement with neither. The poor are hit harder by economic recessions and natural disasters. Earthquakes, hurricanes, and tidal waves that devastate trailer parks spare the sturdy homes of the wealthy.

The existence of inequality cannot be disputed. However, what "class" means is highly disputed. In the United States, those who are neither very rich nor very poor are generally assumed to be middle class. According to author Lillian Rubin,

> …all the talk about the middle class serves to obscure class realities rather than to clarify them…To acknowledge the existence of a working class challenges the long-held American fiction that this nation has conquered the invidious distinction of class. Instead, the political rhetoric supports and strengthens the myth that we are a classless society…[136]

Class is commonly defined by a person's income, wealth, education, and occupation. However, these categories are not useful. Unionized factory workers can make more money than middle-class professionals; top athletes can acquire larger fortunes than Pentagon Generals; and skilled workers can be more educated than small business owners. A gardener could be a unionized worker or own a business, and the category of "white collar" includes the filing clerk and the chartered accountant. Many people think that class is too complicated to define. It doesn't have to be.

Human beings are a social species, and class is a social relationship. Individual characteristics like a person's income, wealth, education, and occupation tell us nothing about a person's relationship to others and to society. We need a social definition of class.

Historically, people have created different social arrangements to secure the necessities of life and raise the next generation. In pre-class, egalitarian societies, everyone shared the work. Sharing the work means sharing the decisions about what will be done, how it will be done, and who will benefit. In class societies, most people work and a few live off their labor. The people at the top make the decisions and everyone else carries them out. The questions of work and power are central to both social arrangements.

A social-based definition of class would measure two variables: the control that people have over their work and the control that they have over other people's work. Using these criteria, we can divide modern society into three classes: the class that rules (the capitalist class); the class that obeys (the working class); and the class in between (the middle class). The following sections flesh out these definitions.

The class that rules

The capitalist class, also called the ruling class, has the most power because it owns or controls the natural resources required to create wealth, the labor process of creating wealth, and the wealth that is created (Seize the Surplus). Because it controls all of these things, the capitalist class decides the overall direction of society, determining what will be produced, how it will be produced, and who will have access to the resulting goods and services. The values of the capitalist class also dominate society. This class has the power to launch a war and to pay for that war by gutting social programs.

People in the capitalist class include CEOs of the largest corporations, presidents and directors of the largest universities and banks, and the highest-ranking politicians, government bureaucrats, judges, and military officers. Each nation has its own capitalist class, and together they form a global capitalist class.

Capitalists are in constant competition for capital (Compete or Die). Larger corporations swallow up smaller ones and grow larger. Stronger nations dominate weaker ones and grow stronger. Ceaseless competition has caused the ruling class to shrink in size while it grows in wealth and power. By 2005, one percent of people at the top of society owned one-third of America's financial wealth.

The class that obeys

The capitalist class controls the means of production; the working class sets it in motion. Although it creates all the wealth in society, the working class has the least power. People in the working class own no land, no factories, no machines, no businesses, nor any other means of making a living. (They can, of course, own personal property such as a home and a vehicle.) Workers can survive only by selling their ability to labor in exchange for a wage. They have no control over how they produce and what they produce. They have no control over the labor of others.

Some people argue that workers can buy into capitalism by purchasing company stocks. In fact, most stocks and bonds are owned by the top ten percent of the population. Furthermore, owning shares does not give people the power to control corporate decisions. Employees who owned shares in United Airlines were powerless to stop the restructuring that cost them their jobs, benefits, and pensions.

While the ruling class has shrunk over time, the working class has grown in size. More than half the global population is urban working class (with the next largest group being small farmers who are middle class because they own a little land). In the United States, about 80 percent of the population is working class — the vast majority. The working class includes clerks, receptionists, book-keepers, cleaners, janitors, cashiers, paramedics, miners, telephone operators, service technicians, mechanics, bank tellers, and also factory, farm, retail, restaurant, hotel, construction, and transport workers.

Over the past 50 years, the composition of the working class has changed. Rising productivity has made it possible to accumulate more surplus from fewer workers. Some of this surplus was used to expand the service sector — finance, transportation, hotels, restaurants, and the education, medical, and penal systems. This shift in capital caused the proportion of industrial workers to fall and the proportion of service workers to rise. Both industrial and service workers are working class. Neither group controls the conditions of its own work or the work of others. Workers' efforts to exert some control over their work through unions will be discussed later on.

The class in the middle

The middle class is the second largest social class. Forming about 20 percent of the North American population, the middle class sits between the two other classes, blending into the capitalist class at one end and the working class at the other end. People in the middle class have an intermediate level of power, having some control over their own work and some control over the work of others. The middle class owns or controls some means of production: the small farmer owns some land; the self-employed artisan owns some tools: the corner-store retailer buys and sells produce. Sections of the middle-class employ and exploit workers — on a small scale.

The 18th century middle class was composed primarily of small farmers and fishermen, artisans, entertainers, lower-level clergy, traders, and owners of small businesses. As capitalism developed, it concentrated capital in fewer hands, obliterating much of the traditional middle class. This process continues today. Giant agricultural corporations (agribusiness) swallow family farms, forcing people off their land and into the cities. Fast-food chains replace family restaurants. Factories flood the market with cheap, mass-produced goods, pushing skilled craftspeople to the fringe of the economy. With no family business to inherit, children of the traditional middle-class have gone to work for the same corporations that put their parents out of business. Some become middle-class managers and professionals.

Modern industry has expanded the role of the salaried professional. The owner of a small factory can personally direct every worker. In large industries, many supervisors are needed to oversee the work of hundreds or thousands of workers. Supervision is needed because bosses and workers have opposite goals. Bosses want workers to produce as much as possible to boost profits. Workers want to slow down to preserve their health. Bosses want to lower wages to cut costs. Workers want higher wages so they can pay their bills. Because the capitalist can stay in business only by forcing the worker to produce more, and to surrender more of the value of what she produces, the worker will always resist producing for the capitalist. The job of middle-managers is to *impose* the will of the boss on the workers—to make sure that workers never think they have the right or the ability to control what happens in the workplace.

The capitalist also needs middle-class financial, legal, scientific, design, and technical experts to find ways to increase profits. While ordinary workers are micro-managed, salaried professionals are encouraged to think creatively and act independently, *within the limits set by the boss.* (How professionals are trained to do this is explained later on.)

Middle-class managers, supervisors, foremen, overseers, and professionals can be distinguished from waged workers by the amount of control they exercise in the workplace. A unionized electrician on a construction site could be more educated, more skilled, and make more money than the site supervisor. However, the supervisor tells the electrician what to do. The supervisor has the power to schedule work, and some have the power to hire and fire. In turn, the supervisor is under the control of the big boss and keeps his job only as long as he carries out the boss's wishes.

The grey zones

An indeterminate number of people inhabit the two grey zones on either edge of the middle class. The zone between the middle and ruling classes includes members of the ruling class who perform upper-level managerial functions, and upper-level managers who are occasionally invited to make big decisions. This layer is of little interest to our discussion.

There is a much larger grey zone between the middle and working classes. At the one end are middle-class professionals whose degraded working conditions resemble industrial assembly lines. Physicians working for Health Management Organizations (HMOs) are permitted to order only those tests and provide only those treatments that the employer approves. By removing their decision-making functions, HMOs force doctors into working-class conditions. In response, thousands of doctors have joined unions and organized collective bargaining units recognized by the National Labor Relations Board.

At the other end of the zone between the working and middle classes are waged workers with small businesses on the side, like the book-keeper with a weekend gig in a dance band. People in the grey zone may alternate between working for others and working for themselves. Consider the restaurant worker with a small catering business on the side. If her business does well, she may hire an apprentice and move into the middle class. If she drops her business to work full time at the restaurant, she moves back into the working class. The prostitute who works for herself is middle class. The one who works for a pimp is working class. When it is difficult to decide if someone is middle or working class, that person is most likely in the grey zone.

Blended-class families are formed when middle- and working-class people marry: a doctor marries a secretary; a musician marries a truck driver; a minister marries a miner. Changes of fortune also create blended-class families: the disbarred lawyer takes a job at the post-office and the steel-worker's daughter goes to medical school.

The grey zone also includes workers who perform managerial functions. These include salaried social workers, nurses, grade-school teachers, prison guards, and active duty soldiers. All are working class because they have little or no control over their own working conditions. At the same time, their jobs give them some control over others. Chapter 12 described how social workers can support or destroy the lives of people who have even less power.

Teachers have power over their students, grooming some for success and abandoning others to failure. Nevertheless, most teachers are working class. They are restricted to an established curriculum and, like their students, their days are regimented to the sound of the bell. In contrast, middle-class university professors generally have more freedom to choose what they teach and how they teach it. Professors also exercise power over other workers, in particular graduate-student teaching assistants. Grade-school teachers have no authority over other school employees.

Ordinary soldiers are working class because they have absolutely no control over the conditions of their work. At the same time, the active-duty soldier has a middle-class function—to control others. Soldiers are not in the same class as police officers. The working-class soldier is drilled to follow commands without thinking, while the police officer is a middle-class professional who is trusted by the higher-ups to know who to target, who to charge, who can be roughed up, and whose life has less value.

When workers who perform managerial functions rebel, they can really rattle the system. Under normal conditions, teachers indoctrinate their students with the values of capitalism. When teachers press for higher wages and better working conditions, they become role models for rebellion. The same holds true for social workers who demand more funds for social services. Soldiers who switch sides can stop wars and topple ruling classes. In 1917, Russian soldiers joined with other workers to pull Russia out of the first World War. A few months later, German sailors sparked a revolution that forced the Kaiser to abdicate and effectively ended the war. In the 1960's, rebelling U.S. soldiers in Vietnam dealt a serious blow to the American Empire.

Unions

Workers form unions to protect themselves from the insatiable demands of employers. A union worker is more likely to have medical coverage, pension benefits, and protection from sexual harassment and wrongful discipline or dismissal. Compared with states with fewer unions, states with more unions enjoy higher wages, more medical coverage, higher life expectancy, lower infant mortality, less poverty, more money for education, and lower workplace fatalities *for everyone*. Patients also do better in hospitals where nurses are unionized. Sadly, the unions of today are a pale shadow of what they used to be. Genora (Johnson) Dollinger describes the confidence of auto workers who organized General Motors in 1937:

Every time something came up that couldn't be settled, or the workers got a tough foreman who told them, "Go to hell," they'd shut down the line. The men were so cocky, they'd say to the foremen, "You don't like it?" They'd push the button and shut down the line.[137]

The power of organized workers frightened and enraged the capitalists, who realized that the only way to tame the unions was to gut them of socialists and other class-conscious militants. With the support of President Roosevelt, employers began to attack unions and union organizers. In 1938 Congress formed the Special Committee on Un-American Activities to rout out "radical subversives." In *Subterranean Fire: A History of Working-Class Radicalism in the United States,* Sharon Smith explains how conservative union officials worked hand-in-hand with the State to drive socialists out of the unions. Stripped of their fighting core, unions were transformed from fighting organizations controlled by workers to bureaucratic organizations run by middle-class professionals.

There are middle-class unions composed of police, doctors, and other professionals. However, most unions function within the grey zone between the classes. *Unions are working-class organizations of self-defense and also part of the management system of capitalism.* Most ordinary union members (known as the rank-and-file) are working class people, while union officials are mostly middle-class professionals. The job of these officials is to mediate between bosses and workers to negotiate the terms on which workers will be exploited.

Most unions have a large working-class base and a much smaller middle-class leadership. Workers who get a few hours off work to conduct union business are still working class. Even some full-time union organizers are working class because they are kept on a short leash by union officials. Other organizers are trusted to know the rules of the game and to make the right decisions, like any other middle-class professional. The higher someone rises in the union hierarchy, the more managerial functions that person performs. Union officials with the power to hire and fire clerical and other support staff are solidly middle class. Top union officials who help the government set policy are upper-middle class.

Union officials (also called union bureaucrats) have the same goal as employers—keeping the company in business—and that means keeping it competitive. The website of America's largest union organization, the AFL-CIO, boasts that "Unions Are Good for Productivity."

> Unions increase productivity, according to most recent studies. The voice that union members have on the job—sharing in decision-making about promotions and work and production standards—increases productivity and improves management practices. Better training, lower turnover and longer tenure also make union workers [up to 38 percent] more productive.[138]

In reality, productivity can increase only by reducing the amount of surplus that goes to the workers who produce it. From the 1940's through to the 1960's, unions supported management drives to raise productivity and profits, bargaining away workers' control on the job in exchange for higher wages and better benefits. This changed in the 1970's, when employers declared war on the working class to push productivity even higher. Most unions did not fight back because the tradition of fighting back was lost when militants were purged from the unions.

Union officials agreed to help employers "downsize" and "restructure" in the hope that if workers helped companies to become more profitable, companies would reciprocate by rewarding workers for their sacrifice. Unfortunately, capitalism is not based on reciprocity but on Seize the Surplus. The more profits rose, the more employers demanded. At each step of this process, union officials protested loudly and then conceded to the employers' demands. As the economy boomed, workers' conditions deteriorated. Some unions did fight.

In December of 1984, members of the United Food and Commercial Workers Union (UFCW) decided not to accept wage cuts at their meat-packing plant in Minnesota. In *Hard-Pressed in the Heartland: The Hormel Strike and the Future of the Labor Movement,* Peter Rachleff writes,

> Over the first half of the 1980's, no local had been able to stand up to the corporate pressure for concessions or the international union's acquiescence. Local P-9's willingness to take a stand thus threatened the international union nearly as much as it threatened the Hormel corporation…P-9 quickly came to symbolize democracy and membership participation, a willingness to oppose corporate demands for concessions, regardless of international union agendas or strategies, and a form of "horizontal" solidarity that threatened the vertical, bureaucratic hold that international unions exercised over their locals. As thousands of workers poured into Austin to express their support, we likened their experience to "catching a virus" from P-9. But the UFCW and the AFL-CIO were determined to prevent the spread of this virus.[139]

In May of 1985, the Executive Board of the UFCW removed the elected leadership of Local P-9, and put a union bureaucrat in charge. As the new Local president, Joe Hansen signed Hormel's concession contract. While conditions in the meat-packing industry continue to deteriorate, Hansen defends his role in the P-9 strike, stating, "It's because of me that there's still a union in that plant." In fact, concession contracts do not preserve unions. By 2005, the percentage of private-sector workers in unions had dropped to under eight percent, the lowest rate in more than a century.

In 2005, the crisis in the labor movement provoked a split in the AFL-CIO. While both sides of this split pledged to organize more workers into unions, neither is committed to fighting the employers. Strikes deplete union funds and risk driving the employer out of business or out of town. As long as union officials accept the logic of capitalism, they will inevitably side with management to put profits before human needs.

In any sane world, a social system that could not function without eroding people's living standards would be replaced. Instead of taking that road, union bureaucrats lower their members' expectations of what can be achieved. The union bureaucracy is a managerial class that fears rousing the rank-and-file. At times, union officials will talk tough and even lead militant struggles, only to crumble under employer pressure. When workers rebel in wildcat strikes, union officials to everything they can to get workers back on the job.

Some people think that unions have become so corrupt and useless that they are not worth defending. This is a big mistake. The capitalist class continues to attack unions because they stand in the way of bosses having complete control over the workplace. Workers need unions, and unions must be defended against those who would destroy them. The best defense would be for workers to take collective control of their unions and transform them into fighting organizations that can win real gains for working people (more on this later). A few solid labor victories would energize the entire working class and raise expectations of what can be achieved.

Unions and the State

Just as union officials partner with employers to manage the workplace, America's top union bureaucrats partner with the American State to manage the world. Without the awareness or consent of their members, top executives in the AFL-CIO have helped to overthrow democratically-elected governments, prop up anti-union dictators, and support right-wing unions against progressive governments. Kim Scipes found that,

> Before the First World War…the American Federation of Labor engaged in counteracting revolutionary forces in Mexico during that country's revolution, actively worked to support and defend U.S. government participation in the First World War, and then led the charge within U.S. foreign policy circles against the Bolshevik Revolution in Russia…The AFL-CIO established its own Latin American operation in 1962, the American Institute for Free Labor Development to better respond to "challenges" within the region. Among other activities, AIFLD helped lay the groundwork for the military coups against democratically-elected governments in Guatemala in 1954, Brazil in 1964 and Chile in 1973…These efforts in Latin America were paralleled in Africa and Asia.[140]

In 1999, the Advisory Committee on Labor Diplomacy (ACLD) was established as a forum for top labor leaders to advise the federal government. Secretary of State Madeleine Albright addressed one ACLD meeting,

> When you undertook your lives as labor leaders…becoming a part of the U.S. Government may have not have been something that you intended…but I do think it has been a very important partnership. I think that is the best way to describe it.[141]

Sections of the labor movement have protested union support for U.S. imperialism. The California Federation of Labor publicly criticized the AFL-CIO for backing right-wing organizations that tried to oust Venezuela's elected President Hugo Chávez. The *class conflict* between union officials and rank-and-file workers is expressed in this statement from the South Bay (California) Labor Council,

> There's no solidarity when labor becomes a go-between, laundering funds and resources from the Bush administration and passing them to groups abroad. That role is more appropriate for government agents—agents of empire…We believe that international labor solidarity must come from the heart of the workers in one country to the heart of workers in another country—a…reciprocal relationship.[142]

Class and consciousness

The capitalist class benefits from exploiting the working class. The working class benefits when it resists the capitalist class. The middle class vacillates, supporting one class and then the other, or both at the same time. The question immediately arises: if the working class is the majority of society, creating all the wealth of society, why does it allow the capitalist class to exploit it? Part 3 explained how the capitalist class imposes its will on society: through outright lies; by blaming the victim; through divide and rule; and by assaulting children. These methods succeed only because people can be bamboozled into thinking that their enemies are really their friends.

The flexibility of human consciousness is both a strength and a weakness. The ability to learn, change, and adapt is a strength. The capacity to be deceived is a weakness. As every con artist knows, people can be deceived into acting against their own interests: priests convince women that using birth control is sinful, and politicians convince the poor to kill each other in wars that benefit the rich. People can also resist indoctrination: most Catholics use birth control despite Church doctrine, and American sailor Pablo Paredes preferred to go to prison than to fight an immoral war in Iraq. People can choose what they think; however, they don't choose in a vacuum.

People in different social classes have different life experiences that influence what they believe. A rich person's experience of being served feeds the belief that she is a superior being. A working woman's life of drudgery feeds the belief that she doesn't deserve better. A shopkeeper's frustration with her employees feeds the belief that workers are lazy and irresponsible. A worker's life of hard work and low pay feeds anger and bitterness.

Even though class strongly influences what people believe, class does not determine consciousness. In theory, anyone from any class can believe anything. To stay in power, the capitalist class must ensure that certain ideas, like private property and inequality, dominate society. However, the ideas that support the capitalist system conflict with most people's experience. The belief that hard work will lead to a better life conflicts with the reality of working two and three jobs for minimum wage and getting nowhere. The belief that the people in charge are superior conflicts with their obvious incompetence when it comes to practical matters.

The capitalist class faces a huge challenge—it must coerce workers into disregarding their own experience in order to view themselves and the world through the eyes of their oppressors. The conflict between the classes must be transformed into a conflict inside the worker, causing confusion and internal doubt. The resulting lack of confidence helps to keep workers subordinate.

Class conflict is rooted in the fact that one class does the work and a different class reaps the benefits. To maintain this inequality, the ruling class promotes the view that everyone has the same interests, that class conflict is no more than an attitude or a state of mind. In reality, as long as humanity is divided into antagonistic classes, people will have to take sides. Those who advocate class neutrality are not neutral at all; they support the status quo that favors the capitalist class. Consider a nurses' strike. Management accuses nurses of harming patients by withdrawing services. Nurses condemn management for harming patients by not hiring enough staff. Both sides claim to represent the patients' interests. Which side would you support?

If the hospital were a metaphor for society, would you be on the side of the capitalist class or the working class? Capitalists insist that what is good for business is good for society. Workers insist that what is good for workers is good for society. Capitalists want a world where profits keep climbing and they are firmly in control. The capitalists' dream is a nightmare for workers who long for meaningful work and freedom from authoritarian control.

The middle class can see both sides and advocates compromise. However, the rule of Compete or Die makes compromise impossible. The employer who agrees to pay higher wages will fall behind his competitor who refuses to compromise. Workers who curb their demands find the employer demanding even more to stay competitive. As long as the two classes are locked in combat over the surplus, there are only three choices: to side with the ruling class; to side with the working class; or to vacillate with the middle class. Let's examine which class best represents the interests of humanity, starting with the class in power.

More of the same?

Despite having all the resources of society at its command, the ruling class is incapable of solving basic problems for two reasons: Seize the Surplus and Compete or Die. Because these two commandments rule society, problems become important only when there is profit to be made or when a threat to profit must be averted. *Nothing else matters.* Consider how the capitalist class responds to epidemics.

The HIV/AIDS epidemic emerged in the mid-1970's in Africa, where it fed on widespread poverty and the devastation of war. Although the disease is preventable and treatable, the rulers of the world have failed to devote sufficient resources to solve the problem. By 2005, more than 20 million people were dead, a further 40 million were infected, and more than 12 million children had been orphaned. As the epidemic continues to grow, the U.S. Council on Foreign Relations warns, "The scale and geographic scope of the HIV/AIDS pandemic has only two parallels in recorded history: the 1918 flu pandemic and the Black Death in the fourteenth century."

In 1996, a potent combination of anti-viral drugs caused a sharp drop in the number of people dying from AIDS in the United States. In 2003, the World Health Organization (WHO) launched a campaign to provide this new treatment to half of the six million people in the world with AIDS. Unfortunately, the rules of capitalism do not allow people to be given the medicine they need; they have to buy it. WHO raised enough money to buy treatment for only one million people. To protect drug company profits, five million were left to die.

In a vicious cycle of deprivation and disease, capitalism creates inequality, inequality creates the conditions for disease, and the refusal to invest in human health contributes to the spread of disease. As the pandemic grows, the response of world leaders continues to be haphazard and ineffective. Stephen Lewis, United Nations special envoy for HIV/AIDS, expresses the frustration felt by many, "People are dying at a rate of three million a year, and we have the capacity to keep them alive, and we can't summon sufficient resources." The response to future epidemics will be no different. As Mike Davis points out,

> The threat of avian influenza maps with uncanny accuracy to the global topography of inequality, debt, and poverty. Like HIV/AIDS, avian flu is a plague that grows directly out of the new ecology of globalization, the world public health crisis, and the obscene misallocation of resources by global capitalism.[143]

Environmental destruction

The only thing constant about life on Earth is change. Two hundred million years ago, a giant land mass began breaking apart to form the separate continents we know today. The continents continue to move past each other, creating earthquakes and tsunamis. Volcanic eruptions transport molten rock from the earth's interior to the surface, destroying and rebuilding the land. The climate alternately cools and warms, covering the planet with ice and then melting it again. Species come into existence, flourish, and then perish. Because Earth has never been stable, survival requires adaptation to changing conditions.

Capitalism's disregard for the environment parallels its disregard for human beings. The single-minded pursuit of profit has depleted the ozone layer, raised carbon-dioxide levels, produced widespread toxic pollution, and contributed to species extinction. While increasing the environmental challenges we face, capitalism also blocks our ability to adapt to those challenges. A prime example is the devastation caused by

Hurricane Katrina. Excessive burning of fossil fuels has warmed the planet and increased the ferocity of hurricanes. Yet, measures to protect people are grossly inadequate. A scientist who investigated the design, construction, and maintenance of the levees in New Orleans concluded,

> People didn't die because the storm was bigger than the system could handle, and people didn't die because the levees were overtopped...People died because safety was exchanged for efficiency and reduced cost.[144]

Some people dismiss concerns about global warming on the basis that warming and cooling cycles are a part of the planet's history. This do-nothing attitude is dangerous. Human beings can adapt to change only by paying attention to what is changing and planning how to respond. The ruling class blocks both responses. The first instinct of public officials in any crisis is to cover their butts. The collapse of the World Trade Center on 9/11 released a million tons of toxic dust, including 2,000 tons of asbestos. The Environmental Protection Agency denied there was any problem, falsely reassured the public that the air was safe, and failed to conduct an adequate cleanup.

While public officials shirk their responsibility, they place inordinate emphasis on individual responsibility. The public is lectured to reduce, reuse, and recycle, while the ruling class does the opposite. Merchants push us to buy goods that are designed to break down or become obsolete so that we will keep on buying. Recycling at the point of production happens only when it is profitable.

Individuals are condemned for littering, while employers dump on a massive scale because dumping is cheaper than safe disposal or recycling. Between World War II and 1970, the U.S. military dumped millions of pounds of toxic nerve gas and mustard gas, along with 400,000 chemical-filled bombs, land-mines, rockets, and tons of radioactive water in more than 26 sites off the coasts of at least 11 states. No one knows the exact location of these sites, let alone their impact. Meanwhile, the most toxic material on earth is flowing from the Hanford nuclear waste dump towards the Columbia river, while the federal government pretends it isn't happening.

The capitalist class can't conserve natural resources any more than a hungry bear can be convinced not to eat his dinner. Capitalists treat natural resources like commodities, where greater use brings higher profits. To boost sales, all energy companies offer lower rates to their higher-use, industrial customers. In 2005, Yankee Gas Services in Connecticut requested a rate increase because customer conservation efforts had caused its profits to drop.

Capitalism blocks the development of clean and renewable energy sources. There is no technical reason why solar-power chips could not be as plentiful as computer chips; however, the capitalist class prefers that society be dependent on oil and nuclear power for political reasons. Whoever controls oil controls those who need it; and nuclear power plants provide material for nuclear weapons. For these reasons, the capitalist class will never allow alternate sources of energy to replace oil and nuclear power.

Challenges are part of life. To survive, we need a social system that helps us to meet these challenges. Capitalism can solve only one problem—how to accumulate capital. By preventing people from solving life's problems, capitalism is leading humanity to extinction.

Descent into barbarism

The capitalist system works perfectly for what it was designed to do—accumulate capital. The cost of this single-minded obsession, in human terms, is barbarism. The more capital accumulates in private hands, the more civil society breaks down. While the majority of people scramble to survive, the two items that dominate world trade are drugs and weapons.

Barbarism is expressed in the enslavement of human beings. In the 21st century, more than 12 million people work as slaves, generating over $30 billion a year in profit. Barbarism is revealed in mass deprivation. Forty percent of the world's population have no access to clean water, and half the world's children live in extreme poverty. In 2003, more than 50 nations were worse off than they were 10 years earlier. Life expectancy is plummeting in AIDS-plagued nations, erasing decades of progress. Instead of producing life-saving medicines, scientists create chemical and biological weapons.

Barbarism is marked by growing investment in means of destruction. The United States is the world's leading arms-exporter, selling six billion dollars worth of weaponry in 2003 alone. Nearly one billion dollars' worth of those weapons went to nations torn by civil war. According to the World Policy Institute, "Twenty of the top 25 U.S. arms clients in the developing world in 2003—a full 80 percent—were either undemocratic regimes or governments with records of major human rights abuses."

Barbarism is undeniable in the trampling of civil rights, secret prisons, systematic torture, and the preference for force over negotiation. America claims the right to attack any nation or government that threatens its interests. A Pentagon document leaked to the *Los Angeles Times* listed seven nations against which the U.S. would be prepared to use nuclear weapons: China, Russia, Iran, Iraq, North Korea, Syria, and Libya. The document also outlined four possible scenarios where the US should be prepared to press the button: In an Arab-Israeli conflict, in a war between China and Taiwan, in an attack by North Korea on South Korea and in an attack by Iraq on Israel or another neighbor.

Those who doubt the willingness of the capitalist class to destroy the future should look at its readiness to destroy the past. Iraq (called Mesopotamia by the ancient Greeks) is known as "the cradle of civilization" because its culture dates back more than 7,000 years. In "The Smash of Civilizations," Chalmers Johnson describes "the greatest cultural disaster of the last 500 years:"

> On April 10, 2003, in a television address, President Bush acknowledged that the Iraqi people are "the heirs of a great civilization that contributes to all humanity." Only two days later, under the complacent eyes of the U.S. Army, the Iraqis would begin to lose that heritage in a swirl of looting and burning.[145]

The National Museum in Baghdad was robbed of its ancient treasures. The museum's entire collection of ancient writings was stolen, including the earliest writings ever discovered. The torching of the National Library and the Library of Korans destroyed a million books and ten million ancient documents—all irreplaceable. More than 10,000 important archaeological sites in Iraq remain unprotected. How could such a disaster happen?

The illegal trade in antiquities is the third most profitable international trade item, after arms sales and drug smuggling. Before the U.S. invaded Iraq, American scholars, museum directors, art collectors, and antiquities dealers met with Pentagon officials who reassured them that Iraq's historical sites and museums would be protected. However, a group of New York-based collectors and dealers lobbied Washington and the Pentagon, arguing that more private trade in Iraqi artefacts would provide the best security for them!

When the invasion of Iraq began, the only building that U.S. forces actually defended was the Ministry of Oil. As American troops watched, the world's cultural heritage was torched by vandals and looted to stock the vaults of rich collectors. Closer to home, a jewel of American culture, the city of New Orleans, was also destroyed when the people in power did nothing to protect it. The question we need to ask is not whether the capitalist class can save humanity, but who will save humanity from the capitalist class.

The middle class

Could the middle class lead humanity to a better future? Middle-class professionals see themselves as natural leaders and advisors. They have more education than the average person and display a personal confidence that comes from commanding others. Some have influence with people in power (or like to think they have). Professionals and student-professionals often head movements for social justice. Unfortunately, the qualities that make a good professional are the opposite of those needed to challenge capitalism.

The ruling class needs its managerial class to be loyal. If employers had to watch their managers the same way they watch workers, there would be no point in having managers. The professional is expected to carry out the boss's wishes when the boss isn't there. In other words, professionals must embrace the goals of their superiors *as if they were their own*. Professional schools are designed to ensure that graduates accept this social role, as I discovered in medical school.

My first few months of medical school were very exciting. It was 1970, and our class was going to change the world. We named our student lounge after Norman Bethune and put up a poster of Ché Guevara. Our heros were doctors like Bethune, Ché, Virchow, Sigerist, and Salvador Allende, who had just been elected president of Chile by a vibrant workers' movement. Three years later, everything had changed. The economy was in recession. A U.S.-backed military coup had murdered Allende and crushed the Chilean worker's movement. If any of us were still rebels, we kept it to ourselves. One outspoken student was forced to repeat her year. A more stubborn one was turfed out. Another dropped out.

In my last year of medical school, I got into trouble for telling a patient that she had almost died from a medical error. She had been given a medicine to which she was allergic, but the higher-ups decided not to tell her in order to avoid a lawsuit. I was concerned that if she ever had that medicine again she would likely die, so I told her the truth. I had been taught, and I believed, that the patients' welfare comes first. Silly me.

The school convened a committee to decide if I should be allowed to graduate. Fortunately, a sympathetic professor interceded on my behalf, reassuring her colleagues that the problem was "a lack of professional socialization" and that she would take care of it. Afterward, she told me that I needed to "learn to play the game." That was when I realized that medical school had two functions—to teach me the skills that I needed to work as a doctor and, *more importantly,* to ensure that I would be loyal to my superiors, regardless of the needs of my patients.

Hospital training provided the perfect brain-washing conditions and the final testing ground for medical graduates. We were run off our feet, deprived of sleep and food, dominated, interrogated, humiliated, and confined to the building for days at a time. Our heads were stuffed with facts. We were taught to give the "right" answers. We were expected to question, but not to question our superiors. We did as they said, even when we thought they were wrong. We learned to cover their butts and our own.

At graduation, my formerly diverse class looked and talked the same. Somewhere along the way, we had traded our dreams of social change for money and status. We were the successful products of the professional training system.

Dreams for sale

In *Disciplined Minds: A Critical Look at Salaried Professionals and the Soul-Battering System That Shapes Their Lives,* Jeff Schmidt explains that most students enter professional schools with the dream of making the world a better place. By the end of their training,

> …deep down something has changed…Students who once spoke critically of the system are…careful not to be provocative—not to do or say anything that might displease individuals in authority. Any opposition is now sufficiently abstract and theoretical to not be provocative.[146]

Whether they are physicists, journalists, doctors, political scientists, psychologists, or engineers, the professional is trained to be "an obedient thinker, an intellectual property whom employers can trust to experiment, theorize, innovate and create safely within the confines of an assigned ideology." Those who question the social context of their work are accused of having a political agenda. Those who keep their heads down are promoted.

Professionals are expected to uphold class divisions and social hierarchies. For members of oppressed groups, the price of admission to the professional class is the willingness to discriminate against members of your own group or go along with that discrimination. The racist, sexist, and homophobic attitudes that pervade professional schools pressure minority, female, and gay students to swallow their dignity and to pressure their fellows to do the same. This happens in medical schools as well as in police academies.

Only three percent of physicians in the United States are Black. Despite their own experience of racism in the medical profession, studies show that Black physicians are just as likely as White physicians to discriminate against Black patients. A study of 4,000 Medicare patients found that White patients were significantly more likely than Black patients to receive a preferred treatment for heart attack, regardless of whether the physician was Black or White. What would account for such a finding?

Students who apply to professional schools are put through a rigorous selection and training process designed to exclude those who challenge the status quo. Black students who want to become doctors must put loyalty to the profession first; those who challenge racist practices are pushed out. The successful medical graduate is a middle-class professional who is willing to ration medical care on the basis of race, class, and gender *or who goes along with that rationing.*

Breaking ranks

Professionals are squeezed between the demands of their employers and the needs of those they manage. As a result, managers who lack professional training can be pulled apart. One of my patients found herself in this dilemma when she was promoted to supervisor. Janice was under pressure from the boss to increase production, but she didn't want her former co-workers to dislike her. There was no way to please both sides.

The stress mounted, and she became too sick to work. Professional training is designed to prevent such outcomes by ensuring professional loyalty to the employer. As added insurance, employers prefer to hire professionally-trained staff from outside the company (putting another barrier in the way of people "working their way up").

Despite their rigorous training, some professionals will break ranks and switch sides. Whoever warned against "the fury of a woman scorned," has never felt the wrath of an employer betrayed. After *Disciplined Minds* was published, Schmidt was fired from his 19-year position as editor of *Physics Today*.

In 1971, military analyst Daniel Ellsberg decided that his first duty was to the public, and so he sent confidential government documents to the *New York Times*. *The Pentagon Papers* exposed the lies that Washington was telling about the war in Vietnam and helped turn the public against the administration and against the war. Ellsberg was charged with theft, conspiracy, and espionage; however, all charges were dropped when it was revealed that one group of federal agents had broken into Ellsberg's psychiatrist's office to steal information to use against him and another group of agents had been assigned to kill him. Assassinating Ellsberg would have sent a powerful message to other government employees not to switch sides.

Rachel Carson was a whistle-blower who worked as a marine biologist for the U.S. Fish and Wildlife Service. Her 1962 classic, *Silent Spring*, documented the damaging environmental impact of DDT and other pesticides. To discredit Carson, the chemical industry threatened any publisher or publication that promoted her findings. She was labeled "a spinster communist, a lesbian, and a scientific amateur." To counter Carson's "distorted" account, the American Medical Association referred doctors with questions about pesticides to the chemical industries who produced them.

In *Fast Food Nation*, Eric Schlosser describes the smear campaign against his exposé of the fast food industry. Despite his meticulous research, Schlosser was denounced as a "dunce" and an "economics ignoramus." His logical conclusions were dismissed as a "hodgepodge of impressions, statistics, anecdotes and prejudices" and he was condemned as a "health fascist."

When Barbara Ehrenreich described the conditions of America's working poor in *Nickel and Dimed*, her book was condemned as a "classic Marxist rant" and a work of "intellectual pornography with no redeeming characteristics." Ehrenreich herself was lambasted as an "anti-Christ," and "a dedicated enemy of the American family" for arguing that families headed by single women deserve the same social support as families headed by married couples.

When professionals criticize the system, they step over the line that capitalism warns them not to cross. As a result, most books that critique society deliver toothless endings. A good example is *The Politics of Cancer*, in which Samuel Epstein documents the harm caused by industrial pollution, concluding, "We must be willing to accept the fundamental reality that a *significant* reduction in exposure to environmental carcinogens will result only from organized political action." He then does an abrupt turn and offers 16 pages of suggestions on how individuals can reduce their risk of getting cancer. Among other things, he advises,

> If you can possibly avoid it, do not live close to a chemical plant, refinery, asbestos plant, or metal, mining, processing or smelting plant, or hazardous waste disposal site even if it claims to be well managed. Also avoid living close to major highways and expressways.[147]

People do not *choose* to live in polluted, industrial areas, they do so because they cannot afford to live anywhere else. Epstein's suggestions blame the victim for getting in the way of capitalist pollution. He also warns, "Unless you are fully and completely prepared to take the consequences, you should not go to work in an uncontrolled, high risk industry, especially one with a bad track record." In reality, people are forced to work at dangerous jobs in order to feed their families. Try telling the families of the dead Sago miners that their loved ones should have worked somewhere else!

Regardless of how thoroughly professionals document the insanity of capitalism, an invisible barrier prevents them from rejecting the system altogether. When the next logical step will take them over that line, there is intense pressure to back off and propose solutions that, *according to their own analysis,* cannot work. I could not understand this phenomenon until I found myself balking at crossing that line and risking my own middle-class privileges by writing this book.

Damage control

When social conditions deteriorate to the point that whole sections of the middle-class threaten to revolt, higher-level managers ensure that lower-level managers remain loyal, as this Canadian example reveals.

Under-funded medical services stress patients and the professionals who treat them. By 1998, 62 percent of Canadian physicians reported that their workload was too heavy, and more than half said that their family and personal life were suffering. By 2003, 46 percent of doctors were "in an advanced phase of burnout, that is feeling that they are ineffective, emotionally overrun and exhausted by their work, and showing clear signs of depersonalization in relationships." The Canadian Medical Association (CMA) attributed these problems to higher work loads, inadequate resources, and loss of control over how medical care is provided.

Warning that "the health care system and those of us who work in it have been seriously traumatized," the CMA pleaded for more funds for the medical system. When moral persuasion proved ineffective, the CMA did not fight for more funding. That would have been "unprofessional." Instead, the CMA did an about-turn to provide damage control for the system. The president of the CMA stated, "occupational stress and burnout have become facts of life," and "physicians…owe it to ourselves and our families to look after our own health." The CMA launched a national program to help doctors cope with stressful working conditions and requested government fund research to answer questions like, "Why does one physician burn out while his colleagues cope well?"

Similar pressures in the United States caused the Joint Committee for the Accreditation of Health Organizations to set new standards requiring hospitals to "identify and manage matters of individual physician health." Doctors were advised that the key to managing stress is "putting yourself first, staying healthy and paying prompt attention to illness. If you do that, no one gets impaired." In Britain, psychologists study the "learning style" of doctors to identify which ones are more likely to "burn out" at work. None of these measures solve the problem of too few people being expected to do too much work.

Because professionals are trained not to question the system, the professional response to social problems has a predictable pattern. The problem is identified and sincere concern is expressed, along with a genuine desire to help ("the health care system and those of us who work in it have been seriously traumatized.") When moral pressure fails to effect change, the professional switches sides. The status quo is accepted ("occupational stress and burnout have become facts of life") and the problem is redefined. Those being victimized are expected to adjust to the new reality ("putting yourself first, staying healthy and paying prompt attention to illness"). Those who succumb to stressful conditions are blamed ("Those who follow recommendations will not become impaired"). And finally, an appeal for help is made to the source of the problem (requesting government-funded research to address the symptoms of a government-created crisis).

More funds could be obtained for the medical system by organizing a united front composed of *all* medical workers (doctors, nurses, technicians, orderlies, cleaners, kitchen staff, clerical workers), patients, and their families—in short, a class fight. Regardless of how effective such a strategy would be, proposals for united action are dismissed as "unprofessional." Professionals are programmed to uphold social divisions, not break them down.

The working class

A dozen CEOs are meeting and the light goes out. It's not their problem and they find another room. A dozen professionals are meeting and the light goes out. As they wait for someone to come from maintenance, they discuss the importance of light and how frustrating it is not to have it. A dozen workers are meeting and the light goes out. They fix the light.

The working class is the only class that society cannot do without. Workers make everything possible: Jane drives the bus; Jorge removes garbage; Maria constructs furniture; and Mike installs plumbing. Without their daily efforts, the world would grind to a halt.

Capitalism created the working class. Before capitalism, most people were farmers. The capitalist revolution forced peasants off the land and into factories. Now the working class is the majority of humanity. By demanding higher productivity, capitalism has forced the working class to produce enough surplus to end human deprivation. Finally, the spread of capitalism throughout the world has created an international working class. *These three characteristics make the interests of the working class identical with the interests of humanity.*

• The majority

Workers are not only the majority class in terms of numbers, they are the most organized class. Regardless of where they were born, the color of their skin, what language they speak, who they vote for, what church they attend (or don't attend), their age, sex, and sexual orientation, workers do all of the socially necessary work in society, and they do it together. Despite the divisions and competition imposed by capitalism, co-operation is essential to the worker's daily experience. On the assembly line of a car factory or of a fast-food restaurant, workers must cooperate to create the finished product. Workers must also cooperate to defend themselves against the employers' demands. This necessity for cooperation has produced the working-class slogans, "An Injury to One is an Injury to All" and "United We Stand; Divided We Fall." These principles fit the needs of humanity equally well. As the organized majority, the working class offers the best hope for humanity to liberate itself from capitalism.

• The producing class

We live in a world shaped by human labor. Goods, services, money, capital—all represent units of human labor. Under capitalism, the working class does not produce for itself but for the capitalist class. The capitalist forces the worker to exchange the collective power to produce for the individual "power" to consume. However, the real power of workers lies not in their wallets but in their ability to stop producing for profit and to start producing for need. When the working class produces to meet its own needs, it also produces to meet humanity's needs because the two are indistinguishable. By taking collective control of production, the working class could end class divisions and unite humanity in the common project of managing society.

• The international class

The international working class already runs the world—for capitalism. Computers are manufactured by Chinese workers, assembled by Mexican workers, sold by American workers, and serviced by Indian workers. The working class is international; every major city contains workers from many different nations. Youngsters around the world watch the same movies, listen to the same music, eat the same (fast) food, and wear the same clothes. However, the persistence of national borders prevents the global integration of humanity. By organizing across national boundaries, the working class could put an end to war and raise everyone's living standards.

Unlike the capitalist class and the middle class, the working class has no interests that conflict with the interests of humanity as a whole. The greatest obstacle to majority rule is the *belief* that it would never work. Fortunately, beliefs can change. The next chapter explores how the working class could take control of society.

Summary

Class divisions block humanity from solving pressing problems. The ruling class obsession with profit endangers human survival. The middle class lacks the power to challenge the ruling class. Only the working class has the size, the organization, and the ability to free humanity from capitalism.

Chapter 14

Seize the Power

> Rise like lions after slumber
> In unvanquishable number.
> Shake your chains to earth like dew
> which in sleep had fallen on you.
> Ye are many — they are few.
>
> *Percy Bysshe Shelley*

If your boss decided to close down your workplace, and no other jobs were available, what would you do? Millions of workers in Argentina faced this problem when the economy collapsed in 2001. The documentary film, *The Take,* follows a group of ceramic workers who decided to take control of their abandoned factory. They organized themselves into a workers' cooperative called FaSinPat (short for *Fábrica Sin Patrónes,* or "Factory Without Bosses") and began to produce for themselves.

The legal owner of the plant had fled the country. Having stashed millions of dollars in foreign bank accounts, Luis Zanón left behind more than $170 million in factory debts, including wages owed to the workers. The Zanón factory had been built with public funds on public land and had operated with public subsidies, yet Luis Zanón had never paid taxes. In light of these facts, the workers felt justified in claiming ownership of the factory.

Under Zanón's management, workers from different sections were prohibited from speaking with each other, and there had been 25 to 30 accidents a month, with an average of one fatal injury every year. One observer reported how, under workers' control, "elected committees oversee the running of the plant and all decisions are made in a general assembly, everyone has the right to be heard, every worker has a vote, all workers are paid equally, and there have been no occupational health and safety crises."[148] The same story was repeated throughout Argentina as medical clinics, book publishers, hotels, supermarkets, bakeries, schools, and tailor shops were taken over and run by workers. Most of these "recovered" industries were able to hire new workers, raise wages, and increase production.

Despite workers proving that they could organize their work better than their former bosses had, or rather, *because they were proving this,* they suffered consistent opposition, from legal eviction notices, to police violence, death threats, kidnaping, torture, and even murder. Workers met these threats with defiant solidarity. Whenever police tried to evict the ceramic workers, a tide of people rose to defend the factory. Outside, unemployed workers formed a physical barrier. Inside, ceramic workers stood on the roof with sling-shots. According to Rosa Rivera, who worked at Zanón for over 15 years, "If a factory is shut down and abandoned, workers have the right to occupy it, put it to work and defend it with their lives."

There has been local, national, and international support for the recovered factory movement. However, a system based on private ownership cannot tolerate a system based on collective ownership for long. Only one class can rule. Eventually, the capitalist class must reclaim control over production, or the working class must take control of society.

The threat of democracy

The word "democracy" literally means "rule by the people." People who take collective control of their work are exercising direct democracy. A social system based on direct democracy has one prime directive: Share. For many thousands of years, humanity lived by this directive, sharing the work, sharing the responsibilities, sharing the problems, and sharing the solutions. Class society is incompatible with direct democracy because one cannot Seize the Surplus and Share it at the same time. The bloody conquest of the Americas proved this to be true.

> In fourteen-hundred and ninety-two
> Columbus sailed the ocean blue.
> The native people were generous and kind,
> and so he murdered all he could find.

Greedy for gold, the Spanish monarchs instructed Christopher Columbus to lay claim to whatever he could. In the West Indies, Columbus found a sharing society and a people who refused to be ruled. Columbus had been instructed to seize, not to share, so over the next 40 years the Spanish conquerors exterminated an estimated 12 to 15 million men, women, and children. The same story was repeated throughout North America and the world until almost all sharing societies were destroyed.

The Franco-Prussian war of 1871 proved that majority rule is such a threat to the ruling class that it will unite with sworn enemies to stay in power. When the Prussian army advanced on Paris, the king of France fled to Versailles with his troops. Determined to defend their abandoned city, the people of Paris created the world's first democratic government, the Paris Commune. The Commune accomplished a tremendous amount during the two short months of its existence. One of its first measures was to abolish the police and the standing army, making the sole armed force the National Guard in which all citizens capable of bearing arms were enrolled. This measure eliminated the forces of repression that had divided and ruled the population, enabling them to unite against their common enemy, the Prussian army.

The Commune decreed that elected representatives could be removed by majority vote at any time and that the highest salary paid by the Commune would be no greater than the average worker's wage. These two measures ensured that representatives would be held accountable for their actions and that people would not seek election for personal gain.

The Commune declared a complete separation of Church and State and ordered abandoned factories to be reopened under workers' control. Women workers insisted on the provision of free education for boys and girls, industrial training for girls, equal pay, equal rights, and day nurseries.

Although the Paris Commune was formed in self-defense, it developed into something unexpected—the means by which ordinary people could shape society. The word "communist" was first used to describe supporters of the Commune. Around the world, the elite and their supporters spat this word with fear and contempt, while working people embraced it with pride and hope.

The French monarchy could not allow a people's government to rule the capital city, so the French king made a despicable deal with his Prussian enemies. France agreed to cease its war with Prussia on the condition that the Prussians allow the French army to enter Paris, destroy the Commune, and retake the city. Not anticipating such treachery, the Commune failed to organize any defense outside of Paris or within the French army. It was a fatal mistake, and the Commune was crushed.

The first working-class revolution

The capitalist class fears majority rule even more than the feudal aristocracy feared it. The industrial revolution organized thousands of workers into giant factories in urban centers. The contradiction between a numerically small capitalist class and a much larger working class was bound to explode. The first major explosion took place during the Russian Revolution of 1917. Because capitalists, East and West, have worked so hard to discredit this revolution, it is worth taking some time to examine what really happened.

At the beginning of the 20th century, Russia was one of the most backward *and* one of the most advanced nations in the world. Ninety percent of the population were poor peasants working the land. The urban working class was tiny but powerful, producing more than half the country's annual wealth. Russia's uneven economic development was the result of state-of-the-art factories being transplanted, "down to the last bolt and screw," from England, Germany, and France. The largest factory in the world was the Putilov munitions factory in St. Petersburg, employing 12,000 workers.

Overworked and poverty-stricken, the Russian working class revolted in 1905. Strikes paralyzed the cities and left the population without basic services. To remedy this problem, every major workplace elected delegates to workers' councils, called "soviets," that ensured the provision of essential services. In deciding such matters, the workers' councils began to function as an alternate government. When the 1905 rebellion was put down, the councils disbanded.

In 1917, workers' councils re-emerged to tackle the crises created by war and government incompetence. This time, councils of workers, soldiers, and peasants converged to form an All–Russian Congress of Soviets. The first meeting of the Congress was attended by more than one-thousand elected delegates, each representing 500 workers. With the monarchy deposed and the capitalist government in disarray, the Congress of Soviets took power. The majority vote in the new workers' government was held by the Bolshevik Party (bolshevik means "majority") based on its program to end the war, give land to the peasants, and put workers in charge of production.

The bulk of the Russian army defected to the side of the working class. In *Ten Days That Shook The World*, American journalist John Reed recounts how a delegation of Cossack soldiers inquired if the Soviets intended to confiscate the estates of the great Cossack landowners and divide them among the Cossack peasants.

> To this Lenin replied. "That," he said, "is for you to do. We shall support the working Cossacks in all their actions…The best way to begin is to form Cossack Soviets; you will be given representation in the [governing body] and then it will be *your* Government too…" The Cossacks departed, thinking

hard. Two weeks later General Kaledin received a deputation from his troops. "Will you," they asked, "promise to divide the great estates of the Cossack landlords among the working Cossacks?" "Only over my dead body," responded Kaledin. A month later, seeing his army melt away before his eyes, Kaledin blew out his brains…"[149]

On taking power, the Congress of Soviets promptly decreed:

- an immediate truce on all fronts of the war
- an end to secret diplomacy and the publication of all secret treaties
- the right to independence for all national groups living in Russia
- workers' control over production
- land to the peasants
- democracy in the army
- an end to capital punishment
- a complete ban on plunder, hoarding, and speculation
- salaries of all government employees fixed at 500 rubles a month (about $50 US).

The rise of mass democracy in Russia shook the capitalist class to the core. Most subversive was Lenin's insistence that ordinary people should not wait to be instructed, but begin to take over the running of society. Around the world, workers responded to this call with a wave of revolt. America's first city-wide strike shook Seattle in 1919. A General Strike Committee formed to organize the strike and provide essential services for the population. Participants of the strike recalled:

the Milk Wagon Drivers consulting late into the night over the task of supplying milk for the city's babies; the Provision Trades working twenty-four hours a day on the question of feeding 30,000 workers; the Barbers planning a chain of co-operative barber shops; the steamfitters opening a profitless grocery store; the Labor Guards facing, under severe provocation, the task of maintaining order by a new and kinder method. When we saw union after union submitting its cherished desires to the will of the General Strike Committee, then we rejoiced. For we knew it was worth the four or five days pay apiece to get this education in the problems of management…[150]

More than a dozen imperial powers sent their armies into Russia to crush the heart of this global revolt. When military measures failed, the revolution was starved to death. Russia's economy had been drained by World War I and was further depleted by the civil war to defend the revolution. Industrial capacity was too low to meet the needs of the population, and an international trade block prevented goods and materials from entering the country. The result was a dire scarcity of food, fuel, warm clothing, soap, medicine, and every other necessity. The cities began to die. Between 1918 and 1919, the number of workers in Moscow dropped by one-third..

Russia's dense concentration of workers laid the basis for revolution. However, the small proportion of workers in a predominately agricultural nation laid the basis for defeat. Had workers taken power in any other industrialized nation, they could have infused Russia with desperately-needed raw materials and technology. Tragically, no other working class was organized enough to take power. Like the Paris Commune, the Russian Revolution was isolated and defeated.

Revolution betrayed

The Russian Revolution opened the door to workers' control of society. The forces of capitalism slammed that door shut. Today, the defeat of the Russian working class is commonly used to dismiss the possibility of workers' revolution ("Look what happened in Russia"). In particular, supporters of capitalism claim that workers' revolutions only bring dictators to power. Let's look at what really happened.

The Bolshevik Party was based on workers' councils. When the factories closed for lack of raw materials, famished workers left the cities to find food in the countryside, and the workers' councils disintegrated. To make matters worse, many leading worker-Bolsheviks had been killed in the civil war. As the Party lost its base in the working class, middle-class opportunists moved in. A strong working class would never have tolerated this, but the working class was decimated.

During the 1920's, middle-class professionals increased their influence within the Party. Because it was in power, the Communist Party became the center for a new ruling class to launch a counter-revolution. During the 1930's, the remaining Bolshevik leaders were isolated and then eliminated. Those who protested this betrayal were imprisoned, exiled, or executed. It took a river of blood to transform the workers' State into a capitalist State. Because the Russian people had sacrificed so much for the revolution, the new capitalist class, led by Stalin, had to *claim* that it was continuing the policies of Lenin and the Bolsheviks, even as it crushed every gain of the revolution.

Capitalism was restored in Russia, but not in its old form. The revolution had abolished private ownership of production and placed it under the collective control of the Soviets. Because control of production was already centralized, the form of capitalism that developed was State capitalism. This was no workers' State. The revolution put the working class in control of the State, and the counter-revolution put the State in control of the working class. "Russia Incorporated" represented the return of private ownership of production, but on a national scale. The State owned everything, and everyone worked for the State. Once again, workers owned only their ability to work for a wage.

Like all capitalist States, Russia Inc. claimed to be a servant of the people, holding the nation's assets in their name. In reality, it served itself. The United States had accumulated its founding capital through slavery. Russia Inc. did the same, accumulating capital through a brutal slave-labor system. To feed the cities, grain was confiscated from farmers who were left to starve. To feed the factories, raw materials were obtained by any means possible. By the end of the 1930's, the Russian economy was booming, based on the prime directive of capitalism, Seize the Surplus.

Russia's economic and military competition with the U.S. during the Cold War fulfilled the second commandment of capitalism, Compete or Die. Russia Inc. was one giant unit of capital, a form of monopoly capitalism, with no economic competition inside the country. All of Russia's competition took place on the international level, against other nation-states. The disintegration of the Russian empire in the late 1980's opened the door to competition inside the nation. This was no fundamental transformation from communism to capitalism; only the form of capitalism changed. The same State bureaucracy, even the same individuals, remained in power.

It was not sufficient for the global capitalist class to defeat the Russian Revolution; every spark of hope that it inspired had to be stomped out. The fact that ordinary people had ruled society for even a brief time had to be erased from history, or so perverted that no one would believe that it had ever happened *and could happen again.*

The history of war is written by the victors. The capitalists want us to believe that any challenge to their system will lead inevitably to a totalitarian nightmare. In fact, the nightmare that followed the Russian Revolution was caused by capitalism crushing the workers' movement and reasserting its dominance over society, trampling the rights of workers, women, gays, and national minorities. Capitalism is better served by disregarding the facts and promoting the view that power always corrupts and that there was no difference between Lenin and Stalin, between the direct democracy of the soviets and the dictatorship of the Communist Party. Fortunately, the actual events of the Russian Revolution were recorded by John Reed, Leon Trotsky, Arthur Ransome, and other witnesses. Through their words, history calls to us, "See what humanity is capable of! Learn from our experience, so that you will not fail."

The Russian Revolution proved that humanity is capable of creating a society run by the producers for the producers, where people democratically decide what is needed and organize themselves to produce it. A socialist society is like a cooperative kitchen, where everyone has a job to do and everyone eats. This is not such an alien concept. The human species has spent most of its existence in classless, sharing societies. Modern socialism would differ from pre-class societies in two important ways: it would be organized on a global scale, and it would be based on abundance, not scarcity. In an historical sense, we could think of capitalism as the road that humanity took to get from a world of shared scarcity to a world of shared abundance.

The Russian Revolution also revealed the obstacles in the way of creating a socialist society. To understand what socialism is and how we can get there, we must be clear about what it is not and what stands in our way. The following sections explain the difference between sham democracy and real democracy, between reform and revolution, between public and common ownership, and why unions cannot be revolutionary. We will then return to the subject of how we can create a genuine socialist society.

Sham democracy

Nuestras sueños no caben en sus urnas
Our dreams do not fit in your ballot boxes

Capitalism can take different political forms: electoral systems like the United States and Canada; religious States like Israel and Iran; one-party States like Cuba and China; monarchies like Saudi Arabia and Nepal; and military dictatorships like Myanmar and occupied Haiti. Capitalism can also change forms over time. France's capitalist economy was born in a republic that reverted to a monarchy that was followed by another republic. Germany's economy was just as capitalist under the left-leaning Weimar Republic as it was under Hitler's fascist dictatorship. All capitalist economies have a common feature: they are run by the bosses for the bosses. As long as the few rule the many, there can be no genuine democracy. However, *the illusion of democracy* is necessary to secure public consent to minority rule.

Students are taught that the New England colonies enjoyed direct democracy based on town meetings; however, as the population grew, direct democracy became unmanageable and was replaced with representative democracy. Nevertheless, the democratic principle is preserved because elections are fair and politicians who don't perform can be voted out of office. This sounds reasonable until you consider how it really works.

The United Sates of America has always been ruled by wealthy property-owners in order to advance their own interests. According to John Jay, the first Chief Justice of the U.S. Supreme Court, the goal of the Constitution was to ensure that those who owned the country controlled the country. As a result, "the world's greatest democracy" is anything but. The president and vice president are not elected by popular vote, but by the Electoral College. In the 2000 election, Al Gore received more votes than George W. Bush. Nevertheless, the Electoral College gave Bush the presidency, and this decision was upheld by the Supreme Court. Supreme Court judges, who wield enormous power, are not elected. They are appointed by the president, approved by the Senate, and can stay in office for life.

Democracy is not served when Congressional districts are based on geography instead of on population. Small and overwhelmingly White states are over-represented while states with larger numbers of Blacks and Hispanics are under-represented. This arrangement has permitted only three Black senators to be elected between 1877 and 2005.

How democratic is it when over half a million people living in Washington, DC, have no voting member of Congress? Four million American citizens living in Puerto Rico are subject to federal law, but they cannot vote in presidential elections, and they have no voting representative in Congress. Millions of foreign-born people living in the U.S. are denied the right to vote. And nearly five million people, including 13 percent of the Black male population, have lost the right to vote because of felony convictions.

In order to be readmitted to the Union after the Civil War, Florida was forced to grant Blacks the right to vote in 1868. That same year, Florida expanded the number of crimes that would cause convicted persons to lose their right to vote, and these crimes disproportionately targeted Black people. Other states also passed "Black Codes." In seven states, convicted felons lose their voting rights for life. One in every four Black men in those states is permanently ineligible to vote.

Amending the Constitution is nearly impossible. The Equal Rights Amendment (ERA) to provide legal equality for women was first proposed in 1923. It was passed by the House of Representatives in 1971 and by the Senate in 1972. Within a year, more than 30 states had ratified the amendment. Even though most Americans supported the ERA, it fell three states short of the 38 required. Today, women living in America still don't have legal equality.

Even if all the above problems were fixed, electoral, parliamentary, and congressional systems would still be sham democracies because they separate politics and economics. The electorate is not allowed to vote for a different social system, only for candidates with different views of how to run the capitalist system. The day-to-day operations of capitalism are decided by executives and bureaucrats who are never elected. As a result, no matter who gets into political office, your job doesn't change. No matter how many rotten politicians are replaced, recalled, or impeached, your life doesn't change. No wonder so many people, especially young people, don't vote. As long as the capitalist class controls production, it doesn't matter who gets elected. Whoever controls production controls society.

To keep the corporate class in power, the electoral process is managed like a horse race. When the leading horse starts to lose its usefulness to the ruling class (too many lies, too much corruption, too many mistakes), a chorus of reformers clamor to kick him out of the race. The electorate is offered a new horse that is presented as different, better, and more reliable. The same track is used, and the new horse continues to run in the same direction as the old one. When people realize that they have been duped, they are told that they must wait for the next race. After several rounds of being seduced into backing one or another "savior," only to be betrayed, people lose hope of any real change—to the delight of the ruling class. As long as democracy is equated with elections, ("You can't complain if you didn't vote"), the ruling class can feel secure.

Sham democracies can be identified by the huge gap between what people want and what leaders deliver. Most Americans want a government-funded medical system, but politicians refuse to provide it. While public officials harp on terrorism, taxes, and crime, a 2005 poll found that terrorism was a priority for only nine percent of Americans, tax and budget issues were a priority for only six percent, and crime was a priority for only three percent. No wonder most Americans think that Congress does not understand people's needs. Instead of acknowledging the abysmal lack of democracy in America, defenders of the system blame the electorate for the state of the nation ("people get the government they deserve").

In a real demoncracy, the people in power are accountable. In a sham democracy, they do pretty much what they want. Domestic spying and torturing prisoners are both against the law, yet Washington has defended its right to do both. A 2006 investigation by the *Boston Globe* found that by adding "signing statements" to legislation,

> President Bush has quietly claimed the authority to disobey more than 750 laws enacted since he took office, asserting that he has the power to set aside any statute passed by Congress when it conflicts with his interpretation of the Constitution.[151]

The President is clearly not accountable to the American people. By 2005, most Americans believed that President Bush had lied to the public about the need to attack Iraq, and 59 percent wanted US troops to leave Iraq. Nevertheless, the president remained in office, "staying the course" he had set for the Middle East. On more than one occasion, the House of Representatives has backed the president by rejecting a proposal to pull American troops out of Iraq. In a real democracy, war would end as soon as the majority opposed it. In this case, the war would never have started.

February 15, 2003 marked the largest anti-war protests the world had ever seen. Millions of people opposed the impending U.S. invasion of Iraq in a chain of demonstrations that circled the globe. Scores of American cities joined protests in Europe, the Middle East, Australia, and Asia. *The New York Times* reported that,

> protesters came from a wide range of the political spectrum: college students, middle-aged couples, families with small children, older people who had marched for civil rights, and groups representing labor, the environment and religious, business and civic organizations.[152]

More than 100 American cities and counties passed anti-war resolutions, including Los Angeles, Chicago, Philadelphia, and Detroit. Unions also passed anti-war resolutions. Sentiment against the war was so strong that the *New York Times* admitted, "there may still be two superpowers on the planet: the United States and world public opinion."

In a display of arrogance, President Bush dismissed world opinion, including huge protests by Iraqis who opposed the invasion of their country, insisting that the world would be better off without Saddam Hussein. Whether or not this was true, *he had no right to make that decision.*

Power and responsibility

Class society severs the link between power and responsibility. Those with the most power take no responsibility, while those with the least power are saddled with the most responsibility. Authorities shirk responsibility with astonishing ease. Who knew that terrorists might hijack commercial air planes and turn them into missiles? Who knew that the levees in New Orleans would crumble during a flood? Who knew that torture was routine in American prisons? The people in charge are supposed to know these things, and it turned out that they did know. It is the height of hypocrisy for them to demand personal responsibility from us when they take no responsibility themselves.

In 2005, General Motors announced plans to eliminate 30,000 jobs at its North American plants. Auto workers had no say over GM's business decisions, yet they were the ones who lost their jobs when those decisions failed to produce enough profit. In a genuine democracy, those with power would be held accountable and no one would be given responsibility without the power to carry it out.

Class society violates the basic right to decide what happens to you. Politicians launch wars that other people's children will fight. Employers authorize the use of toxic materials that other people will handle. Public officials decide how to respond to disasters in which other people risk their lives, homes, and loved ones. The people in power are protected from the harmful consequences of their decisions. The mother of a dead American soldier is not allowed to even question the President who launched the war that killed her son.

In a real democracy, the responsibility for social problems would be shared, along with the power to solve those problems. As it is now, the people in charge care more about the bottom line than they do about meeting human needs. That is why hospitals serve nutritionally-deficient food to sick people. In a real democracy, hospital workers would insist on serving nourishing meals, regardless of cost, and everyone would pitch in to make sure that happened.

Capitalism denies individuals the democratic right to decide personal matters. Sexuality, reproductive rights, personal beliefs, and drug-taking are all considered fair game for political control. Everyone is entitled to an opinion on such matters; however, people in positions of power have no right to *impose* their views on others. Violation of the personal right-to-decide is so taken-for-granted that ordinary people get caught up in debates about *how* the State should control individual behavior. *The right of the State to dictate such matters is never questioned.*

Societies based on genuine democracy treat individual behavior as a strictly personal matter. The Paris Commune abolished "the morality police." The Russian Revolution struck down legislation regulating personal behavior, including laws against homosexuality, prostitution, and abortion. Divorce was granted on request. At the same time, socially harmful behaviors, like hoarding and speculation, were not tolerated. This is the opposite of what happens under capitalism, where employers are free to exploit and oppress, while individual behavior is micro-managed.

Capitalism cannot allow ordinary people to think that they are capable of making *any* decisions. Under the guise of paternalism, slave masters oppress slaves, bosses exploit workers, and States dominate entire populations. In apartheid South Africa, the White ruling class insisted that the Black majority were not ready to manage their own affairs until the Black majority taught them otherwise. Today, Washington claims that it must rule Iraq until Iraqis are ready to rule themselves. Capitalism denies people the right to self-rule, claiming that the majority don't know how to make good decisions. There is an element of truth to this—the majority would not make decisions that are good for the capitalist class. *Conflicting class interests are the real reason why ordinary people are denied the right to decide.*

To stay in power, the ruling class must cultivate the *illusion* that the majority are part of the decision-making process. Washington insists that "our" help is necessary to eliminate the tyrants of other lands (even when "our" government installed them in the first place), and that once "we" have invaded another country, then "we" should stay and clean up the mess. No nation should have the right to decide how another nation functions. We would never want some foreign power invading our country, occupying our land, stealing our things, murdering our people, and telling us what to do. We would want to solve our own problems, including settling with our own dictators. Of course we would accept help, as long as it didn't deprive us of the right to control our own lives. People in the Balkans, Haiti, and the Middle East are no different. A poll conducted by the British Ministry of Defense found that after almost three years of foreign occupation, 82 percent of Iraqis were "strongly opposed" to the presence of foreign troops, and between 45 and 65 percent of Iraqis (depending on their location) believed that attacks against British and American troops were justified.

When ordinary Americans buy the racist lie that some people are too backward to manage their own affairs, they strengthen the system's ability to deprive them of their own right to decide. America's war on terror has destroyed civil society in Iraq *and* shredded civil rights at home. If we want self-determination for ourselves, we must support self-determination for others. When we side with our rulers in depriving other people of their rights, then we are sure to lose our own.

Just as those with power must be held accountable, those who experience the consequences of any decision must be included in the decision-making. In 2003, the people of Spain gave their ruling class a lesson in direct democracy. The Spanish State backed the U.S. invasion of Iraq, despite the objections of 90 percent of the Spanish population. When bombs ripped through the Madrid subway system, killing 200, the population exploded in rage. Demonstrators held their government responsible for the massacre, chanting "Your war; Our dead." The President was thrown out of office and Spain pulled out of the war.

Reform or revolution

Is revolution necessary, or can gradual social improvements result in fundamental social change? In 1900, Rosa Luxemburg addressed this question in *Reform or Revolution*. Luxemburg compares the struggle to reform capitalism with the labor of Sisyphus, a mythical character who was condemned by the Gods to push a boulder uphill only to have it roll back down again. Likewise, people struggle for many years to win reforms, only to see them rolled back or abolished. This back-and-forth movement occurs because the State grants reforms to undercut rebellion and then revokes reforms to promote greater profits (which provokes more rebellion).

Britain's welfare state was created to stabilize the system in response to workers' revolts after World War II. As a Conservative member of the British Parliament warned, "If you don't give the people reform they are going to give you revolution." The best-known American reforms, the New Deal, were a response to the Great Depression. Howard Zinn explains,

> The Roosevelt reforms…had to meet two pressing needs: to reorganize capitalism in such a way as to overcome the crisis and stabilize the system; also to head off the alarming growth of spontaneous rebellion in the early years of the Roosevelt administration—organization of tenants and the unemployed, movements of self-help and general strikes in several cities.[153]

The ruling class prefers reform to revolution. Once social control is restored, the drive for profit takes priority, and the reform boulder is kicked back down the hill. Today, most of the reforms won in the 1930's and in the 1960's have been lost, or are in danger of being lost, so that it seems like we are back at the beginning.

Is it possible to win enough reforms to push that boulder over the top of the hill and create an entirely different society? In 1970, a popular movement in Chile elected a reform government headed by President Salvador Allende, who outraged the capitalist class when he moved to nationalize industry, tax profits, and stop foreign debt payments. In 1973, a U.S.-backed military coup toppled Chile's government, murdered Allende, and imposed a military dictatorship under General Augusto Pinochet. Thousands of people were slaughtered in the wave of terror that followed. The tragedy of Chile proves that the capitalist class will not surrender control over society in response to any vote. On the contrary, it will throw every law out the window to protect its power and its profits.

Some people say that Allende moved too quickly. However, it is absurd to think that the tiger will not devour those who extract his claws more slowly. Allende's mistake was that he relied too much on the rule of law and not enough on the power of workers who were begging him for arms to defend the government. Another mistake was to forget that capitalism is an international system. When any group of capitalists is threatened, the rest view this as an attack on their class, and they suspend their rivalry to defend their class. The working class must also defend itself as a class. Mass support for Chile's reforms within the American working class could have blocked U.S. military intervention.

Not all reformers are murdered; some are incorporated into the State to prevent revolution. This happened in Poland in 1989. Lech Walesa was a leader in Solidarity, the mass workers' movement that toppled the ruling Communist Party. After he was elected president of Poland, Walesa turned against the working class, dismantling the welfare state and promoting corporate control of industry.

Capitalism offers two options to elected reformers: play by our rules or end up like Allende. There are temporary exceptions. Mass support has kept Venezuela's President Hugo Chávez in office despite repeated efforts to depose him. Venezuela is an oil-rich nation; as long as oil prices remain high, Chávez may be able to meet the basic demands of Venezuela's workers and most of its capitalists. When oil prices fall, or when the economy goes into recession, Chávez will be forced to choose which class to support.

Does that mean that reforms are useless? Not at all! Luxemburg argued that the struggle for reforms, *as the primary goal,* cannot transform society. To do that, the struggle for reforms must be waged *as a means to revolution,* where each reform is clearly linked with the aim of putting the working class in power. The distinction is important. The road of reform never challenges the basic rules of capitalism (Seize the Surplus and Compete or Die). In contrast, the road of revolution uses reforms as stepping stones to socialism, building the confidence of ordinary people to take control of society. To travel the road to reform, one must lobby politicians, win influence in high places, and get people out to vote. On this road, the ordinary person is a bystander or a cheerleader backing the "hired guns". To travel the road to revolution, one must mobilize people at work, at school, and in the neighborhood to struggle on their own behalf. On this road, ordinary people take center stage—the more people organize, the more they can win.

Reformers who go hat-in-hand to the people in power must forever settle for crumbs. In 2005, the World Health Organization admitted that it had failed to meet its goal of providing drug treatment for millions of poor people with AIDS. According to Dr. Jim Yong Kim, Director of WHO's HIV/AIDS department, "All we can do is apologize." Had he been outraged and demanded that national leaders cough up the money, or that drug companies provide free medicines, he would have antagonized the people the WHO depends on.

Because reforms must be granted by those in power, reformers must continually compromise in the hopes of getting what they want "down the road." That road is endless and discouraging. As Dr. Kim stated, "I have to say that I'm personally extremely disappointed in myself and in my colleagues because we have not moved quickly enough—we have not saved enough lives."

In contrast, socialists link every struggle with the aim of taking over the bakery and are not deterred from their goal regardless of whether they win or lose a particular crumb. When socialists win a reform, they celebrate their victory and plan the next one. When they lose a reform, they learn from their experience and double their determination to end this heartless system.

Despite countless disappointments, reformism—the belief that gradual improvements will lead to fundamental social change—is kept alive by hatred of the system, combined with the belief that there is no alternative. Capitalism has convinced the majority that revolutions only put new tyrants in power. And many who agree that revolution is necessary will argue that one should fight for reforms *in the meantime*. Whenever I hear this phrase, I think about a patient dying from blood poisoning and the doctor saying, "She needs antibiotics but I will give her aspirin *in the meantime*." No amount of aspirin will cure blood poisoning, and no amount of reforms will transform capitalism. Like Malcolm X said,

> It's impossible for a chicken to produce a duck egg. The system in this country cannot produce freedom for the Afro-American. It is impossible for this system, this economic system, this political system, this social system, this system period.[154]

One big union?

Because it controls the production of goods and services, the capitalist class can impose its rules on society—Seize the Surplus and Compete or Die. By taking charge of production, the working class can impose its rule on society—Share. How could this be accomplished?

The battle for control over production is waged in every workplace every day. When bosses insist that "What's mine is mine, and what's yours is mine too" (Seize the Surplus), workers have no choice but to fight back. When they don't feel confident enough to fight openly, they fight secretly, taking home "company property," damaging equipment, and committing acts of minor sabotage. The more organized workers are, the more confidence they feel to challenge the boss.

Because unions organize workers in self-defence, some people think that unions can be a force for revolution. In 1905, American socialists and trade unionists launched the Industrial Workers of the World (IWW). Their aim was to organize the working class into One Big Union, call a general strike, shut down capitalist production, and restart it under workers' control. It was a great plan with a fatal flaw.

In every workplace people have political differences, so that conflict results when anyone raises an issue like abortion, immigration, or war. To prevent endless disagreements and divisions, the IWW rejected political discussion, insisting that the economic battle was all that mattered. However, problems don't go away because you ignore them. Workers are bombarded by the ideas of the ruling class, including the idea that there is no alternative to capitalism. By boycotting political discussion, the IWW was unable to counter ruling class ideas that maintain social control.

Unions are organizations of reform, not revolution. Their function is to defend workers' rights within the system, not to transform the system. Each union concentrates on improving conditions one contract at a time, in one workplace or one industry. Originally based on specific trades, and then specific industries, unions divide the working class into different and sometimes competing unions, often within the same workplace. Furthermore, union officials perform a management function that makes them hostile to revolutionary change.

The cowardice and betrayal of union officials have prompted groups of workers to build democratic organizations inside their unions. A good example is Soldiers of Solidarity inside the United Auto Workers' Union. In *Democracy is Power: Rebuilding Unions From the Bottom Up,* Mike Parker and Martha Gruelle write,

> Let's be clear: the goal of our movement is not just bigger unions. It's for working people to function as human beings—not bootlicks, not cogs—starting with our jobs, where we spend most of our waking hours. When we leave our jobs at the end of the day, we should be as healthy as when we started. We should be able to look at the next day, and our retirement years, with a feeling of security, not dread. Our larger goal is for workers to exert power collectively in the workplace and society—and for that you need much more than bigger unions. You need powerful workers.[155]

Achieving this kind of power requires union members to organize *across* unions—in workers councils. This step is crucial, not only to fight the bosses and the union bureaucrats, but to lay the foundation for a worker-run society.

Public or Common?

People living in pre-class societies had no concept of property. They had personal-use items, and everything else was shared. No one "owned" the land, the water, the forests, the animals, or the knowledge that had been accumulated through the generations. All this changed with class society. Those who seized the surplus claimed it as their private property for their exclusive use. Today, the term "private property" commonly refers to personal-use items (your house and car) as well as to the means of production (land, water, science, technology, factories, offices, machinery, etc.). This book uses the term "private property" to mean *only* the means of production, not personal property. People have always had personal-use items and will always have them, regardless of the type of social system. The important question is who owns or controls the means of survival—the means of production.

Under capitalism, a distinction is made between private and public property, where private property is owned by a capitalist or group of capitalists and public property is owned by the State. Because the State claims to represent the people, State or public property is assumed to be the property of the people or common property. It is not. *Common property cannot be owned.* Common property is no one's property—it is not "property" at all. It cannot be bought or sold, and its use is democratically determined by ordinary people, the way it was in pre-class societies.

Because public property is falsely equated with common property, most people mistakenly think that an economy that is run by the State must be socialist or communist. Let's look briefly at how this confusion came about.

The first State to command an entire economy developed out of the defeat of the Russian Revolution. When the working class took control of production, it became the common property of the people. When the working class was defeated, the State took ownership of production *in the name of the people.* This may seem like a subtle difference, but it is not. Common ownership means that common people are in control.

Public ownership means that State officials are in control. Common control of production was used to meet the needs of the working class. State control of production was used to exploit the working class.

If the amount of State control of the economy is a measure of socialism or communism, then the United States is as communist as China because the governments of both nations control a similar proportion of their economy (about 30 percent). In fact, neither nation is communist. The U.S. and China are both capitalist countries that exploit their working classes, and both have constitutions that uphold the private ownership of production.

The capitalist State helps the capitalist class to accumulate capital. The stronger the State, the stronger the capitalist class, and vice versa. During the 20th century, the size and scope of the State expanded enormously in all the industrial nations. The World Bank calculated that between 1960 and 1995, total government spending in the wealthiest nations rose from 20 percent to almost 50 percent of their GDP (annual value of goods and services produced). Ironically, the Organization for Economic Cooperation and Development (OECD) has advised the Chinese State to play a *greater role* in developing its economy.

States function as capitalists in their own right, investing at home and abroad, independently and in partnership with private capital. During both World Wars, the American State took direct control of the economy and ran it on behalf of the capitalist class. Public ownership is a form of private property under capitalism, while common ownership is a feature of mass democracy or socialism. There are no socialist economies in the world today, no nations where the working-class collectively controls production. No, not any—not even close.

Social democrats and Heads of State like Cuba's Fidel Castro and Venezuela's Hugo Chávez promote State control as more socially responsive than corporate control. These advocates of "State socialism" prefer that society be ruled by humane reformers instead of by profit-hungry capitalists. They reject majority rule in the belief that society could never be managed by common people.

Fearing the power of the working class, the capitalist class keeps a close eye on workers' cooperatives to make sure that they do not pose a threat to the system. The workers' co-op that managed the Bauen Hotel in Buenos Aires was providing space for political meetings, conferences, and assemblies. City authorities evicted the workers and handed the hotel to a former owner. The Zanón ceramics factory was integrated into the State. The workers were given legal ownership of the factory on the condition that they pay 30,000 pesos (about $10,000) a month in taxes. In essence, the State and the cooperative formed a joint venture. Undoubtedly, this is much better than when Louis Zanón ran the place, but it is not socialism.

Socialism

No living creature is born in a fully developed state, and no new society emerges from the old one fully formed. Socialism is an historical process that occurs in three phases. In the first phase, a social revolution replaces the rule of the capitalist class with the rule of the working class. In the second phase, the working class must secure its rule and prevent the capitalist class from regaining power. The Russian Revolution was defeated because it failed to complete this phase. As majority rule spreads and more people join in the process of managing society, class divisions disappear. In the final phase, humanity is united in the common goal of providing for and developing every human being. Let's take a closer look at these three phases.

Phase I: Let's say that corruption at the top of society, hatred of war, and persistent hardships provoke unrelenting strikes and demonstrations. Let's say that the ruling class cannot agree on how to move forward and that worker's councils have organized at the local, regional, and national levels. After much debate and discussion, the workers' councils decide to take control of society. Once they are sure that the majority supports this decision, especially key sections of the armed forces, then a date is set for the revolution. On that day, everyone goes to work as usual. Once they arrive, workers escort bosses and managers out the door and call a meeting.

Practical tasks are divided up, and worker-managers are elected as coordinators. These people are paid no more than anyone else and are accountable to those who elect them. They can be replaced by majority vote at any time and for any reason. Technical professionals report to worker-managers in the same way they reported to the capitalists. The company's books are posted on the internet for all to see. A debate begins on how to reorganize production, eliminating work that is dangerous (asbestos mining, nuclear power, weapons production), creating safe alternatives, and directing goods and services where they are needed.

Media workers who have taken over their newspapers, magazines, and radio and television stations provide news of the revolution. Soldiers bring their weapons and ammunition to worker-controlled locations. Contingents of armed soldiers and workers guard key sites. The national organization of workers' councils becomes a hub of activity, organizing and coordinating—taking on the functions of a governing body. Groups with no specific workplace (students, seniors, the unemployed, and the disabled) send representatives to the new government.

Phase II: The deposed bosses gather their forces and launch a counter-revolution. They are supported by capitalists in power elsewhere, sections of the middle-class, and whatever media and military forces they still command. The workers' state has prepared for this challenge and mobilizes its forces. The workers' media counters the lies being spread by the capitalists and organizes support for the revolution. The workers' government appeals to those who still waver and calls on the working class to defend itself. An appeal is broadcast to workers of all lands—Join us! Help us! Workers in other countries launch their own revolutions, and the two classes face off on an international stage.

Just as a child learning to walk must fall a number of times before it learns to keep its balance, so too will the working class seize power and fall back on more than one occasion. This process is necessary and unavoidable. As Luxemburg stated,

> It is impossible to imagine that a transformation as formidable as the passage from capitalist society to socialist society can be realized in one happy act. The socialist transformation supposes a long and stubborn struggle, in the course of which, it is quite probable the working class will be repulsed more than once so that for the first time, from the viewpoint of the final outcome of the struggle, it will have necessarily come to power "too early."...Since the working class is not in the position to seize power in any other way than "prematurely," since the working class is absolutely obliged to seize power once or several times "too early" before it can maintain itself in power for good, the objection to the "premature" conquest of power is at bottom nothing more than a *general opposition to the aspiration of the working class to possess itself of State power*.[156]

Phase III: Workers are firmly in control of society on a global basis and can turn their full attention to solving the problems inherited from the old society. There is a desperate need for good food, clean water, medicine, and housing. Polluted areas must be cleaned up. There are many decisions to make, like what forms of energy to use and what to do with people who are so damaged by capitalism that they cannot be safely integrated into society. These matters are debated and decided. Mistakes are made and corrected. The learning curve is steep and exhilarating.

With everyone pitching in, socially necessary work can be done in less time, freeing everyone to explore and develop music, dance, drama, art, literature, and science. Human creativity is expressed in every project, reuniting work and art. People experiment with different ways of living and working together. Every culture brings its riches to the table—a gigantic cultural potluck offering countless dishes to sample. People move where they are needed and travel where they desire.

A new generation is born into a world without classes, without borders, without races, where women and men participate equally in all aspects of social life. From the earliest ages, the young learn to cooperate, to contribute, and to participate in making decisions. School and work merge into a lifelong learning journey. Youngsters are encouraged to find answers to their questions, instead of being injected with pre-set answers. People make their own decisions regarding personal matters. Restricting the right to decide does not prevent mistakes, it prevents learning—the biggest mistake of all.

Creating this new society will not be easy. However, it will be easier than living in a system that prevents people from solving problems. Cooks yearn to feed the hungry. Medical workers long to treat the sick. Teachers want to excite their students. The unemployed hunger to work. Parents desire good lives for their children. Everyone aches to create, to contribute, to belong, to be appreciated. Unable to meet these needs, the system lurches from crisis to crisis and class anger grows. People are fed up with incompetent leaders, perpetual insecurity, and endless war. The seed of socialism strains to free itself from the suffocating husk of capitalism. Only one thing is missing—the means by which the working class can organize itself to take power.

The revolutionary party

The capitalist class in the United States has two vanguard parties: the Republicans and the Democrats. The key members of these parties are the most class-conscious advocates for capitalism. The working class needs its own vanguard party, composed of all who understand the need to fight capitalism and are actively organizing against it at work, at school, and in their neighborhoods.

Capitalist parties promote the interests of the capitalist class. Workers need a political party that promotes their interests. Capitalist parties aim to get elected to public office. A workers' party must aim to put the working class in power. Capitalist parties attract wealthy and influential people. The workers' party looks for ordinary people who want to change the world. Capitalist parties wheel and deal to get ahead. The workers' party must be totally honest about its goals, regardless of how unpopular they are. People who compromise their principles cannot be trusted, and the workers' party must gain the trust of the working class.

Capitalist parties are controlled by well-connected insiders at the top; ordinary party members have little or no influence. The workers' party is organized very differently, more like the human body. Think about it. Each organ in the body is continually communicating its condition to all the other organs that use this information to coordinate body functions. The brain serves as the executive center that collects information from all the organs, analyzes it, and then sends out instructions that meet the needs of the body as a whole. The brain itself is composed of different centers that take on executive functions according to the needs of the situation. Like the body, the workers' party needs to hear from all of its members. The party also needs executive centers to organize that information into plans of action that serve the whole. This form of organization is called democratic centralism.

Democratic centralism links maximum discussion with unity in action. The democracy portion of democratic centralism lies in the communication that moves horizontally and vertically, between people and up and down the chain of command. All of this information is important to the functioning of the whole. If leaders take the organization in the wrong direction, members can call a meeting to elect a new leadership.

Centralism is rooted in the need for many different elements to act as one. The brain tells the body to move in one direction so that it doesn't try to go in different directions at the same time. After the move, the brain collects feedback from all the organs regarding their experience. The brain may be assured that it moved the body correctly or that it made a mistake (like bumping into a wall) and should move differently next time. Either way, the brain-body is constantly learning. The workers' party does the same. Once a decision is made, everyone moves together. Afterwards, everyone discusses the experience. If the move was not good, then the following move can be different. Either way, leaders and members are engaged in a continuing learning process. (Under repressive conditions, the workers' party needs to be more centralist to survive. This was the case in Russia under the rule of the Tsars. When organizing is legal, the best results flow from balancing centralism and democracy.)

Consider what would happen if the body was run like capitalism, where the brain played the role of the ruling class and the organs represented the working class. I can see it now…

Brain: Liver! No talking to the Kidneys. Heart, stick to the rhythm I laid out for you! I am the brains of this operation, not you. OK, Gut, it's time to push out the crud. What did you say? How dare you question my timing?

Under such conditions, it would not take long for everything to break down. An authoritarian system where information travels only one way—from top to bottom—is a rigid system. Examples include the refusal to heed the warning that terrorists might use commercial airplanes as missiles and that the levees protecting New Orleans would fail in a flood. In flexible systems, information goes up as well as down. The needs of people "on the ground" must be heeded at the top so that resources can be sent where they are needed.

Socialism is like the human body, a complex biological organism that is self-organizing, self-regenerating, totally integrated, and with a flexible leadership that changes depending on the needs of the situation. Capitalism is like a cancer, where a few cells serve their own needs regardless of the damage done to the whole.

Anarchism and violence

Revolutionary organizations of the working class have nothing in common with revolutionary organizations of the middle class. Anarchism (literally "anti-power") represents the needs of small-scale producers who are squeezed between big business and organized labor. Anarchists reject all forms of central authority as undemocratic. In typical middle-class style, anarchists want to do their own thing and oppose workers controlling society as much as they oppose capitalists controlling society. In terms of the body metaphor, anarchists want the organs to communicate among themselves, with no brain to coordinate the whole.

Insisting that small is beautiful, anarchists long to return to the time of small farmers, artisans, and shopkeepers. Anarchy would fragment the world economy into small spheres of local production and exchange that were typical during the Middle Ages. Even if we could turn back the clock, the process of capital accumulation (described in earlier chapters) would eventually bring us back to where we are now—monopoly capitalism.

While anarchism is commonly associated with violence, most anarchists are not violent. However, anarchism does lend itself to dramatic gestures and extreme acts that aim to shock people into action. Militant anarchists hurl themselves against the State, the police, and every other symbol of authority. The basic difference between anarchists and socialists is that anarchists favor individual actions to change society, while socialists rely on the organized power of the working class.

Capitalism is the most violent society ever created. Every day, millions suffer and die needlessly. The violence of those who fight the system is minuscule in comparison. Nevertheless, capitalism cannot be defeated through military means because the ruling class controls far more military means than ordinary people could ever lay their hands on. *The power of the working class lies in its ability to stop capitalist production and to begin producing for human need.* The working class is such a large majority that a well-organized revolution need not be violent at all. In *Ten Days That Shook the World*, John Reed observed that on the day of the Russian Revolution, fewer people than normal died in St. Petersburg. However, the capitalist class will not surrender its power without a fight, forcing the working class to defend itself.

History lessons

Those who do not learn from history will repeat its mistakes. The workers' party serves as the memory of the working class, applying the lessons of the past to the problems of the present. Some of the most important lessons are:

- Whoever controls production controls society.

- Only one class can rule. Either the capitalist class imposes its directives (Seize the Surplus and Compete or Die) or the working class imposes its directive (Share). No society can follow two conflicting rules at the same time.

- Capitalism is an international system, so that socialism must also be international. Socialism is not possible in one workplace, one city, one state, or one country. Failure to spread the revolution will lead to its defeat.

- The conditions of capitalism force the working class to rebel. When and how these rebellions break out cannot be predicted in advance.

- The middle class will always compromise. (See the next chapter).

- The working class needs a revolutionary party to organize the seizure of power.

Workers' councils are the foundation on which socialism is built, and they form spontaneously during general strikes. Some better-known examples include Spain in 1936-37, Hungary in 1956, Portugal in 1974-75, Chile in 1973, and Iran in 1979. While workers' councils form spontaneously, they do not take power spontaneously because there is so much pressure against such a move. Workers' councils have formed a government only once, in revolutionary Russia, when the Bolshevik Party *convinced* the All–Russian Congress of Soviets to take power.

A successful working-class revolution requires support from the armed forces. Recall that soldiers are workers who provide a management function for capitalism. Because they stand between the classes, civil conflict pulls the armed forces apart; they are disciplined to follow orders, yet naturally balk at killing their own people. The outcome of the revolution depends on winning the loyalty of the ordinary soldier. During the Russian Revolution, the armed forces defected to the Bolshevik Party because it was committed to ending the war and because it was pushing the workers' councils to take power. The determination to take power is critical to prevent the capitalist class from regaining control and exacting the most ruthless vengeance on those who rebelled against it.

To win the argument for workers' revolution, the workers' party must organize as far in advance as possible. Earlier chapters explained the pressures that prevent people from thinking clearly and from feeling confident enough to fight for their rights. Such pressures can be resisted only by standing together. The workers' party provides a place where people can clear the mental confusion that capitalism generates and practice solving problems collectively. A workers' party breaks down divisions based on race, sex, nationality, and sexual orientation by bringing people together to fight as a class against capitalism and all the forms of oppression that it generates.

The strength of a workers' party lies in marrying political clarity with growing numbers. More people pulling together leads to more clarity, more success, and more people joining. Big is definitely better. When the workers' party finally wins the support of most of the working class, the date for the revolution can be set. Capitalism generates so much self-doubt within workers that most people will not believe that revolution is possible, even up to the day of the revolution. However, a determined minority who fight *consistently* for the interests of the majority can convince that majority to take power, because *it is the working class, not the party, that must take control of society*. As Rosa Luxemburg argued,

> Socialism will not and cannot be created by decrees; nor can it be established by any government, however socialist. Socialism must be created by the masses, by every worker. Where the chains of capitalism are forged, there they must be broken. Only that is socialism, and only thus can socialism be created.[157]

Self-emancipation

No ruler, politician, bureaucrat, intellectual, professional, expert, or reformer can liberate humanity from capitalism. The majority must liberate itself for two reasons. Only the working class can take control of production away from the capitalist class. And only through the process of changing society can people become fit to rule that new society.

Human beings are shaped by what they do, and people transform themselves in the process of changing their world. Nadya Krupskaya captures this change in her memoirs,

> The streets in those days [of the Russian Revolution] presented a curious spectacle: everywhere, people stood about in knots, arguing heatedly and discussing the latest events… The house in which we lived overlooked a courtyard, and even here, if you opened the window at night, you could hear a heated dispute. A solider would be sitting there, and he always had an audience—usually some of the cooks, or housemaids from next door, or some of the young people…These street meetings were so interesting, that it once took me three hours to walk from Shirokaya Street to the Krzesinska Mansion.[158]

Capitalism degrades the human spirit by excluding the majority from control over their lives. When people fight for a better world, they develop the capacities that capitalism suppresses. They discover their courage, their strength, their intelligence, their hope, and their power. As people pull together for a common goal, suspicion, isolation, and fear are transformed into trust, solidarity, and confidence. After the 1937 occupation of General Motors, Dollinger recalls,

> the auto worker became a different human being. The women that had participated actively became a different type of woman, a different type from any we had ever known anywhere in the labor movement and certainly not in the city of Flint. They carried themselves with a different walk, their heads were high, and they had confidence in themselves. They were not only mentally different, but physically different. If you saw one of those women in the beginning and then saw her just a short period after going through this experience, learning and feeling that she had things she could fit together in her life, it would be an entirely different woman.[159]

When human beings experience their collective power, they discover a world of possibilities. They also find themselves to be more honorable than they thought possible. During the Russian Revolution, the first workers to enter the Winter Palace were dazzled by the treasures of the Tzars. Being very poor, their first impulse was to grab what they could carry. John Reed was there and described what happened,

> The looting was just beginning when somebody cried, "Comrades! Don't take anything. This is the property of the People!" Immediately, twenty voices were crying, "Stop! Put everything back! Don't take anything! Property of the People!" Many hands dragged the spoilers down. Damask and tapestries were snatched from the arms of those who had taken them; two men took away the bronze clock. Roughly and hastily the things were crammed back into their cases, and self-appointed sentinels stood guard. It was all utterly spontaneous.[160]

Most of what was taken from the Winter Palace was retrieved. Today, the treasures of Russia are exhibited in museums and art galleries around the world. (Compare this outcome with the permanent loss of the treasures of Iraq.) The Russian Revolution taught John Reed three things:

> That in the last analysis, the property owning class is loyal only to its property. That the property owning class will never readily compromise with the working class. That the masses of workers are capable not only of great dreams, but they have in them the power to make dreams come true.[161]

Yes, but

In times of social crisis, when the ruling class has lost credibility and the working class is fed up with being oppressed, people begin to shake off the ideas that hold them in bondage. The experience of collective organizing opens possibilities that normally seem like pipe dreams. The working class has the power to create a society that can meet human needs. It would not be a perfect society, because human beings are incapable of being perfect; however, no class could do a worse job at managing society than the capitalist class. At this point, the middle class jumps up in protest. The next chapter explains why the middle class is so hostile to majority rule.

Summary

Workers don't need bosses. Ordinary people are capable of producing under a system of democratic self-management. The working class can become fit to manage society only by going through the transformative process of liberating itself.

To prevent mass democracy, capitalism offers a sham democracy that separates economics and politics. The capitalist class is united in its determination to hold onto power. The revolutionary workers' party must ensure that the working class is more united and more determined.

Chapter 15

Beware the Middle Ground

Compromise Always Favors Those Who Have More Power

In *The Cancer Stage of Capitalism,* John McMurtry compares capitalism to a cancer that threatens the human species. Like a cancer, capitalism seeks to expand regardless of what it destroys. McMurtry concludes that, like a person suffering from cancer, humanity must unite to repel the disease. Here the metaphor breaks down. A person with cancer has one goal — to defeat the illness. In contrast, humanity is split into classes with conflicting goals. As the cancer of capitalism grows, the capitalist class grows richer and more powerful. From the perspective of the working class, the capitalist class *is* the cancer because it imposes its sick rules on society. The middle refuses to admit that the conflict between the other two classes is irreconcilable. Middle-class appeals for unity disarm the working class — the only force that can cure the cancer of capitalism.

The capitalist class has no problem supporting appeals for peace and unity that do not challenge its power. In 1999, the General Assembly of the United Nations passed a Declaration "to promote and strengthen a culture of peace in the new millennium." In 2000, the UN launched the International Year for the Culture of Peace, and the following ten years were declared the International Decade for a Culture of Peace and Non-Violence for the Children of the World. While the UN talks peace, it wages war. For the past 70 years, the UN has provided a humanitarian cover for the military aggression of the world's most powerful nations. During the 1990's, the UN imposed an economic embargo on Iraq that resulted in the deaths of more than half-a-million children. In 2004, UN forces helped to crush the democratically-elected government of Haiti and establish a murderous military dictatorship. The UN message of peace works like a drug to dull the pain of imperialism. Soothing phrases about peace seduce people into supporting a system addicted to war.

There can be no peace without justice. As long as the capitalist class wages war on the working class, asking people to cultivate peace in their hearts is asking them to accept exploitation and oppression.

The noisy middle class and the invisible working class

Despite forming only 20 percent of the population, the middle class makes a lot of noise. Middle-class people write books, make films, set fashions, and are heavily represented in the media. They are consulted as professionals and experts, as people who know things, and they exhibit the confidence that accompanies this social role. The middle class makes so much noise that it exerts a far greater influence over society than its numbers warrant.

The working class is four times larger than the middle class, yet it is much less visible. Television is populated overwhelmingly by middle-class characters. When they appear at all, working-class people are generally portrayed as buffoons, bimbos, and deviants. The relative invisibility of the working class contributes to the mistaken belief that working people are not intelligent or important, let alone a force that could remake society.

The middle class cannot imagine any system other than capitalism, having no respect for the ability of the working class to create a different world. Consequently, the middle class embraces the myth that the Russian Revolution was a palace coup, not a mass revolution. Without a shred of evidence, economic reformer Jeffrey Sachs states, "Lenin and a small group of conspirators were able to seize power with very little support."[162] Sachs cannot imagine ordinary people fighting for their own liberation; therefore, it could not happen. The Russian ruling class made the same mistake.

In *Ten Days that Shook the World*, American journalist John Reed recounts how Kerensky's army marched on Petrograd, demanding that the workers' government surrender. Who would oppose them? Two days before the battle, Petrograd was full of leaderless bands of armed workers, sailors, and soldiers. Yet, on the morning of the battle, this scattered, rag-tag army had organized itself into a formidable force. Reed describes how it happened.

> Over the bleak plain on the cold quiet air spread the sound of battle, falling upon the ears of roving bands as they gathered about their little fires, waiting…So it was beginning! They made towards the battle; and the worker hordes pouring out along the straight roads quickened their pace…Thus upon all the points of attack automatically converged angry human swarms, to be met by [revolutionary officers] and assigned positions, or work to do. This was *their* battle, for *their* world; the officers in command were elected by *them*. For the moment, that incoherent multiple will was one will…Those who participated in the fighting described how the sailors fought until they ran out of cartridges, and then stormed; how the untrained workmen rushed the charging Cossacks and tore them from their horses; how the anonymous hordes of the people, gathering in the darkness around the battle, rose like a tide and poured over the enemy…Before midnight the Cossacks broke and were fleeing, leaving their artillery behind them.[163]

The muddle in the middle

Because the middle class has so much influence in society and dominates (or tries to dominate) the social movements, we need to understand the conflicting pressures that shape it. The middle class is in constant conflict, being pushed and pulled by the other two classes — squeezed by banks and finance capitalists on the one side and by workers' demands for higher wages on the other. The conflicting interests of the middle class result in conflicted loyalty. On the same day, the middle class will side with workers against capitalists (opposing the loss of civil liberties) and with capitalists against workers (opposing a rise in the minimum wage).

The conflict within the middle class creates conservative and liberal sections. The part closer to the ruling class promotes capitalism as the best of all systems. The part closer to the working class is more critical and wants capitalism to meet human needs. As conflict between capitalists and workers increases, the middle class is pulled apart, with one section backing the ruling class and another section siding with the working class.

Let me repeat that class does not *determine* a person's beliefs. Anyone from any class can be right-wing, left-wing, conservative, liberal, or revolutionary. However, people find it easier to hold beliefs that fit with their class function than to hold beliefs that conflict with their class function. And the function of the middle class is to manage capitalism, not replace it. The beliefs and behaviors most consistent with this function are: opportunism and compromise; individualism; moralism; liberalism; and idealism.

Opportunism and compromise

Because of its intermediate position, the middle class waffles between support for the ruling class and support for the working class. The capitalist class has no choice but to exploit the working class — ending exploitation would end capitalism. The working class has no choice but to resist exploitation — submission would result in being worked to death. The middle class is the only class that can choose which side to support.

Like a middle child, the middle class sees both sides and wants everyone to get along. Compromise is valuable in a family or among friends with common interests. However, in a class-divided society, compromise favors those with more power. When push comes to shove, the bulk of the middle class will abandon its principles and side with the more powerful class. Such opportunism makes the middle class an unreliable ally. In times of peace, middle-class liberals deplore war. As soon as war is declared, they are the first to support it. In *PR!*, Stewart Ewen describes how middle-class intellectuals were recruited to promote World War I, "People who had once believed in the ability to use creative intelligence to bring about a more humane social order [became] dutiful technicians of mass persuasion, craven manipulators of consent."

The middle class believes that it is possible to support both sides of a war, to back a military invasion and also to provide medical care for the civilian wounded. In the real world, one cannot be on the side of the invaders and on the side of the invaded at the same time. The best way to help the victims of war is to prevent war or to stop it as soon as possible. The capitalist class sets up clinics and other helping services to provide humanitarian dressing for its military aggression. The middle class keeps falling for this ruse, believing that it is helping the victim, when it is actually supporting the perpetrator.

Politically, the middle class swings back and forth as the balance of forces shifts between the classes on either side of it. When the ruling class is on the offensive, the middle class falls in line. When the working class is gaining ground, the middle class becomes more radical. Unwilling to acknowledge their own opportunism, liberals refer to this back-and-forth movement as "the political pendulum." The Claude Pepper Museum actually has a Political Pendulum exhibit, with the following description:.

> Over the years, America has altered between liberal and conservative ideals…Each year, Pepper Museum staff set the pendulum to reflect the country's current leanings. Though the pendulum on occasion may swing disagreeably to one extreme, though we may sometimes display an attitude of which we will be ashamed subsequently, always the steady, pulsing heart of the American people will ensure that America does not lose its balance or its traditions.[164]

The pendulum metaphor reassures the powerless that, no matter how bad things get, they will (somehow) get better in time. In 2006, *New York Times* columnist Bob Herbert lambasted a federal policy that excluded poverty-stricken Americans, especially poor Blacks, from Medicaid. His conclusion was,

"Someday the pendulum will swing back, and the government of the United States will become more representative and more humane." Used in this way, the pendulum metaphor frees liberals from any obligation to organize against the system they criticize.

Individualism

Workers can improve their work and their lives only through collective action. A single factory worker who asks for more pay has a snowball's-chance-in-hell of getting it. In contrast, individual professionals advance by acquiring higher education and by making personal connections. The middle-class experience of individual advancement supports the belief that everyone should be able to advance the same way. Those who promote individual effort and ignore the constraints of the social pyramid end up blaming the victims of the system for their own misfortune.

The individualist approach to social problems is basically selfish. A common middle-class argument is that people who can pay for medical care should not have to wait in line with everyone else. The result of such thinking is a two-class medical system that offers top-of-the-line care for the wealthy and bargain basement care for everyone else. The collective alternative, providing top notch medical care for everyone, is rejected on the basis that the well should not have to pay higher taxes to support the sick.

Sections of the middle class are close enough to the working class to understand the importance of providing basic medical care for everyone. However, they stop short of demanding that everyone get the best possible care. The middle class accepts social inequality in the mistaken belief that society cannot provide for everyone. (The final chapter counters this belief.)

The individual outlook of the middle class ignores social factors and promotes health as an individual responsibility. A doctor advises a hotel worker suffering from overwork to take a vacation. A working mother with headaches is told to take more time for herself. How a hotel worker would pay for a vacation and when a working mother would find time for herself are not the doctor's problems. Instead of challenging a society that demands too much and provides too little, the middle class lectures the victim.

Moralism

> ...the warring classes will seek to gain victory by every means, while middle-class moralists will continue to wander in confusion between the two camps. Subjectively they sympathize with the oppressed—no one doubts that. Objectively, they remain captives of the morality of the ruling class and seek to impose it upon the oppressed instead of helping them to elaborate the morality of revolution.[165]
>
> *Leon Trotsky*

Moralism—the assumption that there is only one right way to behave—is a powerful form of social control. In reality, conflicting classes have conflicting moral views. Most working people would support Robin Hood stealing from the rich to give to the poor. They would also be sympathetic to a mother who stole food for her children. In contrast, the capitalist would condemn Robin Hood, throw the mother in prison, and put her children in foster care. *The morality of each class represents what is right for that class.* The capitalist class has only one morality—accumulate capital—and accepts all means to that end, legal or illegal (torture), moral or immoral (wars of acquisition).

To stay in power, the capitalist class must present its "morality" as a universal morality (What's good for business is good for America). When the authorities condemn stealing as wrong, they mean that stealing by workers is wrong because their own thievery is sanctioned by law (Seize the Surplus). When the people in power condemn murder as immoral, they mean that murder committed by ordinary people is immoral, because the cold-blooded murder they commit is completely legal (war and State executions).

Middle-class moralists help the capitalist class to impose its priorities on the working class. Consider these moralistic statements: Giving drug addicts clean needles only condones drug addiction. Educating young people about sex only encourages them to have sex. Providing access to abortion only makes it easier for people to be irresponsible. In real life, individuals behave as they see fit, and we all suffer when they are prevented from doing so safely. Clean needles and sex education reduce the harm to individuals and society that is caused by criminalizing drug use and keeping young people sexually ignorant. However, the ruling class is willing to risk individual and social safety to prevent people from making their own choices, and moralists supply the arguments that support this stance.

Middle-class moralism is rooted in the belief that we cannot change society; therefore, we must change ourselves by making the right choices and by living the right lifestyle. In reality, choice is determined by class. Under capitalism, the people with the most money have the most choices and the most power to shape society.

Liberalism

Liberal politics suit the middle class. The word "liberal" derives from the Latin word *liber*, meaning "free." The middle class wants the freedom to conduct its individual affairs, unhampered by the demands of the capitalist class *and* by the demands of the working class.

Liberalism was a progressive force in the fight against feudal restrictions and in the fight against colonial rule during the American Revolution. Liberalism is also progressive in its demand to extend democratic rights, like the right to vote and the right to gay marriage. However, the contradictory position of the middle class creates a conflict in the heart of liberalism. Liberalism champions equality and individual rights *and* the right to privately own the means of production. These principles conflict in the case of slavery, where two people cannot be equal if one owns the other. The right to own slaves violates the rights of slaves. In industrial terms, the private ownership of production makes capitalists and workers unequal. The right of employers to control the labor process conflicts with the right of workers to control their work.

Under capitalism, medical formulations are privately owned (patented) to ensure that drugs will be profitable. The only way to defend the property rights of drug companies *and* the individual right of people to have medicine is to raise enough money to buy medicines for those who cannot pay. Such efforts are typically insufficient so that, in practice, the "right" to medicine is enjoyed only by those who can afford it. Liberals reject the collectivist alternative of providing free medicines to all because that would violate the right of drug companies to privately own medical formulations.

On social issues, liberals vacillate between pro-business conservatives on the right and pro-labor socialists on the left. Where conservatives want to restrict the right to abortion, liberals defend a woman's right to choose. However, liberals reject the socialist demand for all women to have access to abortion (free abortion on demand). Liberals talk left and move right. By rejecting social measures that would give everyone the same rights, liberals uphold individual rights only for those who can pay for them.

Idealism

> When you wish upon a star, makes no difference who you are
> Anything your heart desires will come to you.

A lack of power nourishes a belief in magic. The middle class has neither the command power of the ruling class nor the organized power of the working class. Being the least powerful class, the middle class is steeped in idealism, religion, spiritualism, and wishful thinking. For the middle class, wanting something badly enough should be enough to make it happen.

Lacking power on its own, the middle class wants the State to protect it by curtailing the power of big business *and* the power of labor unions. This desire is expressed in the liberal demand that the State be a neutral force that favors neither capital nor labor. When the State displays its bias for the capitalist class, the middle class is shocked and outraged. For the middle class, the *need* for a neutral State becomes a moral imperative—the State *should* be neutral—followed by the magical belief that the State *is* neutral. Perpetual frustration results when the State does not behave the way it *should*.

Overwhelming evidence that the State serves the capitalist class is dismissed with a variety of excuses: the right people aren't in power; they don't know what they're doing; there are always a few bad apples. For the middle class, belief in the neutrality of the State is a matter of faith—a religion. No matter how much evidence accumulates to prove that the State is an instrument of class rule, the middle class cannot acknowledge what it feels powerless to change.

The idealism of the middle class feeds the magical belief that the world could change if people behaved as if it were already different. ("Be the change you want to see in the world.") In this cozy fantasy, class divisions and State repression don't exist. Cooperatives and utopian societies embody this kind of idealism.

Cooperatives and utopian societies

Capitalism makes life seem empty and meaningless by alienating people from their work, from each other, from themselves, and from the natural world. Understandably, some people try to create islands of equality and cooperation within capitalism. One of the better known examples is the Mondragon Cooperative Corporation in Spain.

> From its origins forty years ago as an employee-owned cooperative manufacturing paraffin stoves, Mondragon has grown to 160 employee-owned cooperatives, involving 23,000 member owners, with sales grossing three billion dollars (US) in 1991. Statistics show the Mondragon cooperatives to be twice as profitable as the average corporation in Spain with employee productivity surpassing any other Spanish organization. It has its own bank, a research institute, an entrepreneurial division, insurance and social security institutions, schools, a college, a health maintenance system and a health insurance cooperative. It is focused on relational cooperatives dedicated to the common good.[166]

Can the cooperative model be an alternative to capitalism? Unfortunately, the answer is no. Like any other business, a co-op must compete as a capitalist enterprise. Those that cannot compete successfully go out of business; those that stay in business are forced to exploit themselves. The Mondragon Bookstore and Coffeehouse in Canada provides a good example.

Everyone who works there is a co-owner, all work is shared evenly, there are no bosses or hierarchies and everyone earns the same wage. After nearly six years of operation...collective members, even those who have been part of the project since day one, still make only minimum wage—perhaps part of the reason some members have left so quickly....All but a handful of the original 10 have moved on.[167]

Most importantly, cooperatives in a capitalist system are not free to produce what people need, only what can be sold or traded within the co-op network or larger market. As Rosa Luxemburg pointed out 100 years ago,

Producers' co-operatives are excluded from the most important branches of capital production—the textile, mining, metallurgical and petroleum industries, machine construction, locomotive and shipbuilding. For this reason alone, co-operatives in the field of production cannot be seriously considered as the instrument of a general social transformation...Within the framework of present society, producers' co-operatives are limited to the role of simple annexes to consumers' co-operatives.[168]

Most cooperatives consider themselves to be models of how society should function. Through the centuries, a variety of ideal or utopian communities have been constructed, based on the philosophies of their founders. During the Middle Ages, religious monasteries and convents offered sanctuary, learning, cooperation, and service. During the 19th century, reformers like Charles Fourier, Etienne Cabet, and Robert Owen created detailed blueprints for ideal communities that would be managed by intellectuals and financed by far-sighted capitalists.

Cooperatives and utopian communities offer working models of how society should operate, but they offer no way to transform society on a global scale. The assumption is that these models will be so attractive that, *somehow*, they will grow to encompass all of society. This is naive. The capitalist class will not abandon its power and profits for a more humane model of society.

A second problem with utopian societies is that they are pre-planned, offering one right way to live and organize society. In real life, people have plans of their own. The job of planning society properly belongs to those who live in it, using whatever theories and methods seem best at the time. In contrast, utopian societies impose behaviors on people based on the founder's values. A good example is PARECON, a model society based on participatory economics.

In *PARECON: Life After Capitalism,* Michael Albert describes his version of an ideal society. Like all anarchists, Albert opposes central planning as inherently authoritarian and undemocratic. He cannot imagine workers coordinating global production for the benefit of humanity. However, in a genuine democracy, people would be free to choose the method of organizing that works best in any situation. Some things, like fresh produce, are better produced locally, while other things, like pharmaceuticals, are better produced centrally. Restricting people's choices in advance is bureaucratic.

PARECON is not based on the socialist principle, "from each according to ability and to each according to need," because Albert distrusts that people could actually put this into practice. Instead, he proposes a complex "system of remuneration for effort and sacrifice," in which those who work harder get more. How will effort and sacrifice be measured and by whom? Albert's insistence on the need for an external measure leads to only two options: either a professional class of bureaucrats weigh and measure who does what or everyone is involved in weighing and measuring and no work gets done!

Despite its vision of equality, PARECON produces a two-class system where some are rewarded on the basis of effort and others are provided for on the basis of need or charity. The only way to ensure a truly egalitarian society is for everyone to contribute what they can and for everyone to get what they need.

Reformers who reject the only force that can defeat capitalism—the power of the working class—are left with only idealism. Albert insists, "we need to incorporate classless values and structures in our demands, our process, our projects, and our movements." This variation on "Be the change you want to see in the world" is bad advice for the working-class. The more workers ignore class divisions and cooperate with their bosses, the more they are exploited.

We cannot transcend capitalism by pretending that it doesn't exist. Capitalism is not like a suit of clothes that can be removed at will. Like fish swimming in water, people live in a sea of relationships that are shaped by the rules of society (Seize the Surplus and Compete or Die). We can't see these relationships, any more than fish can see the water in which they move. We can know how much capitalism has affected us on a personal level only after we are free of it. Of course, we should aim for equality and mutual respect in our personal relationships; however, people will fail to achieve this ideal, not because of bad character or poor motivation, as moralists insist, but because *capitalist social relations are in our bones*. The ability to sustain cooperative relationships requires personal confidence and emotional security—the very qualities that rulers suppress in those they dominate.

Consensus

Organizing methods are linked with class. The ruling class makes back-room deals and pays people to do what it wants. When acting in its own interests, the working class organizes at the point of production and on the broadest possible scale. The middle-class prefers organizing methods that suit small-scale activities carried out by like-minded people. A good example is consensus decision-making, or deciding by general agreement.

Consensus is the preferred method to use when deciding what to eat for dinner. When it comes to political questions, aiming for consensus favors those with the time and energy for lengthy discussions. Compared with students and professionals, working-class people have much less time and energy. When you have to get up early for work, you cannot talk all night. As a result, groups that promote lengthy decision-making discussions are usually dominated by middle-class people.

The consensus model claims to protect the minority, but it actually gives the minority the power to block the majority; a few dissenters can hold an entire group hostage. To prevent such paralysis, those who disagree are often pressured to go along with the majority, even when they are not truly convinced. The result can be false unity and underground dissent.

> Indeed, systems of formal consensus often only work in practice by developing systems of informal control that will allow the majority to limit the ability of individuals to thwart the will of the majority. In North American native groups that use consensus, for example, it is often the case that tribal elders are able to exert enormous informal pressure on individuals who tend to disrupt consensus. (This is often missed by outsiders.) In some organizations using formal consensus, there is an informal process where people who do not "toe the party line" on issues seen as key to the organization's identity or purpose are encouraged to leave.[170]

Consensus decision-making is promoted as more democratic than majority rule, when it is actually less democratic. Under the consensus model, everyone is presumed to be equal and there are no leaders, only facilitators. However, the more unwieldy the decision-making process becomes, the more likely a small clique will develop to make decisions behind the scenes. Because these people are not voted in, they cannot be voted out. The result is unaccountable leadership.

Large groups of people are better served by the working-class methods of majority rule and democratic centralism (discussed in the previous chapter). After a certain amount of discussion, where disagreements can be aired openly, a vote is called, a decision is made by majority rule, and *everyone* abides by the decision. The decision can be re-evaluated at any time, and leaders can be replaced at any time.

The consensus model avoids group discipline by imposing the discipline of social pressure. Under consensus, people are discouraged from expressing disagreements for fear of holding up the decision-making process. The result can be "groupthink," where no one objects to a bad decision for fear of breaking consensus. Under truly democratic majority rule, people are encouraged to state their opinions because doing so does not hold back the decision-making process. After a decision is made, dissenters can continue to hold opposing views as long as they carry out the will of the majority. When a decision turns out to be wrong, and when dissenters turn out to be right, then the organization can change direction.

The consensus model can work for small groups, but not for large organizations. Groups that insist on using consensus *as a matter of principle* cannot grow beyond a few hundred people, at most. No method of organizing is more important than the need to organize millions of people to replace capitalism with socialism. On this, the middle class disagrees, preferring small over large, exclusive over inclusive, process over results, and talk over action. The middle class aims to change society, not by organizing masses of people to exercise their own power, but by relying on experts or dedicated individuals, playing to the media, orienting to the people in power, and not expecting too much. Consensus decision-making lends itself to these goals. The extent to which consensus decision-making is imposed on organizations indicates the extent to which middle-class politics dominate those organizations. Truly democratic organizations are free to choose their method of decision-making and their leaders, and they are also free to review and change their decisions *as they see fit*.

Actions speak louder than words

The best way to change society cannot be discovered through debate and discussion alone. At some point, people must decide on a course of action, carry out that action, and evaluate the results. Testing theories in practice provides new and *unanticipated* information about your abilities and limitations and those of your opponents. This new information leads to more informed discussion and more effective strategies, which must again be tested in practice, in a continual learning process.

What people say and what they do is often different because society is steeped in deception. When talk is cheap, how can you know who is really on your side and who is not? Fortunately, actions speak louder than words. During a strike, the co-worker you thought was your friend crosses the picket line while one you disliked remains loyal. On a demonstration, Officer Friendly pepper-sprays your face, while a homeless beggar comes to your aid. As the following example shows, experience is the best teacher.

During the British miner's strike of 1984-1985, a group called Lesbians and Gays Support the Miners collected so much money in gay clubs and pubs that it became the single largest financial donor to the strike. On picket lines and demonstrations, lesbians and gays stood with miners and their families. Both were attacked by police, and both were transformed by the experience. According to one gay activist,

A few months ago if anyone had asked us if this kind of alliance was possible we would never have believed it…All the myths and all the barriers of prejudice were just broken down. It makes me feel quite moved by the possibilities. You can unite and fight![169]

After the strike, hundreds of miners and their families traveled to London to join the Lesbian and Gay Pride March. That same year, the National Union of Miners campaigned to incorporate gay rights into trade union policy. As one miner's wife put it, "We've suffered over the last year with the police what they've been suffering all their lives and are likely to continue to suffer unless we do something about it."

The process of struggle produces a depth of personal change that cannot occur through discussion alone. Co-ops and utopian communities struggle internally, removing people from the larger fight against capitalism. Why take on the system, when you can live and work in a feel-good community with like-minded people?

In 1880, Frederick Engels wrote *Socialism: Utopian and Scientific*, explaining how the working class could replace capitalism with an egalitarian, classless society. Having no confidence in the working class, the middle class prefers to concoct ideal societies that spring fully-formed from the minds of their creators.

Contempt for the working class

Most middle-class people look down on the working class. When a few are put in charge of the many, it is assumed that the few are more capable. The experience of managing others, and the belief that such management will always be necessary, leads the middle and upper classes to dismiss the possibility of majority self-rule.

The middle class cannot see the working class as a force for social change. In the 1980's, economic reformer Jeffrey Sachs helped Poland's mass working-class movement (called Solidarity) reconcile with the capitalist class because, as he put it, "What, after all, were the alternatives? Civil war? A quick descent into a new tyranny? Anarchy? A new conflict with the West?"[171] The possibility of workers controlling society in their own interests was not on his radar screen. Michael Albert thinks that the working class is strong enough to defeat capitalism, but too weak to prevent itself from being pushed out of power by a small group of ambitious bureaucrats, what he calls a "coordinator class."

The conditions of work under capitalism reinforce the belief that workers could never manage themselves. Workers take no pleasure in being commanded by others to exert themselves to the utmost to produce in monotonous fashion for someone else's profit. Those who consider the capitalist organization of work to be natural and inevitable observe workers' resentment of their daily grind and mistakenly conclude that labor itself is repulsive to workers and must be imposed on them.

The alienated condition of workers causes them to keep their heads down and their eyes focussed on what is directly in front of them. Workers who are resigned to feeling powerless in this way are viewed as dull and incompetent instead of realistic. One manager told me, "Workers are not interested in the big picture. I spend a great deal of time explaining to my staff how what they do affects what others have to do and where they are in the big picture. More than once I've been told flat-out 'I don't care. Just tell me what to do.'" The depressed spirit of workers is wrongly assumed to be a lack of social interest, instead of the result of daily hardship, humiliation, and defeat. Failure to recognize the psychological impact of class oppression leads to the mistaken conclusion that workers could never direct production.

Contempt for the majority permeates society and all of its institutions. Contempt shows up in the panic myth, where authorities withhold vital information from the population on the basis that ordinary people have nothing to contribute and would only make things worse. Contempt is revealed in the systemic neglect of human needs, in the failure to provide for women and children, for the sick, disabled, homeless, and elderly.

Another form of contempt for working people is "consumer power"—the belief that people have more power as consumers than they have as producers. This is nonsense. Would it be more effective to protest Wal-mart's policies by organizing 2,000 people not to shop there, or by organizing 2,000 Wal-mart workers into a union? Would General Motors feel more pressure to reduce fuel emissions if 2,000 people refused to buy SUVs, or if 2,000 auto workers went on strike? Some people argue that the best way to protest the horrendous condition of food animals is to convince people not to eat meat. In fact, the meat-processing industry is notoriously inhumane for workers and for animals. The 2006 strikes in support of immigrants' rights achieved what vegetarians have never accomplished; shutting down the nation's feedlots and slaughterhouses.

Top-down reformism is also based on contempt for the working class. Middle-class reformers believe that experts and other professionals are the only ones who can solve social problems. The majority of people are perceived only as victims, with no power to solve their own problems. Top-down, "leave-it-to-us" reformers include charitable organizations (give us your money and we will take care of the needy), union bureaucrats (give us your money and we will deal with the boss), utopians (follow our model for society), politicians (elect us and we will take care of you), and advocates for politicians (elect them and they will make life better). Top-down efforts to transform society, however well-intentioned, keep the majority powerless.

Liberal lectures

The capitalist class cannot solve the most basic social problems: the need for jobs, peace, security, and a better future. A determined majority could expose the ruling class as corrupt and powerless and lay the foundation for an egalitarian society. However, the influence of the middle class makes it difficult to form a determined majority. The middle class wants to manage capitalism, not replace it. Instead of challenging the system, middle-class reformers lecture the people in power.

New York Times columnist Bob Herbert writes, "A fierce and bitter war—not bloody like the war in Iraq, but a war just the same—is being waged against American workers." He describes workers suffering from unemployment, low wages, few or no benefits and overly stressful working conditions. He tells us that "…the right of workers to form unions and bargain collectively has been under assault for years" and that union-busting "…has been bolstered by the full force and power of the federal government, which puts struggling workers at a hopeless disadvantage." At this point, one might expect a call to revolution. Offered instead is this jaw-dropping conclusion, "The president of the United States should be allied with working families in this struggle [against corporate union-busting]."[172] When hard-hitting arguments collapse in a moral whimper, people are left feeling confused and powerless. The more skilled professionals are at criticizing the system, the more confusion and powerlessness they generate when they fail to offer solutions.

One *New York Times* editorial on homelessness chides, "the administration should stop hacking away at housing for the poor." Another admonishes, "Banks do not have to gouge their customers just because the law permits it." These appeals fall on deaf ears because capitalism is deaf to human need. The State takes from the poor to give to the rich (Seize the Surplus), and banks that do not gouge their customers are left behind by those that do (Compete or Die).

Liberal lectures can be invaluable in advancing the careers of the lecturers. Al Gore's book, *Earth in the Balance: Forging a New Common Purpose,* was published in 1992. A year later, Gore was elected vice-president under the Clinton administration. During the eight years of his vice-presidency, environmental protections were dismantled at an alarming rate. In 2006, Gore released his film, *An Inconvenient Truth: The Planetary Emergency of Global Warming and What We can do about it.* This documentary highlights Gore's commitment to environmental issues, while neatly avoiding any criticism of big business, of capitalism, or of the abysmal environmental record of the Clinton administration. This is public relations at its finest.

However accurate their criticisms, liberal lectures do not change the behavior of capitalists and politicians; *they foster the delusion that the people in power can be persuaded to do the right thing.* Appeals to the ruling class to have a conscience are like coaxing a rapist into providing rape-counseling for his victims. Liberal appeals to the working class are like persuading rape-victims to give the rapist-turned-counselor another chance.

The middle class serves capitalism *despite its good intentions.* If this were not so, capitalism would cease to exist, because the ruling class is too small to control society on its own. The following sections explain how middle-class politics block human progress and why those who want to transform society must reject those politics.

Liberals and the Democratic Party

> The two-party system depends on the ability of one party to serve the corporate agenda when the other party is too discredited to do so.
>
> *Lance Selfa*

In 2000, masses of people demonstrated against global corporate control. The anti-globalization movement formed the spring-board for a vigorous anti-war movement that challenged the U.S. invasion of Iraq before it even began. Four years later, the American anti-war movement was in a coma. How did this happen?

When social movements challenge the capitalist agenda, middle-class liberals push for unity with "progressive" capitalists. In the lead-up to the 2004 elections, the Democratic Party pressured anti-war activists to back their pro-war candidate, John Kerry. The only genuine anti-war candidate, Ralph Nader, was viciously attacked by Democrats who insisted that "a vote for Nader is a vote for Bush." Leaders of the anti-war movement bought the argument that anybody would be better than Bush and that Kerry was the "lesser evil." Anti-war protests were suspended to prevent embarrassment to Kerry. As a result, there was no organized outrage against the torture of Iraqi prisoners by U.S. forces and virtual silence when chemical weapons were dropped on the Iraqi city of Fallujah. The Democratic Party was willing to sacrifice the anti-war movement to get its candidate elected, and liberal leaders of the anti-war movement went along.

The Democratic Party is a graveyard for social movements. Every two years, liberal leaders divert the energy of social activists into electing capitalist politicians, *no matter how many times this has proved to be a dead-end.* The strategy of acquiring friends in high places becomes more important than grass-roots organizing, and activists are pressured to tone down their demands. The resulting silence on critical issues makes it easier for conservatives to advance their pro-war, anti-women, anti-gay, and racist agendas. The result is a more right-wing atmosphere that helps the "greater evil" politician get elected. In 2004, President Bush won his second term in office, *because there was no principled opposition.* Instead of taking responsibility for this outcome, liberals blamed the electorate for being too conservative!

Liberals show their contempt for ordinary people when they insist that not alienating voters is more important than maintaining a principled position. It never occurs to them that voters are alienated by electoral campaigns that lack principles. Because liberals remain loyal to the capitalist system, no matter what happens, they are reduced to searching for minute differences between pro-capitalist candidates, none of whom will keep their promises after they are elected.

Sections of the anti-war movement continue to embrace liberal Democrats in the hope that they can change the Party as a whole. This will not happen. The Democratic Party will keep moving right until a serious and sustained movement from below forces it to the left. It will never move to the left on its own because the Democratic Party serves the capitalist system.

There is no basic difference between the Democratic Party and the Republican Party. Both supported slavery and continue to support the oppression of Black people; both are backed by big business; both support America dominating the world; both break strikes, persecute immigrants, attack women's rights, and assault the poor. Both work to defeat any challenge to the two-party system.

Democrats are just as eager as Republicans to expand the American Empire by military means. In 1998, Democratic President Bill Clinton signed the 1998 *Iraq Liberation Act*, formally launching Washington's plan to force regime-change in Iraq. Less than two months later, Clinton ordered the bombing of Baghdad. And it was Clinton who presided over the deadly UN embargo against Iraq. Republican President George W. Bush could not have invaded Iraq if the groundwork had not been laid by the Democratic Party. In 2005, all but three Democratic representatives voted to continue the war. Whatever Democrats promise when they are not in power is negated by what they do in office.

Emphasizing divisions

It is obvious that women are oppressed in relation to men, that Blacks are oppressed in relation to Whites, and that homosexuals are oppressed in relation to heterosexuals. However, the middle-class does not see that the majority suffer by being forced into a social pyramid. The middle class assumes that those who stand a little higher up must benefit from the fact that others stand lower down. According to middle-class ideology, if men were not sexist, Whites were not racist, and heterosexuals were not homophobic, then equality could be achieved.

The middle class emphasizes the vertical divisions of humanity (sex, race, sexual orientation, nationality) while ignoring or minimizing the horizontal class divide. *Yet, every oppressed group is divided by class.* In all oppressed groups, the majority is working class, some are middle class, and a tiny few are ruling class. While middle-and-upper-class women, Blacks, and homosexuals suffer discrimination (their proportion at the top of society being considerably less than their proportion in the population), their lives are completely different from the lives of their working-class counterparts. As a Black woman, Secretary of State Condoleezza Rice experiences oppression. At the same time, she belongs to a class that rules by oppressing the majority. Described as "the most powerful woman in the world," her experience of oppression cannot be equated with the experience of the average Black woman. More than that, Rice's elevated position depends on the degraded position of the majority of women and men, Blacks and Whites.

In every oppressed group, those who belong to the middle-and-upper-classes have conflicting interests from those who belong to the working-class. This conflict is expressed in different strategies to fight oppression. Consider the gay liberation movement.

In June, 1969, New York City police raided a gay bar in Greenwich Village called the Stonewall Inn. Unexpectedly, several thousand gay people and their supporters fought back. The Stonewall Rebellion inspired the formation of the Gay Liberation Front (GLF)—named in solidarity with the National Liberation Front against the U.S. invasion of Vietnam. GLF chapters sprang up in cities and on college campuses around the country. The GLF was inclusive, containing gay men, lesbians, transsexuals, and people of color—many Blacks and Hispanics had participated in the Stonewall Rebellion. The GLF also worked with other groups, including the Black Panther Party. There was a sense of strength in unity, a common fight against a common enemy. All this changed as the ruling class reasserted its control.

By the mid-1970's, gay liberation groups began to fragment under the influence of identity politics—the belief that oppression is a personal matter that cannot be understood by those who don't experience it. As differences became more important than similarities, groups split to form separate organizations based on different forms of oppression. The fight for sexual freedom for everyone faded into the background and then disappeared.

In 1990, Queer Nation launched itself with the slogan, "We're here. We're queer. Get used to it." The word "queer" was deliberately used to emphasis the difference between gays and straights. Heterosexuals could not be members of Queer Nation; they were the enemy. Needless to say, the organization never grew beyond a few hundred predominately middle-class Whites. Queer Nation offered no strategy for working-class gays to fight their oppression.

Gay Pride Day was launched in June, 1970, to mark the first anniversary of the Stonewall Rebellion. Today, the fight for gay liberation has been sidelined by celebrations of "queer identity." Pride Day has become a profitable event for gay-owned bars, clubs, bookstores, restaurants, travel companies, and other retailers seeking the gay dollar. An end to gay oppression would threaten this "pink economy." Gays who felt welcome everywhere would have no need to patronize gay-owned establishments.

The middle class benefits by emphasizing the divisions created by oppression. Middle-class members of oppressed groups can be big fish in the small pond of their "community," instead of having to compete as small fish in the much larger pond of society. Like all businesses, gay-owned businesses profit by denying equal rights, job security, and freedom from harassment on the job. In contrast, these remain key issues for all workers, gay and straight. One day of feeling free to be yourself, as good as it feels, is no substitute for a world in which you could be yourself *every day*.

Sexism and the feminist middle class

Winning the legal right to abortion in 1973 increased the ability of women to work outside the home. In *Backlash: The Undeclared War Against American Women,* Susan Faludi describes how the New Right (which wasn't new at all) fought to push women back into the home by making abortion inaccessible. As anti-abortionists picketed, harassed, and bombed women's clinics, Christian fundamentalists and their supporters fought to restrict legal access. In 1976, the *Hyde Amendment* eliminated funding for abortions for poor women on Medicaid. Since Hyde, a web of restrictive laws have made it increasingly difficult for women to obtain legal abortions. Between 1995 and 2002, states enacted 335 anti-abortion measures. By 2004, 22 states had imposed waiting periods for women wanting abortions, 21 states required parental permission, and another 14 required parental notification. In 2006, Democrats and Republicans worked together to outlaw abortion in South Dakota.

Regardless of your personal views on abortion, it is a big mistake to support any legal restriction on a woman's right to choose. The right to control your body is a fundamental democratic principle. If the State can deny women the right to control their fertility, then no one's rights are safe. A genuine democratic society provides all the options—sex education, contraception, abortion, support for having children—and trusts that people will make the best decisions for themselves. Of course, some people's decisions will turn out badly. However, such outcomes cannot be avoided by restricting people's choices. On the contrary, women who cannot obtain safe abortions have unsafe abortions, with their much greater risk of infection, infertility, and death.

American women are losing the battle to control their bodies. Employers can refuse to provide contraceptive coverage in their health plans, pharmacists can refuse to dispense oral contraceptives, and medical professionals can deny patients' requests for birth control information. More than one-third of all American women live in the 87 percent of counties with no abortion providers at all. The Defense Department has a permanent ban on abortion, except to save the life of the mother. And more than four thousand female Peace Corps volunteers are not covered for abortion under their government-provided insurance plan, even in cases of rape or when their lives are endangered.

Whenever abortion is restricted or illegal, women with money have always been able to obtain safe abortions. Restrictions on abortion hit working-class women hardest. In New York City, before abortion was legalized, Black women accounted for half of the deaths caused by illegal abortions, while Puerto Rican women accounted for 44 percent of those deaths. Today, tighter restrictions on contraception and abortion are causing poor women to suffer more unwanted pregnancies and a greater risk to their lives from delayed and illegal abortions.

While women lose the right to abortion, middle-class women's organizations refuse to mount a serious defense of abortion rights. On the contrary, feminist author Naomi Wolf calls abortion a form of violence against women and a crime against women. She wants pro-choice supporters to join with abortion opponents to lower the nation's "shamefully high" abortion rate and has even proposed a ban on abortion after the first trimester. This attack on women's right to abortion is despicable and dangerous. Right-wing forces have restricted access to birth control information and technology, including the morning-after pill, so women need *more* access to abortion, not less. The question is not whether abortion is good or bad, but whether women have the right to decide for themselves. The real crime against women—the real violence against women—is denying them the right to make choices that protect their health and their lives.

The nation's largest pro-choice organization does not defend abortion as a democratic right, rather, "NARAL Pro-Choice America works to reduce the need for abortions." When a million supporters attended the 2004 March for Women's Lives in Washington, DC, NARAL organizers did not use the occasion to launch a nation-wide defense of women's rights. Instead, participants were instructed to get out the vote for Democratic presidential candidate, John Kerry. The event also featured Democratic Senator Hillary Rodham Clinton as an "honored guest"—a woman who calls abortion a "sad, even tragic choice" that shouldn't "ever have to be exercised, or only in very rare circumstances."[173] Instead of criticizing Clinton, NARAL's former president praised her for "reaching out to anti-choice Americans." This is no way to fight for women's rights!

Feminism contends that women of all classes have more in common than men and women in the same class. This is not true. When push comes to shove, middle- and upper-class women side with the men of their class. In 2006, Louisiana Governor Kathleen Blanco told reporters that she would sign a near-total ban on abortion in her state on the basis that "the Legislature has spoken."

Liberal women's organizations view abortion primarily as a legal matter. However, in countries like Canada, where there are no legal restrictions on abortion, working-class women still have difficulty obtaining abortions because the medical system does not guarantee the right to any procedure. Being "pro-choice" is not good enough. Without access to abortion, women have no choice. As long as people have to pay for medical care, those with money will have more choices than those without. We need free abortion on demand, so that *all* women have the right to choose. This working-class demand is flatly rejected by middle-class liberals whose loyalty to capitalism is greater than their commitment to women's rights.

Racism and the Black middle class

Before the civil rights movement, many people assumed that Blacks were less intelligent than Whites because so few Black people were middle or upper class. When the civil rights' movement forced open the door to higher education and better jobs, a few Black people moved up the social pyramid. Between 1972 and 1991, the number of Black professionals increased 470 percent. Between 1964 and 2005, the number of Black elected officials rose from fewer than 200 to more than 9,100. Black people became mayors of major cities including New York, Chicago, Houston, Detroit, Philadelphia, Los Angeles, and San Francisco. A few Blacks entered the ruling class: Secretaries of State Colin Powell and Condoleezza Rice, Supreme Court Justice Clarence Thomas, and a sprinkling of CEOs in top U.S. corporations.

Unfortunately, the growth of the Black middle class and the inclusion of Blacks into the ruling class have not benefited the majority of Black people, whose living conditions continue to deteriorate. There are two possible explanations. Some argue that the civil rights' movement did not go far enough and a more vigorous struggle is needed. Others blame the victim by arguing that poor Blacks are just too lazy to better themselves. Many middle-and-upper-class Blacks adopt this second attitude because the system is structured to ensure that those who rise in the system adopt the values of the system, including the belief that anyone can make it if they try.

Capitalism uses a carrot and stick to divide and rule. Allowing a few people from oppressed groups to rise in the social pyramid is the carrot. The war on the poor is the stick. Those who get the carrot are expected to support those who use the stick. In this way, middle-class sections of oppressed groups are recruited to keep the rest down.

In the 1990's, Black physician Louis Sullivan, Secretary of Health and Human Services for the first Bush administration, helped to launch the "Violence Initiative" that presumed Blacks to be genetically more prone to violence. Black mayor Thomas Bradley was in charge of the racist police force that provoked the Los Angeles rebellion of 1992. Former Black Panther leader Elaine Brown describes the current situation in Atlanta, Georgia.

> What Blacks in Atlanta do is act as overseers and serve the interests of the rich whites…They serve as police, as jailers, as clerks in the county, state, city and federal offices—all to grease the wheels and make sure that no one steps out of line and messes with the money. We have a situation where a Black person in the city council is calling for the criminalization of the homeless by saying that they're offensive in their behavior to the good tourists that come through Atlanta. ..You have a Black district attorney who started out his career as the first Black district attorney in the state of

Georgia by prosecuting mainly young Black men under the new law that allows the state to try children as adults...It's Black people themselves, elected and appointed, who have taken the machinery of government and instead of using it to serve the interests of Black and other poor and oppressed people, they have used it to serve the interests of the developers, the capitalists, the business owners and the big boys in Atlanta.[174]

Politically powerful Blacks like Clarence Thomas and Condoleezza Rice oppose affirmative action and other social measures to counter discrimination; they argue that Black people should elevate themselves through hard work and personal responsibility. In 1995, Black millionaire Ward Connerly led a successful crusade to ban affirmative action admissions' policies at the University of California. This measure caused the number of Black and Latino students to drop sharply throughout the University system.

On the 50th anniversary of the Supreme Court's *Brown v. Board of Education* decision (that ruled segregated schools to be illegal), wealthy Black comedian Bill Cosby slammed poor Blacks for not "keeping up their end of the bargain." Feeding every racist stereotype, Cosby delighted conservative America by condemning Black youth and their parents for keeping themselves down. In attacking poor Blacks, Cosby joins a chorus of Black professionals including *New York Times* columnist Bob Herbert, who rails against "the mass flight of black men from their family responsibilities, especially the obligation to look after their children."[175] Herbert barely pauses to acknowledge systemic racism as he attacks its victims.

Society is unfair and racism is still a rampant evil. But much of the suffering in black America could be alleviated by changes in behavior....much of the most devastating damage to black families, and especially black children, is self-inflicted...we have entire legions of black youngsters turning their backs on school, choosing instead to wallow in a self-imposed ignorance that in the long run is as destructive as a bullet to the brain.[176]

Harvard professor Henry Louis Gates, Jr. chides, "We can't talk about the choices people have without talking about the choices people make."[177] Herbert calls for a new civil rights movement, not to challenge racism but to change the values and behaviors of Black people.

The truth is that a racist War on Drugs has incarcerated Black men in unprecedented numbers, tearing apart millions of Black families in the process. The truth is that decades of mass layoffs have eliminated most good-paying jobs and devastated Black families. In some places, like New York City and parts of Chicago, half of all Black men are unemployed. The truth is that most parents, Black and White, are working so hard to make ends meet that they have no time for their kids.

Black students don't do as well as White students, not because they are lazy, but because America's school system is segregated by class and by race. The wealthiest ten percent of school districts spend almost ten times more on their students than the poorest ten percent. Less money for students means larger classes, less experienced teachers, crumbling buildings, inadequate libraries, and reduced academic achievement for poor youngsters, who are also more likely to be non-White.

Investing more money in students leads to higher academic achievement. A policy to economically integrate schools in Wake County, North Carolina, showed amazing results for Black and White students. A decade before the integration began, only 40 percent of Black students in grades three through eight scored at grade level. Ten years later, 80 percent did. Overall, 91 percent of students in grades three through eight scored at grade level, up from 79 percent 10 years earlier. The truth is that all youngsters want to learn and will do well when given the chance. Instead of condemning the racism of the system, Black middle-class liberals lecture the victims.

Malcolm X used the following parable to explain the relationship between the Black middle class and the Black working class:

> The house Negroes — they lived in the house with master, they dressed pretty good, they ate good because they ate his food — what he left. They lived in the attic or the basement, but still they lived near the master; and they loved the master more than the master loved himself. They would give their life to save the master's house – quicker than the master would. If the master said, "We got a good house here," the house Negro would say, "Yeah, we got a good house here." Whenever the master said "we," he said "we." That's how you can tell a house Negro. If the master's house caught on fire, the house Negro would fight harder to put the blaze out than the master would. If the master got sick, the house Negro would say, "What's the matter, boss, we sick?" We sick! He identified himself with his master, more than his master identified with himself. And if you came to the house Negro and said, "Let's run away, let's escape, let's separate," the house Negro would look at you and say, "Man, you crazy. What you mean, separate? Where is there a better house than this? Where can I wear better clothes than this? Where can I eat better food than this?"[178]

Treachery

There can be no doubt that middle-class reformers are genuinely concerned about social problems. Many dedicate their lives to making the world a better place and sacrifice much to do so. However, the belief that change comes only from the top of society causes liberals to betray their ideals and their followers by demanding that we "give the system a chance." This happened in the spring of 2006, when leaders of the immigrants' rights movement initially opposed a bill that criminalized immigrants only to back another bill that was not much different. The same betrayal occurs in the labor movement, where union bureaucrats talk tough one day and collapse in response to employer pressure the next day. Anti-war liberals who opposed the prospect of war against Iraq did a 180-degree turn when the war began. As one liberal confessed, "I was against the invasion of Iraq, but now that we're there, we need to finish the job." This is nonsense. The longer the U.S. occupies Iraq, the worse things get. We need to get out NOW. The billions being spent on the war can be given to the Iraqi people as reparations to rebuild their country.

In any real fight, liberals choose the road of least resistance — the status quo. When Mumia Abu-Jamal was sentenced to death after an unfair and politically-motivated trial, the National Association of Black Journalists refused to support him, even though Abu-Jamal was president of the Philadelphia chapter of the organization at the time of his arrest! This cowardly betrayal was attributed to members being "attuned to the subtle grunts and imagined nods of their employers in the corporate media."[179]

In great social upheavals, sections of the middle class advocate caution and moderation, evolution, not revolution. This liberal "voice of reason" betrays the working class by holding back the struggle while the capitalist class regroups its forces. During the Russian Revolution, when the ruling class was thoroughly discredited, the middle class did all it could to prevent workers, farmers, and soldiers from forming their own government. In Germany, the middle class supported the Nazi Party's efforts to rescue capitalism from the threat of workers' revolution. Once the Nazis took power, professional associations of engineers, lawyers, doctors, psychiatrists, scientists, and other professionals rushed to pledge their support. Jeff Schmidt concludes,

> Generally speaking, the greater the power, whether corporate or state or even oppositional, the more eager professionals are to subordinate themselves to it. The power's morality or immorality has only a secondary effect on the professional's eagerness to serve, because good subordinates don't make moral judgements about their superiors.[180]

Countering middle-class politics

The middle class is not a uniform class with uniform ideas. Sections of the middle class can be convinced to fight capitalism, and most of the people in the grey zone between the middle and working classes can also be convinced. Socialists developed the tactic of the "united front" to help people with different ideas work together on matters of common concern.

Too often, people let their disagreements about society hold back their efforts to change it. Human beings prefer to cooperate; conflict makes us anxious so when political disagreements arise, we tend to make one of two mistakes:

The first mistake is to be sectarian—to refuse to associate with people you don't agree with. Hanging out with like-minded people is comfortable; however, organizations that avoid conflict by shutting out dissenters cannot grow beyond a small circle of friends.

The second mistake is to minimize disagreements ("we all want the same thing"). Unfortunately, unity that is built by papering over real disagreements always breaks down under stress. Those who are loyal to capitalism and those who oppose it will forever be in conflict. When people can't agree on the fundamentals, their organizations become paralyzed or split.

Conflict is distressing. Suppressing dissent is undemocratic. Pretending we have no differences is unrealistic. So how can we proceed? The first thing to determine is whether the disagreement is fundamental or not. That can be determined by deciding if a person has more to gain by preserving capitalism or by replacing it. Those who have more to gain by preserving capitalism will never be convinced to oppose it. In contrast, all workers and the more oppressed sections of the middle class would be better off in an egalitarian society. Therefore, despite the contradictory ideas in their heads, most people can be convinced of the need for socialism.

The united front allows people to fight together without having to agree on everything and without having to be in the same organization. For example, everyone and all organizations who want U.S. troops out of the Middle East should work together to build an anti-war demonstration. The anti-abortionist who opposes the war should be welcomed, despite her views on abortion. Working together against the war provides a space to discuss how the right of people to run their own countries is linked with the right of women to control their own bodies. Similarly, the racist worker must be welcomed on the picket line, where it is possible to convince him that his racist views hurt his class interests. The key is to be honest and open about differences *and* work together on specific activities, to acknowledge disagreements without letting them hold back the struggle. Over time, such discussions-within-activity help people to clarify and resolve their differences.

Movements against oppression contain people from different classes. As the struggle heats up, these movements inevitably split along class lines. The middle and upper classes will limit their demands to what can be obtained within capitalism. Such demands do not meet the needs of working-class people whose liberation requires an end to capitalism. These splits are inevitable. Socialists reject pleas for unity that would subordinate the interests of the working class to the interests of the middle and upper classes. A united front is not coercive; it is a free association where organizations holding different views can work together. Organizations participating in a united front retain their political independence, including the right to break away if that becomes necessary.

A workers' party must represent the interests of the working class *without compromise*. Because middle-class views and methods undermine the fight for socialism, people who hold onto such views and methods cannot be members of a workers' party. Membership must be restricted to those who are committed to putting the working class in power. A workers' party cannot be a debating society or a platform for opportunists; it must be a party of action. Voting rights must be restricted to those who are *actively organizing* for socialism. Those who do the work must make the decisions or they will be continually outvoted by those who assume the right to make decisions for other people to carry out.

Socialists are often accused of having an agenda that undermines the struggle against oppression. On the contrary, socialists provide a unique and valuable contribution; they work to accomplish the goals of the movement by linking struggles against oppression and grounding them in the power of the working class. Socialists raise the slogan "Gay, Straight, Black, White; One Struggle; One Fight." That one fight is the fight to liberate humanity from capitalism and end all oppression. To win that fight, we need to build the broadest possible unity within the working class across divisions of sex, race, nationality, sexual orientation, religion, and so on. Socialists insist on bringing everything back to class because class is what unites the majority and gives us the power to change the world. The next chapter explains how the material base already exists to create a classless, socialist society.

Summary

The middle class is full of well-intentioned people who want a better capitalism. Being socialized to manage the working class, the middle class rejects the possibility of workers managing society. The middle class works to lower expectations and limit demands to what can be achieved within the system. To win their rights in the present and their liberation in the future, the working class must organize independently of the middle class and its politics of compromise.

Chapter 16

Claim the Surplus

> In our hands there is a power greater than their hoarded gold,
> Greater than the might of armies magnified a thousand fold.
>
> from the song *Solidarity Forever*

Artificial scarcity

Like other physicians, I struggle with the problem of too many patients and not enough time. Every day, I tell people wanting my help that they must go on a waiting list or that my waiting list has grown too long, and they must find help elsewhere. I cannot tell them who to call because every doctor I know has the same problem. One man suffering from depression sat on my waiting list for four months. When I finally offered him an appointment, he told me that he felt better and no longer needed therapy. He killed himself the following week.

Denying people treatment and making people wait for treatment are forms of rationing. Why does rationing exist? One writer insists, "The demands of society are infinite, but its capacity to meet those demands is finite."[181] If this were true, rationing would make sense. In *Can We Say No?: The Challenge of Rationing Health Care,* Henry Aaron and William B. Schwartz argue that rationing is necessary to contain costs, even if that means denying medical treatments to sick people. They never consider rationing profits, which are the main reason why medical costs are escalating.

What if there were no profit system? What if a worker-run society provided medical treatment on the basis of need? Consider the fastest growing medical expense—the cost of pharmaceuticals. A socialist society would promote cooperation in scientific research instead of today's wasteful competition. There would be no useless drugs developed, no endless variations of already-existing drugs, and no advertising to drive up drug consumption. The most effective medications would be produced and provided to all who need them. With the profit motive removed, more resources could be devoted to promoting health and preventing disease.

What if medical care were provided as a human right instead of being bought and sold as a commodity? There would be no medical insurance bureaucracies to weed out those who might actually need treatment and to restrict what treatments people got. Everyone would get the best care without question.

Doctors in a socialist society would not practice "defensive medicine," ordering unnecessary tests and treatments to reduce the risk of being sued, because there would be little or no suing. Today's medical law suits are costly because medical care is so expensive. Patients who have been harmed by shoddy treatment need lots of money to pay for continuing care and to compensate them for lost income. When medical care is free and people's needs are socially provided, the only suits would be for punitive damages. These would be rare for several reasons: Errors would be minimized by medical staff working cooperatively in teams that include patients and their primary supports. Of course, accidents will always happen. However, people don't sue because accidents happen; they sue because they feel badly treated. And that would be rare in a system that put people first.

The "need" to ration medical care and other necessities arises from the need to preserve the capitalism system. By claiming the social surplus as its private property, the capitalist class creates an artificial scarcity for everyone else. It seems like too many people are chasing too few goods and services. However, this seeming scarcity is the result of deliberate social policies. In 2006, two days after the House approved $40 billion in cuts to health, welfare, and education, the Senate passed a $70 billion dollar tax cut for the rich. Within one week of warning that "The retirement of the baby boom generation will put unprecedented strains on the federal government," President Bush called for more money for the military and "nearly $300 billion in tax cuts over the next five years, and $1.5 trillion over the next 10 years." For the people in power to get what they want, the rest of us must get less.

There is no real scarcity. Gross Domestic Product (GDP) measures the annual value of all goods and services produced. Between 1950 and 2000, the American population increased 86 percent, from 151 million to 281 million. During the same period, the U.S. GDP soared 3,239 percent, from $294 billion to $9,817 billion. In other words, the production of wealth in America grew 38 times faster than the population. Most of that wealth was confiscated by the capitalist class, creating a huge gap between the super-wealthy few and everyone else.

If the total wealth produced by American workers in 2003 had been shared, every U.S. resident would have received the equivalent of $38,000 that year. Because that sum would have been paid to everyone regardless of age, a family of four would have received $152,000. This payment would be much larger if it included interest on the past wealth produced by workers. And much more could be produced if everyone who wanted to work were employed.

Under capitalism, there is no sharing. The top one percent of the U.S. population owns more than one-third of the nation's wealth. Meanwhile, one in four Americans earns poverty-level wages, and one in six children lives in poverty. In the world's richest nation, 60 percent of workers report having enough savings to last just a few months. While some enjoy fabulous wealth, most Americans are just a paycheck or two away from being homeless.

Containing demand

> With. Without.
> And who'll deny that's what the fighting's all about.
>
> *Us And Them — Pink Floyd*

To maintain control over the surplus, the capitalist class must curb the demands of the majority by driving down their expectations. The myth of scarcity was invented for this purpose. Supporters of capitalism insist that the rich didn't get rich by robbing the poor; there was never enough to go around. They say that scarcity is a law of nature, like gravity; that society could never produce enough to meet everyone's needs, and so there will always be have-lots and have-nots. They reject the idea that social progress should mean rising living standards for everyone, not just the rich. Using the myth of scarcity, employers cry that they can't afford to raise wages, even as their profits soar. Politicians claim that there is no money for health care, while spending billions on war. Economists warn that there are not enough young workers to support those who are retiring. Meanwhile, the wealth that older workers labored their entire lives to produce sits in the bank accounts of the super-rich.

Like real scarcity, artificial scarcity breeds competition and conflict. "Cost-containment-measures" pit the needs of medical staff against the needs of patients. Under-funded schools pit the needs of teachers against the needs of students. Employers reduce staff to the lowest numbers possible, pitting workers against customers. The unfairness of being made to wait creates anger that workers direct against each other. People forced to wait at the post office gripe about lazy postal workers. When supermarket check-out lines get too long, people grumble about slow cashiers. Retail workers complain about rude and abusive customers. As workers attack each other, the bosses enrich themselves.

The pretense of scarcity is used to pit needy people against one another. In 2005, the Bush administration proposed cutting social programs to reduce a record budget deficit. As the *New York Times* pointed out,

> In effect, Mr. Bush's budget pits veterans against the 660,000 women, infants and children whose food assistance is on the chopping block; against the 120,000 preschoolers who would be cut from Head Start; against the 370,000 families and disabled and elderly individuals who would lose rental assistance; against whole communities that would lose support for clean air and drinking water; and so on.[182]

None of these groups should have to sacrifice a thing. Diverting money from the military and reversing tax cuts for the super-rich would provide more than enough for all of them.

People will compete for jobs, housing, access to higher education, and every other necessity if they believe that there is not enough to go around and that the prize will be awarded on the basis of hard work and personal merit. Understandably, intense resentment results when some people are seen as "not playing by the rules" or gaining an unfair advantage. In reality, the system is structured to produce a few winners and many more losers. The ruling class deflects the inevitable bitterness away from the system and onto society's scapegoats: the unemployed, Blacks, immigrants, foreigners, people on welfare, single mothers, unions, etc.

Artificial scarcity leads to false choices. A newspaper article warns that money going to fight obesity will not be available to fight smoking. A pediatrician insists that it is preferable to fund research into the causes of premature births than to "waste money" supplying pregnant women with milk, eggs, and orange juice. During the 2005 Canadian national election, the Liberal Party promised to fund more child-care spaces, while the Conservative Party countered with promises of a cash payment for each child under age six. It is simply assumed that there isn't enough money to fund anti-obesity programs *and* anti-smoking programs, to support medical research *and* provide food supplements, to pay for child-care programs *and* give parents more cash.

The experience of scarcity lowers expectations. Instead of wishing you had a better job, you are grateful to have a job at all. Instead of voting for someone you want, you vote for someone you don't want in order to keep out someone you want even less. A pervasive sense of scarcity makes having it all seem impossible. In fact, there is no real scarcity at all.

A world of abundance

According to the myth of scarcity, poverty is caused by there being too many people in the world. The facts say otherwise. Between 1800 and 2000, the global population increased six times. Over the same period, the total amount of wealth produced increased 49 times. Because production is privately owned, most of this wealth went to a few at the expense of the many (Seize the Surplus). In 2001, there were 497 billionaires with a combined wealth of $1.54 trillion—greater than the total annual income of all the nations of sub-Saharan Africa ($929 billion) and more than the combined incomes of half of humanity. At the same time, more than a billion people live on less than one dollar a day and nine million people die from hunger and other preventable causes every year—that's 24,000 people, or the equivalent of eight World Trade Center bombings *every day*.

Poverty persists because a few privately own what should be socially shared. If the total amount of wealth produced in the world in 2005 were divided by the world's population, every human being on the planet would have $9,212 or $36,848 for a family of four. This amount would be many times higher if everyone who wanted to work were employed and if workers were better fed. The United Nations estimates that reducing hunger by half would produce $120 billion more wealth every year from workers living longer, more productive lives.

Production would also increase if poor nations had access to the same methods of production used in rich nations. Currently, 30 percent of the world's population produces 90 percent of the world's wealth. If everyone produced at the higher level, world production would triple, providing every person with a minimum of $27,636, and a family of four with more than $110,554 every year.

The only reason deprivation persists is because the world's wealth is privately owned and not shared. However, there is intense pressure to deny this fact and to dismiss the possibility of sharing. When justice for all is taken off the agenda, people will settle for some justice, for some people, some of the time.

One at a time?

> A man walks to the beach and discovers thousands of starfish stranded on the shore. He picks up one and tosses it back into the water. He picks up another and throws that one in, and then another. A woman sees what he is doing and asks, "What does it matter if you save a few starfish? Thousands will still die." The man picks up another starfish, and as he casts it back into the ocean he replies, "It matters to this one."

Like the story of the medical worker who rescues drowning people, the parable of the starfish describes the role of the "clean-up crew" for capitalism—crisis workers, medical workers, psychologists, social workers, and charities. They don't have the power to change the system, and they don't have enough resources to help everyone in need. Like the man saving starfish, they console themselves with saving a few. And, if that were all that could be done, it would be a fine and generous thing. But what if it were possible to do more?

Let's suppose that the people living by the sea put their heads together and devised a way to prevent the starfish from becoming stranded. However, they needed more people to make the method work. Let's suppose that the woman walking along the beach is wondering how to involve more people in the project. She sees the man tossing starfish into the water, one at a time, and she explains how all the starfish could be saved if enough people joined in the project. He replies, "That sounds like a great plan. *In the meantime*, I will save this one, and that one, and the one over there...."

An ounce of prevention is worth a pound of cure. Before doctors understood that cholera was a waterborne infection, they treated people as they got sick. Now that we know that cholera is caused by contaminated water, it would be irresponsible to treat sick people and fail to treat the water supply. Yet, that is what the clean-up crew for capitalism does—they help the needy while feeling helpless to change the social system that generates so much neediness.

When Rosa Luxemburg posed the question—reform or revolution?—she was not dismissing the value of helping people; she was arguing that *how* we fight for reforms depends on whether our goal is to replace capitalism or to improve it. To replace capitalism, the oppressed must organize on their own behalf and link their struggles together in a united front. Reforms won this way do not end the struggle; they make it stronger. In contrast, the middle-and-upper classes want to make capitalism more humane through individual sacrifice, by winning influence in high places, and by convincing people to give money to help this one, and that one, and the one over there….

Robin Hood charity

The amount of pain and suffering in the world is intolerable, and people want to do something about it. One physician launched a fund-raising campaign for life-saving projects in Africa under the slogan, "Africa's Dying Can't Wait." We need to question why Africans have been made to wait; who benefits from their waiting; and what can be done about a system that makes people wait, not only in Africa but here at home. If all we do is raise money to reduce waiting-times for some people, capitalism will keep making the rest wait.

Significant social change has never happened without mass mobilization. However, charities fondly quote Margaret Mead who wrote, "Never doubt that a small group of thoughtful, committed people can change the world. Indeed, it is the only thing that ever has." It's good to encourage people to do what they can. However, charities thrive by promoting the myth that the good will and good deeds of a few individuals are all that is needed.

Charities are modeled after Robin Hood, who took from the rich and gave to the poor. Robin Hood was an outlaw, not a revolutionary; he did not consider ordinary people to be capable of fighting for themselves, and he never organized them to do so. He was loyal to the "rightful king" who was expected to right all wrongs on his return. Charitable organizations, including non-governmental organizations (NGOs), function like modern-day Robin Hoods—working to redistribute some of the surplus from the rich to the poor, while they dream of benevolent leaders who will set things right.

Charities work within the boundaries of the system and pose no threat to it. To make sure that they don't, the federal tax code prohibits charitable organizations from being politically active. When a rector delivered an anti-war sermon during the 2004 election, the Internal Revenue Service warned that his church could lose its tax-exempt status. No pro-war church was similarly warned.

Charity can be big business. According to its web site, America's Second Harvest (ASH) is the "largest charitable hunger-relief organization" in the United States, supporting

> …approximately 35,000 programs operating 50,000 feeding agencies nationwide, including food pantries, soup kitchens, women's shelters, and Kids Cafes. These local organizations provide emergency food assistance to 23 million hungry Americans, including more than nine million children and nearly three million seniors each year.[183]

ASH fights hunger by "Feeding America's Hungry, One Meal at a Time." ASH does not question why so many people go hungry in the world's richest nation, nor is it alarmed that the number of hungry Americans keeps growing. On the contrary, ASH celebrated the fact that it distributed 1,000 times more food in its 25th year than it did in its founding year. ASH is also proud of the support it receives from Congress, the Food Marketing Institute, and the Grocery Manufacturers of America—who all profit from high food prices. Robin Hood would turn over in his grave. The powerful get rich by taking bread from people's mouths. Charities perpetuate the problems they claim to solve when they partner with those who caused the problems in the first place.

Charity is good public relations. In 1998, when Microsoft was charged with unfair and illegal practices, Bill Gates was painted as a ruthless monopolist. The Bill & Melinda Gates Foundation was launched a year later. Four years after that, Gates was praised for being a generous philanthropist committed to the betterment of humanity. In 2003, the world's richest man met with a group of prostitutes in Botswana to promote safe sex as a way to combat AIDS. The media praised Gates for his compassion, but never questioned why his fortune is four times larger than the entire GDP of Botswana, and why some women are so poor that they must prostitute themselves to survive. In a world where a few become wealthy by taking from everyone else, Gates' fortune and Botswana's poverty are related. The more we praise the super-rich for dispensing crumbs of charity, the less we notice that they have stolen the bakery.

Capitalism deprives people faster and in greater numbers than charities will ever be able to counter. As a result, charities must decide where to put their limited resources. The result is a rationing process that essentially discriminates between the deserving and the undeserving poor. Holding the poor accountable for their poverty in this way allows the system that creates their poverty to go unchallenged.

Charity cannot solve the problems created by capitalism. The more social support charities provide, the more resources the State can divert to the capitalist class. Ordinary people are bamboozled into paying three times: producing surplus that is taken by the capitalists instead of being given to the needy; paying taxes that subsidize the capitalist class instead of funding social services; and donating money to charity to provide needed services.

The end of poverty?

> A part of the capitalist class wants to redress social grievances in order to secure the continued existence of capitalist society.
>
> *Karl Marx & Frederick Engels*

Jeffrey Sachs is an economic advisor to the United Nations and a passionate promoter of the UN Millennium Goals. His campaign against poverty has become popular, partly because of his association with U2 rock star Bono, who wrote a glowing forward to Sachs' book, *The End of Poverty: Economic Possibilities for Our Time*. Sachs' main argument is that too much poverty threatens the security of the rich nations, causing wars and insurrections that cost far more than it would cost to reduce poverty. This argument is an old one—give the poor a little more so they won't rise up and take it all. Despite the title of his book, Sachs does not want to end poverty. As he says,

The goal is to end *extreme* poverty, not to end all poverty, and still less to equalize world incomes or to close the gap between the rich and the poor. This may eventually happen, but if so, the poor will have to get rich on their own effort.[184]

Sachs calls for charity, not justice. He thinks the rich should help the poor out of "enlightened self-interest," not because the rich *owe* compensation to the poor for getting rich at their expense. The word "reparations" never appears in this book. Sachs explicitly denies that the capitalist class is responsible for creating poverty.

Africa's problems, I have noted repeatedly, are not caused by exploitation by global investors but rather by its economic isolation, its status as a continent largely bypassed by the forces of globalization.[185]

Sachs does not deny that Africa has been devastated by three centuries of slavery, a century of colonial rule, post-colonial exploitation, and crushing debt. Nevertheless, he believes that these burdens do not explain Africa's "long-term developmental crisis." He argues that the economic Grand Canyon between Africa and the United States is the result of different growth rates—Africa is poor because its economy has grown slowly, while the U.S. is rich because its economy has grown quickly. He admits that having more wealth to start with contributes to faster growth, but he never links America's more rapid growth with the massive wealth it accumulated from the labor of African slaves! His racist conclusion is that Africa has been "poor since time immemorial."

Africa's massive debt burden has been called a modern form of slavery. Nigeria has paid over $16 billion on its original $5 billion loan, and it still owes $32 billion on that same debt. Kenya pays six times more to service its debt than it receives in foreign aid. The prevalence of HIV/AIDS is linked directly with inequality, poverty, and debt. Sub-Saharan Africa pays $15 billion a year in debt service—four times more than it spends on health care. *Just two days' of debt payments flowing from poor nations to the IMF and World Bank would pay for AIDS treatment for everyone in Africa.* Sachs admits these facts, then, incredibly, he concludes, "As of today there is no solid explanation for why Africa's AIDS prevalence is at least an order of magnitude higher than anywhere else in the world."

Sachs is equally baffled by the soaring income gap in America, claiming "The reason for this dramatic shift toward the rich is not really known." This refusal to acknowledge that the rich get rich by exploiting the poor is political. As long as Sachs denies the link between power and powerlessness, he can deny any fundamental problem with capitalism. In his mind, "Technology has been the main force behind the long-term increases in income in the rich world, not exploitation of the poor." Sachs advises more multi-national corporations to invest in poor nations, reassuring them that such investment would be profitable. As he puts it,

Ending poverty is a grand moral task, and a geopolitical imperative, but at the core, it is a relatively straightforward investment proposition.[186]

Sachs advocates industrial free-trade zones run on low-cost labor, in the belief that "sweatshops are the first rung on the ladder out of extreme poverty." *New York Times'* columnist, Nicholas D. Kristof agrees. He insists that, "Anyone who cares about fighting poverty should campaign in favor of sweatshops."[187] Both Sachs and Kristoff believe that working under horrific conditions is better than dying from starvation, *as if that were the only choice.* The working class has already created more than enough wealth for the capitalist class and should not have to produce for it a minute longer. The real alternative to poverty and starvation is not sweatshop labor but socialist revolution to remove from private hands what should be socially shared—the surplus and the means of producing it. Capitalist reformers like Sachs and Kristoff want the impossible—to improve workers' conditions without sacrificing capitalist control of production, without compromising profits, and without social revolution.

Sachs accuses the anti-globalization movement of being "too pessimistic about the possibilities of capitalism with a human face." He offers nine steps to "heal the world" including "Redeem the Role of the United States" as a "leader and inspiration in democratic ideals" and "Rescue the IMF and the World Bank" by restoring their roles as "champions of economic justice and enlightened globalization." Achieving socialism would be easier!

Sachs' devotion to capitalism makes his message a dangerous one. He wants to join rich and poor in "a common bond of humanity, security, and shared purpose across cultures and regions." However, real unity requires equal rights, which are impossible in a class-divided society. Sachs wants the kind of unity that maintains the power of the capitalist class and perpetuates the poverty of the working class.

Changing the rules changes the game

> If our leaders were as generous in helping people as they are in killing them, no one would ever go hungry.
>
> *George Monbiot*

People like Jeffrey Sachs insist that capitalism could work, "If governments would do their job in setting up the right rules." Economic reformers want to change the rules but not the game. They have no problem with capitalists seizing the surplus; they just don't want them taking so much. They have no problem with capitalist competition; they just don't want so many poor people dying. It seems so reasonable. The World Bank estimates that $124 billion, little more than $100 per poor person per year, could end extreme poverty by increasing food yields, providing basic health care and education, providing clean water and sanitation systems, and establishing basic energy, transportation, and communication systems. The amount needed would be less than 0.7 percent of the GDP of the 22 rich "donor" nations.

Washington pledges foreign aid with such fanfare that most Americans think the United States spends more than 20 percent of its budget to help poor countries. However, politicians are more interested in promoting a benevolent image than in handing over any real money. In 2002, President Bush created the Millennium Challenge Account to dispense $10 billion to impoverished African nations over three years. By 2005, not a single dime had been paid out. Even the *New York Times* condemned the U.S. as "stingy," noting that "Victims of the earthquake in Bam, Iran, a year ago are still living in tents because aid, including ours, has not materialized in the amounts pledged." Ordinary Americans don't know that the U.S. never gives enough to make a real difference. So, when poverty persists, people fall victim to lies that blame poverty on the poor. In fact, the capitalist class has no interest in eradicating the poverty on which its wealth is built.

In 1992, the United States agreed to pledge 0.7 percent of its GDP ($84 billion) in direct financial aid to poor countries every year. This promise has never been kept. Between 2001 and 2003, the U.S. donated just $15 billion a year to foreign aid, barely more than 0.1 percent of its GDP. The Department of Defense got more than 30 times that amount.

What the U.S. provides in foreign aid is not designed to alleviate poverty but to promote U.S. interests. The 2003 *United States Leadership Against HIV/AIDS, Tuberculosis, and Malaria Act* links international medical assistance with the acceptance of U.S. agricultural products that contain genetically modified organisms (GMOs). Foreign aid also takes the form of subsidies that help U.S. corporations relocate or expand into countries with a lower-waged workforce and fewer environmental restrictions. Foreign aid includes military support for friendly States that, in turn, ensure a compliant workforce.

Those who give can also take away. Withholding foreign aid is a potent weapon to enforce U.S. policies. On his first official day in office, President George W. Bush re-imposed the "Global Gag Rule" that restricts foreign non-governmental organizations (NGOs) that receive American aid from using their own, non-U.S., funds to provide legal abortion services, lobby their own governments for abortion law reform, or even provide medical counseling or referrals that mention abortion. When the people of Palestine elected the Hamas Party into government, the U.S. and its allies stopped humanitarian aid to Palestine and refused to resume it until Hamas renounced its opposition to Israel. In contrast, the billions of dollars flowing from the U.S. to Israel every year in foreign aid were not threatened when Israel bombed and invaded Lebanon in 2006. As long as Israel carries out U.S. policies, the U.S. will continue to fund Israel.

When you consider how capitalism actually functions (Seize the Surplus and Compete or Die), the expectations of reformers like Sachs are completely unrealistic. He argues,

> The $450 billion that the U.S. will spend this year on the military will never buy peace if it continues to spend only one-thirtieth of that, just $15 billion, to address the plight of the poorest of the poor, whose societies are destabilized by extreme poverty and thereby become havens of unrest, violence and even global terrorism.[188]

This would be a reasonable argument in a sane world. However, capitalism is a form of social insanity. The capitalist class is not investing billions of dollars in the military to secure peace. The war on terror, like the war on the poor, is the capitalists' response to inequality and injustice. They seize the surplus; they do not share it. They crush their victims; they do not rescue them.

In their passion to put a human face on an inhuman system, reformers are like the hopeful spouses of alcoholics, believing the promises made to them, being disappointed, hoping again, having those hopes dashed, trying again, being encouraged by little signs, and so on. The people in power provide enough intermittent reinforcement to keep the hope of change alive. Like gamblers at a casino, reformers are convinced the payoff will come. But the game is stacked and the house always wins

The rules of capitalism are fixed, not flexible. Capitalism cannot change the rules on which it is based and still be capitalism. No matter how much you want to play baseball, if you play by the rules of hockey you are playing hockey, not baseball. Different social rules create different social arrangements.

Chapter 5 explained how simple rules can create complex social patterns. A flock of birds will undulate through the air as a single entity based on two simple rules: follow your neighbor and stay the same distance apart. Convincing a few birds to follow a different flight plan will not redirect the flock as long as the basic rules stay the same. Reformists want to change the social patterns created by the rules of capitalism without changing the rules themselves. They want to eliminate poverty without eliminating private ownership of production. They want peace without eliminating the competition for profit that leads, inevitably, to war.

The key to fighting oppression is solidarity, not charity. Nothing changes when we only provide what the system fails to provide. When the ruling class fails to meet people's needs, we must hold them accountable, organizing in every town hall, school, and workplace in the nation. The movement for immigrants' rights has shown the importance of demonstrations and strikes to demand justice. There is no scarcity. *There is more than enough for us all.* If the capitalist system cannot meet human needs, then we need to create a system that can.

Production for need

The only way to eliminate poverty is to revolutionize the system of production. Under capitalism, the goal of production is profit. Nothing is produced unless it is profitable, and nothing can be obtained unless it is paid for. Human need is irrelevant. In advance of Hurricane Katrina, 80 percent of nursing homes chose not to move their residents to safety because they would not have been reimbursed for the cost of evacuating if the storm did not materialize. Only a society that produces for need can prevent such problems. A worker-run society would have the following characteristics:

- Production for need not for profit.

- No exploitation. Free association of the producers. Full employment.

- No oppression. Equal rights.

- Protection of the environment.

- No national borders. Global cooperation. No war.

A socialist society would direct production to solve social problems and respond to human needs and desires. Let's look at how the problem of malaria might be handled in a worker-run society.

Under capitalism, 90 percent of the $106 billion spent annually on medical research goes to diseases affecting just 10 percent of the population. Socialism would make it a priority to tackle all diseases, starting with those that afflict the most people. More than 40 percent of the world's population lives in areas where malaria is epidemic, and more than a million people die of malaria every year, mostly in sub-Saharan Africa. Ninety percent of those killed by malaria are children under age five. Effective treatments exist, but the cost (40 cents per child and $1.50 per adult) is more than most Africans can afford. The first step to eradicating malaria would be to produce anti-malarial medicines for all who need them. Subsequent steps would concentrate on prevention. The mosquito that transmits malaria bites primarily at night, and insecticide-treated bed nets have proven effective in preventing the spread of the disease. However, eradicating malaria requires more than the production and distribution of medicines and bed nets.

At the beginning of the 20th century, malaria was common in the United States, especially in the Southeast. By 1949, America was declared to be malaria-free. This feat was accomplished through a State-funded campaign that included digging ditches to drain water where mosquitoes bred and spraying insecticides. By the end of 1949, over 4,650,000 houses had been sprayed. Rising living standards after the war also played a role.

A socialist campaign to eradicate malaria would be different. Insecticides would not be selected on the basis of cost, but for maximum effect against the mosquito and minimal harm to people and mosquito-eating predators. Alternatives to insecticides would be developed, including strengthening the mosquito's own resistance to the malaria parasite. To raise human resistance against malaria and other diseases, people would be provided with plentiful amounts of nutritious food, initially imported until it could be locally produced. Depleted soil could be enriched with compost, and irrigation systems could be built. Greenhouse technology would make it possible to produce a variety of foods in any climate. Clean water delivery systems could be constructed, along with indoor plumbing and sanitary waste disposal. Hospitals, clinics, and schools could be built, stocked and staffed. The best materials would be used and the highest standards applied. Most importantly, *control over the process would be in the hands of those most affected*. Are you wondering how these projects would be financed?

Claim the surplus

Once the workers' revolution has spread throughout the world and the capitalist class is no longer a threat, people can turn their full attention to constructing a socialist society. Tons of stockpiled food and other goods could be distributed. If it is necessary to pay people to produce goods and provide services, there would be no problem finding the money. Seventy-four U.S. banks have assets of over $10 billion each. The top ten have combined assets of more than two trillion dollars. Two-and-a-half trillion dollars in Third World debt would be cancelled. The one trillion dollars that the world spends every year on war would be available, along with the billions spent on spy agencies like the CIA, and all corporate profits. Workers formerly employed in these industries could be re-employed in more socially useful ways.

Money does not solve social problems, people do. Money is a symbol for human labor. Think about it. Our world is shaped by human labor: this book you are reading; the room you are in; the furnishings around you; the clothing you wear; and the food that sustains you. The roads you travel, the bicycle, car, bus, or train you travel in, the planes overhead and the buildings you pass have all been created by human hands. At work, at home, and at school, the tools and machines that you use were all produced by human beings. Capital also embodies labor-time. Capital is the surplus that the capitalist class confiscates from the working class and uses to produce more surplus (profit). Capital can include buildings, machinery, natural resources, science, technology, money, and commodities. This wealth was produced by the working class and rightfully belongs to all; the working class is completely justified in confiscating it.

Capitalism is based on private property—the private ownership of the means of production. Private property can also take the form of public property that is owned by the State and remains outside the control of ordinary people. A socialist revolution would end class divisions by transforming private and public property into common property. When anything is owned in common, it is no longer owned at all. People would not forfeit ownership over personal-use items; however, no one can be allowed to own the means of production and thereby gain the power to exploit other people's labor. *Holding social resources in common is the only way to prevent some people from acquiring power over others.*

The first task of a socialist society would be to eliminate hunger, disease, and deprivation. The rule of "Share" would mandate that no one gets two of anything until everyone has one (or the choice of having one). Both the need for goods and services and their availability could be posted on the internet for all to see. Entire cities already provide wireless internet access, so it should be possible to provide the same service across the globe. Someone has already designed a wind-up laptop computer that requires no electricity and sells for $100. Such devices could be mass produced to connect people in remote areas to the internet. With everyone linked in a world-wide web, production can be coordinated to meet human needs with a minimum of waste.

At some point, the production of goods and services will exceed what people need. This will happen in different parts of the economy at different times. There will begin to be a surplus of food, housing, educational opportunities, medical care, tools, machinery, and so on. Capitalism suffers from regular crises of overproduction, called recessions, where more is produced than the market can absorb. This is not true overproduction, because many people still need and want those goods and services—they just can't afford them. Capitalist overproduction results in economic stagnation, bankruptcies, and mass unemployment.

Under socialism, overproduction will be cause for celebration. As long as desired goods and services are scarce, they will be bought and sold—legally or illegally. Once a surplus is achieved, goods and services can be distributed freely. As overproduction extends throughout society, the money economy can be replaced with a simple system of exchange, where everyone contributes to society, and everyone takes what they want. The result will be a freedom that is inconceivable today.

As basic needs are met, more people will be able to participate in shaping their lives and society. People can decide how much time they spend producing what they want and how much time they devote to other activities. Those who want more material goods can produce more. Those who want more time to play, explore, and discover can choose to make do with less. At different times and in different places, people will make the decisions that suit their needs and desires. People could choose the kind of life they want, based on what matters most to them.

You might be wondering who would do the tough, dirty, uncomfortable jobs. If the military can develop robot soldiers that kill, it should be possible to design robots to collect toxic waste and clean sewage systems. Necessity is the mother of invention. When the producers are in control, they will find creative ways to reduce shit-work to a minimum. However, cleaning up shit is a necessary part of life, as anyone with children or pets understands; everyone must do some of it.

What if people are greedy and take too much? Some people need more and others want more, but hoarding makes no sense in conditions of plenty. Consider smorgasbord or buffet-style restaurants where there are piles of food and no limit on what you can eat. At first, people get excited and take too much, producing stomach aches and wasted food. After a few visits, they get used to the idea of abundance and adjust what they take based on what they can comfortably consume. Hoarding makes sense when there are limited supplies of desirable goods. When there is plenty to go around, hoarding provides no benefit.

Reestablishing the rule of reciprocity will transform human beings in ways that we cannot imagine. The life-long deprivation that kills dreams and corrupts relationships will be unknown to our descendants. Cooperative management of society will completely change how people feel about themselves, how they relate to each other, and how they perceive and relate to the environment. The following sections look at what this will mean.

The end of exploitation

IT'S EVERYWHERE: road rage, airplane rage, mail rage. And news reports abound with accounts of angry, stressed-out workers with hair-trigger tempers who erupt in fits of office rage. Yelling. Punching computers. Fist-fighting. And worse.[189]

The goals of capitalism conflict with the goals of human beings. Capitalism aims to produce profit. Human beings hunger for creative work that is challenging, fun, and appreciated by others. The capitalist class makes a deal with the working class: give up what you want and give us what we want instead. In exchange, we will give you wages to purchase what you want. In the 19th century, this arrangement was imposed on workers who were forced into factories by the threat of starvation. Subsequent generations found themselves bound by a social contract they never signed. That contract is inherently unfair. No matter how high wages go, they can neither buy the deep satisfaction that results from meaningful work nor compensate for the lack of it. The result is mass resentment and anger. This anger contributes to interpersonal aggression at work and at home and a host of medical problems including anxiety, depression, digestive difficulties, immune system disorders, and cardiovascular disease.

Under capitalism, those who make the decisions don't do the work, and those who do the work don't make the decisions. In surrendering their labor to the capitalist class, creative, intelligent human beings are reduced to cogs in a machine. When people control their own labor, they infuse it with creativity, joy, and comradery. When people choose what they produce and how they produce it, they become complete human beings, fully engaged in the creative process. By taking control of production, the working class will end alienated labor and the dissociated life that it demands.

A socialist society will end the divide between producers and consumers. Consider how most people relate today. We get wages in exchange for working a certain number of hours. (We are paid less than the value of what we produce so the capitalist can make a profit.) We exchange our wages for goods and services that are priced according to the labor-time that went into them. The exchange of money makes it seem that the primary relationship in society is between producers and consumers. However, if the money part of the transaction is removed, what remains is a simple exchange of labor for goods and services, with the capitalist skimming profits off the top. If we remove the capitalist, then we have a mutually beneficial relationship between producers. This is socialism, where people can feel proud of what they produce for others and gratitude for what others produce for them.

It seems strange to think about life without money and capitalists, even though humanity has spent most of its history in societies without both. I first encountered moneyless exchange as a child, when my brother needed regular transfusions of blood products that my family could not afford. My aunt worked for the Kodak Corporation and appealed to the factory workers for help. They lined up to donate their blood, and my brother survived. No money changed hands. Their blood was exchanged for my brother's life, and my family responded to their generosity with immense gratitude.

Under capitalism, money is a source of stress, conflict, and wasted energy. Consider how much time you spend worrying about not having enough money and how many arguments about money you have with family and friends. Think of how much time you spend paying bills, filing tax returns, going to bank machines, and rummaging for change for the bus, the newspaper, the parking meter. Now multiply that by billions of people. Include the time and effort that advertisers devote to parting people from their money. Whole industries are devoted to banking and finance, to balancing books and investigating money fraud, to preventing theft and protecting private property. These social resources could be used much more productively to provide what people need.

Consider what a visit to a food store might be like in a moneyless society. (The food store would be the place where food is stored.) As you enter, you are greeted by people you know, because you also work there. Let's say that most of the time you eat in communal restaurants (think McDonald's convenience with gourmet quality). However, tonight you are planning a private meal. You make your selections and leave. There are no line-ups, no cashiers, and no items removed from your basket because you can't afford them. On your way out, you write your name on the list of jobs. You might spend a few hours restocking shelves, working in the nearby greenhouse, or cooking in the community dining room. Either way, the work will be relaxed and pleasant.

Being forced to produce and collect money for everything sours relationships. Consider the bus driver in a socialist society. She drives around picking up people and dropping them off. No one is turned away because they can't pay. No one feels entitled to be rude because they did pay. No one is stressed about making ends meet. Many people take turns driving the bus, and all appreciate the service.

As the goal of production shifts from making profits to solving problems, the barriers between different areas of expertise will break down. Different perspectives and different skills can be pooled to solve problems that seemed unsolvable before. Freely-shared information will eliminate the duplication of effort that currently wastes so much time and materials. Research can tackle problems with no concern to produce a profitable outcome. There will be no benefit from faking research results or from covering up mistakes and failures.

Liberating science and technology from capitalist control will unleash a flood of creative energy and produce an explosion of discovery and invention. If someone has a good idea, the first response would not be "Is it profitable?" but "How could we do it?" The "cost" of any project would be measured by people's willingness to devote the necessary time and materials. Different solutions could be implemented in different places. My 11-year-old granddaughter suggested that instead of cutting the grass, we should get a goat to crop the lawn and fertilize it at the same time. Under socialism, she could raise her suggestion at a community meeting. Those who like the idea could collaborate on where to obtain goats, how to keep them healthy, and how to prevent them from wandering. Those who didn't like that idea could do something else, like share a neighborhood lawn mower, or get rid of their lawns altogether. Unlike today, people wouldn't be pressured to do the same things in the same way. Socialism would encourage flexibility and individual creativity.

When production is commonly controlled, life will never be boring. Everyone will participate in planning what needs to be done and in carrying out the plans. Everyone will do a variety of jobs and activities so that mind and body will be fully exercised. The mental and physical disorders of today that result from doing the same thing repeatedly over many hours (or having nothing to do) will no longer exist. The pace of life will slow down and accommodate to human rhythms. Better nutrition, fulfilling work, and real social security will contribute to more people experiencing good health. This may sound too good to be true because, under capitalism, abundance of anything other than profit is considered to be a problem, not a success.

Redundancy

The word "redundant" comes from the Latin verb *redundare*, meaning "to overflow." The word redundant is frequently used in the negative, to indicate what is superfluous, not useful, not needed. With the exception of profits, abundance is a problem for capitalism. A trade surplus creates international friction. An abundance of products lowers prices. An abundance of workers lowers wages. An abundance of medicine also presents a problem. Most drugs are easily mass produced. The pharmaceutical industry estimates that it loses seven billion dollars every year from unauthorized replications of its products. The drug industry is not pleased that more people are getting their medicines; they want to protect drug patents that keep medicine out of the hands of people who cannot pay inflated prices.

To push up profits, employers reduce the number of employees to the minimum. In order to extract the most surplus from the fewest workers, the rest must be made "redundant." These "excess" workers are the unemployed, and there are a growing number of them. In 2006, a new Wal-Mart in Chicago received

25,000 job applications for 325 positions, most of which were part-time and low-paid. Far more people want to work than capitalism can *profitably* employ. The need is there. Poor nations are desperate for tools and machinery. Classrooms are overcrowded, hospitals are understaffed, and there are not enough childcare centers. At the same time, unemployment offices overflow with people eager to work. There is an abundance of need for goods and services, and an abundance of people wanting to provide them, yet capitalism cannot put the two together.

A socialist society would provide full employment. Everyone can contribute something of value, from the smallest child who can shuck peas to the oldest person who can tell stories. Under capitalism, people are prevented from contributing to society. This is a huge loss to society as well as to the individual. The more people contribute, the better life can be. As the proverb says, "Many hands make light work." Full employment will reduce the amount of time needed to do socially necessary work, providing more leisure time for everyone.

In redundant systems, components are duplicated so that if one fails, the entire system does not crash. This principle is essential in electronics and communications. In contrast, capitalism seeks to eliminate redundancy altogether. Efficiency experts reduce staffing levels to the absolute minimum so that no one is ever idle (not producing profit). The result is more stress, more mistakes, more accidents, and reduced quality of work. Hospitals forced to function at full capacity under normal conditions cannot handle emergencies.

A socialist society would aim for lots of redundancy. Systems with built-in redundancy are more flexible and resilient. Eliminating the profit motive will slow the pace of work. With time pressure removed, work can be done more safely and enjoyably. People will have time to think about what they are doing and to consult with others to solve problems more effectively. Hospitals in a socialist society would be deliberately overstaffed, with people working minimal hours under normal conditions and more intensely as needed. When people aren't needed to work at the hospital, they would be free to do other things on and off the premises. Patients, medical workers, and society would all benefit.

The end of lies, bureaucracy, corruption, and crime

Capitalism is based on lies because it cannot be admitted that profits come before people. Advertisers lie all the time to sell products. Businesses lie when they assure us that customer satisfaction is their primary concern. This is nonsense—profits come first. Children are introduced to a life of lies by way of Santa Claus and the Easter Bunny. Kids are encouraged to believe that these fictitious characters are real, when they are actually marketing tools for retailers. Youngsters learn that adults lie and that protesting these lies is considered antisocial and anti-fun. At school we lie about what's going on at home. At work, we lie to protect our jobs and our co-workers. We lie to our parents, our lovers, and our kids. We lie to ourselves. We are so immersed in lies that we don't know what is true. A society run by the producers for the producers would make lying unnecessary and counterproductive.

Capitalism creates bureaucracy. When people must line up for what is scarce, bureaucrats are needed to maintain order in the line. Bureaucracies devote a tremendous amount of time, effort, and money to rationing goods and services. In the United States, every applicant for medical insurance and every patient needing treatment is scrutinized to make sure no one gets anything to which they are not "entitled." The immense resources that capitalism devotes to depriving people could be used to provide what people need instead. Where there is abundance there is no need for rationing and no need for bureaucracy.

Competition corrupts, and the competition for profit is especially corrupting (Compete or Die). The greater the prospect of profit, the greater the corruption. The drug trade, the arms trade, the slave trade, and the extraction of "debt" payments from starving nations are proof of this. As Bob Dylan pointed out in *Highway 61 Revisited*, a businessman will sell tickets to the end of the world if he could make a profit by doing so.

When some have power over others, corruption is inevitable, and no amount of rules and regulations can eliminate it. According to the FBI, corrupt behavior by public officials is deeply rooted and widespread. A writer for the *New York Times* discovered that "In 2004 and 2005, more than 1,060 government employees were convicted of corrupt activities, including 177 federal officials, 158 state officials, 360 local officials and 365 police officers."[190] The FBI's web site concludes that greed is "the principal motivating factor in public corruption." When power is shared, there is no room for corruption. There is no advantage in taking advantage when people have what they need.

Competition also corrupts ordinary people who must contend for jobs, access to higher education, housing, childcare, and other necessities that are kept artificially scarce. Cheating, lying, and stealing are inevitable when people think that is the only way to get what they need. The bitterness that flows from losing out poisons peoples' lives and relationships.

A worker-run society will eliminate corporate crime by eliminating private ownership of production and the competition for profit. Common crime will disappear along with inequality and deprivation. In 1902, Clarence Darrow wrote,

> If every man and woman and child in the world had a chance to make a decent, fair, honest living, there would be no jails, and no lawyers and no courts. There might be some persons here and there with some peculiar formation of their brain, like Rockefeller, who would do these [anti-social] things simply to be doing them; but they would be very, very few, and those should be sent to hospital and treated, and not sent to jail; and they would entirely disappear in the second generation, or at least in the third generation.[191]

By freeing the forces of production, socialism will free human beings to do right by each other. A socialist society will dismantle the capitalist penal system and integrate prisoners into society, providing them with education, employment, medical treatment, and housing. The few who present a danger to others would be placed in protective custody, which would not be punishment. A society based on human dignity would be repulsed by unnecessary violence and cruelty. Healthy people avoid behaving in ways that cause them to feel guilt and shame; they treat others the way they would want to be treated.

What if some people refuse to cooperate? Peer pressure provides powerful motivation for cooperation. When the well-being of each depends on the well-being of all (all for one and one for all), the motivation to protect the whole is strong. And when cooperation brings positive results, the desire to cooperate gets even stronger. In all cooperative societies, those who refuse to cooperate *for no good reason* are rightly considered to be sick.

Under capitalism, only winners are allowed to feel good about themselves. An abundant and cooperative society will make everyone a winner. For the first time in human history, everyone can experience real social security, not only in the material sense but also in the emotional sense of *belonging* from cradle to grave. People in pre-class societies prided themselves on being members of tight-knit communities. Capitalism equates needy with pathetic. To reduce demands on the system, people are ridiculed and shamed for not being able to manage on their own. Showing that you don't need others is a badge of honor. Socialism will restore honor to giving *and* receiving. Once again, belonging will be prized and bonds will be cherished.

The end of oppression

> Freedom from hunger and poverty (without which all other freedoms mean nothing), freedom from war, from endless toil, from exploitation, from racial and sexual oppressions—these are the real freedoms we fight for. They can be made real only by establishing the positive freedom of the working class to run society.
>
> John Molyneux

In any competition, some people will be disadvantaged. Members of oppressed groups have less access to good jobs, decent housing, higher education, medical treatment, etc. The result is a measurable hierarchy of access. Within four years of a heart attack, 50 percent of Black women will die, 23 percent of White women will die, 15 percent of Black men will die, and 13 percent of White men will die. The hierarchy varies with what is being measured. The 2003 unemployment rate for Black men and women was more than double the rate for White men and women. At the same time, White youth of both sexes (16 to 19 years of age) suffered 50 percent more unemployment than adult Black men, while Black youth had the highest unemployment rate of all (one in three). Regardless of how one measures oppression, people experience it as daily humiliation, poorer health, shorter lives, and broken dreams.

Oppression cannot be eliminated by arguing over who is more oppressed or by fighting over the crumbs that fall from the capitalists' table—White against Black, male against female, adult against youth, citizen against immigrant, employed against unemployed. Oppression is rooted in artificial scarcity and will end when we claim the surplus for human need. Take the example of women's oppression.

If the condition of women and children is a measure of social development, capitalism is a barbaric system indeed. Every year, more than three million babies are stillborn, and most of these deaths are preventable. Every year, more than half a million women die in pregnancy or childbirth, and millions more are crippled. High infant and maternal death rates are linked with poverty. In the year 2000, the number of maternal deaths per 100,000 women was two in Sweden, 17 in the United States, 330 in Asia, and 920 in Sub-Saharan Africa. If all women had equal access to social resources, the maternal death rate in every area would fall to the lowest achievable rate.

Women will be oppressed as a sex as long as they have primary responsibility for the care of small children. Employers pay women lower wages than men on the assumption that women are not permanent members of the workforce (which they are), that their primary responsibility is to their families (even though one of those responsibilities is to bring home a wage), and that they will take time off work to care for their families (because social services are insufficient). When someone must leave work to tend to the young, the old, and the sick, it is usually the woman, because her wages are lower. In short, women are unfairly burdened with socially necessary work and also penalized for doing that work.

Women are half of the working class, and a socialist revolution could never happen without their active participation. One of the first priorities of a worker-run society will be to meet the needs of women and children. Full and free access to reproductive technology will ensure that every child is a wanted child. No one would be forced to bear a child against her will, and those who want children would be provided with everything they need to produce healthy infants. New mothers would be supported to take as much time off work as they wanted. The availability of 24-hour childcare facilities, communal eateries, and drop-off laundries will free women to participate in society as equals with men, liberating both sexes from constricting gender roles.

In pre-class societies, everyone helped to raise the next generation. Socialism will revive this ancient tradition. At every workplace, food center, meeting hall—everywhere people go—there would be child-care centers staffed by people with a passion for caring for children. No child would ever again be trapped in an isolated family unit, vulnerable to neglect and abuse. Every child would have an extended family of many caring people.

Under capitalism, child-support laws force hostile parents to interact, trapping children in a psychological war zone. Socialism will sever the link between parenting and material support. When society attends to the material needs of all children, biological parents can choose how they relate to each other or not to relate at all. Much unnecessary misery will be ended by this measure.

Economic equality is the foundation for social equality. During World War II, factory work was redesigned for women. Under socialism, tasks can be engineered to enable anyone to do them, regardless of height, weight, or physical abilities. People with disabilities could be fully integrated into society, producing along with everyone else. Full employment would end the practice of selling sex to survive or accepting bad treatment in exchange for material support. Romantic and sexual connections would last only as long as they were mutually desired. A surplus of housing would provide the freedom to move at will. Full equality for women will allow sexuality to be separated from reproduction and end the oppression of gay people. People's sexual preferences will become no more important than their food preferences

Socialism will transform education. In a sharing society, everyone doesn't need to know everything. Instead of forcing all youngsters to learn the same thing, a socialist education system would adapt to the needs of each student. Because today's schools produce a few winners and many losers, authoritarian measures are needed to control the losers. A learning system that cultivates the interests and abilities of all youngsters would have no problem holding their attention and winning their cooperation.

Socialism will break down the artificial barriers between school and work. At work, everyone would take part in planning, problem-solving, and producing. Youngsters would prepare for this process by working in teams to solve real-world problems geared to their interests and abilities. There will be no ranking, no grading, no high-stakes testing, no gold stars, and no individual failures. When problems are solved cooperatively, everyone wins. When problems remain unsolved, they present a continuing challenge. Learning will become a life-long process for everyone.

One world

> The path of solidarity must be built through daily concrete actions, with a lot of love, tolerance, patience, and education, and with a good dose of courage. In this way, we will create the world about which we workers dream.
>
> *Mexican union leader*

The capitalist class has divided the world into competing nation-states. However, these boundaries are completely arbitrary. When astronauts look down on the Earth, they see no national boundaries. Nor are there any boundaries to the problems facing humanity—infectious disease, pollution, ozone depletion, climate change, and so on. To defeat capitalism, the working class must organize across national boundaries.

Supporters of capitalism go berserk at the thought of abolishing national boundaries. They warn that billions of impoverished people will flood into the better-off nations and drag down everyone's living standards. This is absurd. Most people don't want to leave their homes and families; they migrate from necessity. Workers survive by selling their ability to work for a wage. If there is no work at home, they must find it somewhere else. When they are prevented from crossing borders legally, they will cross them illegally. Living standards are falling, not because more people are entering the U.S., but because the capitalists' hunger for profit impoverishes workers at home and abroad. As Lee Sustar points out,

> The economic reality for U.S. workers today bears increasing similarities to their counterparts in less developed countries: a small and shrinking sector of better-paid workers amid a sea of low-paid and often temporary labor, a country where unions are weak and any economic gains for workers are under constant threat, and where the state has abandoned almost all pretense of a social safety net.[192]

Employers play workers of different nations against each other to lower the cost of labor, leaving working people no choice but to organize as an international class. The living standards of American workers will keep falling until they fight to raise *all* workers' living standards, including their own.

Supporters of capitalism fear that abolishing borders will generalize poverty. On the contrary, socialism will free the global economy and generalize abundance. In a world without borders, goods and services developed in one location can quickly become available everywhere. When a decent life is possible everywhere, people will travel for pleasure. Former border stations can become welcome stations for travelers.

The coming to power of the working class will end the miseries generated by national divisions—war, imperialism, national oppression, border patrols, smuggling, human trafficking, and family separation. Every year, an estimated 48,000 children from Mexico and Central America illegally enter the U.S. searching for mothers who had to leave to find work. When the borders come down, families can reunite, as people, products, and services move freely through the world.

For a working-class revolution to succeed, ordinary people must learn that what unites them is greater than what divides them. The prejudice and distrust bred by capitalism must be overcome by the solidarity necessary to win. Racism is incompatible with socialism. Racism feeds on national divisions and scarcity. Socialism is based on global integration and abundance. The racist doctrine that people are more different than similar cannot survive in a cooperative society. A new generation will grow up with no experience of nationalism or racism; they will have difficulty understanding why we let ourselves be divided for so long.

Humanity and the environment

> No species has ever had such a wholesale control over everything on earth, living or dead, as we now have. That lays upon us, whether we like it or not, an awesome responsibility. In our hands lies not only our own future, but that of all other living creatures with whom we share the earth.
>
> *David Attenborough*

People are right to be concerned about the environment. However, most environmentalists locate the problem in consumption not in production. Individuals are lectured to reduce, reuse, and recycle, while governments policies permit industry to abuse the environment on a grand scale.

Blaming individuals for social problems lets policy-makers off the hook. People have no choice but to drive cars in towns and cities that lack public transportation. Where public transportation does exist, it takes twice as long to get anywhere, and working people are already squeezed for time. The worker who takes a job in a chemical plant cannot be equated with the employer whose management decisions poison workers and the environment. The kid who drops a candy wrapper on the street cannot be equated with the CEO who profits from polluting the world.

The capitalist class is responsible for the environmental crisis because it is in power. To keep profits flowing, raw materials are ripped from nature as cheaply as possible. Toxic chemicals flood into the environment because they are cheap and profitable to use. Manufactured goods are designed to be disposable, to break down, and to become obsolete so they can be replaced. Advertising generates dissatisfaction to sell products that people don't need.

The working class is not responsible for creating environmental problems; however, workers can save the environment by taking control of society. The working class suffers most from pollution and is in the best position to end it. Workers can redesign industry to use only safe materials, protecting people and the environment. The tons of toxic waste left by capitalism can be loaded onto missiles and incinerated in the Sun's furnace. The world's nuclear arsenal can be disposed of in the same way.

When crops are grown to meet human needs, there will be no need to use poisonous pesticides and herbicides. More than enough food can be produced without worrying about birds and bugs consuming some of it. The tons of human and animal waste that pollute our waterways could be collected, composted, and delivered to farmers as quality fertilizer. This single measure would reduce pollution, improve soil fertility, eliminate the need for harmful chemical fertilizers, and reduce the need to clear new land. A need-based society would not force-feed cows to bulk them up or inject them with hormones to produce more milk. Such practices create sick cows and sick people. If we provide food animals with a decent and healthful life, they will provide us with healthful nourishment in return.

Capitalism links energy policy to profit and power, not to need. When it is profitable to do so, goods are transported many thousands of miles from where they were produced, without regard to how much energy is wasted in such transportation and how much pollution is caused in the process. Employers locate work in the most profitable location, forcing workers to spend hours commuting every day in vehicles that pollute the air on roads built over prime agricultural land.

A socialist society will locate production where it is most beneficial. Food that is produced close to where it is consumed does not require toxic chemical preservation and can be harvested at its peak, improving taste and nutrition. People will live near their work and have access to good public transportation. These measures alone will reduce pollution and save huge amounts of time and energy.

If we remove considerations of profit and power, there is no energy shortage. We live between two virtually inexhaustible sources of energy—the Sun and the molten core of the Earth. Most life on earth is already driven by solar energy, and giant solar collectors could be mounted in space. A combination of centrally-produced and locally-produced energy would provide maximum flexibility. Socialism will free people to develop whatever form of energy works best in any given situation.

Some people insist that there are too many people to provide for everyone's needs and protect the environment at the same time. This is not true. Many species on earth are more numerous than human beings. *How we live is the central issue.* Socialism will eliminate the immense amount of waste generated by capitalism. Excessive packaging to prevent theft is unnecessary in an abundant society. Why steal what is freely available? Advertising represents colossal waste. The time, effort, and materials devoted to creating artificial needs could be used to fill real needs instead. Capitalism floods the market with duplicate products. How many different kinds of soap do we need? A producer-controlled society would eliminate waste by producing only what people decide they want. Recycling can be designed into the production process. Landfill sites are over-flowing with materials that could be recycled.

Those who can imagine no social system other than capitalism have no solution for environmental problems; they can only despair. Extreme environmentalists argue that the planet can be saved only by dismantling civilization and dramatically reducing the human population. Such profound pessimism only serves the ruling class.

The rule of reciprocity cannot be restored in relation to the natural world until it is first restored in human society. As long as the capitalist class can exploit and oppress human beings, it will also pillage and pollute the environment. A worker-run society will produce to meet human need, and that includes the need for a healthy environment. Socialism will improve living conditions for human beings *and* revitalize the environment. A socialist society will eliminate toxic waste, restore forests, reclaim deserts, and provide areas for wildlife to flourish. Humanity and the environment are inextricably linked, and only a global worker's revolution can save both.

Another world is possible

Some people believe that humanity cannot be redeemed. Albert Einstein recalls being asked, "Why are you so deeply opposed to the disappearance of the human race?" Some religions predict that humanity will face an Apocalypse, an Armageddon, or a final judgment in which our fate will be decided by supernatural forces. However, as Chomsky warns, "assume the worst and it will surely arrive: commit oneself to the struggle for freedom and justice, and its cause may be advanced." Low-paid tomato pickers in Imokolee, Florida, were told that they were crazy to take on Taco Bell. They did anyway and won a contract that doubled their wages. Now they are challenging McDonald's.

Human beings are social creatures; we find meaning in devoting ourselves to improving society. Capitalism sabotages the need to contribute, causing the human spirit to deteriorate. As Einstein pointed out,

> The individual has become more conscious than ever of his dependence upon society. But he does not experience this dependence as a positive asset, as an organic tie, as a protective force, but rather as a threat.[193]

Life is not fair. Accidents happen and people die. However, society can be fair because it is created by human beings. Cooperation, not competition, has been the key to human evolution. If we think of humanity's journey through time, class society is an aberration that propelled production forward, shortening the path between the ancient system of reciprocity based on scarcity to a future system of reciprocity based on abundance. This short-cut has cost us dearly, and we cannot survive if it continues much longer.

Some people cry that it's too late, that war is unstoppable. This is not true. The American Empire can be stopped, *if we understand what is at stake and do what is required*. Washington pursues its wars in the Middle East, despite public opposition, because backing off would mean a defeat for U.S. capitalism. The way to force such a defeat would be to build a perfect storm of opposition—linking rebellion inside the U.S. military with a massive civilian anti-war movement. Only the working class has the interest and the power to stop this or any war. The Democratic Party is committed to the American Empire, and the union bureaucracy will not break its ties with the Democratic Party. Our soldiers need the support of an anti-war movement that actively campaigns to bring them home *now*.

Some people despair that we have passed the "tipping point," the point of no return, that the earth is damaged beyond recovering. Such a point can be known only in hindsight. On more than one occasion, past catastrophes have dramatically altered the planet and wiped out the majority of existing species. Nevertheless, life has recovered and new species have flourished. It's never over until it's over. A socialist society will inherit many serious problems. It will also inherit creative solutions that were not applied because they were unprofitable or politically risky. Someone once told me, "I would rather believe in people and make a mistake than not believe in people and make an even bigger mistake."

Some people say that revolution is impossible ("Been there; Done that"). The protest movements of the 1960's failed to defeat capitalism because McCarthyism crushed the socialist tradition in America. As a result, people moved into struggle without knowing the lessons of the past. Other people point to the failure of the Russian Revolution. The fact that past revolutions have not succeeded is no reason to give up, especially when the alternative is certain extinction.

History is full of surprises. No one predicted that ordinary people would tear down the Berlin Wall in 1989, or that immigrants would rise up in the millions to shake America in 2006. As long as capitalism exists, the working class will rebel. The critical question is whether there will be a workers' organization that is strong enough to convince the working class to take power.

Capitalism is dragging humanity into an abyss of barbarism, but we can choose another road. Humanity is Nature's youngest child, standing on the threshold of the most exciting journey imaginable. We can build the world that our ancestors dreamed about, struggled, and died for. The few who act for the many will never be as powerful as the many who act as one. We will go forward together or not at all. *¡Sí Se Puede!* Working people of the world unite!

The real solution to the problems of people in general and working class people especially is socialism, social ownership of the means of production. That is the way to stop the ruling class from dominating humanity, and for working people to achieve their liberation.

Genora (Johnson) Dollinger

What Now?

Books don't change the world—people do. You have three options: to feel overwhelmed and give up in despair; to exhaust yourself fighting every battle; or to begin organizing at work, at school, and in your neighborhood. No one can stand alone against capitalism and its backers. Find one other person who agrees with you. Two people can more easily find a third. The fourth is easier still. The more people work together, the more they can do.

Many forces conspire to keep us divided and feeling powerless. Nevertheless, if we understand what we are up against and what we are fighting for, we can succeed. The resources listed below will get you started. We have a world to win.

Susan Rosenthal

Resources

- Military Project (www.militaryproject.org) produces *GI Special* and *Traveling Soldier*, supporting service men and women against the war. Contact Tom Barton, telephone: 212.749.1673.

- Campaign to End the Death Penalty. (cedp@nodeathpenalty.org) Organizes against the death penalty and publishes *The New Abolitionist*. Telephone 773.955.4841

- *International Socialist Review* (www.isreview.org) Bimonthly magazine offers news and analysis from a socialist perspective.

- *Democracy Now!* (www.democracynow.org) Daily radio and TV news program hosted by Amy Goodman. Breaking news that the mass media ignores.

- *Labor Notes* (www.labornotes.org) Monthly newsletter covers the American and international labor movement. A biannual conference brings international labor activists together.

- Haymarket Books (www.haymarketbooks.org) Offers socialist books on current and historical topics. Telephone 773-583-7884

Questions and comments welcome

Visit www.powerandpowerlessness.com
Email author@powerandpowerlessness.com or powerandpowerlessness@rogers.com
Telephone 647.435-6585

Notes

1. Moyers, B. (2004). Battlefield Earth. *AlterNet*, December 8.
2. CBC. (2004). 40 per cent of world's population has no basic sanitation: WHO. August 26.
3. Cited in Teixeira, R. & Rogers, J. (2000). *America's forgotten majority: Why the white working class still matters.* New York: Basic Books, p.13.
4. Haley, L. (2002). Blood donations following Sept.11 strained resources, communications. *The Medical Post* (Toronto), September 17.
5. MacCharles, T. (2002). 'Plane people' recall kindness of strangers: Gander opened heart to stranded passengers. *Toronto Star*, September 12.
6. Pullman, J. (2003). Enlightening medical students. *CMAJ*, May 27. p.1390.
7. American Psychiatric Association. (1994). *Diagnostic and statistical manual of mental disorders.* Washington: Author. pp.649-650.
8. Dowie, M. (1977). Pinto madness. *Mother Jones*. September/October, pp. 18-32.
9. Sternberg, M. & Schnall, M. (2001). *The stranger in the mirror: Dissociation—the hidden epidemic.* New York: HaperCollins. p.xiii.
10. American Psychological Association. Handling anxiety in the face of the anthrax scare. http://helping.apa.org/daily/anthrax.html accessed June 6, 2002.
11. Schumpeter, J. (1919/1951). *Imperialism and social classes.* New York: Augustus M. Kelley, p. 66.
12. Hall, et. al. (2002). Psychological and behavioral impacts of bioterrorism. *PTSD Research Quarterly*. Vermont: The National Center for PTSD. p.2
13. Bradshaw, L. & Slonsky, L.B. (2005). The real heroes and sheroes of New Orleans. *Socialist Worker* (U.S.) September 9, pp.4-5.
14. Editorial. (2004). We have some planes. *New York Times*, June 19.
15. Bradshaw, L. & Slonsky, L.B. (2005). The real heroes and sheroes of New Orleans. *Socialist Worker* (U.S.) September 9, pp.4-5.
16. University of Sussex. (2002). Protesting is good for you, say psychologists. Press release December 16. http://www.sussex.ac.uk/press_office/media/media270.shtml
17. Martin, M. (2003). Winning in Illinois: How we got there. *The New Abolitionist*, No.27, February, p.2.
18. Lee, R. (1979). *The !Kung San.* Cambridge. p.118
19. Lee, R. (1988). Reflections on primitive communism, in Ingold, T., Riches, D. & Woodburn, J. (Eds). *Hunters and gatherers.* Vol. I. Oxford.
20. Ferguson, B.R. (2003). The birth of war. *Natural History*, July/August.
21. Leakey, R. & Lewin, R. (1992) *Origins reconsidered: In search of what makes us human.* London: Little Brown & Co., p.234.
22. Zinn, H. (2006). After this war. *ZNet* January 3. http://www.zmag.org/sustainers/content/2006-01/03zinn.cfm
23. Harman, C. (1991). The state and capitalism today. *International Socialism 51*, quarterly journal of the Socialist Workers Party (Britain), p.7.
24. Editorial. (2004). Corporate tax holidays. *New York Times*, April 13.
25. Quoted in Rubin, L.B. (1992). *Worlds of pain, Life in the working-class family.* New York: Harper Collins, p.155.
26. Ruskin, J. (1897). *The stones of Venice.* Boston: Estes and Lauriat, Section II, Chapter VI, p.162.
27. Braverman, H. (1974). *Labor and monopoly capital: The degradation of work in the twentieth century.* New York: Monthly Review Press, p.195.
28. Braverman, (above), p.229.
29. Sides, M. (2005). Mandated programs push classroom de-skilling. *Labor Notes* (Detroit), January, p.7. http://www.labornotes.org/archives/2005/01/articles/d.html
30. Braverman, H. (1974). *Labor and monopoly capital: The degradation of work in the twentieth century.* New York: Monthly Review Press, p.133.
31. Sennett, R. & Cobb, J. (1972) *The hidden injuries of class.* New York: Random House. p.94.
32. Lee, R. (1979). *The !Kung San.* Cambridge, p. 244
33. Chan, S. (2004). Inquiry finds secret deal between workers for L.I.R.R. and Garden. *New York Times*, December 25.
34. Schor, J.B., (1991) *The overworked American: The unexpected decline of leisure.* USA: HarperCollins, p.2.
35. Schor, (above), p.1.
36. Waldron, T., Roberts, B. & Reamer, A. (2004). *Working hard, falling short: America's working families and the pursuit of economic security.* Baltimore, MD: Annie E. Casey Foundation.
37. Roberts, S. (2005). In Manhattan, poor make 2¢ for each dollar to the rich. *New York Times*, September 4.
38. Dunning, T.J. (1860). *Trades' unions and strikes: Their philosophy and intention.* pp.35-36. Quoted in Marx, K. (1867/1977). *Capital Vol I.* New York: Vintage, p. 926.
39. Transparency International. (2006). *Global corruption report 2006: Corruption and health.*
40. Schmidt. J. (2000). *Disciplined minds: A critical look at salaried professionals and the soul-battering system that shapes their lives.* Rowman & Littlefield, p.104-105.

41. Braverman, H. (1974). *Labor and monopoly capital: The degradation of work in the twentieth century.* New York: Monthly Review Press, p.284.
42. Engels, F. (1844) *The condition of the working-class in England.* In *Essential classics in politics: Karl Marx and Frederick Engels.* (1998) London: ElecBook. pp.15, 255.
43. Hakim, D. (2004). Carmakers face huge retiree health care costs. *New York Times*, September 15.
44. Cited in Mass, A. (2004). Wal-Mart workers need help to get by. *Socialist Worker* (US), October 1, p.2
45. Friedman, T. (1999). A manifesto for the fast world. *New York Times*, March 28.
46. Butler, S.D. (1933). *On interventionism.* Federation of American Scientists. http://www.fas.org/man/smedley.htm accessed February 6, 2004.
47. Eggebroten, A. (2002). A biblical feminist looks at the Andrea Yates tragedy. *Evangelical and Ecumenical Women's Caucus Update*, Vol.25, No.4, Winter 2001-2002.
48. Baker, A. (2004). *Life and debt: Why American families are borrowing to the hilt.* New York: The Century Foundation, pp.9-10.
49. Warren, E. & Tyagi, A.W. (2003). *The two-income trap: Why middle-class mothers and fathers are going broke.* New York: Basic Books.
50. Gold, S. N. (2000). *Not trauma alone: Therapy for child abuse survivors in family and social context.* Philadelphia: Brunner/Routledge, pp.77-78.
51. Steinmetz, S.K. & Straus, M.A. (1975). *Violence in the family.* New York: Dodd, Mead & Co., p.3.
52. Randell, L. (2001). Athlete death toll rises after summer training. *Yale Herald.* www.yaleherald.com/archive/xxxii/09.07.01/sports/p25randell.html accessed October 6, 2001.
53. Dutton, D. G. (1998). *The abusive personality: Violence and control in intimate relationships.* New York: Guilford, pp.142-145.
54. Leacock, E. (1981). *Myths of male dominance: Collected articles of women cross-culturally.* New York: Monthly Review Press, p.279.
55. Editorial. (2003). Occupational hazards. *New York Times*, December 23.
56. *The Economist.* (2002). Productivity growth: To these the spoils. May 9.
57. Schneider, M. (1975). *Neurosis and civilization.* New York: Seabury Press.
58. Cohen, P. (2004). Forget lonely. Life is healthy at the top. *New York Times*, May 15.
59. McCaughey, B. (2005). Coming clean. *New York Times*, June 6.
60. Welch, N. (2004). Health care system in crisis. Interview with David Himmelstein, *Socialist Worker* (US), October 22, p.11
61. Physicians for a National Health Plan. (2002). Harvard study finds government health spending in U.S. higher than in any other nation. Press release, July 9.
62. Promotional letter from Stephen Giroud, Director, Professional Communications, Merck Frosst Canada and Co., April 2001
63. Pearson, C. (2002). Response to the announcement that health risks outweigh benefits for combined estrogen plus progestin. National Women's Health Network. July. http://www.womenshealthnetwork.org/hrtupdate.htm accessed July 7, 2003.
64. Poussaint, A.F. & Alexander, A. (2000). *Lay my burden down: Suicide and the mental health crisis among African-Americans.* Boston: Beacon Press, p.125.
65. Spitzer, R.L., Sheeney, M. & Endicott, J. (1977). DSM III: Guiding principles. In (Eds). Rakoff, V., Stancer, H. & Kedward, H. *Psychiatric diagnosis.* New York: Brunner Mazel.
66. Caplan, P. (1995). *They say you're crazy: How the world's most powerful psychiatrists decide who's normal.* New York: Addison-Wesley, pp.180-181.
67. Caplan, P.J. (2002). Expert decries diagnosis for pathologizing women. *Journal of Addiction and Mental Health* (Toronto). September/October 2001, p.16.
68. Editorial. (2004). Subverting science. *New York Times*, October 31.
69. Cited in Ewen, S. (1996). *PR!: A social history of spin.* New York: Basic Books, p.66.
70. Martin, E.D. (1920). *The behavior of crowds: A psychological study.* New York, pp.10-11.
71. Beard, C.A. & Beard, M.R. (1927). *The rise of American civilization.* New York. Cited in Ewen, S. (1996). *PR!: A social history of spin.* New York: Basic Books, p.119.
72. O'Dell, J.H. (2005). Operation Dixie: Notes on a promise abandoned. *Labor Notes*, April, pp.5-6.
73. Keach, W. (2000). Rehabilitating McCarthyism. *International Socialist Review*, No.12, June-July, pp. 53-60.
74. Schrecker, E. (1998). *Many are the crimes: McCarthyism in America.* Boston: Little, Brown, p.x..
75. Keach, W. (2000). Rehabilitating McCarthyism. *International Socialist Review*, No.12, June-July, pp.53-60.
76. Cited in Schulte, E. (2003). The trial of Ethel and Julius Rosenberg. *International Socialist Review*, No.29, May-June
77. Harman, C. (1999). *A people's history of the world.* London: Bookmarks, p.546.
78. Zinn, H. (2006). Lessons of Iraq war start with U.S. history. *ZNet*, March 18. http://www.zmag.org/sustainers/content/2006-03/18zinn.cfm
79. David L. Robb interviewed by Fleischer, J. (2004). Operation Hollywood: How the Pentagon bullies movie producers into showing the U.S. military in the best possible light. *Mother Jones.* September 20.
80. Quoted in Colson, N. & Maass, A. (2005). Inside the media propaganda mill. *Socialist Worker* (U.S.), March 25.
81. Steinbeck, J. (1959). *Once there was a war.* London: Heinemann.
82. Quoted in John McArthur. (2003). An Orwellian pitch: The inner workings of the war propaganda machine. *LA Weekly*, March 21-27.
83. Chase, A. (1977). *The legacy of Malthus: The social costs of the new scientific racism.* Chicago: R.R. Donnelley & Sons, p.6-7.
84. Chase, (above), p.8.

85. Zinn, H. (1980/95). *A people's history of the United States: 1492 – present*. New York: HarperCollins. p.406.
86. Chase, A. (1977). *The legacy of Malthus: The social costs of the new scientific racism*. Chicago: R.R. Donnelley & Sons, p.381.
87. Quoted in Cockburn, A. & Silverstein, K. (1996). *Washington Babylon*. London: Verso, p.8.
88. Darrow, C. (1902/2000). *Crime and criminals: Address to the prisoners in Cook County jail*. Chicago, Charles H. Kerr, pp.24 & 20.
89. Horn, S. (2005). Counting corporate crooks. *New York Times*, July 16.
90. Beiser, V. (2001). How we got to two million: How did the Land of the Free become the world's leading jailer? *Mother Jones*, July 10.
91. Jackson, J. (2001). Liberty and justice for some: Mass incarceration comes at a moral cost to every American. *Mother Jones*, July 10.
92. Weed, W. (2001). Incubating disease: Prisons are rife with infectious illnesses—and threaten to spread them to the public. *Mother Jones*, July 10.
93. Rev. Martin Luther King Jr. (1967). *Beyond Vietnam: Address delivered to the Clergy and Laymen Concerned about Vietnam*. April 4.
94. Quoted in Williams, J. (1994). Violence, genes, and prejudice. *Discover*, November, p.100.
95. Cited in Amnesty International: Racial Profiling: Questions and Answers on racial profiling. http://www.amnestyusa.org/racial_profiling/qanda.html accessed June 12, 2006.
96. American Anthropological Association. (1998). American Anthropological Association statement on race. *American Anthropologist*. Vol. 100, pp.712-3.
97. Williams, E. (1944/1990). *Capitalism and slavery*. London: André Deutsch Limited. p.19.
98. Fields, B.J. (2001). Race: The power of an illusion. Edited presentation to the producers of *RACE*, a PBS documentary. http://www.pbs.org/race/000_About/002_04-background-02-02.htm
99. Quoted in Zinn, H. (1980/95). *A people's history of the United States: 1492 – present*. New York: HarperCollins. p.186.
100. Camp Calcium. www.surgeongeneral.gov/library/bonehealth/Appendix_B.html accessed May 16, 2005.
101. Prunier, G. (1995). *The Rwanda crisis: History of a genocide*. New York: Columbia University Press, pp.38-39.
102. Greenhouse, S. (2005). Immigration sting puts 2 U.S. agencies at odds. *New York Times*, July 16.
103. Taylor, K-Y. (2003). Civil rights and civil wrongs: Racism in America today. *International Socialist Review*, No.32, p.30.
104. Amnesty International. (2004). *Threat and humiliation: Racial profiling, domestic security, and human rights in the United States*. New York: Author.
105. Sante, L. (2004). Tourists and torturers. *New York Times*, May 11.
106. Goff, S. (2004). An open letter to GIs in Iraq: Hold on to your humanity. *International Socialist Review*, No.33, p.36. January-February.
107. Lembcke, J. (2003). Spitting on the troops: Old myth, new rumors. *The Veteran*, Vol.33, No.1, p.22.
108. Perlo, V., Eisenhower, D., Weiss, L. & Perlo, E. (1996). *Economics of racism II: The roots of inequality. USA*. New York: International Publishers.
109. Kawachi. I., Kennedy, B.P., Gupta, V. & Prothrow, S.D. (1999). Women's status and the health of women and men: A view from the States. *Soc Sci Med*, Vol.48, No.1, pp.21-32.
110. Roberts, D. (2002). *Shattered bonds: The color of child welfare*. New York: Basic Books, p.233.
111. Roberts, (above), p.235.
112. Bernstein, N. (2001). Left behind: Tens of thousands of children have a parent behind bars. What are the social costs of their loss? *Mother Jones*, July 10.
113. cited in Roberts, D. (2002). *Shattered bonds: The color of child welfare*. New York: Basic Books, p.89.
114. National Coalition for Child Protection Reform. Who is in the system—and why. http://www.nccpr.org/newissues/5.html accessed June 29, 2004.
115. Roberts, D. (2002). *Shattered bonds: The color of child welfare*. New York: Basic Books, p.35.
116. Cited in Roberts, (above), p. 52.
117. Roberts, (above), p.91.
118. Riccardi, N. (1999). Grandmother blames county in latest death of foster child. *Los Angeles Times*, June 15, p.B1.
119. National Coalition for Child Protection Reform. Foster care vs. family preservation: The track record on safety. Accessed June 28, 2004. http://www.nccpr.org/newissues/1.html
120. Smith, M.G. & Fong, R. (2004). *The children of neglect*. New York: Brunner-Routledge, p.243.
121. National Coalition for Child Protection Reform. Who is in "the system"—and why. http://www.nccpr.org/newissues/5.html accessed June 28, 2004.
122. Roberts, D. (2002). *Shattered bonds: The color of child welfare*. New York: Basic Books, p.134.
123. Cited in Du Bois, W.E.B. (1935/1998). *Black reconstruction in America: 1860-1880*. New York: Free Press, p.641-642.
124. Cited in Gatto, J.T. (2003). *The underground history of American education: An intimate investigation into the prison of modern schooling*. New York: Oxford Village Press, p.38.
125. Cited in Gatto, (above), p.105-106.
126. Gatto, J.T. (1992/2002). *Dumbing us down: The hidden curriculum of compulsory schooling*. Gabriola Island, BC: New Society Publishers, p.xxii.
127. Kozol, J. (1991). *Savage inequalities*. Crown Publishers.
128. Cited in Sides, M. (2005). Mandated programs push classroom de-skilling. *Labor Notes* (Detroit), January, p.7.
129. Human Rights Watch. (2001). *Hatred in the hallways: Violence and discrimination against lesbian, gay, bisexual and transgender students in U.S. schools*. www.hrw.org/reports/2001/uslgbt/toc.htm accessed June 13, 2004.

130. Woodworth, T. (2000). DEA Congressional Testimony: Before the Committee on Education and the Workforce: Subcommittee on Early Childhood, Youth and Families. May 16.
http://www.usdoj.gov/dea/pubs/cngrtest/ct051600.htm accessed February 19, 2004
131. Fuentes, A. (2003). Discipline and punish: Zero tolerance policies have created a 'lockdown environment' in schools. *The Nation*, December 15.
132. Fuentes, (above).
133. Males, M. (2001). The Myth of the Grade-School Murderer: Contrary to camera-ready experts, child killers are rarer than ever. *Extra!* Vol. 14, No. 3. p30.
134. Drug Reform Coordination Network. (2003). Interview: Youth sociologist Mike Males. November 21.
www.stopthedrugwar.org/chronicle/312/males.shtml accessed July 10, 2004.
135. Quoted in *Socialist Worker* (Canada). (2001). Killed for fighting back. August 1, p3.
136. Rubin, L.B. (1992). *Worlds of pain, Life in the working-class family*. New York: Harper Collins, p.xvii.
137. Rosenthal, S. (1996). *Striking Flint: Genora (Johnson) Dollinger remembers the 1936-37 General Motors sit-down strike*. pp.25-26. Chicago: Haymarket.
138. Belman, D. (1992). Unions, the quality of labor relations, and firm performance. In Mishel, L. & Voos, P.B. [Eds.]. *Unions and economic competitiveness*. Armonk, NY: M.E. Sharpe, Inc., pp. 41-107.
139. Rachleff, P. (1993). *Hard-pressed in the Heartland: The Hormel strike and the future of the labor movement*. Boston: South End Press, p.82.
140. Scipes, K. (2005). Labor imperialism redux?: The AFL-CIO's foreign policy since 1995. *Monthly Review*. May.
141. Albright, M. (2000). Transcript: Remarks by Secretary of State Madeleine K. Albright at meeting of Advisory Committee on Labor Diplomacy. U.S. Department of State. Office of the Spokesman. November 8.
142. Hirsch, F. (2005). AFL-CIO foreign policy in Venezuela. *ZNet*, June 18.
143. Davis, M. (2005). Avian flu: The monster at our door. *International Socialist Review*. Vol.43, September–October, pp.51-55.
144. Quoted in Schwartz, J. (2006). New study of levees faults design and construction. *New York Times*, May 21.
145. Johnson, C. (2005). The smash of civilizations. *Mother Jones*, July 7.
146. Schmidt. J. (2000). *Disciplined minds: A critical look at salaried professionals and the soul-battering system that shapes their lives*. Rowman & Littlefield, p.120.
147. Epstein, S. (1998). *The politics of cancer revisited*. Freemont Center, NY: East Ridge Press, p. 306.
148. Rosa, Y. (2005). A new form of resistance: Argentina's recovered factories. *NonViolent Activist*, May-June.
149. Reed, J. (1919/1977). *Ten days that shook the world*. New York: Penguin. pp.250-251.
150. History Committee of The General Strike Committee. (1919). An account of what happened in Seattle and especially in the Seattle labor movement, during the General Strike, February 6 to 11, 1919.
151. Savage, C. (2006). Bush challenges hundreds of laws: President cites powers of his office. *Boston Globe*, April 30
152. McFadden, R.D. (2003). From New York to Melbourne, protest against war on Iraq. *New York Times*, February 16.
153. Zinn, H. (1995). *A people's history of the United States: 1492— present*. New York: Harper Collins, p.383.
154. Malcolm X. (1965). *Malcolm X speaks: Selected speeches and statements*.
155. Parker, M. & Gruelle, M. (2005). *Democracy is power: Rebuilding unions from the bottom up*. Detroit: Labor Education and Research Project, p.xi.
156. Luxemburg, R. (1900/1908). *Reform or revolution*. London: Bookmarks, pp.80-81.
157. Luxemburg, R. (1918). *On the Spartacus Programme*. Delivered at the Founding Conference of the Communist Party of Germany, Berlin, December 30.
158. Krupskaya, N.K. (1933/1979). *Reminiscences of Lenin*. New York: International Publishers, pp.351-352.
159. Rosenthal, S. (1996). *Striking Flint: Genora (Johnson) Dollinger remembers the 1936-37 General Motors sit-down strike*. Chicago: Haymarket, p.25.
160. Reed, J. (1919/1977). *Ten days that shook the world*. New York: Penguin, p.108.
161. Cited in Newsinger, J. (Ed.). (1998). *Shaking the world: John Reed's revolutionary journalism*. London: Bookmarks, p.132.
162. Sachs, J.D. (2005). *The end of poverty: Economic possibilities for our time*. Penguin Press, p.44.
163. Reed, J. (1919/1977). *Ten days that shook the world*. New York: Penguin, pp.200-201.
164. The Claude Pepper Museum: Political Pendulum exhibit. www.claudepepper.com/museum/site/exhibit21.cfm accessed June 15, 2006
165. Trotsky, L. (1939/1986) *Their morals and ours*. New York: Pathfinder Press, 5th edition, p.59.
166. Mondragon Corporacion Cooperativa, Spain www.iisd.org/50comm/commdb/list/c13.htm accessed June 15, 1006.
167. Leibl, D. (2002). Café Resistance. *This Magazine*, July. http://www.a-zone.org/mondragon accessed June 15, 2006.
168. Luxemburg, R. (1900/1908). *Reform or revolution*. London: Bookmarks, p.66.
169. Cited in Field, N. (1995). *Over the rainbow: Money, class and homophobia*. East Haven, CT: Pluto, p.163.
170. http://en.wikipedia.org/wiki/Consensus_decision-making accessed January 9, 2006.
171. Sachs, J.D. (2005). *The end of poverty: Economic possibilities for our time*. Penguin Press, p.135.
172. Herbert, B. (2003). Another battle for Bush. *New York Times*, December 15.
173. Cited in Healy, P.D. (2005). Clinton seeking shared ground over abortions. *New York Times*, January 25.
174. Schulte, E. (2005). An interview with Elaine Brown: A former Panther's Georgia campaign. *Counterpunch*. October 15 /16.
175. Herbert, B. (2005). Dad's empty chair. *New York Times*, July 7.

176. Herbert, B. (2005). A new civil rights movement. *New York Times*, December 26.
177. Gates, H.L.Jr. (2004). Breaking the silence. *New York Times*, August 1.
178. Malcolm X. (1965). *Malcolm X speaks: Selected speeches and statements.*
179. Ford, G. (1995). The final betrayal of the NABJ. *Philadelphia New Observer*, July 26, pp.11-12.
180. Schmidt. J. (2000). *Disciplined minds: A critical look at salaried professionals and the soul-battering system that shapes their lives.* Rowman & Littlefield, p.207.
181. Maynard, A. (1993). Are mental health services efficient? *International Journal of Mental Health,* vol. 22, no. 3, p.3.
182. Editorial. (2005). A fighting strategy for veterans. *New York Times*, March 5.
183. www.secondharvest.org accessed May 28, 2005.
184. Sachs, J.D. (2005). *The end of poverty: Economic possibilities for our time.* Penguin Press, p.289.
185. Sachs, (above), p.356.
186. Sachs, J.D. (2005). The end of the world as we know it. *Guardian* (UK), April 5.
187. Kristoff, N.D. (2006). In praise of the maligned sweatshop. *New York Times*, June 6.
188. Sachs, J.D. (2005). *The end of poverty: Economic possibilities for our time.* Penguin Press, p.1.
189. Genusa, A. (2001). Rising anger in the workplace. CIO 5/1.http://www.itworld.com/Career/4198/CIO010501workplace/ accessed June 15, 2006.
190. Johnston, D. (2006). F.B.I.'s focus on public corruption includes 2,000 investigations. *New York Times*, May 10.
191. Darrow, C. (1902/2000). *Crime and criminals: Address to the prisoners in Cook County jail.* Chicago, Charles H. Kerr, p.18.
192. Sustar, L. (2005). The one-sided class war: Working harder for less while business lines its pockets. *Socialist Worker* (US). April 22, p.5.
193. Einstein, A. (1949). Why socialism? *Monthly Review*, No.1. May.

Index

A

aboriginal genocide, 114, 128, 165
abortion, 101, 172, 175, 189, 198-200, 203, 213
Abu Ghraib Prison, 91, 123
Abu-Jamal, Mumia, 202
"accident-prone," 108
ADD (ADHD), 140
affirmative action, 101, 121, 135, 201
Afghanistan, 1, 14, 20, 21, 90, 91, 93, 94, 118, 123, 125
AFL-CIO, 151-153
Africa, 75, 90, 112-115, (Rwanda, 117-118), 153, 155, (South Africa, 20, 172), 208, 209, (Botswana, 210), 211-212, 214, (maternal mortality, 221)
agriculture, 17, 29-30, 33, 41, 149, 224
AIDS — see HIV/AIDS
Albert, Michael, 191-192, 194
Albright, Madeleine, 124, 153
alienation, 13, 35-37, (and dissociation, 37-39), (definition, 40), 190, 194, 197, 217
Allende, Salvador — see Chile
Al Qaeda, 22, 118
altruism, 2-3, 10
American Civil War, 115
American Medical Association (AMA), 160
American Psychiatric Association (APA), 7, 57, 77, 98
America's Second Harvest, 209-210
anarchism (see also cooperatives), 180-181, 191
anger, (function of, 19-20), (shame and rage, 62-63)
anti-war movement, 85-86, 101, 125-126, 150, 166-167, 171, 196-197, 202, 203, 225-226
Ashcroft, John, 123
attachment (social bonds), 16-17, 24-25, 39-40, 58-59, 68-70, 131

B

bankrupt(cy), 55, 71
Bayer, 71
bed-wetting, 74
Bernays, Edward, 85
BiDil, 116
Black Codes, 107, 170
Black Panther Party, 101, 198, 200
Blair, Tony, 123
bonding — see attachment
Braverman, Harry, 36, 37
Breggin, Peter and Ginger, 106
British Miners' Strike (1984-1985), 193-194
Brown, Elaine, 200
BSE — see Mad Cow Disease
bullying, 62, 138,
Burge, Jon, 123
Bush, George W., 9, 14, 21, 52, 79, 90, 94, 119, 122, 124, 157, 170, 171, 196, 206, 207, 212, 213
Business Roundtable, 102
Butler, Smedley, 50-51

C

Caldicott, Helen, 4
Campaign to End the Death Penalty, 25
Canadian Medical Association (CMA), 161
cancer, 68, 69, 70, 108-109, 117, 180, 185
capital (definition), 34, 215
capitalism (definition), 34, 215
Caplan, Paula, 77-78
Carson, Rachel, 160
Carter, Jimmy, 52
Charcot, Jean-Marie, 12-13
charity (see also foreign aid), 2-3, 195, 208-210, 213
Chase, Alan, 96, 99
Chavez, Hugo, 153, 174, 177
childhood trauma (abuse), 58-63, 128-144
child welfare system, 129-134, (and prison system, 143)
Chile (Allende, Pinochet), 90, 153, 158, 174, (workers' councils, 181)
China, 51-52, 105, 157, 177
Chomsky, Noam, 84, 90, 92, 225
CIO, 86-88
circumcision, 61-62
Civil Rights Act, 101
civil rights, (struggle for, 101, 135, 200-201), (reversal of, 106-107, 143)
class, (origin, 30-31), (struggle, 101), (mobility, 146), (definition, 146-150), (and consciousness, 153-154)
Clinton, Bill, 110, 120, 134, 138, 197
Clinton, Hilary Rodham, 199
CNN, 93
Cold War, 51, 88-89, 109, 118, 121, 168
Columbia River, 156
Columbine High School, 62, 138, 142
Committee on Public Information (CPI), 85-86
compassion, 2-3, 6-7, 9-11
consciousness and class, 153-154
consensus, 192-193
consumer power, 195
cooperation (reciprocity, egalitarian), 17, 19, 29, 39-40, 44-45, 55, 69-70, 147, 153, 162, 193-194, 215-216, 220-22, 225
cooperatives (and utopian societies), 164-165, 177, 190-192, 194
Corporation, The, 7
corruption, 1, 44, 219-220
Cosby, Bill, 201
crime (criminal(s), penal system), 103-107, 110, 143, (end of, 220)
Cuba, 177

D

Darrow, Clarence, 103-104, 220
Davenport, Charles, 97
Davis, Mike, 155
death penalty (execution, capital punishment), 25, 101, 105, 167, 189
Debbs, Eugene, 86
democratic centralism, (definition, 179-180), 193
Democratic Party (Democrats), 47, 48, 94, 101, 179, 196-197, 199, 225-226

deregulation, 95, 102
dissociation, 12-15, 18-19, (and alienation, 37-39), (definition, 40), 59, 62, 68, 73, 110, 137-138, 217
Dollinger, Genora (Johnson), 150, 183, 226
doublespeak (doublethink), 14
Douglass, Frederick, 112, 115, 126
drugs—see pharmaceutical industry, War on Drugs
DSM, 77-78, 139
Dunlap, Al (Chainsaw), 7-8
Duster, Troy, 116
Dutton, Donald, 63
dyslexia, 17

E

education system, 134-141
egalitarian—see cooperation
Ehrenreich, Barbara, 160
Einstein, Albert, 225
Ellsberg, Daniel, 160
Emancipation Proclamation, 115
emotions (function of), 18
empathy—see compassion, altruism
employers' offensive, 102-107, 151-152
Engels, Frederick, 48, 194, 210
Enron, 17-18, 49
environment, 4, 38, 100, 108, 155-156, 196, 223-225
Epstein, Samuel, 4, 160-161
Equal Rights Amendment, 170
Erlich, Paul, 99
eugenics (forced sterilization), 97-99
Ewen, Stewart, 85, 187
exploitation, (definition, 34), 187, (the end of, 216-218), 221

F

Fallujah (see also Iraq), 196
"family values," 57-58
farm subsidies, 50, 100
FaSinPat, 164
FDA, 46, 71-72, 74-76, 78
Ferguson, Brian R., 29-30
fertility rates, 100
Fields, Barbara J., 84, 115
flu, 79, 155
Ford, Henry, 8, 109
Ford Motor Company, 8, 19, 104
foreign aid, 212-213
foster care—see child welfare system
Fox Network, 91-92
free trade (and protectionism), 50
French Revolution, 41, 83, 89, 95-96
Freud, Anna, 131
Freud, Sigmund, 12-13, 77, 85
Friedman, Thomas, 51
Fuentes, Annette, 141

G

Galton, Francis, 96-97
Gates, Bill, 35, 210
Gatto, John Taylor, 135
gay—see homosexual, lesbian
Gay Liberation Front (GLF), 198
gay marriage, 189
Gay Pride Day, 198, (Lesbian and Gay Pride March (UK), 194)
General Electric (GE), 92, 102, 104
General Motors (GM), 48, 49, 90, 150, 172, 183, 195
genetically modified organisms (GMOs), 213
Genovese, Kitty, 10
Global Gag Rule, 213
global warming, 97, 155-156, 196
Goff, Stan, 123-124
Gold, Steven, 53, 57
Gonzales, Alberto, 91
Goodwin, Amy, 92
Gore, Al, 170, 196
Gottman, John, 65
grey zone (between middle and working class), 149-151, 203
greed(y), 5, 9, 29, 31, 44, 70, 96, 104, 216, 220
Guantanamo, 123
Guiliani, Carlo, 144

H

Haiti, 51, 89, 173, 185
Halliburton, 47
Hanford Nuclear Reservation, 156
Herbert, Bob, 187-188, 195, 201
herd instinct—see panic myth
Hill and Knowlton, 92
Himmelstein, David, 72
Hiroshima (Nagasaki), 51
Hispanic(s), 69, 107, 116, 120-121, 135, 198
HIV/AIDS, 20, 68, 70, 71, 105, 125, 155, 174, 210, 211, 213
Hollywood, 8, 29, 86, 90-91, 110
Homeland Security, 47, 67, (Endgame, 120)
homophobia, (homophobic bullying, 62), 56-57, 77, 113, 127, 138, 159
homosexual(s)(ity), 17, 56-57, 61, 77, 172, 191-192, 197-198
Hormel Strike, 152
hormone replacement therapy (HRT), 75-76
hospital(s), 6-7, 37, 70, 154, 158, 172, 219
Human Genome Project, 113
human nature, 2-5, 9-10, 16-20, 24-26, 29-30

I

idealism, 190
identity politics, 197-198
ideology and class, 101
Illich, Ivan, 108
illiteracy, 135-136
immigrant(s) (immigration), 42, 47, 97, 98, 119-121
immigrants' rights (struggle for), 121, 138, 194, 202, 214, 223, 226
imperialism, 50-52, 89-90, 117-118, 124-125, 185, 222-223
India, 100, 118
individualism, 188

individuality, 24, 218
industrial revolution, 28, 48, 56, 114
inequality (see also racism, sexism, homophobia, oppression), 19-20, 39-40, 43-44, 68-70, 96-99, 146-147
International Monetary Fund (IMF), 118, 212
internet (www), 215
Iran, 118, 157, (workers' councils in, 181), 212
Iraq (U.S. war against), 4, 22, 90-94, 118, 121-125, 157-158, 172-173, 185, 196-197, 202
Ireland (Irish), 121
IRS, 50, 209
Israel, 22, 33, 90, 213
IWW, 175-176

J

Jackson, Donovan, 138
Jackson, Jesse, 105
Jackson State University, 101
Janet, Pierre, 12-13
Jefferson, Thomas, 89
Jim Crow, 107, 115
Johnson, Chalmers, 157
Johnson, Lyndon, 89, 101
Johnston, David Cay, 49
juvenile detention, 129, 130, 143

K

Katrina, Hurricane, 9, 23-24, 38, 117, 125, 155-156, 180, 214
Kennedy, John, 89, 102
Kent State University, 101
Kerry, John, 196, 199
King, Martin, Luther, 101, 106
Kozol, Jonathon, 135, 136
Ku Klux Klan, 115, 120

L

Lanham Act, 48
Latin America, 89, 90, 112, 121, 153, 223
Latino(a)s — see Hispanic, Mexico, immigrants
Law, Cardinal Bernard, 8
Leacock, Eleanor Burke, 29, 64
lead poisoning, 108
Leakey, Richard, 29, 30
learned helplessness, 25
Lebanon, 213
Lee, Richard, 29, 39
Lembcke, Jerry, 125-126
Lenin, 166-169, 186
lesbian (see also gay, homosexual), 61, 77, 198
Lesbians and Gays Support the Miners, 193-4
Lewis, Stephen, 155
liberal(s)(ism), (definition, 188), 195-196, (and the Democratic Party, 196-197), 202-204
Lincoln, Abraham, 115
Los Angeles Rebellion (1992), 200
Ludlow Massacre, 84-85
Luxemburg, Rosa, 173, 174, 178, 182, 191, 209
lynch(ing), 115, 123

M

Mad Cow Disease, 46
malaria, 214-215
Malcolm X, 101, 132, 175, 202
Males, Mike, 142
Malthus, Robert, Thomas (Malthusians), 96-97, 99-100
Marx, Karl, 41, 121, 210
McCarthy, Joseph, (McCarthyism), 87-88, 226
McMurtry, John, 185
McVeigh, Timothy, 121, 125
media (mainstream), 4, 13, 14, 21, 23, 58, 85-86, 91-93, 95, 141-142, (in revolution, 178), 185
medical-school lottery, 45-46
menopause — see HRT
Mexico (Mexican), 51, 89, 120, 153, 222
Middle East, 22, 52, 90, 94, 118, 121-122, 173, 203, 225
military (war, Pentagon) (see also Iraq war), 1, 4, 14, 20-24, 29-30, 32, 47, 50-52, 85-93, 108, 121-126, 138, (chemical dumping, 156), 157-158, 185, 213, 225-226
minimum wage, 9, 120
Mondragon Cooperative, 190
Monsanto Corporation, 91
Moore, Michael, 4
moralism, 188-189
Moyers, Bill, 2, 38
Murray, Charles, 103
Muslim (Arab), 118, 122, 126

N

Nader, Ralph, 94, 196,
NAFTA, 119-120
NARAL, 199
National Museum, Baghdad, 157
nationalism (patriotism), 87-89, 119-121, 222-223
National Union of Miners — see British Miners' Strike
Nature — see environment
Nazi (Hitler), 98, 202-203
neoliberalism, 102
New Age, 108
"9/11" (World Trade Center), 4, 9, 21-24, 52, 93, 105, 122, 156, 208
Nineteen Eighty-Four, 14, 82
Nixon, Richard, 89, 101, 105
nuclear (power, 4, 23, 101, 108, 156), (weapons, 51, 108), (waste, 156)

O

occupational illness, injury, death, 66-69
one drop rule, 116
Operation Gatekeeper, 120
opportunism, 187-188
oppression (oppressed) (struggle against), (see also inequality, racism, sexism, homophobia), 77-78, 112-113, 126-127, 159, 169, 172, 197-198, 203-204, 209, (end of, 221-222)
Orwell, George — see *Nineteen Eighty-Four*
overpopulation (myth of), 99-100, 208, 224

P

Palestine, 213
panic myth, 22-24, 85, 194-195
PARECON, 191-192
Paredes, Pablo, 154
Paris Commune, 165-166, 172
Pasteur, Louis, 70
patriotism—see nationalism
pellagra, 97
Pentagon—see military
Perot, Ross, 35
pharmaceutical industry, 20, 71-72, 73-76, 78-79, 218
Pinochet, Augusto—see Chile
Pinto—see Ford Motor Company
political pendulum, 187-188
Poussaint, Alvin, 77
pre-class (societies), 29, 32, 38, 147, 176
prison(er)(s), (see also crime), 37, 91, 103-107, 110, 123, 129, 141, 143, 220
productivity, 6-8, 41-44, 54-55, 66-67, 107-108, 148, 151-152, 162
profit (definition), 34
property (private), 31-32, 33-35, 168, 189, 206, 213, 220, (difference between private, public, personal, and common property, 176-177, 215)
Prozac, 75, 78
psychopath(s), 7-9, 14
Puerto Rico(ans), 99, 170, 199

Q

Queer Nation (queer), 198

R

racial profiling, 106-107, 122
racism (racist), (see also slavery), 68-69, 76-77, 79, 89, 96-100, 103, 106-107, 113-124, 126, 128-129, 131-132, 134-136, 140, 143, 159, 170, (and the Black middle class, 200-202), (end of, 221-223)
Reagan, Ronald, 11, 103
reciprocity—see cooperation
redundancy, 218-219
Reed, John, 166, 169, 181, 183, 186
reformism (see also Luxemburg, Rosa), 173-175, 195
religion, 94
reparations, 202, 211
Republican Party (Republicans), 47, 48, 179, 196-197, 199
Rice, Condoleezza, 112, 197, 200
Ritalin, 140
Roberts, Dorothy, 128, 131, 132, 143
Robin Hood, 49, 188, 209-210
Rockefeller, 84, 85, 97, 108, 220
Rockefeller Drug Laws, 105
Roosevelt, Franklin D., 51, 151, 173
Roosevelt, Theodore, 98
Rosenbergs, Ethel and Julius, 87-88
Rubin, Lillian, 35, 147
Rumsfeld, Donald, 79
Russian (Bolshevik) Revolution, 88, 150, 153, 166-169, 172, 176, 177, 181, 182-183, 186, 202
Rwanda—see Africa
Ryan, George, 25
Ryan, William, 106

S

Sachs, Jeffrey, 186, 194, 210-213
salaried professionals (role of), 149
scarcity (artificial, myth of), 95-96, 205-207, 219-220
Schanberg, Sydney, 92
schizophrenia (schizophrenic), 79, 117
Schlosser, Eric, 160
Schmidt, Jeff, 45-46, 159, 203
schools—see education system
Schor, Juliet, 43
Seattle General Strike, 167
sectarian (definition), 203
Sennett, Richard, 37
sexism, (see also women's oppression), 61-62, 65, 137-138, 159, (and the feminist middle class, 198-200)
shame (shaming), 6, 7, 18, 19, 20, 40, 62-63, 74, 137
Shay, Jonathon, 91
Sheehan, Cindy, 124, 172
Siegel, Daniel, 16
Sir! No Sir!, 125
Sklar, Holly, 19
slave(s)(ery), 19, 32, 48, 76-77, 83-84, 99, 110, 114-115, 128-129, 132, 134, 157, 168, 189, 197, 211
Social Darwinism, 97
soldier(s) (veterans), 9, 18-19, 20, 86, 90-91, 123-126, 150, 178, 181-182, 186, 207, 225-226
Soldiers of Solidarity, 176
Soltero, Anthony, 138
Spain, 173
spanking, 60-61
Spencer, Herbert, 97
Spiderman, 8, 40
spying, 1, 121-122, 137, 171
Stalin, 168-169
Star Trek, 7, 24
State (origin and function), 32, 46-52, (nation-State, 118-119)
State capitalism, 168
Steinbeck, John, 92
sterilization (forced)—see eugenics
Stockholm Syndrome, 94
Stonewall Rebellion, 198
strike(s) (see also unions), 37, 86-87, 166, 173, 186, 193-194
Supreme Court, 32, 98, 101, 105, 115, 120, 129, 170
surplus, 31-32, 34-35, 148, 151, 162, 205, 215-216
Survivor, 45
sweatshops, 211-212

T

Take, The, 164
Taliban—see Afghanistan
Tate, Lionel, 143
Tauzin, Billy, 73
Taylor, Frederick Winslow (Taylorism), 36-37
tend and befriend (see also cooperation), 24-25

terrorist (terrorism), (definitions, 14, 90), 21-22, 67, 88, 93, 122, 124, 171
torture, 1, 91, 123, 171, 196
Trotsky, Leon, 169, 188
Truman, Harry, S., 87, 89
tsunami, 2, 155

U

UAW, 150, 176, 183
UFCW—see Hormel strike
union(s) (see also strikes), 42, 49, 84, 86-88, 102, 120, 127, 150-153, 171, (One Big Union, 175-176), 190, 194, 195, 202, 207, 225
United Airlines, 50, 148
united front, 162, 203-204, 209
United Nations, 14, 93, 99, 118, 155, 185, 197, 210
utopian societies—see cooperatives

V

Venezuela—see Hugo Chavez
Verizon, 44
veterans—see soldiers
video news releases, 92-93
Vietnam (U.S. war against), (see also soldiers, veterans), 89-90, 101, 160, 198
violence, (see also war, military, childhood trauma), (interpersonal, 12, 59-64), (systemic, 103-104), (violence gene, 106, 200), (and youth, 141-142), (and anarchism, 180-181)
Vogt, William, 99

W

Walesa, Lech, 174
Wal-Mart, 49, 195, 218-219
war—see military
War on Drugs, 105, 107, 110, 201
War on the Poor, 105, 200, 213
War on Poverty, 101
War on Terror, 88, 173, 213
water, 3, 28, 33, 206, 214
Watergate, 101
Webb, Gary, 92
welfare (as social control), 133-134
Wilkinson, Richard, 68-69
Williams, Eric, 114
Wilson, Woodrow, 85, 135
Wolf, Naomi, 199
women's oppression, (origin of, 32), 55-57, 78, 126-127, (end of, 221-222)
Woolhandler, Stephanie, 73
workers' councils, 166-167, 176, 177-178, 181
workers' party (revolutionary), 179-180, 204
World Bank, 118, 212
World Health Organization, 155, 174-175
World Trade Center—see "9/11"

Y

Yates, Andrea, 53, 60, 109
Yugoslavia (Balkans), 90, 118, 138, 173

Z

Zanon, 164-165, 177
zero tolerance (in schools), 141
Zinn, Howard, 30, 89, 98, 114, 146, 173

ISBN 1412056918